Crisis and Inequality

For Saul

Crisis and Inequality

The Political Economy of Advanced Capitalism

Mattias Vermeiren

polity

The right of Mattias Vermeiren to be identified as Author of this Work has been asserted in accordance with the UK Copyright, Designs and Patents Act 1988.

First published in 2021 by Polity Press

Polity Press
65 Bridge Street
Cambridge CB2 1UR, UK

Polity Press
101 Station Landing
Suite 300
Medford, MA 02155, USA

ISBN-13: 978-1-5095-3768-6
ISBN-13: 978-1-5095-3769-3 (pb)

A catalogue record for this book is available from the British Library.

Typeset in 10.5 on 13pt Swift by
by Fakenham Prepress Solutions, Fakenham, Norfolk, NR21 8NL
Printed and bound in Great Britain by T J Books Limited

The publisher has used its best endeavours to ensure that the URLs for external websites referred to in this book are correct and active at the time of going to press. However, the publisher has no responsibility for the websites and can make no guarantee that a site will remain live or that the content is or will remain appropriate.

For further information on Polity, visit our website:
politybooks.com

Contents

Figures, Tables and Boxes

All figures and tables were created by the author for the book. Credit lines refer to the source of the underlying data.

Figures

Tables

Boxes

Abbreviations

ABCP	asset-backed commercial paper
ABS	asset-backed security
AOC	Alexandria Ocasio-Cortez
APP	Asset Purchase Programme
BoP	balance of payments
CDO	collateralized debt obligation
CEO	chief executive officer
CME	coordinated market economy
CPE	comparative political economy
CPI	consumer price index
CRA	credit rating agency
ECB	European Central Bank
EEC	European Economic Community
EFSF	European Financial Stability Facility
EMDC	emerging markets and developing countries
EMS	European Monetary System
EMU	Economic and Monetary Union
EU ETS	European Union Emissions Trading Scheme
FCIC	Financial Crisis Inquiry Commission
FDI	foreign direct investment
FIRE	finance, insurance and real estate
FOMC	Federal Open Market Committee
G7	Group of Seven
G20	Group of Twenty
GATT	General Agreement on Tariffs and Trade
GDP	gross domestic product
GND	Green New Deal
GVC	global value chain
IBRD	International Bank for Reconstruction and Development
ICT	information and communication technologies
IMF	International Monetary Fund
IPCC	Intergovernmental Panel on Climate Change
IPE	international political economy

IPO	initial public offering
IPRs	intellectual property rights
ISCO	International Standard Classification of Occupations
KWS	Keynesian welfare state
LME	liberal market economy
MBA	Master of Business Administration
MBS	mortgage-backed security
MEW	mortgage equity withdrawal
MIP	Macroeconomic Imbalance Procedure
MME	mixed market economy
MNE	multinational enterprise
MPC	marginal propensity to consume
MSP	minority shareholder protection
NAFTA	North American Free Trade Agreement
NIIP	net international investment position
OECD	Organisation for Economic Co-operation and Development
OPEC	Organization of the Petroleum Exporting Countries
PEPP	Pandemic Emergency Purchase Programme
PPP	purchasing power parity
PRRP	populist radical right party
QE	quantitative easing
R&D	research and development
repo	repurchase agreement
RoA	return on assets
RoE	return on equity
S&P	Standard and Poor's
SBTC	skill-biased technological change
SGP	Stability and Growth Pact
SIV	structured investment vehicle
TARP	Troubled Asset Relief Program
ULC	unit labour costs
VoC	varieties of capitalism [approach]
WTO	World Trade Organization

Introduction

In 2008 the world economy was shattered by the deepest financial crisis since the Great Depression of the 1930s (and, according to some criteria, even the severest financial crisis in global history). For more than a decade, capitalism in the advanced market economies has been in the throes of a threefold crisis.[1] The global financial crisis was first and foremost a *banking crisis* stemming from the fact that private banks extended too much credit to households, creating bubbles in housing markets. When these bubbles collapsed, many large US and European banks had to be bailed out by their governments. Public debt ratios skyrocketed in the wake of the crisis as governments had to borrow massive amounts of money to save the banking industry and stabilize the economy, triggering a *fiscal crisis* in the weaker member states of the Eurozone. To reduce the public debt burden and regain the confidence of the markets, governments in the entire advanced capitalist world imposed drastic cuts in social spending and other harsh austerity policies on their citizens. This resulted in a *crisis of the real economy*, which manifested itself in persistently low economic growth (or even stagnation) and, in some countries, stubbornly high unemployment levels. The economic fallout of the lockdown measures in 2020 to contain the spread of the coronavirus further deepened these instabilities and plunged advanced capitalism into the worst existential crisis since the Great Depression of the 1930s.

The 'Great Lockdown' of 2020 came as an external, 'exogenous' shock to the advanced capitalist system. The structural causes of the global financial crisis of 2008, by contrast, were 'endogenous' to this system: what happened in 2008 has to be understood as an outgrowth of the financialization of the economy and the outcome of growing levels of income and wealth inequality. In almost all rich countries, since the 1980s the gains of economic growth were distributed unequally. In 2016, the share of total national income accounted for by just the top 10 per cent of earners (that is, the top 10 per cent income share) was 37 per cent in Europe and 47 per cent in North America (even higher than in Russia and China, where the top 10 per cent income share was respectively 41 and 46 per cent of total national income).[2] From 1980, income inequality increased rapidly in North America, while inequality grew more moderately in continental Europe. From a broad historical perspective, the rise in inequality marks the end of a post-war 'Golden Age' of egalitarian capitalism. Many lower- and middle-class consumers in the United States and other Anglo-Saxon countries like Ireland and the United Kingdom increasingly had to borrow to maintain and finance their consumption patterns in the face of stagnating incomes. In this way, the rise in inequality contributed to the global financial crisis of 2008 by leading to an unsustainable rise in household debt. Fiscal austerity reinforces these dynamics of inequality by cutting spending on social programmes that primarily benefit the bottom half of the income distribution. Finally, high levels of inequality can be a cause of low economic growth and 'secular stagnation', as even mainstream neoclassical economists at the Organisation for Economic Co-operation and Development (OECD) and the International Monetary Fund (IMF) have increasingly acknowledged.[3]

There is a growing consensus that excessive levels of inequality could also endanger the endurance of liberal democracy. Based on their analysis of recent public opinion data, political scientists Roberto Stefan Foa and Yascha Mounk come to a sobering conclusion:

> Citizens in a number of supposedly consolidated democracies in North America and Western Europe have not only grown more critical of their political leaders. Rather, they have also become more cynical about the value of democracy as a political system, less hopeful that anything they do might influence public policy, and more willing to express support for authoritarian alternatives.[4]

Since the 1980s, both voter turnout and trust in democratic institutions such as independent parliaments and judicial courts have sharply declined across the established democracies of North America and Western Europe: 'As party identification has weakened and party membership has declined, citizens have become less willing to stick with establishment parties. Instead, voters increasingly endorse single-issue movements, vote for populist candidates, or support "anti-system" parties that define themselves in opposition to the status quo.'[5] An increasing number of recent studies claim that the rise in 'populism' in most Western societies is closely connected to the rise in income inequality, the stagnation of middle-class wages and growing economic insecurity linked to financial and economic globalization.[6]

The economic instability of capitalism and its inherent tendency to fuel inequality are therefore topics that should be of interest to any student and scholar in social sciences. This book aims to deepen our understanding of these two central challenges of advanced capitalism from a political economy perspective. Political economy is a field of study that is based on the assumption that it is impossible to say much sensible about the economy and the functioning of 'markets' without taking into account the broader political and institutional context in which these markets are always embedded. It is a research tradition whose principal objective is to break down disciplinary boundaries between economics, political science and sociology and to ask basic questions about the distribution of resources in capitalist 'market economies'.

Thus, political economy applies Harold Lasswell's classic definition of politics – the study of 'who gets what, when and how' – to the economy and is, as such, a research approach that is ideally suited to identify the political and social causes and consequences of rising inequality and instability.

Perhaps the best way to clarify the distinctive features of political economy as a field of study is by setting it against its main contender: neoclassical economics, which has become the dominant approach to study the economy in our contemporary society: it is the research tradition in which most economics students are nowadays educated. Neoclassical economics has become increasingly formalistic, developing mathematical models and quantitative methods that are completely detached from the social, political and historical context of economic dynamics in the real world. The global financial crisis exposed the failures of neoclassical economics.[7] Understanding and deepening our knowledge of the global financial crisis and its longer-term causes and consequences should be central objectives in the social sciences, but neoclassical economics seems to have failed in reaching these objectives. In a famous event symbolizing this failure, Queen Elizabeth II of the United Kingdom asked, during a briefing by economists at the London School of Economics in 2008, why nobody had seen the crisis coming. Since then a growing group of students (and teachers) have started to complain that existing textbooks in economics had not done a sufficiently good job of explaining what exactly had happened and – even more importantly – why it had happened. In many countries, groups of students have demanded an overhaul in how economics is taught, with more pluralism and more emphasis on real-world problems like inequality and financial instability.

Critics of neoclassical economics have argued that the assumptions behind its mathematical models are often simplistic and unrealistic, revealing a conservative bias that is overly optimistic about the efficiency of free markets and pessimistic about the effectiveness of government intervention. The *homo economicus* is one of the most contested of these unrealistic assumptions: individuals are seen as rational and self-interested actors who maximize their utility by making decisions that are based on full information. This assumption allows neoclassical economists to design mathematical and law-like models of human behaviour and economic decision-making: these economists tend to engage in a logical exercise based on assumptions that are adopted because they can be *quantified* and *modelled*, not necessarily because they are true or even sensible. For example, in order to predict consumer behaviour, neoclassical models assume that all people have perfect information about all of the goods that they might want to buy: they know all of the prices and qualities involved and they know how much satisfaction they would receive from every product. Another assumption of neoclassical economics, closely associated with the first one, is that free markets balance supply and demand in the long term and are self-adjusting: it is presumed that the economy disturbed by a shock will always return to a new equilibrium (see chapter 1 on the meaning of market equilibrium). There is, obviously, a liberal bias to this line of thinking: if markets are assumed to be stable and self-correcting, it is better to allow them to function on their own, without excessive government intervention. This efficient market hypothesis provided, as we will see, ideological support for the excessive deregulation of the banking system, which – together with the rise in inequality – was an important cause of the global financial crisis.

In response to such criticisms, neoclassical economists usually reply that the main purpose of their mathematical models is to predict economic behaviour rather than formulate realistic assumptions about how the world really works. In his essay on the methodology of positive economics, US economist and Nobel laureate Milton Friedman argues that it does not really matter that the assumptions behind a theory are unrealistic as long as the theory's predictions are correct:

> the relevant question to ask about the 'assumptions' of a theory is not whether they are descriptively 'realistic', for they never are, but whether they are sufficiently good approximations for the purpose in hand. And this question can be answered only by seeing whether the theory works, which means whether it yields sufficiently accurate predictions.[8]

Friedman's argument was reiterated by William Prescott – another Nobel laureate – in his 2016 paper *RBC Methodology and the Development of Aggregate Economic Theory*: 'Reality is complex, and any model economy used is necessarily an abstraction and therefore false. This does not mean, however, that model economies are not useful in drawing scientific inference.'[9]

Nonetheless, neoclassical economists have a bad track record in making correct predictions. The global financial crisis of 2007–9 caught most neoclassical economists by surprise. As Ben Bernanke, former president of the US central bank, conceded, neoclassical economists 'both failed to predict the global financial crisis and underestimated its consequences for the broader economy'.[10] To be fair, some experts warned about the dangers of housing bubbles. But in the final analysis, the consensus was that the situation was not as bad as it seemed. In the wake of the crisis, research staff at the IMF or central banks have also been notoriously wrong regarding their projections of economic variables like gross domestic product, inflation and unemployment. Political economy as an academic discipline might be equally bad at making predictions about the future, but tends to be much better in explaining post hoc why economic events occurred in the way they did. The reason is that political economists do not base their theories on unrealistic assumptions and that they take into account non-economic factors that all too often ignored by neoclassical economists.

One of these factors is power and politics: political economists are critical of the neoclassical presumption that economic phenomena can be separated from relations of power and politics. Neoclassical economists believe that someone's wage or income is a reflection of the marginal productivity of his or her labour – that is, the additional revenue a firm gets from hiring that particular individual (see chapter 1). As a typical example from neoclassical reasoning, consider the following statement by Greg Mankiw – author of one of the most famous introductory handbooks in neoclassical economics, *Principles of Economics*:

> Most of the very wealthy get that way by making substantial economic contributions, not by gaming the system or taking advantage of some market failure or the political process ... Take the example of pay for chief executive officers (CEOs). Without doubt, CEOs are paid handsomely, and their pay has grown over time relative to that of the average worker ... [However], the most natural explanation of high CEO pay is that the value of a good CEO is extraordinarily high.[11]

Yet this neoclassical conception of CEO compensation ignores the role of the government, the legal system and all other institutions and norms that underpin the political power of CEOs and might have played a role in helping them receive high incomes. For instance, the highest federal marginal tax rate in the United States fell from 91 per cent for all personal income in the 1960s to less than 40 per cent in the 2000s. Such changes in the US tax system were vital in boosting top incomes of CEOs. In their book *Winner-Take-All Politics: How Washington Made the Rich Richer – and Turned Its Back on the Middle Class*, political scientists Jacob Hacker and Paul Pierson argue that the dramatic increase in income inequality in the United States since 1978 has been the result of political forces, rather than the natural and inevitable result of technological innovation and increased competition associated with globalization. They note that the balance of political power shifted sharply in favour of those at the very top of the economic ladder. Financial and economic elites have used their political clout to dramatically cut taxes, dismantle social welfare and liberalize labour markets, reduce the power of labour unions and deregulate the financial industry.[12]

In the following chapters of this book, we will provide a comprehensive overview of the many policy and institutional changes that have shifted political power from workers to the top managers of firms and their shareholders and have contributed to the rise in inequality in income and in wealth. These changes fall under the rubric of neoliberalism – a set of policies grounded in neoclassical economic theory and aimed at maximizing the role of markets in the allocation of economic resources and reducing the role of the state to the principal enforcer of 'market efficiency' in the economy.[13] Neoliberalism tried to undo the Keynesian compromises of the post-war era of egalitarian capitalism through a process of marketization – such as lifting restrictions on international economic transactions and subjecting governments and workers to the discipline of global market forces (see chapter 2). The compromises of the Keynesian era arose from the Great Depression of the 1930s, which had created a new consensus among economists and policymakers that activist state intervention in the economy and a more equitable distribution of income and wealth were the most effective ways to sustained prosperity:

> The key to full employment and economic growth, many at the time believed, was high levels of aggregate demand. But high demand required mass consumption, which in turn required an equitable distribution of purchasing power. By ensuring sufficient income for less well-off consumers, the government could continually expand the markets for businesses and boost profits as well as wages.[14]

This Keynesian consensus unravelled during the economic crisis of the 1970s, giving rise to a neoliberal turn in economic thinking and policymaking that heightened income and wealth inequality and ultimately contributed to the global financial crisis of 2008. In this book we will trace neoliberal transformations in four policy domains that have played a pivotal role in fuelling economic inequality and financial instability over the past four decades:

1 macroeconomic policy, which refers to the tools of the government to manage the business cycle, fight unemployment during economic recessions and maintain price stability;
2 social policy and industrial relations, which is about the organization of the welfare state and labour market;
3 corporate governance, which consists of formal and informal rules and norms shaping firms' business strategies and the distribution of profits between their main stakeholders (i.e. shareholders, managers and workers); and
4 financial policy, which is about the regulation of the banking and credit system.

This book is the first to give a comprehensive and systematic overview of neoliberal transformations within these four policy domains since the 1980s and show how these transformations have made advanced capitalist societies in Europe and the United States both more unequal and unstable.

The book will examine these changes from a 'growth model' perspective. It will provide a synthesis of a nascent comparative and international political economy literature that has linked the global financial crisis to the formation of two mutually dependent but unsustainable growth models: the Anglo-Saxon liberal market economies (LMEs) as well as several Southern European mixed market economies (MMEs) pursued *debt-led* growth models, whereas the Northern and Western European coordinated market economies (CMEs) adopted *export-led* growth models. The development of these growth models was deeply connected to distinctive patterns of income and wealth inequality in these advanced capitalist countries – patterns that have been shaped by divergent institutions that both reflect and shape the bargaining position of various classes and groups in these countries. From the growth model perspective elaborated in this book, these institutions reflect temporary and fragile attempts to resolve structural tensions and conflicts between different classes and groups, making the capitalist system intrinsically unstable and prone to crisis.

The book is structured in eight chapters. In **chapter 1** we introduce various economic concepts and measures needed for a systematic study of these challenges. The most important objective of the chapter is to give a comprehensive and empirically grounded overview of the cyclical patterns and interlinked nature of economic instability and inequality since the birth of democratic capitalism in the beginning of the twentieth century. We will discuss different measures of income inequality, highlighting the important distinction between personal income distribution and functional income distribution and their connection to wealth inequality. Empirically, we will show that dynamics of inequality are deeply connected to varieties of capitalism: the Anglo-Saxon LMEs have more unequal *personal* income distribution and experienced a much sharper increase in the national income share of the top 1 per cent than the Northern and Western European CMEs, which witnessed a starker decline in the share of national income going to labour (which is the main measure of *functional* income distribution). Moreover, we discuss the neoclassical interpretation of rising inequality in the advanced capitalist world since the 1980s and criticize its neglect of power relations, the role of institutions and the structural instabilities that permeate capitalist economies. As such, the chapter explains why (comparative and international) political economy is needed for a deeper understanding of rising inequality, and of how it is connected to the global financial crisis of 2008 through the development of two unsustainable growth models.

In **chapter 2** we give an overview of the rise and fall of egalitarian capitalism, which is linked to the expansion of the Keynesian welfare state (KWS) during the 1950s and 1960s and its subsequent demise since the 1970s. The KWS, which arose in the wake of the Great Depression, was based on a wage-led growth model that had three features: (1) there was a cross-party political consensus that achieving full employment via activist macroeconomic policymaking had become a central responsibility of the government; (2) the KWS aimed at expanding social security and advancing collective bargaining, empowering labour unions in ways that ensured wages grew in line with average productivity; (3) the KWS was supported internationally by the Bretton Woods regime, which established rules for managing post-war international financial relations and offered a conducive external environment for domestic state intervention. In this chapter we also discuss how the KWS came to a halt in the wake of the breakdown of the Bretton Woods regime and the stagflation crisis in the 1970s, which undermined the legitimacy of the Keynesian paradigm and set the stage for the rise of neoliberalism as a new framework for economic policymaking in the advanced capitalist world. The KWS collapsed due to inflationary pressures associated with intensified industrial conflict in the 1970s and longer-term secular trends of globalization, deindustrialization and financialization, which forced governments in the advanced capitalist world to find a replacement for the wage-led growth model in the form of either debt-led or export-led growth. In chapter 2 we sketch out why a post-Keynesian account of these growth models is more suitable to clarify the linkages between rising inequality and the global financial crisis than the account delivered by the 'varieties of capitalism' literature.

In **chapter 3** we examine the neoliberal shift in macroeconomic policy-making, from the Keynesian focus on full employment towards a 'sound money' consensus about the necessity to pursue low inflation and public debt levels. Monetary policy was delegated to politically independent central banks with a principal mandate to maintain price stability, leading to a regime of monetary dominance in which fiscal policy was subordinated to that mandate. The shift towards neoliberal macroeconomic policy is often interpreted as the result of the deficiency of Keynesian ideas during the 1970s stagflation crisis and the fiscal crisis of the welfare state during the 1980s, which set the stage for monetarist and neoclassical views on macroeconomic policymaking that eventually culminated in the New Keynesian macroeconomic policy paradigm. We go beyond such an ideational interpretation by pointing to new institutional constraints on Keynesian macroeconomic policymaking, as well as to the distributional effects of neoliberal macroeconomic policy. By subordinating fiscal policy to the inflation target of central banks, governments became entirely dependent on foreign investors in transnational sovereign bond markets to fund their public deficits. This put new constraints on the capacity of governments to pursue reflationary Keynesian macroeconomic policies, making governments more attentive to the preferences of sovereign bond investors and credit rating agencies for low inflation and public deficits. Drawing on class-based perspectives, we will clarify why restrictive macroeconomic policies served to weaken the bargaining power of workers and labour unions, allowing firms to restore their profitability (and contributing to a falling labour income share in the industrialized economies). Drawing on sectoral perspectives, we will explain why the transition towards low inflation particularly advanced the interests of banks, asset managers and their wealthiest clients.

Conflict between employers and labour unions during the 1970s resulted in a crisis of the wage-led growth model that had been central to the Keynesian Golden Age of capitalism. From a neoliberal perspective, the crisis of wage-led growth and the ensuing rise in long-term unemployment rates were caused by structural rigidities in labour markets – for example, the excessive influence of labour unions in the wage-setting process – and overly generous welfare states. While there continue to be persistent institutional differences between the Anglo-Saxon LMEs and the European CMEs in terms of social policy, the crisis of the wage-led growth model put pressure on *all* the advanced capitalist countries to liberalize their labour markets and dismantle their social security systems. In **chapter 4** we will review different theoretical perspectives on these liberalization pressures. Class-based power resource approaches maintain that globalization and regional integration have forced the CMEs to liberalize their social model by strengthening the exit power of capital and weakening the power of labour and left-wing political parties. Employer-centred varieties of capitalism (VoC) approaches contend that pressures for liberalization predominantly arose in the domestically oriented service sectors, since employers in the internationally exposed industrial sectors of the CMEs continue to benefit from centralized labour markets and relatively generous social security systems. The chapter subsequently traces different pathways to liberalization in the Scandinavian social-democratic CMEs, the conservative-corporatist CMEs and Anglo-Saxon LMEs. By surveying these diverse trajectories of neoliberalization, it will become clear that all varieties of capitalism – even the more social and redistributive CMEs – have evolved into less egalitarian forms.

Neoliberal globalization also fostered a shareholder model of corporate governance, according to which the maximization of shareholder value and returns should be the principal objective of firms' business strategy. The shareholder model of corporate governance was more eagerly adopted by firms in the Anglo-Saxon LMEs than in other countries, which explains why the national income share of the top 1 per cent rose much faster in the former than in the latter economies. In **chapter 5** we will trace these divergent patterns by looking at institutional differences in corporate governance and associated executive compensation practices. First of all, we will attribute the neoliberal shift towards shareholder value maximization in the US economy to growing international economic pressures faced by large US vertically integrated corporations, financial ideas (the growing popularity of the neoliberal agency theory of corporate governance) and interest group politics (weakening of labour unions and rent-seeking by managers). Subsequently, we will link divergences in corporate governance and executive compensation practices in the CMEs and LMEs to the distinctive institutional complementarities between their financial systems (bank-dominated versus capital market-dominated), labour markets (centralized versus decentralized), educational systems (promoting industry-specific versus general skills) and firm innovation strategies (incremental versus radical innovation). By linking the shareholder model of corporate governance to the increasing financialization of non-financial firms, we go beyond overly functionalist and static VoC approaches of corporate governance and discuss regulatory changes – for example, the European Union's promotion of the shareholder model as part and parcel of its efforts to integrate European financial markets – that portend an at least partial erosion of the institutional complementarities of CMEs.

Financial globalization promoted a shift towards market-based banking in ways that increasingly blurred the boundaries between national financial systems dominated by capital market financing and those predominantly reliant upon banking credit. Whereas, in the traditional model of financial intermediation, banking credit is funded by retail deposits, market-based banks increasingly rely on the market to enable their lending (e.g. by financing themselves in wholesale funding markets and/or by developing 'originate-to-distribute' techniques like securitization). In **chapter 6** we will discuss the emergence of market-based banking since the 1980s and its distinctive manifestation in the Anglo-Saxon LMEs and European CMEs, linking diverging dynamics in household debt and housing markets to diverging patterns of income inequality and growth models. In the United States and the United Kingdom these dynamics have been linked to the formation of asset-based welfare regimes that allowed poor and middle-class households to extract easy credit from the rising market value of their homes. In this chapter we will also explain how large banks from the European CMEs were deeply implicated in these dynamics, as they massively invested in these complex securitized assets and funded these investments by borrowing from other banks in short-term US money and eurodollar markets. By offering an overview of these developments in the European financial system, we will challenge the core assumptions on which the bank-based/capital market-based dichotomous framing in the comparative political economy (CPE) literature – especially in the VoC tradition – rests. Moreover, we will highlight strong growth in household debt in several CMEs (especially the Netherlands and Denmark) and clarify why the accumulation of household debt in these countries did not culminate in a fully fledged housing crisis like those in the United States and the United Kingdom.

Two distinctive growth models ensued from these changes in macroeconomic policy, industrial relations, corporate governance and financial policy: debt-led growth models in the LMEs and Mediterranean MMEs and export-led growth models in the CMEs, all of which have been shaped by distinctive patterns of income inequality. **Chapter 7** reviews recent analytical approaches to CPE that focus on the relative importance of different components of aggregate demand and dynamic relations among these demand drivers of growth, thereby paying due attention to the instability of these growth models and their diversity within distinct groups of varieties of capitalism. We will sketch out the main political-economic pillars of these growth models and explain how the mutually interdependent relationship between debt-led and export-led growth gave rise to unsustainable macroeconomic imbalances that were an important source of the global financial crisis of 2007–8 and Eurozone debt crisis of 2010–15. Furthermore, we examine the varying capacity of the industrialized countries to avoid the burden of macroeconomic adjustment after the crisis, highlighting the importance of monetary sovereignty – that is, the capacity to issue debt in a currency controlled by the national central bank. The Eurozone countries have surrendered this capacity by issuing debt in a currency that is controlled by the European Central Bank (ECB), which was more reluctant than the Federal Reserve and the Bank of England to engage in large-scale asset purchase programmes known as quantitative easing (QE; see chapter 7). In the United States and the United Kingdom QE reflected an attempt to minimize the macroeconomic adjustment costs of the crisis by restoring the key pillars of finance-led growth. The ECB's reluctance to pursue QE offered the northern CMEs a mechanism to deflect the burden of macroeconomic adjustment onto the southern MMEs, which were forced to pursue very painful austerity measures.

The asymmetrical adjustment to the global and regional macroeconomic imbalances after the crisis resulted in persistently weak and fragile economic growth, leading to a revival of the hypothesis that advanced capitalist countries face a period of secular stagnation. In **chapter 8** we will discuss the risk of secular stagnation and other key challenges these countries will be confronted with in the near future: the rise in radical right-wing populism, global warming and the economic fallout of the coronavirus crisis. In doing so, the final chapter assesses the prospects for the emergence of a more egalitarian and more sustainable form of democratic capitalism, arguing that a fundamental revision of the neoliberal macroeconomic policy framework should be central to addressing these challenges.

1

Rising Inequality in Advanced Capitalism

In this chapter we will provide a brief overview of some issues related to rising inequality in advanced capitalist countries. First, how is it measured? There are many ways that inequality can be measured, but we will restrict ourselves to those measures that are most frequently used in contemporary debates on inequality: (1) measures of *personal income distribution* like the Gini index and the shares of different groups in national income; (2) measures of *functional income distribution* like the labour and capital share in national income; (3) measures of *wealth distribution*. By all measures, economic inequality has risen sharply in many advanced capitalist economies. Nevertheless, significant cross-national differences can be observed in terms of both the level of inequality and the evolution of inequality since the 1980s: patterns of inequality have been shaped by national varieties of capitalism, with the Anglo-Saxon LMEs displaying higher inequality and growth of inequality than North and West European CMEs.

Second, how can rising inequality be explained? Cross-national divergences in patterns of inequality suggest that the neoclassical interpretation remains inadequate. Neoclassical economists have emphasized exogenous market forces like skill-biased technological change (SBTC) and globalization to explain the rise in inequality. Since advanced capitalist economies have more or less equally been exposed to these market forces, they fail to clarify why the trajectory of inequality has been so markedly different in the Anglo-Saxon countries and the other advanced countries. So while technological change and globalization may act as powerful forces for income inequality, continued cross-national diversity suggests that other factors influence both the magnitude and the rate of change in inequality and top income shares. From a political economy perspective, the effects of technological change and globalization on the distribution of income and wealth in the advanced economies have been shaped and mediated by a variety of government policies and economic institutions that will be examined in subsequent chapters.

Finally, why does rising inequality matter? A growing body of research in social sciences and political economy suggests that excessive inequality can have different kinds of undesirable social and political effects. While it is important to be aware of these effects, the main focus of this book will be on another adverse consequence of rising inequality: financial instability. There is a growing consensus that the rise in income and wealth inequality was one of the deeper, structural causes of the global financial crisis of 2007–9. In this chapter we briefly discuss the main mechanisms behind this connection and sketch out why heterodox political economy is more adequate to understand the causes and consequences of rising inequality than neoclassical economics.

Measures of economic inequality

Personal income distribution

For many decades, both the IMF and the OECD have collected data on the evolution of income inequality, which they usually measure by the Gini index, developed by the Italian statistician and sociologist Corrado Gini (1884–1965). Essentially, the Gini index measures the extent to which the actual distribution of disposable household income deviates from the situation in which every household has the same income, ranging from zero (indicating 'perfect equality') to one (meaning 'complete inequality'). In order to understand the origin of the Gini index, we need to have a look at the Lorenz curve – shown in figure 1.1. The Lorenz curve depicts the cumulative percentage of households (from poor to rich) on the horizontal x-axis and the cumulative income share

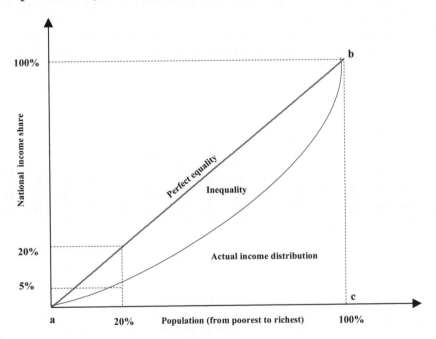

Figure 1.1 The Lorenz curve and the Gini index

of these households on the vertical y-axis. For instance, the poorest 20 per cent of households earn 5 per cent of total income in our example. The Gini index is then calculated by the ratio of the area between the line of perfect equality (the 45-degree diagonal line) and the observed Lorenz curve to the area between the line of perfect equality (line ab in the graph) and the line of perfect inequality (line acb). The higher the index, the more unequal the distribution is.

The Gini index used by the OECD, which is depicted in figure 1.2, measures the distribution of disposable income after all taxes have been paid and government transfers have been received. It includes income from labour (wages and salaries, profit-sharing bonuses and other forms of profit-related pay, income from self-employment) and capital (income from non-financial assets like real estate and financial assets like banking accounts, bonds and stocks). Several conclusions can be drawn from this figure. First of all, Anglo-Saxon countries tend to have higher levels of income inequality than most continental European countries and Japan. Inequality also rose faster in the former countries between 1985 and 2017 than in the latter. Although Finland and Sweden are an exception to this trend, their Gini indices were the lowest in the 1980s and they remain among the most equal countries according to this measure. France and Belgium are the only two countries whose Gini index remained more or less the same during this period. So while the rise in income inequality was an almost universal phenomenon in the advanced capitalist world, there are substantial cross-national differences between OECD countries in terms of both the level of inequality and the pace at which it has increased since the 1980s.

One problem with statistical indices like the Gini index is that they summarize the entire income distribution in one single number, making it

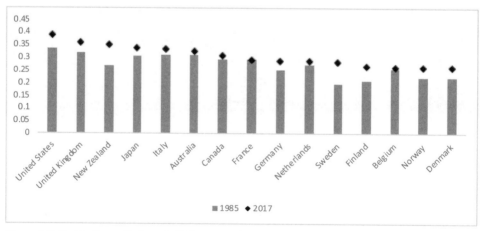

Figure 1.2 Gini indices of selected OECD countries, 1985 and 2017

Source: OECD

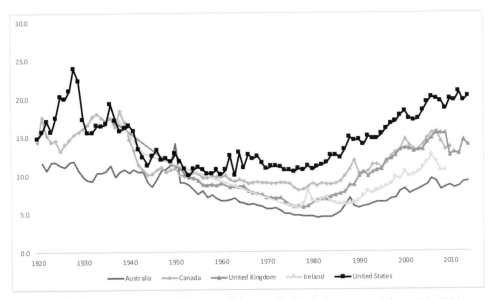

Figure 1.3 Share of the top percentile in total income in Anglo-Saxon countries, 1920–2014

Source: World Inequality Database, https://wid.world

a relatively abstract measure of inequality. For this reason, it is more illumi-nating to rely on distribution tables, which present data on the shares of different income groups in the total income that is earned every year in a particular country and how these shares have evolved over time. French economists Thomas Piketty and Emmanuel Saez collected such data, using tax records that enabled them to track changes in the levels of inequality over very long periods of time – even going back for more than two centuries for some countries. These authors are best known for their historical data on the evolution of the share of the 'top 1 per cent' in total income, which are shown in figures 1.3 and 1.4.

There is a considerable difference between the Anglo-Saxon countries and other rich OECD countries in terms of the income share of the top 1 per cent. The Anglo-Saxon countries – Australia, Canada, Ireland, the United Kingdom and the United States – all show a U-shape. Over the period 1980 to 2012, the top 1 per cent income share more or less doubled in these five countries (and rose by more than 50 per cent in New Zealand, not shown). According to this measure, income inequality is highest in the United States, where the top 1 per cent's income share rose from 10.6 per cent in the 1970s to 20.8 per cent in 2012. The experience is again markedly different in continental Europe and Japan, where the long pattern is closer to an L-shaped curve. The income shares of the top 1 per cent have also risen in these countries in recent years, but they are not extremely far today from their levels in the late 1940s.

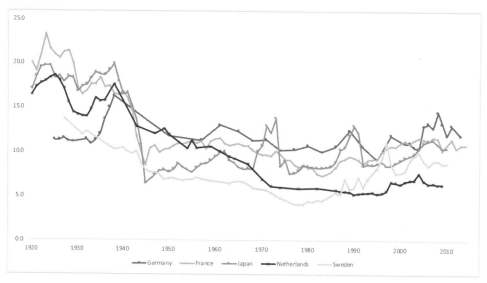

Figure 1.4 Share of the top percentile in total income in continental Europe and Japan, 1920–2014

Source: World Inequality Database, https://wid.world

In his best-selling book *Capital in the 21st Century*, Piketty rightly notes that 'the share of income (or wealth) going to the top decile or centile is a useful index for judging how unequal a society is, because it reflects not just the existence of extremely high incomes or extremely large fortunes but also the number of individuals who enjoy such rewards'.[1] The group is, by definition, a very small minority of the population, but is nevertheless far larger than the dozens or hundreds of 'super elites' who are tracked by Forbes' or Bloomberg's billionaires lists. In a country like the United Kingdom with more than 60 million citizens (of whom about 45 million are adults), the top centile contains about 450,000 people. In a country like the United States with about 250 million adults, the top centile consists of 2.5 million individuals. These are numerically large groups of people who inevitably have the most social and political influence in their country, which is why Piketty labels this group as the 'dominant class'.[2]

Similar cross-regional differences emerge if we look at the evolution of the income shares of people in the bottom 50 per cent – who can be called the 'lower classes' – and the middle 40 per cent – the 'middle classes', who stand between the fifth and ninth decile of the income distribution. Table 1.1 presents accumulated income growth rates in Europe and North America from 1980 to 2016 for these income groups. Real national income growth per adult – that is, income growth adjusted for inflation – during this period reached 40 per cent in Europe and 63 per cent in North America (the United States and Canada). In both regions income growth is systematically higher for upper

Table 1.1 Total income growth and inequality, 1980–2016

	Total cumulative income growth per adult		Share of total accumulated income growth captured by income groups	
	Europe	United States and Canada	Europe	United States and Canada
Full population	40%	63%	100%	100%
Bottom 50%	26%	5%	14%	2%
Middle 40%	34%	44%	38%	32%
Top 10%	58%	123%	48%	67%
Top 1%	72%	206%	18%	35%
Top 0.1%	76%	320%	7%	18%
Top 0.01%	87%	452%	3%	9%
Top 0.001%	120%	629%	1%	4%

Source: Alvaredo et al. 2018, https://wir2018.wid.world

income groups. But in Europe the growth gap between the bottom 50 per cent and the full population is much lower, as is the gap between the bottom 50 per cent and top income groups. To better understand the significance of these unequal rates of growth, it is useful to focus on the share of total growth captured by each group over the entire period. The top 1 per cent captured 35 per cent of total growth in the United States and Canada, whereas it 'merely' seized 18 per cent of total growth in Europe. In Europe, the fruits of income growth have also been shared more equally with the bottom 50 per cent: 14 per cent against a meagre 2 per cent in North America. While the middle 40 per cent also reaped a higher share in total accumulated income growth in Europe than in the United States and Canada (38 per cent against 32 per cent), it is especially the experience of the bottom 50 per cent that has been strikingly different.

But the same table also shows that the inequality in North America has been markedly higher in the top end of the income distribution. This difference becomes larger the higher we go in the hierarchy: the share of total income captured by the top 1 per cent is twice as large in the United States and Canada as in Europe, whereas it is three times as large for the top 0.01 per cent and four times as large for the top 0.001 per cent. To be sure, the top 0.01 per cent and top 0.001 per cent are much smaller groups than the top 1 per cent: in the United States, these two groups amount to, respectively, 25,000 and 2,500 individuals. Focusing on the evolution of the income share of this group is nevertheless highly important for our understanding of the structure of inequality: individuals belonging to these groups are 'super elites' who derive most of their income from capital rather than from their labour. Remember that the Gini index is a measure of *total* income inequality: it measures the distribution of income from *both* labour (wages, salaries, bonuses, etc.) *and* capital investments (banking accounts, stocks, bonds, real estate and other assets). This is also the case for the income share of different groups discussed above. The key issue here is that income from capital – for example, interest rate income on savings accounts and bond investments, dividend income on stock investments (see box 1.1), rental income on real estate, etc. – becomes increasingly important for groups at the top end of the income hierarchy.

Box 1.1 Stocks and bonds

Stocks and bonds are financial assets that can be bought and sold on financial markets. Firms issue stocks and bonds to attract funding, which can be used to finance their operations or expand their production. Stocks and bonds have different implications both for the firm and for the owner of these assets. The purchaser of a company's stocks becomes a partial owner of the firm – a shareholder – who receives a part of the company's profits every year in the form of a dividend. The purchaser of a company's bonds is only a lender to that company: bonds are a certificate of indebtedness that specifies the obligations of the borrower to the owner of the bond; it identifies the time at which the loan will be repaid (called the maturity) and the rate of interest that will be paid periodically until the loan matures. As such, investing in a company's bonds is less 'risky' than investing in its stocks, as bond investors can be sure to get all their money back if the company does not go bankrupt. The returns for a stock investor, by contrast, depend on the profitability of the firm and its performance on the stock market. See chapter 5 for a more elaborate discussion.

Most individuals do not own stocks or bonds on their own account. In most cases, individuals invest their money in stocks and bonds (or other types of financial assets) through institutional investors like private pension funds and mutual funds. These institutional investors pool money from both small savers and wealthy individuals to purchase a variety of financial assets in order to diversify risk. Although many middle-income households have invested some of their savings in financial assets through these institutional investors, the ownership of financial wealth remains highly unevenly distributed in every society. In the United States, for instance, the top 10 per cent of US households owns more than 80 per cent of all the stocks that have been issued by publicly listed US corporations.

Functional income distribution

Why does this matter? The relative importance of capital income for the top 1 per cent – and especially for the top 0.1 per cent and top 0.01 per cent – suggests that these groups are the main beneficiaries of the declining labour share and parallel rising capital share in national income. The statistics on income inequality that we have discussed so far are measures of the *personal* income distribution – that is, the distribution of income between the various individuals or households in a country. Another important indicator for our purposes is the *functional* income distribution, which measures the distribution of income between the two factors of production – that is, the inputs that are needed by firms to produce goods and services: capital (which also includes land) and labour. In capitalist economies, firms make profits by adding value to the raw material and intermediate goods consumed in the production process, using both labour (workers and managers) and capital (factory and administrative buildings, machines and equipment). The gross domestic product (GDP) is the market value of all final goods and services produced within a country in a given period of time, where 'final' means that the value of intermediate goods – that is, parts and components that are used to produce final goods – is not included (to avoid double accounting). GDP is, perhaps, the single most important concept in economics, because it represents the economic size of a country as well as the national income that is generated in a country every year. Hence, GDP is a reflection of a country's material well-being: GDP per capita gives an approximate idea of how much money an average citizen earns in a particular year.

A key problem with the concept of GDP and national income is that it tells us nothing about the distribution of that income. While the average annual income of a US citizen was about US$59,000 in 2017, a top manager of a large US firm received a multiple of that amount while a retail worker earned much less. Measures of *personal* income distribution like the Gini index or the income share of the top percentile give us information about the degree of income inequality, and should always be considered together with data on GDP and GDP per capita in order to get a full picture of a country's economic well-being. Measures of *functional* income distribution represent a different type of income distribution: the *labour share* and *capital share* of GDP or national income indicate how the national income of a country is distributed between the two factors of production in that country; they measure how much of the added value that has been generated in a country is seized either by the sellers of labour (in the forms of wages, salaries and other employment-related income) or the owners of capital (in the form of profits, rents and other investment-related income). The best way to understand a country's labour and capital share is that they offer an idea of how the value added and profits of firms in that country are, on average, divided between its workers and managers (who supply labour) and its shareholders (who own the firms and supply capital). Since labour and capital are both needed to produce goods and services, the labour and capital share indicate how much of the profits from selling these goods and services goes to either labour or capital.

The labour share of national income seems to capture the Marxist notion that capitalism features intrinsically competing interests between the working class and the owners of capital (see below) – that is, that there is a 'zero-sum' conflict between capital and labour over the division of the national income pie: the gain of one production factor is the other one's loss.[3] While the Eurozone's labour share was, for instance, 68 per cent in 2010 – meaning that 68 per cent of Eurozone GDP went to wages and other types of labour income

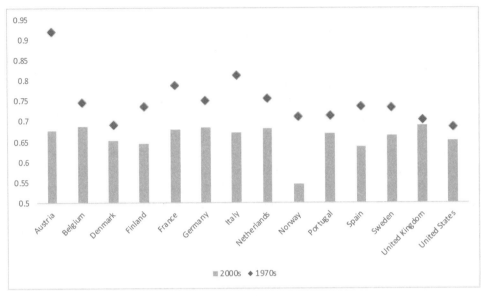

Figure 1.5 Average labour income share, 1970s and 2000s
Source: OECD

and the rest to profits and other types of capital income – the ratio has not been stable over time: figure 1.5 shows that the labour income share has been falling in the advanced capitalist world since the 1970s. A falling labour share implies that workers have been getting a shrinking piece of the pie and the owners of capital a growing piece.

It is interesting and important to note that the fall in the labour income share has been more pronounced in the continental European countries than in the United States and the United Kingdom. There are two complementary explanations for this observation. On the one hand, the labour income share is a broad measure that integrates the incomes of employees working on very different pay scales and in different economic sectors: it includes the low wages of workers located in traditionally low-pay sectors such as food and retail as well as the exorbitantly high salaries of chief executives and senior managers. So given the fact that management pay rose more sharply in the Anglo-Saxon countries than in the continental European countries (as we will see in chapter 5 on corporate governance), it is not really surprising that the labour share fell less prominently in the former group of countries than in the latter. Yet the sharper rise in wage inequality makes the fall in the labour share in the Anglo-Saxon economies look more modest than it is in reality for the majority of wage earners.[4] For this reason, it is more appropriate to compare the evolution of *median* wages with the evolution of *average* labour productivity – that is, the amount of real output (GDP) produced by an hour of labour. Since the 1980s a growing *productivity–wage gap* has emerged in the US economy: from 1973 to 2015, net productivity rose by 73.4 per cent, while the hourly pay of the typical median wage earners essentially stagnated – increasing

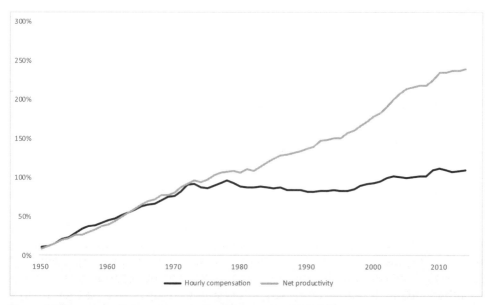

Figure 1.6 The productivity–pay gap in the US economy, 1948–2014

Source: Economic Policy Institute analysis using data from the Bureau of Economic Analysis and Bureau of Labor Statistics

Data are for average hourly compensation of production/nonsupervisory workers in the private sector and net productivity of the total economy. Net productivity is the growth of output of goods and services minus depreciation per hour worked.

only 11.1 per cent over forty-two years (after adjusting for inflation). So while US workers are more productive than ever, the fruits of their labour have primarily accrued to corporate profits (which were distributed to US corporations' shareholders *and* their managers) (figure 1.6).[5]

On the other hand, the greater fall of the labour income share in the continental European economies reflects a more hidden path of rising income inequality related to the weakening of labour power. During the post-war era labour unions were particularly strong in the Eurozone countries and in the Scandinavian countries, but their bargaining power has declined significantly since the end of the 1970s due to a number of developments that will be discussed in the following chapters. One of these developments is economic globalization, which put more pressure on labour unions to contain their wage demands in order to preserve the competitiveness of internationally oriented manufacturing firms, and gave these firms more 'exit options' to shift their production to countries with lower labour costs. Another important development is the rise in unemployment in the wake of the neoliberal shift in macroeconomic policy targets away from 'full employment' towards the lowering of inflation and public debt levels. As we will see in chapter 3, the Northern European countries have adopted more restrictive monetary and fiscal policies since the 1980s than the Anglo-Saxon countries, as a way to contain the wage demands of their more powerful labour unions and to strengthen the competitiveness of manufacturing sectors, which play a central role in the export-led growth models of the Northern European countries.

Distribution of wealth

Wealth inequality refers to the unequal distribution of a country's net national wealth – that is, all the financial and non-financial assets (mostly land and real estate) owned by the residents of a country minus all the liabilities owed by them. For a typical rich country, it consists of about 50 per cent real estate wealth and 50 per cent financial wealth like savings on banking accounts, stocks and bonds.[6] Traditionally, *wealth* inequality is significantly higher than *income* inequality. There are several reasons for this. By definition, an individual's wealth is income that has been saved and accumulated during his or her lifetime. Because individuals with high incomes tend to save and invest more than individuals with low incomes (who have insufficient income to save and invest), inequality of income translates almost automatically into inequality of wealth. Moreover, wealthy individuals tend to enjoy larger investment returns because they are in a more financially comfortable position to invest in riskier assets and have higher levels of financial expertise and access to professional investment assistance. Finally, and most importantly, wealth can be *inherited* across generations. In short, as the OECD notes in a recent report, 'A key aspect of wealth accumulation is that it operates in a self-reinforcing way; wealth begets wealth.'[7]

Table 1.2 shows the household net wealth shares held by the 10 per cent, 5 per cent and 1 per cent of households at the top of the wealth distribution in each country, along with the shares of those held by the bottom 40 per cent and 60

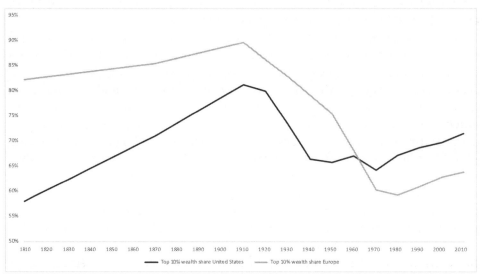

Figure 1.7 Wealth shares of top 10 per cent in Europe and the United States, 1810–2010
Source: Piketty 2014

Table 1.2 Distribution of net wealth in the OECD world, 2015 or latest available year

	Bottom 40% share	Bottom 60% share	Top 10% share	Top 5% share	Top 1% share
Australia	4.9	16.5	46.5	33.5	15.0
Austria	1.0	8.0	55.6	43.5	25.5
Belgium	5.7	19.0	42.5	29.7	12.1
Canada	3.4	12.4	51.1	37.0	16.7
Denmark	-8.6	-3.9	64.0	47.3	23.6
Finland	2.2	13.6	45.2	31.4	13.3
France	2.7	12.1	50.6	37.3	18.6
Germany	0.5	6.5	59.8	46.3	23.7
Greece	5.3	17.9	42.4	28.8	9.2
Ireland	-2.1	7.2	53.8	37.7	14.2
Italy	4.5	17.3	42.8	29.7	11.7
Japan	5.3	17.7	41.0	27.7	10.8
Luxembourg	3.9	15.3	48.7	36.3	18.8
Netherlands	-6.9	-4.0	68.3	52.5	27.8
New Zealand	3.1	12.3	52.9	39.7	...
Norway	-3.0	7.3	51.5	37.8	20.1
Portugal	3.2	12.4	52.1	36.5	14.4
Spain	6.9	18.7	45.6	33.3	16.3
United Kingdom	3.4	12.1	52.5	38.8	20.5
United States	-0.1	2.4	79.5	68.0	42.5

Source: OECD

per cent. Based on top wealth shares, household net wealth is most unequally distributed in the United States, where the top 10 per cent of households owned 79 per cent of total wealth and the top 1 per cent held a staggering 42 per cent in 2015. By comparison, the bottom 60 per cent of the wealth distribution in the United States owned a meagre 2.4 per cent of net national wealth. Looking at the concentration of wealth at the other end of the distribution, the share held by the bottom 60 per cent of households was *negative* in some countries, meaning that, on average, these households had liabilities exceeding the value of their assets (because, for instance, the value of their house was lower than the value of their mortgages and other real estate debt).

The level of wealth inequality has also been rising since the 1980s. Figure 1.7, drawn from Piketty's *Capital in the 21st Century*, reveals that wealth inequality was extremely high in the beginning of the twentieth century – even higher in Europe than in the United States. For reasons we will explore in this book, the level of wealth inequality was brought down in the United States during the interwar years and continued to decline in Europe until the 1970s. In other words, the post-war Golden Age of capitalism was the most egalitarian period in human history in terms of both income and wealth distribution. The period from the 1930s to the 1970s saw the emergence of what Piketty calls the 'patrimonial middle class' – 'the principal structural transformation of the distribution of wealth in the developed countries in the twentieth century': the wealth share of the middle 40 per cent reached 35 per cent in the 1970s in the United States and as much as 40 per cent in several European countries. Since the end of the 1970s, the share of the middle classes has been declining, while the share of the top 10 per cent – and especially of the top 1 per cent – has been rising in the United States and, to a lesser extent, in other advanced capitalist countries. One of the central objectives of this book is to explain what happened during this unique period of democratic capitalism, why this egalitarian period came to a halt in the course of the 1970s, and why a less egalitarian period has followed ever since.

The central thesis in Piketty's book is that wealth inequality in the United States and Europe is set to rise because, historically, the net rate of return to capital (r) exceeds the growth rate of output (g): if we assume that the annual increase in medium wages reflects the growth rate of output (GDP), the relationship $r > g$ basically means that the annual growth of the capital income of the medium capital owner will be higher than the annual growth of the wage income of the medium worker. However, the relationship $r > g$ is not a natural or deterministic feature of the capitalist economy but is deeply influenced by public policies, institutions and regulations. As we will see in the next section, a political economy perspective deviates fundamentally from a neoclassical interpretation by making the analysis of these policies, institutions and regulations central to the explanation of past and future patterns of income and wealth inequality.

Neoclassical interpretations of rising inequality in advanced capitalism

Two interlinked explanations are usually put forward by neoclassical economists to explain the re-widening of income gaps. The prevailing interpretation is SBTC: innovation in technology, especially the increasing use of computers, has increased demand for skilled labour relative to that for unskilled labour, and hence pushed up the wages of highly educated employees with university degrees relative to those of poorly educated workers who merely have high school diplomas (or less). This explanation is first and foremost based on the neoclassical view that a worker's wage should be equal to the *marginal product of labour* – that is, his or her individual contribution to the output and profitability of the firm he or she works for. In this regard, high-skilled workers are believed to be more productive than low-skilled workers, who have a lower marginal product of labour and therefore should be paid less by their firm.

The other dimension of the SBTC interpretation is that a worker's marginal product of labour depends not only on his or her skills but also on the supply and demand for these skills in the labour market – that is, the market where employers and workers interact as, respectively, buyers and sellers of labour. Although SBTC created more demand for high-skilled labour like engineers and software developers, the educational system failed to generate enough 'supply' of high-skilled labour. In some countries, like the United States, 'educational progress' – that is, the degree to which children attain levels of education higher than those of their parents – has even come to a standstill since the 1980s. Claudia Goldin and Lawrence Katz's book *The Race Between Technology and Education* (2008) is the key reference text for this interpretation of rising income inequality in the advanced capitalist world:

> During the first three-quarters of the twentieth century, the rising supply of educated workers outstripped the increased demand caused by technological advances. Higher real incomes were accompanied by lower inequality. But during the last two decades of the century the reverse was the case and there was sharply rising inequality. Put another way, in the first half of the century, education raced ahead of technology, but later in the century, technology raced ahead of educational gains.[8]

The neoclassical theory of SBTC is a clear attempt to explain the rise in income inequality by way of 'market forces' that are regulated by the 'law of supply and demand': if demand for a specific good (in this case, skilled labour) increases for any given supply of that good, the price of that good (in this case, the wage of skilled workers) will increase. The alleged efficiency of the 'price mechanism' to balance supply and demand in markets for goods and services (in this case, labour markets) is one of the key principles of neoclassical economics (box 1.2).

Box 1.2 The market price mechanism

Figure 1.8 presents a simple illustration of how the market price of a good or service is determined by the relationship between supply and demand. Demand is indicated by the downward-sloping curve, representing the phenomenon whereby a falling price of a good or service leads to a greater willingness among consumers to buy more of that good or service: if the price of a good increases, consumers will buy less of the good and purchase alternatives; if the price of a good drops, they will consume more of it. Supply is indicated by the upward-sloping curve, reflecting the phenomenon whereby rising prices make it more attractive and profitable for firms to increase their production: if the price of a good increases, producers of the good will produce and try to sell more (not because they like the consumers, but because they can make more profit); lower prices discourage supply because firms will make less profit. In a free market there will be a single price which brings demand and supply into balance, called the equilibrium price. The equilibrium price is also called the market clearing price, because it is the price at which the exact quantity that producers supply to market will be bought by consumers. This is efficient because there is neither an excess of supply and wasted output, nor a shortage – the *market clears efficiently*.

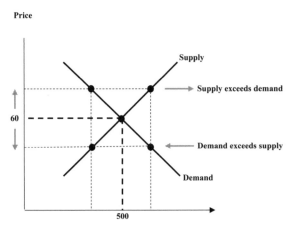

Figure 1.8 The market price mechanism

In figure 1.8 the market will be in equilibrium at a price of 60. At this price the demand equals the supply, and the market will clear: a quantity of 500 units will be offered for sale at 60 and 500 units will be bought – there will be no excess demand or supply at this price. Market prices have a key *signalling function*, as changes in prices provide information to producers and consumers about changes in market conditions. If prices are rising because of high demand from consumers, this is a signal to suppliers to expand production to meet the higher demand; if there is excess supply in the market, the price mechanism will help to eliminate a surplus of a good by allowing the market price to fall.[9]

In order to allow markets to clear efficiently, one important condition needs to be in place: free competition. According to neoclassical economists, the most effective 'regulator' of firms is competition in the free market system, which forces firms to produce goods and services that are demanded by consumers and sell these goods and services only at the price that consumers are willing to pay for them. Suppose in the above example that a producer wants to make an excess profit by asking a higher price than the equilibrium price of 60. If there is free competition, the producer will be unable to sell his goods as consumers can always buy the same good from another producer at the lower equilibrium price: if a producer raises his price above the equilibrium price to gain extra profits, competitors will step in and undersell him. Even if many producers unite and agree to charge an unduly high price, the collusive coalition will be broken by new firms entering the market: if there is free competition, the excessively high price will be a signal to entrepreneurs that it will be highly profitable to manufacture the good and steal the market from the colluding firms by underselling their price. Due to the entry of new competitors in the market, the price will return to the equilibrium price.

Another presumed benefit of free markets and the price mechanism, according to neoclassical economists, is that demand and supply adjust to external shocks until a new market equilibrium has been reached. Because free markets are believed to be *self-adjusting*, they work best without excessive government intervention. As Robert Heilbroner summarizes the self-adjusting and self-regulating nature of markets in his widely acclaimed book *The Worldly Philosophers* (1953):[10]

The beautiful consequence of the market is that it is its own guardian. If output or prices stray away from their socially ordained levels, forces are set into motion to bring them back to the fold. It is a curious paradox that thus ensues: the market, which is the acme of individual economic freedom, is the strictest taskmaster of all. One may appeal the ruling of a planning board or win the dispensation of a minister; but there is no appeal, no dispensation, from the anonymous pressures of the market mechanism.

Figure 1.9 offers an explanation of how SBTC raises income inequality through the operation of the price mechanism in labour markets for low-skilled and high-skilled workers. Due to the availability of new technologies and machineries that substitute for low-skilled workers, employers will demand fewer of these workers: graphically, the demand curve for low-skilled labour shifts to the left from D0 to D1 until a new equilibrium (E1) is reached, with lower wages and quantity (numbers) hired than in the original equilibrium (E0). Since the same new technologies and machineries are a complement to high-skill workers – such as engineers – there will be more demand for these types of workers: the demand curve for high-skilled labour shifts to the right from D0 to D1 until a new equilibrium (E1) is reached, with higher wages and quantity hired than in the original equilibrium (E0).

Akin to SBTC, economic globalization reduced demand for low-skilled workers and boosted demand for high-skilled workers in advanced capitalist countries. Increased competition with low-wage countries has forced firms in labour-intensive sectors of these countries – for example, textile and apparel – to close their business or move parts of the production process – for example, the stitching of clothes or the assembly of consumer electronic goods such as personal computers and smartphones – to developing countries. In a widely discussed study, US economists have estimated that the rise of China in the

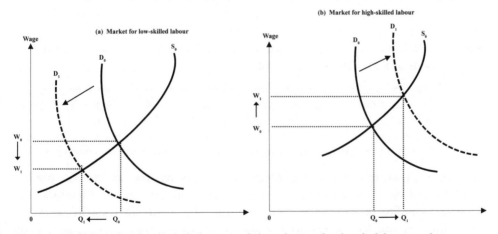

Figure 1.9 Skill-biased technological change and the price mechanism in labour markets

world economy destroyed about 40 per cent of manufacturing jobs in the US economy.[11] While globalization also opened up opportunities for firms and led to the creation of new jobs in competitive (usually capital-intensive) industries and business service sectors of the advanced economies, these jobs predominantly went to high-skilled workers. In this way, economic globalization reinforced the effects of SBTC on income inequality.

From a neoclassical perspective, rising income inequality due to SBTC and economic globalization is both unavoidable and desirable. It is unavoidable because of structural shifts in demand for low-skilled and high-skilled workers in competitive labour markets, where wages correspond to workers' marginal product of labour. But it is also to a significant degree desirable because people respond to incentives triggered by the market price mechanism: if people know that they will be rewarded with higher income, they will be more eager to develop skills (via education) for which there is high demand in the labour market. In the long term the greater supply of scarce skills will boost the growth potential of the economy by providing the human capital that is needed for technological innovation. There is a broad consensus among neoclassical economists that *the long-term growth of GDP is dependent on labour productivity growth*, which refers to the quantity of goods and services that a worker can produce per hour: 'it reflects our ability to produce more output by better combining inputs, owing to new ideas, technological innovations and business models'.[12] The availability of new machines and technologies has radically improved the efficiency of the production process over the past two centuries, raising the labour productivity of the average worker as well as the average standards of living (measured by GDP per capita) in advanced capitalist countries. Economic globalization is also believed to have boosted productivity by facilitating technology transfers and competition.

The relationship between labour productivity and living standards has profound implications for public policy. According to most neoclassical economists, governments face a trade-off between equality and efficiency. First famously elaborated by US economist Arthur Okun in his 1975 book *Equality and Efficiency*, the existence of this trade-off has become so commonly accepted that it was labelled by Greg Mankiw as one of the ten *Principles of Economics* in his widely used introductory textbook:

> When the government redistributes income from the rich to the poor, it reduces the reward for working hard; as a result, people work less and produce fewer goods and services. In other words, when the government tries to cut the economic pie into more equal slices, the pie gets smaller. This is the one lesson concerning the distribution of income about which almost everyone agrees.[13]

Policymakers should therefore focus on enlarging the economic pie by adopting policies that make markets and firms operate more efficiently and boosting average productivity – for example, by ensuring that workers are well educated and have access to the best available technologies, as well as by freeing up markets and intensifying competition in ways that push firms to adopt these technologies (e.g. by liberalizing trade).[14]

Towards a political economy perspective on rising inequality

Power and institutions as determinants of inequality

It would be wrong to believe that technological innovation and globalization are unrelated to inequality. Yet, from a political economy perspective, the neoclassical interpretation remains deficient for various reasons. As discussed above, income inequality has also increased within the top 10 per cent, between the 9 per cent and the top 1 per cent, which is difficult to explain on the basis of the theory of marginal productivity. Indeed, as Piketty notes in his book, 'when we look at the changes in the skill levels of different groups in the income distribution, it is hard to see any discontinuity between the 9 percent and the 1 percent, regardless of what criteria we use: years of education, selectivity of educational institution, or professional experience'.[15] The SBTC is even less well-equipped to explain differences in income gains within the top percentile (see table 1.1 above), whose members display even greater uniformity in skills than the top 10 per cent.[16]

Moreover, the neoclassical interpretation fails to explain why the trajectory of inequality has been so markedly different in the Anglo-Saxon countries and the continental European countries. After all, these advanced capitalist economies have been more or less equally exposed to exogenous market forces like technological innovation and globalization, making it difficult to understand why wage differentials between high-skilled and low-skilled workers rose faster in the former group of countries than in the latter. In fact, the more egalitarian countries of Northern Europe have been *more* open to international trade and more export-oriented than the less equal Anglo-Saxon economies. So although technological change and globalization may act as powerful forces for income inequality, continued cross-national diversity suggests that other factors influence both the magnitude and the rate of change in inequality and top income shares: from a political economy perspective, the effects of technological change and globalization on the distribution of income and wealth in the advanced economies have been shaped and mediated by a variety of public policies and economic institutions that should be central to debates on inequality.

Finally, the neoclassical view that labour productivity growth translates into a growth of wages and living standards for the average worker is clearly at odds with the fall in the labour income share since the 1980s. The constancy of the labour share of GDP was long seen as one of the 'stylized facts' in neoclassical economics: being equal to the marginal product of labour, wages are expected to grow in step with productivity growth, and the labour share of GDP should remain more or less stable over time.[17] The fact that the labour share remained stable during the post-war era of egalitarian capitalism until the 1970s and has fallen ever since is a clear vindication of a central claim in the political economy literature, which states that the distribution of national income between the two factors of production is a function of shifting relations of bargaining power between capital and labour.

The typical starting point in the political economy literature is therefore that the distribution of income and wealth in an economy is intrinsically political, in the sense that it is always determined by the distribution of political and economic power between different groups and classes in that economy. All capitalist economies have an intrinsic propensity to fuel economic inequality due to the asymmetric relations of power between the owners of capital and the owners of labour, as Karl Marx argued forcefully in the first volume of *Capital*. Marxist political economists believe that owners of capital always have structural power in market economies through their control over the means of production: a fundamental feature of the capitalist mode of production is the commodification of labour; the majority of people have to sell their labour to capitalist employers to make a living, leading to a dependent relationship that allows employers to exploit the working classes by extracting 'surplus value' from their labour. For Marx and his followers, the exploitation of labour power through extraction of surplus value is the ultimate source of capitalist profits: workers' wages will always be lower than the value added they produce for their firms. As such, Marxists reject the neoclassical view that wages tend to reflect the marginal product of labour: due to asymmetric bargaining relations between capitalist employees and wage earners in competitive labour markets, wages of the majority of workers will be typically below the value they produce for their firms.

The capitalist class also often has a structural power over the formation of the public policies of the government, which is reliant on the decisions of private businesses to invest in the economy and create a sufficient amount of economic growth and jobs: 'a major, perhaps *the* major, function of government is to encourage businessmen to invest and produce, thus increasing GDP and improving everyone's standard of living'.[18] As Charles Lindblom argued in his 1977 book *Politics Against Markets*, the structural power of capital has two components.[19] First, the owners of capital are able to cause economic disruption by organizing investment strikes – for example, postponing decisions to expand production or moving production abroad – whenever they disapprove of the government's economic policies. The mere threat of such an investment strike can often be sufficient to convince the government to pursue policies that are more favourable to capital. Second, the capitalist class is able to exert ideological control by representing private business interests as synonymous with the national interest. Seen from this angle, economic globalization fuelled income inequality not by reducing demand for unskilled labour but by strengthening the structural power of capital: the removal of cross-border restrictions on trade, investment and financial flows enabled the owners of capital to threaten their government with capital flight to countries with more favourable conditions. The owners of capital were supported in this by the neoliberal ideology that served to change 'expectations about the appropriate role of government, the importance of private enterprise, and the virtues of markets'.[20]

However, as Jacob Hacker and Paul Pierson have noted, 'the structural power of business is variable, not constant'.[21] A variety of developments in the first half of the twentieth century enabled the working classes to strengthen their bargaining position vis-à-vis capital. On the one hand, workers organized in the form of trade unions to engage in collective bargaining, the key purpose of which is to make sure that the wages of the working classes grew in step with labour productivity. When universal and equal suffrage was introduced in the early years of the twentieth century in most industrialized countries (in most cases initially only for male voters), left-wing political parties striving to defend the interest of the working classes also gained influence and became increasingly successful in shaping public policies (either in government or in national parliaments) – particularly after the Great Depression of the 1930s, which revealed the blatant need for more extensive state intervention to protect citizens against the vagaries of markets.[22] From the 1930s to the 1970s these democratic class struggles culminated in the development of national welfare states, ushering in a new era of egalitarian capitalism based on collective bargaining, full employment and expansion of social safety nets. These equality-promoting institutions were supported by restrictions of cross-border capital flows, which weakened the structural power of capital by constraining the ability of firms and capital owners to escape these institutions.

The post-war settlement broke down during the stagflation crisis of the 1970s, when a combination of economic stagnation and rising inflation pushed governments of the industrialized countries to liberalize trade, investment and cross-border capital flows. A central question for the emerging CPE and international political economy (IPE) literature since the end of the 1970s is to what extent economic globalization and the ensuing intensification of competition between firms and between states would undermine the main institutional pillars of egalitarian capitalism. Scholars of the VoC school have rightly noted that there continues to be a significant amount of institutional divergence between the Anglo-Saxon economies and the continental European economies in terms of organization of their labour markets, welfare state and corporate governance.[23] These persistent institutional differences go a long way to explain why income inequality rose faster in the former group of countries than in the latter. Nevertheless, economic globalization weakened the power of labour and strengthened the power of capital in ways that spawned varying tendencies towards neoliberalization – even in the more egalitarian European countries.[24] In the upcoming chapters we will examine these tendencies in various policy domains that have been most consequential in fuelling economic inequality in the advanced capitalist world.

Rising inequality as a structural cause of the global financial crisis

Not only should the neoclassical interpretation of the *causes* of rising inequality be disputed; its rather sanguine views of the *consequences* of inequality can be criticized as well. Remember that the rise in income inequality is believed to boost long-term growth insofar as it creates incentives for individuals to develop scarce skills and human capital, and for firms to invest in more efficient technologies, which will enhance the growth in productivity and living standards. Yet a growing number of studies have shown that, other things being equal, a rise in income inequality hampers long-term economic growth and increases financial instability.[25]

There are two different interpretations of this observation. A 'supply-side' interpretation stresses the negative effects of rising inequality on educational opportunities for children in lower-income households, leading to a decline in human capital development that reduces long-term productivity growth. According to this view, higher income inequality translates into higher educational inequality, with low-income children ending up in low-quality schools and having less access to higher education. This slows the rate of economic growth relative to a counterfactual scenario where all children have equal educational opportunities, given that children of poor households accumulate less human capital and will become less efficient and productive future workers. Econometric analysis by the OECD suggests that income inequality has had a negative and statistically significant impact on economic growth, offering empirical evidence for the hypothesis that inequality hampers human capital formation: increased income disparities depress skills development among individuals with poorer parental education background, both in terms of the quantity of education attained (e.g. years of schooling) and in terms of its quality (e.g. skill proficiency).[26]

A 'demand-side' interpretation, by contrast, points to the negative effects of rising income inequality on *aggregate demand* in the economy (box 1.3). Because individuals with higher incomes have a lower marginal propensity to consume (MPC) – that is, they consume a smaller part of their income (see also chapter 3) – than individuals with lower incomes, an upward redistribution of income from poor households to rich households reduces the level of aggregate consumption in the economy. The fall in the labour income share has the same effect, as the MPC of workers is higher than that of capital owners. The lower level of aggregate consumption, in turn, pushes firms to curtail their investment expenditures, as weaker consumer demand offers a signal to businesses that there is less need to raise their capital stock (e.g. factories, machines and equipment) to meet demand for their goods and services.[27] Conversely, rising income inequality since 1980 has generated a large increase in saving by the top of the income distribution, which Atif Mian and his colleagues refer to as 'the saving glut of the rich'. Because firms have had less incentive to raise their investment and capital stock in the face of weaker consumer demand associated with rising inequality, these savings of the wealthy have been invested in financial assets that were linked to and hence contributed to the substantial dis-saving and large accumulation of household debt of the bottom 90 per cent: in the United States, the savings of the top of the income distribution increasingly financed borrowing by the rest of the population.[28]

Box 1.3 Supply-side versus demand-side macroeconomics

What are the main sources of economic growth and economic crisis? This question determines the ultimate dividing line between different schools of (political) economic thought. Classical and neoclassical economists emphasize the role of the supply side of the economy, which refers to those factors that underpin the efficiency of the production process of firms – for example, taxation, product and labour market regulation, and the availability of (human) capital. A key assumption of supply-side economics is that entrepreneurship in the private business sector is the ultimate driver of economic growth and capital accumulation: only when private firms and individuals are willing to take risks and invest capital are jobs created and income (profits and wages) generated. From a supply-side perspective, the key to economic growth is profitability: firms will only invest in new factories, machines and production facilities when it is profitable to do so.

Demand-side economists, on the other hand, emphasize the importance of sufficient aggregate demand in the economy: firms will only invest and produce goods and services when they believe their goods and services will effectively be sold. These economists also recognize the importance of private investment spending, but they add that firms will only undertake new investments and raise output if there is adequate demand. In macroeconomics, the following sources of aggregate demand (and therefore economic growth) are identified:

$$Y \text{ (GDP)} = C + I + (G - T) + (X - M),$$

where C refers to household consumption (i.e. purchases of *consumer* goods and services), I to private investment (i.e. purchases of *capital* goods), (G – T) to the government balance (i.e. government spending minus tax revenues) and (X – M) to the trade balance (i.e. exports minus imports).

A key reason for continuing disagreement between supply-side and demand-side economists is the contradictory role of wages as an important – if not the most important – source of both aggregate household consumption and firms' production costs. From a supply-side perspective, governments should get rid of 'distortionary' regulations of the labour market, like minimum wage laws, that lead to excessive labour costs for firms and diminish their incentives to invest and employ people by hurting their profits. From a demand-side perspective, these labour market regulations are needed to empower workers and boost their wages, which is necessary to support aggregate consumption in the economy. A similar argument exists with regard to taxation: while supply-side economists tend to be in favour of cutting taxes on firms to make investment more profitable, demand-side economists point to the redistributional role of tax revenues and the fact that they enable transfers to poor households with a high MPC.

Any capitalist economy faces a potential contradiction between the need for firms to contain production costs and make profits and the need to support the consumption capacity of lower- and middle-income households. This contradiction lies at the heart of Marxist theory that capitalism is inherently prone to economic crisis and instability due to the recurring problem of 'underconsumption' and 'overproduction'.[29] As Marx wrote, 'the ultimate reason for all real crises always remains the poverty and restricted consumption of the masses as opposed to the drive of capitalist production to develop the productive forces'.[30] Marx noted that there is a fundamental contradiction in the capitalist system between the competitive need for capital owners to extract as much surplus value as possible from the working classes and the need to find enough buyers for their goods. Modern 'underconsumption' theory is closely associated with John Maynard Keynes, who believed that any deficiency in aggregate demand can be resolved by the intervention of the state: the government can always support aggregate demand during falls in household consumption (C) and corporate investment (I) by engaging in 'deficit spending' (G > T).

During the post-war 'Keynesian era' of egalitarian capitalism, aggregate demand was supported not only by governments' macroeconomic policies geared towards 'full employment', but also by relatively strong labour unions and collective bargaining institutions that ensured wages grew in line with average labour productivity – a complex of institutions that reflected a historical compromise between the industrial fractions of capital and the working classes (see chapters 2 and 3). Marxist scholars are sceptical about the political and economic sustainability of these equality-promoting institutions in a capitalist system that continues to be driven by profit maximization.

While these two interpretations are complementary, a demand-side interpretation is better able to explain the connection between rising inequality and the global financial crisis. The central claim that will be developed throughout this book is that governments in the advanced capitalist economies had to find new sources of aggregate demand in the wake of the stagflation crisis of the 1970s, which was widely interpreted as a crisis of the wage-led growth model of the post-war Keynesian era (chapters 2, 3 and 4).[31] Growth in the Anglo-Saxon countries and several Southern European countries became increasingly reliant on household consumption. But rather than relying on rising wages or income transfers provided by the welfare state, poor and middle-income households became increasingly dependent on credit to finance their consumption.[32] The expansion of household debt was only possible after the extensive liberalization and deregulation of the financial sector in the 1980s and 1990s, which boosted the supply of credit to households (as well to firms and governments) by nourishing competition between banks and encouraging them to take more risk. The unsustainable increase in household debt was a proximate cause of the global financial crisis of 2008. Economic growth in the Northern European countries, on the other hand, increasingly came to rely on external demand via increased exports: a combination of wage restraint and selective labour market flexibilization depressed household consumption, but it also strengthened the competitiveness of the export-oriented manufacturing firms by decreasing their labour costs.

In sum, two distinctive growth models emerged in the advanced capitalist world in the wake of the stagflation crisis of the 1970s. Most Anglo-Saxon and Southern European countries adopted debt-led growth models based on a credit-financed expansion of household consumption, whereas Northern European countries adopted export-led growth models, if we look at the contribution of these two sources of aggregate demand to GDP growth. Figure 1.10 illustrates the distinction between these two growth models by showing the average annual contribution of household consumption and net exports (i.e. exports minus imports) to GDP growth between 1985 and 2007. The average annual contribution of net exports was negative for debt-led economies, implying that their trade balance – that is, the difference between their exports and imports – was negative throughout this period: they imported more than they exported. A negative trade balance is a typical consequence of debt-led growth, as the expansion of household consumption 'leaks out' to the rest of the world in the form of increased imports: after all, households buy goods and services that are produced by domestic *as well as* foreign firms. Northern European countries were export-led in the sense that their trade

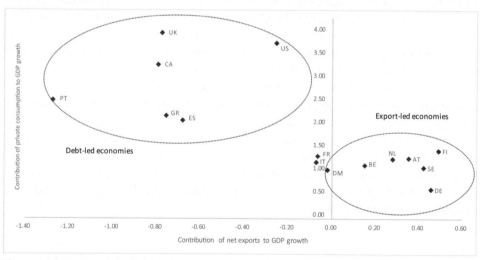

Figure 1.10 Average annual contribution of private consumption and net exports to GDP growth, 1985–2007

Source: AMECO; OECD

AT = Austria; BE = Belgium; CA = Canada; DE = Germany; DM = Denmark; ES = Spain; FI = Finland; GR = Greece; JP = Japan; NL = Netherlands; PT = Portugal; SE = Sweden; UK = United Kingdom; US = United States.

surplus supported aggregate demand, whereas private consumption played a less important role in fostering economic growth during this period. Only a couple of countries like France and Italy were neither debt-led nor export-led, as depressed private consumption and a slightly negative trade balance contributed to relatively low *overall* growth between 1985 and 2007.

The debt-led and export-led growth models became mutually dependent: buoyant domestic demand in the debt-led economies translated into higher imports from export-led economies and helped to sustain their growth model; trade surpluses in the latter economies translated into excess savings that were reinvested in the financial system of the debt-led economies and facilitated their growth. The key problem was that these interdependencies culminated in widening and unsustainable trade imbalances that many economists consider to be an important international cause of the global financial crisis and subsequent euro crisis: running persistent and rising trade deficits implied that the debt-led economies accumulated unsustainable amounts of foreign liabilities by borrowing in net terms from private banks in the export-led economies. In chapter 7 we analyse the linkages between the formation of these two growth models and the widening of unsustainable imbalances, which has imposed a painful macroeconomic adjustment process on many industrialized countries since the eruption of the crisis – but particularly so on peripheral Eurozone countries.

The growth model perspective elaborated in the following chapters deviates from neoclassical models in three fundamental ways. First, it is based on heterodox economic theories that emphasize the role of aggregate demand dynamics not only in affecting the short-term fluctuations of economic activity (i.e. business cycles) but also in determining the long-term growth potential of the economy. Second, these dynamics are to a great extent determined by the distribution of national income and wealth in the economy, which is exogenously affected by social conditions and institutions that both reflect and shape the bargaining position of various classes and groups in capitalist societies. Third, these institutions reflect temporary and fragile attempts to resolve structural tensions and conflicts between these classes and groups, making the capitalist system intrinsically unstable and prone to crisis. These three features make a growth model perspective theoretically appropriate for understanding the rise and fall of egalitarian capitalism, as the following chapter sets out to argue.

2

The Rise and Fall of Egalitarian Capitalism

In the previous chapter we have seen that the era between the 1930s and the 1970s was the most egalitarian period in the history of advanced capitalism: income inequality fell in the entire industrialized world. In this chapter we zoom in on the rise and fall of egalitarian capitalism, providing an overview of the rise and demise of the KWS. The KWS arose from the ashes of the Great Depression, which devastated the world economy and undermined the legitimacy of the classical-liberal pillars on which the institutional organization of capitalist economies had been based. Faced with soaring levels of unemployment and a sharp contraction of economic activity, governments abandoned their laissez-faire beliefs and started to experiment with new forms of state intervention informed and legitimized by new economic ideas and theories that are now identified as 'Keynesianism'. The KWS had the following three features:

1 There was a cross-party political consensus that actively managing aggregate demand and bringing the economy towards its full potential and towards full employment had become a central responsibility of the state.
2 The KWS was oriented towards the expansion of welfare rights through steady growth in social spending and the advancement of collective bargaining in ways that ensured wages grew in line with average productivity.
3 The KWS was supported internationally by the Bretton Woods regime, which set out rules for managing international financial relations and provided a conducive external environment for domestic state intervention.

The rise of the KWS was both cause and effect of the post-war economic expansion, which lasted until the recession of 1973–5 and came to be known as the 'Golden Age' of capitalism. Its expansion came to a halt in the wake of the breakdown of the Bretton Woods regime and the first oil shock of 1973, which precipitated a stagflation crisis that undermined the legitimacy of the Keynesian paradigm and set the stage for the rise of neoliberalism as a framework for economic policymaking and institutional reorganization in the advanced capitalist world. In this chapter we sketch out how a growth model perspective accounts for the rise and fall of the KWS, and how it relates to other theoretical approaches in comparative and international political economy. We will argue that a growth model perspective not only clarifies the dynamics of economic inequality and instability in advanced capitalism over the past century but also offers a valuable synthesis of interest-based, institutional and ideational approaches in CPE and IPE. The central message is that national growth models are shaped by a variety of institutions seeking to mediate tensions arising from market inequalities in ways that reflect the interests and ideas of dominant classes and groups but always remain unstable.

The rise of the Keynesian welfare state

The Great Depression: from laissez-faire to state intervention

By the end of the nineteenth century, political elites in the Western world had fully embraced the principles of classical liberalism. These principles prescribed a very restricted role for the state in the economy: governments reduced their involvement in the economy by introducing market mechanisms for the allocation of resources. The principal purpose of the state was to maintain public order to ensure a proper functioning of the free market system and supply 'public goods' – that is, non-rival and non-excludable goods that remained underprovided by the market system, such as national security, public roads and infrastructure. State protection of property rights, especially, was absolutely essential: without the ability to transfer and exchange property and enter into contracts, there could be no markets and hence no market economy; the right to own physical capital and land and the ensuing capacity to capture the value of what is produced using that capital and land were of fundamental importance to the expansion of markets and the accumulation of capital.[1] The state also enabled the commodification of labour and the creation of 'free' labour markets by organizing repressive actions against worker revolts. In this sense, the liberal doctrine of laissez-faire was, in practice, at least as much about the state *imposing* and *creating* free markets as it was about abolishing restrictions on markets. As Polanyi argued in *The Great Transformation*: 'There was nothing natural about *laissez-faire*: free markets could never have come into being merely by allowing things to take their course ... The road to the free market was opened and kept open by an enormous increase in continuous, centrally organized and controlled interventionism.'[2]

Classical liberals saw the creation of national wealth during the nineteenth century as the ultimate reflection of the benefits of free markets and globalization: GDP per capita rose exponentially in the industrializing countries for the first time in human history. Yet the sharp rise in GDP did not say anything about the distribution of national income and wealth. National wealth was distributed extremely unequally at the beginning of the nineteenth century, but wealth inequality grew even further and reached record levels at the beginning of the twentieth century: the share of the top 1 per cent and top 10 per cent in national wealth reached, respectively, 45 and 81 per cent in the United States on the eve of World War I, and in Europe 64 and 90 per cent.[3] This belle époque of patrimonial capitalism ended with World War I, when the rise in public debt to fund war expenditures destroyed the real value of financial wealth by fuelling inflation (see chapter 3 for an analysis of the distributional implications of inflation). Political elites attempted to restore the liberal economic order during the 1920s but their efforts eventually ended in the Great Depression of the 1930s, which started in the US economy after the October 1929 Wall Street Crash and rapidly spread to Europe and the rest of the world.[4]

The Great Depression had a devastating impact on the US economy: real GDP fell for four consecutive years and unemployment reached more than 25 per cent in 1933. The persistent downturn in economic activity discredited the belief of political elites in the self-adjusting capacity of markets, whereby the price mechanism would automatically restore market equilibrium and allow the economy to return to its full potential. When it became increasingly clear that typical policies of the classical-liberal paradigm – with its straitjacket of tight money and balanced budgets – exacerbated the crisis, governments began to experiment with less orthodox forms of state intervention based on increased public spending, expansion of social rights and reforms of the banking system.

The first country to do so was Sweden, where domestic political conditions were conducive to state intervention: unions were increasingly influential and the government was led by the Social-Democratic Party. In the United States the government led by Democratic president Franklin D. Roosevelt enacted the 'New Deal', consisting of banking reforms, spending programmes and new social insurance and labour rights. The banking crisis was contained by bank bailouts and the 1933 Banking Act, which divided deposit banks from those that invested on Wall Street, and established the Federal Deposit Insurance Corporation to protect the savings of ordinary Americans. In March 1935, the US Congress approved its largest peacetime allocation ever, putting millions of people back to work to build roads, airports and other infrastructural projects. A few months later, Congress passed the Social Security Act, the country's first national social insurance system.[5] Other industrialized countries implemented a similar mixture of banking reforms, spending programmes and expanding social security rights.

Embedded liberalism: the Keynesian welfare state after World War II

While these new forms of state intervention were crucial to revive the economy by restoring aggregate demand, countries increasingly turned inwards: governments erected trade barriers and all kinds of restrictions on international capital movements – called 'capital controls' – that led to a disintegrated world economy and exacerbated the fallout of the Great Depression. After World War II the Allied forces aimed to rebuild an open international economic order that would leave national governments room for state intervention and enable them to protect their citizens from market instabilities. At the time, it was clear that the United States would emerge from the war as the dominant economic power: US policymakers were determined to play a leadership role in building and sustaining a more open and multilateral international economic order than the one that had existed during the 1930s. But rather than returning to the classical-liberal order of the pre-1930s, they hoped to find a way to reconcile liberal multilateralism with the new, domestically orientated priorities to combat unemployment and promote social welfare that had emerged with the New Deal. John G. Ruggie famously termed this compromise 'embedded liberalism': 'Unlike the economic nationalism of the thirties, it would be multilateral in character; unlike the liberalism of the gold standard and free trade, its multilateralism would be predicated upon domestic interventionism.'[6] The Bretton Woods system, which established governing rules for post-war international economic relations, reflected this compromise of embedded liberalism.[7] It had the following features:

- Signatories to the Bretton Woods agreement agreed to fix ('peg') the exchange rate value of their currency in relation to the US dollar, which was the only currency to be freely convertible into gold at a fixed price of US$35 per ounce. The Bretton Woods architects aimed to re-establish a world of international currency stability without returning to the rigidity of the irrevocably fixed exchange rates of the nineteenth-century international gold standard. Countries were given the option of adjusting their countries' exchange rate whenever their country was in 'fundamental disequilibrium'. As such, the Bretton Woods system was a kind of 'adjustable peg' system, in which countries could devalue their exchange rate when they experienced sustained deficits in their trade balance. Currency realignments of up to 10 per cent could be approved automatically, but larger ones required the permission of the newly created IMF. In short, it was a discretionary exchange rate regime that allowed for internationally negotiated state intervention in currency markets.

- Countries were given the right to control international capital movements by means of a variety of restrictions on moving money in or out of the country. These capital controls were not applied to long-term private capital movements like foreign direct investments to build factories; they were only to discourage short-term capital flows that often have a speculative character – for example, international bank lending or international trade of financial assets like stocks and bonds. It was generally accepted that unrestricted capital mobility would not only destabilize exchange rates, and disrupt international trade, but also undermine the autonomy of national governments to fight economic recessions and develop the welfare state. The regulation of international capital movements via capital controls became the prevailing orthodoxy: the right of members of the IMF, the European Community and the OECD to regulate and control movements of capital was protected by the IMF's Articles of Agreement (1945), the European Community's Treaty of Rome (1957) and the OECD's Code of Liberalization of Capital Movements (1961).

- The Bretton Woods architects also established two public international financial institutions: the International Bank for Reconstruction and Development (IBRD, part of the World Bank) and the IMF. Broadly, these institutions were given the task of promoting international economic co-operation. The IBRD was designed to provide long-term loans for reconstruction and development after the war. The IMF was to provide short-term loans to help countries with international payment difficulties – a function that was designed explicitly to reinforce those countries' policy autonomy and challenge the kind of external discipline that private international financial flows and the gold standard had imposed before the 1930s.[8]

- The Bretton Woods system promoted the gradual liberalization of trade, which took place through the General Agreement on Tariffs and Trade (GATT). In April 1947, participating countries agreed to cut trade tariffs by more than one-third on average and agreed not to discriminate among countries. This was enshrined in the principle of unconditional most-favoured-nation

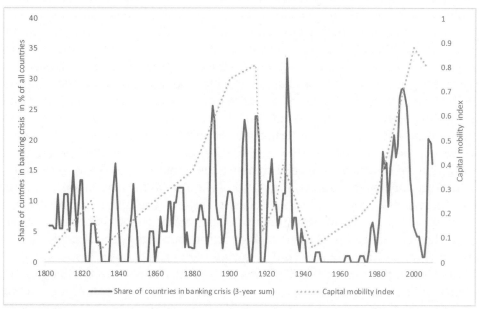

Figure 2.1 Index of capital mobility and percentage of countries in a banking crisis, 1800–2010

Source: Rogoff and Reinhart 2009

treatment: any reduction in trade barriers between two GATT signatories was automatically offered to all GATT members; countries could not discriminate against the products of one member in favour of the products of another. The result was a gradual international liberalization of trade, which grew exponentially after 1950.[9]

Arguably, the most significant feature of the Bretton Woods system – the one that most clearly reflected the compromise of embedded liberalism – was its explicit endorsement of the use of capital controls. As figure 2.1 shows, there seems to be a clear correlation between the degree of cross-border capital mobility in the world – measured by an index that captures all the restrictions on international short-term capital flows and ranges from zero (no capital mobility) to one (perfect capital mobility) – and the share of countries experiencing a banking crisis (three-year moving averages): the Bretton Woods era, which features capital controls and very low cross-border capital mobility, was the most financially stable period over the last two centuries.

Financial stability concerns were not the principal reason for installing capital controls, though. Restrictions on the international mobility of financial capital particularly aimed to preserve the autonomy of governments to build a KWS based on (1) countercyclical macroeconomic policymaking and (2) higher taxes to fund social spending. A key dimension of the welfare state was that the government had to adopt expansionary fiscal and monetary policies geared towards the attainment of 'full employment' in the economy: during economic recessions, higher public spending and lower interest rates were needed to boost household consumption and corporate investment until there were enough jobs for the working classes. The problem was that these expansionary fiscal and monetary policies could lead to higher inflation, potentially eroding the returns of private investors, who would have every incentive to move their capital to higher-yielding countries (see chapter 3). Indeed, as Keynes argued, 'the whole management of the domestic economy depends on being free to have the appropriate rate of interest without reference to the rate prevailing elsewhere in the world'.[10] In short, capital controls were required to avoid 'capital flight' from undermining the effectiveness of Keynesian macroeconomic policies oriented towards full employment. But the containment of capital flight was also needed to assist the expansion of the welfare state, which entailed higher levels of taxation (of both capital and labour) to fund the increasingly generous social security system: the architects of Bretton Woods sought to shield governments from capital flight that was initiated with the goal of evading domestic taxes or the 'burdens of social legislation' – as the chief US delegate proclaimed during the negotiations.[11]

Another dimension of the KWS was the expansion of collective bargaining rights: a growing number of workers came to be represented by labour unions which negotiated with employer organizations over the setting of wages, working hours and other working conditions. For several reasons, collective bargaining contributed to a more equal income distribution. First, it facilitated the compression of inter-firm and inter-sectoral wage differentials by including different firms and sectors in a single wage agreement: workers doing similar jobs would be paid similar wages across various firms and sectors. Second, collective bargaining also ensured that the *annual growth of wages* would be similar for workers and employees across different firms and sectors: national-level and sectoral-level agreements aligned nominal wage growth with, respectively, nation-wide and sector-wide average real productivity growth. As a result, workers in firms and sectors with below-average productivity received the same annual pay rises as workers in firms and sectors with above-average productivity (see chapter 4 for more details). As such, national industrial relations systems characterized by strong trade unions and collective bargaining provided 'crucial institutional mechanisms ensuring the transfer of productivity gains into real wages and household consumption', allowing 'aggregate demand to expand in lockstep with the expansion of the productive potential of the economy for some time'.[12]

Fordist wage-led growth: interests, ideas and institutions

Keynesian macroeconomic policymaking, collective bargaining and the rise of the welfare state provided the institutional underpinnings of what came to be known in the political economy literature as the *Fordist accumulation regime*. Named after the founder of the Ford Motor Company, who aimed to combine assembly-line mass-production methods with mass consumption, it consisted of a range of policies and institutions to support the accumulation of wealth by ensuring that there would be sufficient and stable demand for the standardized consumer goods produced by the system, with high wage growth acting as the engine of aggregate demand and economic growth.

The concept of the Fordist accumulation regime is particularly associated with the French Regulation School, a Marxist-oriented political economy approach that focuses on the historical, geographical and institutional specificities of capitalist development in an attempt to explain why capitalism is more durable than anticipated in orthodox Marxist theory. Central to the approach is the analysis of how an ensemble of institutions, state practices and norms – called a 'mode of regulation' – can stabilize a capitalist 'regime of accumulation', which can be defined as 'a complementary pattern of production and consumption which is reproducible over a long period'.[13] Key elements of the Fordist mode of regulation were:

1 an institutionalized compromise between organized labour and capital whereby workers accept management prerogatives in return for rising wages;
2 state intervention to maintain full employment and expand a welfare state;
3 an overall strong presence of the state in the economy through an extensive

regulatory apparatus and public control over and/or public ownership in key industries (e.g. public utilities and banking); and

4 the embedding of national economies in a liberal yet financially restrictive international economic order centred on US hegemony via the Bretton Woods system.[14]

For three reasons, the Regulation approach can be seen as an important intellectual precursor of the growth model perspective elaborated in this book. First of all, it shares the notion that capitalist development is intrinsically unstable and can only be stabilized by institutional forms and practices that provide a temporary resolution to the endemic crisis tendencies of capitalist accumulation processes: '[Modes of regulation] represent temporary institutional "fixes", they do not neutralize crisis tendencies completely.'[15] Second, the concept of the accumulation regime underscores the importance of aggregate demand for long-term economic growth: the accumulation of capital was only possible in the context of sufficiently growing demand, which required workers to get their fair share of economic growth. Figure 2.2 shows the Fordist wage-led growth cycle: collective bargaining converted labour productivity growth into wage growth, which stimulated consumption and further enhanced productivity growth by encouraging firms to invest in the expansion of production. Rising wage costs also directly boosted productivity growth by pushing firms to adopt the most efficient production methods and technologies. Figure 2.3 shows that in the United States the period between 1945 and 1973 was one of extraordinarily high productivity growth and low levels of unemployment compared to both the preceding classical-liberal era and the succeeding neoliberal period.[16] Finally, inspired by Antonio Gramsci, authors in the Regulation approach have argued that the mode of regulation has to be supported and legitimized by a 'hegemonic social bloc' – that is, a coalition between social groups or fractions within these groups capable of representing and selling their interests as those of society as a whole.[17]

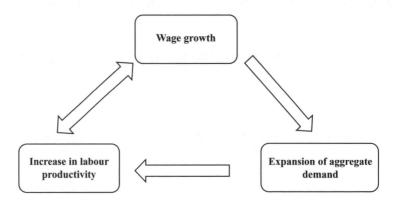

Figure 2.2 Fordist wage-led growth cycle (adapted from Baccaro 2020)

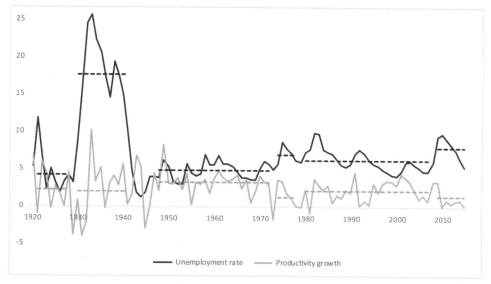

Figure 2.3 Unemployment and productivity growth in the United States, 1914–2015

Source: https://www.core-econ.org

Dashed lines refer to moving averages.

Who were the key social groups belonging to the Fordist social bloc and how did they forge a hegemonic consensus? The answer to this question suggests that a synthesis of interest-based, ideational and institutional perspectives is needed to attain a comprehensive understanding of the establishment and expansion of the KWS and its subsequent demise in the 1970s. Cataclysmic events like the Great Depression can act as critical junctures that lead to a fundamental revision and transformation of existing economic policy paradigms and their underlying institutions. In the CPE and IPE literature, three approaches are usually distinguished to account for such instances of fundamental institutional refurbishment: interest-based, ideas-oriented and institutional approaches. These three 'I's – interests, ideas and institutions – should not necessarily be seen as separable ways to explain outcomes but 'represent different but not mutually exclusive ways to focus attention in explaining political economy'.[18] Indeed, interests, ideas and institutions all played a central role in the formation of the Fordist wage-led growth model during the post-war era.

In terms of material interests, the rise of the labour movement in the first half of the twentieth century was paramount to curb the structural power of capital, as advocates of the power resources approach have argued. The core contention of the power resources approach is that the working class could improve its bargaining position vis-à-vis capital by collectively mobilizing in the form of labour unions and left-wing political parties.[19] Table 2.1 presents

Table 2.1 Union membership as a percentage of non-agricultural workers, pre-World War I to 1975

	Before World War I	Interwar	1945–75
Australia	19.7	40.3	50.9
Austria	6.0	42.2	62.0
Canada	4.7	8.9	27.7
Denmark	15.3	33.6	59.3
Finland	5.0	8.0	38.5
France	7.0	11.5	22.0
Germany	16.0	35.9	34.3
Italy	11.0	19.0	32.5
Ireland	-	15.0	36.5
Japan	-	20.0	34.5
Netherlands	16.9	30.6	38.8
New Zealand	17.0	25.0	41.5
Norway	5.5	19.4	58.0
Sweden	6.0	34.3	69.1
United Kingdom	13.2	29.6	42.2
United States	6.8	14.0	29.8

Source: Donado and Wälde 2011; Korpi 1983

Table 2.2 Left percentage of valid votes, pre-World War I to 1980

	Before World War I	Interwar	1945–80
Australia	37.0	45.0	48.5
Austria	23.0	41.0	48.0
Canada	0.0	3.0	15.0
Denmark	26.0	39.0	45.5
Finland	40.0	39.0	47.0
France	13.0	32.0	42.0
Germany	31.0	40.0	37.5
Italy	18.0	26.0	38.0
Ireland	-	32.0	42.0
Japan	-	-	36.5
Netherlands	13.0	25.0	34.5
New Zealand	5.0	35.0	46.0
Norway	15.0	36.0	51.0
Sweden	13.0	46.0	51.5
United Kingdom	5.0	33.0	46.5
United States	4.0	5.0	0.5

Source: Korpi 1983

some historical data on the evolution of union membership in sixteen OECD countries. The level of unionization doubled during the interwar years and increased further during the post-war period. The Great Depression increased the appeal of labour unions that served to protect the interests of the working class through collective mobilization. Rising unionization strengthened the ability of the working class to organize strikes and push through labour demands. The working class also mustered power resources in the political arena by pushing through universal suffrage and engaging in partisan politics. Table 2.2 shows the increasing popularity of left-wing parties among the electorates in most industrialized societies. During the interwar years, the strongest social-democratic parties were found in the Nordic countries. They were reformist parties based on the principle that

> those who do not own instruments of production [e.g. workers] consent to the institution of the private ownership of the capital stock, while those who own productive instruments consent to political institutions [e.g. free elections with universal suffrage, right of workers to organize in labour unions, etc.] that permit other groups to effectively press their claims to the allocation of resources and the distribution of output.[20]

A united working class was a necessary precondition for the promotion of social-democratic reforms, but a divided capitalist class was also critical: 'A singular feature of the 1930s was the prominence of corporate backers of the macroeconomic, social, and labour reforms associated with social democracy.'[21] Above all, capitalists saw the benefits of giving the government more responsibilities in terms of macroeconomic management, as the Great Depression undermined their profits by destroying demand for their goods. Many capitalist employers also favoured an expansion of state-provided social insurance.[22] This argument, which clarifies the rise of the KWS in countries like the United States that lacked a powerful labour movement, is particularly associated with the work of Peter Swenson. In his book *Capitalists Against Markets* Swenson made the case that the KWS was actively promoted by business leaders for various pragmatic reasons.[23] Capitalists recognized that the impact of expanding social security on their profits and competitive position would be minimal if all firms were required to contribute to unemployment and pension programmes. In some sectors, employers already paid out higher wages and provided in-house unemployment and pension benefits as a way to attract skilled workers. This explains why capitalist support for social insurance was particularly strong in capital-intensive industries – for example, automobiles and consumer electronics – where there was more need for a skilled workforce and where labour costs were a relatively small part of total production costs (see chapter 4 for a detailed discussion of corporate interests in collective bargaining and welfare spending).

While support from some fractions of the capitalist class was probably needed for the development of the KWS, it is clear that the system did not benefit the entire capitalist class. The financial sector was obviously disadvantaged by the

KWS, particularly by the restrictive financial regulations that underpinned its development. As Eric Helleiner has argued, the widespread enthusiasm for restricting the mobility of financial capital via capital controls reflected a 'structural break' with how financial affairs were managed before the 1930s: 'Discredited by the crises, the private and central bankers who had dominated financial politics before the 1930s were increasingly replaced at the levers of financial power by a new class of professional economists and state managers whose social base was among labour and national industrial leaders.'[24] These new producer group coalitions favoured interventionist policies that made finance the servant and not the master of the economy. In sum, interest-based approaches point towards the formation of a historical compromise between the working class and the industrial fractions of the capitalist class as the key political underpinning of the KWS. This compromise rested on 'the mutual contributions of the parties to increase economic growth': 'They would co-operate in "making the pie larger in order that there would be more to divide". Through control of the government, the labour movement could influence the distribution of economic growth. Business enjoyed favourable conditions for investment and expansion.'[25]

Ideas-oriented approaches draw attention to the role of Keynesian ideas either in shaping powerful actors' preferences regarding the KWS or in legitimizing new forms of state intervention. From a neo-Gramscian perspective, a key function of ideas is to allow the dominant social groups to establish a hegemonic bloc, which involves 'the institutionalisation of a set of ideas and practices ... not only by representing the narrow interests of the dominant class *as the general interest* but by genuinely incorporating opposing interests into its discourse, although in such a manner that they are subordinated to the interests specified by the original class ideology of the hegemonic group'.[26] Keynesian ideas legitimized and offered intellectual support to social-democratic parties' desire to build a KWS:

> Social democrats everywhere soon discovered in Keynes' ideas, particularly after the appearance of his *General Theory*, something they urgently needed: a distinct policy for administering capitalist economies. The Keynesian revolution in macroeconomics [see box 2.1] provided social democrats with a goal and hence the justification of their governmental role and simultaneously transformed the ideological significance of distributive policies that favoured the working class.[27]

In West European countries Keynesianism gave social-democratic politicians not only a reason to be in office; it also enabled them to forge a cross-party consensus about the benefits of the KWS and the appeal of macroeconomic demand management.[28]

Box 2.1 The Keynesian revolution in macroeconomics

The prolonged fall in economic activity and persistently high levels of unemployment during the 1930s undermined the legitimacy of the classical-liberal policy paradigm, leading to a profound loss of confidence in laissez-faire:

> The Great Depression politicized economic issues and ideas, and demonstrated the potentially dire adverse consequences of the kinds of untrammelled free markets that the liberal creed advocated. It also illustrated more eloquently than any academic treatise could that the underlying assumptions of neo-classical economics ... do not necessarily obtain in the real world, certainly not in the short run.[29]

One of these assumptions is that free markets tend towards equilibrium at full employment – a principle known as Say's Law, named after the nineteenth-century French classical economist Jean-Baptiste Say. Say's Law postulates that 'supply creates its own demand', as in the process of producing output businesses also create enough income for workers and the owners of capital to ensure that all the output will be sold.[30]

The classical-liberal doctrine and its laissez-faire policy prescriptions were almost universally accepted by economists and policymakers until the Great Depression, which shattered the classical belief that any unemployment would be moderate and short-lived. The most forceful critic of Say's Law – and the entire classical-liberal model of the economy – was John Maynard Keynes. Keynes did not believe that a market economy could be relied on to automatically preserve full employment, and held that the central government had to *manage the level of aggregate demand* to achieve those objectives. He developed the following arguments for government intervention and management of the business cycle in his magnum opus *The General Theory of Employment, Interest and Money*:[31]

- In trying to explain the depth of the Great Depression, Keynes argued that economies could fall into a slump for long periods if there was a *collapse in confidence* among consumers, and if firms chose to save and hold on to their money (rather than consume and invest) until they perceived that the economy was improving. When a lack of confidence leads firms to reduce their spending on buildings and equipment, firms and workers who had been supplying these products before would be out of jobs and income. As a result, the effects of their declining spending would spill over into the consumption sector, causing a decline there as well.
- Given this view of how the *aggregate* economy could quickly slide into a recession, the solution seemed obvious to Keynes: as investment and consumption spending fell, the government should take up the slack in demand by reducing interest rates to encourage spending in other sectors of the economy – that is, through an expansionary *monetary policy* – and/or by borrowing money to increase its own expenditures – that is, through an expansionary *fiscal policy*. For reasons explained in the next chapter, Keynes believed especially in the effectiveness of fiscal policy, based on increased government spending, to revive the economy and reduce unemployment during a deep economic recession. As public spending worked its way through the economy, it would ultimately produce a better outlook for businesses, which would restore their confidence and lead them to spend and invest more.

The rise of egalitarian capitalism from the 1930s materialized in different *national varieties* of the KWS with different degrees of collective bargaining and welfare state expansion. In historical-institutionalist accounts, capitalist diversity is brought about and sustained by the way in which labour is institutionalized as a *countervailing power* in the organization of production: 'productive cooperation between capital and labour takes different forms and produces different results depending on how labour is organized and included'.[32] In Nordic countries, workers organized in 'peak-level' labour unions representing workers with different skill profiles (low-skilled; medium-skilled; high-skilled) and employed in different sectors (high-productivity versus low-productivity sectors; domestically focused services versus export-oriented manufacturing sectors). These countries developed national business associations, encompassing a large share of the potential membership and enabling employers to co-operate with each other as well as with representatives from labour unions and government. In countries with *sectoral* coordination, such as Germany, employers and labour unions wield power largely at the industry level: given that the encompassing peak organizations were much weaker, employer organizations with specific industries engaged in collective bargaining with corresponding labour unions – largely without any state involvement. In *pluralist* countries, such as the United States and the United Kingdom, unions organized along the crafts and skill sets of their members, and employers were represented 'by a panoply of conflicting groups, with many purporting to aggregate business interests and with none having much policy-making authority'.[33]

National varieties of the KWS were also shaped by divergences in political institutions, which affect the number of effective political parties and types of cabinets as well as the relative strength of different types of parties. In this context the key distinction is between *proportional* and *majoritarian* electoral systems: while proportional systems generate multi-party competition and coalition cabinets, majoritarian/plurality systems tend to have two major parties alternating in cabinets.[34] Majoritarian political regimes involve alternations of single-party governments, which may entail relatively frequent and abrupt changes in economic policy in these countries. This in turn made credible commitment to collective bargaining and a generous welfare regime more difficult. Proportional systems, on the other hand, created a political environment favourable to co-operation between political and economic actors. A great number of political and economic actors are veto-players with access to the political and policy process, leading to a more stable and consensus-oriented policy constellation that facilitates commitment to collective bargaining and welfare expansion. Moreover, proportional systems have a bias towards centre-left governments, as centrist parties are more likely to form coalitions with left-wing parties and it is often more difficult to form majorities without these parties' participation.[35]

These differences in collective bargaining institutions and electoral systems gave rise to national varieties of capitalism that adopted different forms of

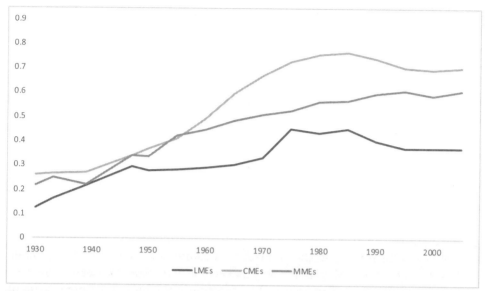

Figure 2.4 Average replacement rates for pensions and unemployment and sickness benefits, 1930–2005

Source: Social Citizenship Indicator Program 1930–2005

the KWS. While all industrialized countries witnessed a significant increase in social spending during the Golden Age of capitalism, there were substantial differences in terms of the *generosity* of social benefits between groups of countries that would later be identified as CMEs), LMEs and MMEs (see chapter 4 for more details). Figure 2.4 shows the evolution in average replacement rates – that is, the proportion of individual income that is paid out via social transfers – for public pensions and unemployment and sickness benefits: replacement rates were similar between these models of capitalism until 1950, but Northwestern European CMEs then began to develop increasingly more generous systems of social transfers than the Anglo-Saxon LMEs. The generosity of social transfers in the Mediterranean MMEs lay somewhere in between the other two models during this period.

The fall of egalitarian capitalism

Economic globalization

The rise of the KWS came to a halt in the 1970s, when a number of challenges constrained its further expansion. First of all, the decision of the US government led by Richard Nixon to devalue the exchange rate of the US dollar in 1971 and 'close the gold window' – that is, suspend the convertibility US dollars into gold at the fixed price of US$35 per ounce – marked the end of the Bretton Woods system, ushering in a new era of international monetary disorder (see box 2.2

for the causes of the demise of the Bretton Woods system).[36] As a result of the 'Nixon shock', the world's major currencies – the US dollar, the Japanese yen, the Deutschmark and the British pound – became *flexible* currencies whose value would be determined by market forces rather than by state intervention. This transition towards a floating exchange rate regime was triggered partially by the growing size of speculative international financial flows, which complicated the efforts of governments to defend their currency pegs.

In 1974 the US government was also the first to remove its remaining capital controls, which played a central role in the Bretton Woods system by supporting the autonomy of national governments to develop a KWS. The United Kingdom dismantled its capital control regime in 1979; other industrialized countries soon followed in the 1980s. As cross-border financial flows grew dramatically, exchange rates were often subject to considerable short-term volatility. For this reason, a number of member states of the European Economic Community (EEC) decided to establish a new regime of fixed exchange rates, which they believed was necessary to promote deeper regional economic integration. The less stable international monetary environment made a commitment to Keynesian macroeconomic management of aggregate demand more difficult (see chapter 3).[37]

Box 2.2 The demise of the Bretton Woods system

The Bretton Woods system collapsed during the early 1970s, when the US government suspended the gold convertibility of the US dollar and the adjustable-peg exchange rate system broke down.[38] The most important cause of the Bretton Woods system was the inherent instability of the dollar–gold standard. Already in 1960 the Belgian economist Robert Triffin had argued that the dollar-gold standard faced an intrinsic dilemma between the world's need for US dollars and the capacity of the United States to maintain foreign confidence in the stability of the US dollar. The United States could only supply dollars to the rest of the world by running a deficit on its balance of payments – that is, on the record of all financial and trade transactions between the residents of a country and the rest of the world (see box 7.1 in chapter 7 for an explanation of the balance-of-payments). But the more the US economy ran balance-of-payment deficits, the more it would undermine confidence in the dollar's convertibility into gold. Triffin's predictions were increasingly borne out during the 1960s, when the amount of dollars circulating in the world economy far exceeded the amount of gold the US government held to back it up.

The United States enjoyed significant benefits from the international status of the US dollar, as the country was able to finance its increasing external deficits simply by printing dollars. At the same time, however, the country became increasingly vulnerable to a confidence crisis: a growing amount of investors began to convert their dollars into gold, as it became abundantly clear that the United States would not be able to back all the circulating dollars. Moreover, the dollar's fixed value in gold undermined the international competitiveness of US-based firms by making their goods more expensive to foreign consumers. Declining confidence in the gold convertibility of the US dollar and concerns about the effects of the US dollar's overvaluation on the competitiveness of US firms eventually pushed the US government to close the gold window and devalue the US dollar.

Second, the stagflation crisis of the 1970s damaged the legitimacy of the KWS. Between 1973 and 1979, members of the Organization of the Petroleum Exporting Countries (OPEC) raised the price for oil from US$2.5 to US$33 per barrel, massively increasing the energy costs of oil-importing industrialized countries and feeding into a general increase in the price level of goods and services. However, rising inflation was also endogenously connected to the workings of the KWS: governments' commitment to full employment had strengthened the bargaining power of labour to such an extent that the wage demands of workers started to exceed productivity growth by the end of the 1960s. Faced with falling profit margins, private firms increasingly embarked on investment strikes by curtailing their spending on new capital goods and diminishing their production capacities. As such, the post-war accord between capital and labour and its Fordist rationale of enlarging the 'overall economic pie' broke down into a renewal of distributional struggles over the size of the slice each group could seize. The resulting stagflation crisis undermined the legitimacy of the Keynesian macroeconomic policy paradigm, as expansionary monetary and fiscal policies fuelled inflation instead of reducing unemployment. Rising unemployment and falling economic growth also increased the fiscal burden of the KWS. In short, '[t]he mid-1970s brought much slower growth rates in the OECD as a whole, combined with high inflation, squeezed profits, industrial strife, high government deficits, unstable exchange rates, weak investment, and very low levels of employer confidence'.[39]

From a neoliberal perspective, the stagflation crisis and growth in public debt were clear manifestations of the inefficiencies of the KWS and its lack of responsiveness to market exigencies. Neoliberal solutions to the perceived ills of the KWS became increasingly attractive for right-wing conservative parties in the 1980s and even for left-wing social-democratic parties in the 1990s. Indeed, as David Harvey notes in his *A Brief History of Neoliberalism*, 'almost all states ... have embraced, sometimes voluntarily and in other instances in response to coercive pressures, some version of neoliberal theory and adjusted at least some policies and practices accordingly'.[40] A central dimension in this respect was the pursuit of neoliberal globalization, the key features of which can be summarized as follows:

- *Trade liberalization*: Further liberalization of tariffs and non-tariff barriers to international trade at the global level were accompanied by efforts towards even deeper regional integration. In different rounds, GATT negotiations led to new agreements that extended trade liberalization to new issues and drew in new and future members from the developing and formerly Communist nations. The Uruguay Round in 1994 also created a new institution, the World Trade Organization (WTO), to replace the GATT. The WTO is a permanent organization with powers of its own, largely to mediate trade disputes. Its founding consolidated the open trading system.[41] At the regional level, members of the European Union approved the Single European Act in 1986. The United States and Canada had long-standing investment and trade ties, and in 1987 they signed a free trade agreement. Five years later Mexico joined in, and in 1994 the North American Free Trade Agreement (NAFTA) went into effect. Trade liberalization brought a huge expansion of world trade.

Combined with the innovations in information and communication technologies (ICT) and transportation (especially the great breakthrough of containerization, which revolutionized shipping by putting traded goods into standardized containers), the liberalization of trade enabled a transnational organization of production by multinational enterprises (MNEs): finished products increasingly result from manufacturing and assembly in multiple countries, with each step in the process adding value to the end product and with growing participation by developing countries in these global value chains (GVCs). One of the most important aspects of these GVCs is that they rest on a continuously evolving international division of labour:

> While the consumption of finished products remains concentrated in the West, the production of this increasing range of commodities is increasingly conducted by workers located across the far reaches of global capitalism ... This division of labour incorporates a great number of diverse and spatially separated workforces who undertake specific compartmentalised tasks and who are connected to the larger process through various forms of social organisation – ranging from the bureaucratic control of multinational firms, to market exchanges, social networks of subcontracting firms, and intricate webs of financing – that facilitate complex flows of goods, money and information.[42]

• *Financial liberalization*: Since the early 1970s there has been a trend towards globalization of private financial markets. Recall that the Bretton Woods architects endorsed an international financial order in which governments could control cross-border private financial flows. Apart from the dismantling of capital controls, innovations in ICT and the digitalization of finance enabled money to be moved around the world much more easily than in the past. The dramatic expansion of international trade and the rise of MNEs and GVCs from the 1960s onwards also generated a growing demand for private international financial services. Private firms and investors were encouraged to diversify their assets internationally by the increasingly volatile currency environment after the breakdown of the Bretton Woods regime in the early 1970s, when governments of the major industrialized countries moved towards flexible exchange rates. Financial globalization brought more volatility in exchange rates and interest rates, creating an urgent need for various financial innovations to mitigate these new risks, such as the creation of currency futures, options and swaps.

Freedom of movement for capital became the new orthodoxy once again and can be seen as the key pillar of neoliberal globalization. Neoliberals were less sympathetic to the Bretton Woods idea that governments' national policy autonomy had to be protected against capital flight. While the architects of Bretton Woods had endorsed the use of capital controls for this purpose, neoliberals applauded the fact that international financial markets might impose an external discipline on governments pursuing policies that were not 'sound' from a neoliberal standpoint. Neoliberals have also criticized the role that capital controls might play in interfering with market freedoms and preventing the efficient allocation of capital internationally. The liberalization of capital controls was seen as a kind of competitive strategy of governments to attract mobile financial business and capital to their national territory.[43]

Varieties of capitalism: towards neoliberal convergence?

To what extent did economic globalization undermine the main institutional pillars of egalitarian capitalism? One of the most widely debated propositions in the CPE and IPE literature is the globalization thesis, which states that 'globalization is bearing down on all welfare states with equal force, inducing retrenchments of programs and convergence on minimalist neoliberal welfare norms'.[44] In its strongest form, the thesis argues that competition between nation states to attract mobile capital spurred a 'race to the bottom', with globalization unleashing downwards convergence pressures towards the lowest common denominator of the neoliberal model. Global economic integration intensified the quest of national governments to attract mobile capital to the domestic economy, increasingly transforming the welfare state

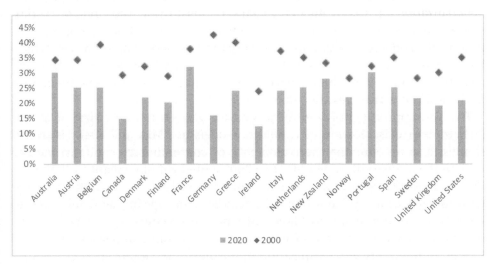

Figure 2.5 Statutory corporate income tax rate in selected OECD countries, 2000–20
Source: OECD

into a neoliberal *competition state*: while the welfare state had created a fairly self-contained national economy insulated from international markets from the 1940s to the 1970s, the competition state opened up to international trade and capital flows, and transformed itself from an instrument of national self-government into an enforcer of the interests of global capital vis-à-vis domestic society.[45] One of the most important outcomes of this process is the declining progressivity of taxation in the advanced capitalist world, as governments cut tax rates on mobile capital in order to attract foreign investors or prevent domestic investors from moving their capital to countries with lower taxes.[46] As an illustration, figure 2.5 shows that statutory tax rates on corporate income fell in all the selected OECD countries between 2000 and 2020.

The globalization thesis has been strongly criticized for overstating both the extent of global economic integration and the convergence pressures resulting from that integration. The VoC school – exemplified in a series of essays in the 2001 book *Varieties of Capitalism: The Institutional Foundations of Comparative Advantage*, edited by Peter Hall and David Soskice – became the dominant CPE approach to reject the view that different national varieties of capitalism would inevitably converge towards a neoliberal model.[47] Based on different sets of *complementarities* between different institutional domains like the labour market, corporate governance and the financial system, VoC scholars identified two ideal-types of capitalism: the LMEs of the Anglo-Saxon countries and the CMEs of continental Europe and Japan.[48] These scholars' key argument is that each of these two models of capitalism has its own 'comparative institutional advantage', with firms in LMEs engaging in *radical* innovation and those in CMEs in *incremental* innovation. For this reason, firms in these two distinct varieties of capitalism will try to maintain or at most modestly adjust existing institutions to external pressures of change. An important implication of this argument is that firms in the CMEs – at least those from manufacturing sectors – will prefer to keep rather than overhaul the equality-promoting institutions like collective bargaining structures and welfare state spending, which have bolstered their international competitiveness and comparative advantage (chapters 4 and 5). This should clarify why, since the 1980s, income inequality in the CMEs has risen less fast than in the LMEs.

The VoC approach has been contested for various reasons. First of all, its dichotomous classification of capitalist models as LMEs and CMEs is overly simplistic to account for the complexity of contemporary capitalist variety even in the industrialized world.[49] In a 2007 edited volume meant to refine the VoC framework, Oscar Molina and Martin Rhodes tried to overcome the LME–CME juxtaposition by identifying the Southern European countries (Greece, Italy, Portugal and Spain) as MMEs, in which the state played a key role in facilitating the coordination of economic activity and compensating for the lack of autonomous self-organization of business and labour. As such, Molina and Rhodes echoed arguments elaborated by other scholars of comparative capitalisms, who also included France in this group of state-influenced market economies.[50] In the original Hall and Soskice 2001 volume it had already been conceded that France and the Southern European countries were 'in more ambiguous positions' and did not easily fit into either the CME or the LME model.[51] Since these countries were found to be less coherent in their domestic institutional setup than countries belonging to the LME or CME model, MMEs were generally seen to be less successful in adapting to the challenges of globalization than the other two models: in Southern MMEs, 'state inter-vention supports an economic system which pays out rents to economic actors in the face of economic shocks, rather than giving economic actors the means and incentives to adjust their competitiveness to a new situation'.[52]

By taking this position, VoC is seemingly stuck in an overly functionalist interpretation of economic institutions, whose main function is to solve collective action problems faced by firms in their mission to remain compet-itive in the world economy. From a rationalist-functionalist perspective, economic globalization can be seen as a source of institutional divergence, as institutional differences between CMEs and LMEs enable local firms in these countries to establish a comparative advantage by specializing in particular products and processes (i.e. incremental versus radical innovation). However, equality-promoting institutions like collective bargaining and welfare spending programmes should rather be seen as collective (yet fragile) solutions to distributional conflicts arising from market activities; the performance-enhancing effects of these institutions are a *by-product* of these solutions rather than their ultimate *purpose*.[53] The functionalist interpretation is at odds with the historical observation that capitalists only came to accept these institutions after a series of worker revolts and strikes.[54] The growing strength of the working class was a necessary condition for capitalists in the CMEs to become convinced of the idea that collective bargaining and the welfare state can also be 'beneficial constraints' that might enhance their competitiveness by enabling incremental innovation strategies (see chapters 4 and 5). Yet 'whether or not capital is willing to "learn" and explore alter-native, more labour-accommodating production and marketing strategies is significantly affected by available opportunities to exit from a regime under which labour has the capacity to impose obligations on capital'.[55] Economic globalization can be a source of institutional convergence precisely because it offers capital more opportunities to escape these obligations. One of the most pressing critiques of VoC's functionalist approach is that it does not sufficiently account for institutional change.[56] If firms in CMEs are so much in favour of preserving equality-promoting institutions, why do we see in many cases – if not all – a gradual transition towards a less egalitarian model? Income inequality has risen significantly even in many CMEs, so accounting for institutional change is essential for understanding their distinctive trajectory. The social models of the CMEs have been subjected to various forms of liberalization in response to attacks by employer organizations (see chapter 4).

These observations underscore a common criticism of the VoC approach: that it pays excessive attention to the persistent differences between varieties of capitalism and turns a blind eye to remaining similarities. More specifically, VoC tends to ignore the fact that any capitalist system continues to feature structural tensions and conflicts between the capitalist class and the working class, which can only temporarily be alleviated by institutional compromises that will always be highly fragile.[57] Institutional change and stability are a function of the distribution of power resources between the main political-economic classes in capitalist societies, as advocates of the power resources approach have argued. Although there is still considerable cross-national variation in the distribution of political power between the capitalist class and the working classes, economic globalization strengthened the power resources of the former and weakened those of the latter in ways that spawned varying tendencies towards neoliberalization in *all* the advanced capitalist countries – as we will see in the following chapters.[58]

Neoliberalism and varieties of growth models

VoC's supply-side focus on the role of institutions in shaping national production regimes ignored the importance of aggregate demand dynamics in determining long-term economic growth. The central aim of VoC was to explain how firms' business strategies in CMEs and LMEs are shaped by institutional differences in labour market organization, skill formation systems and corporate governance, and how they have contributed to divergent national production regimes. However, as Herman Mark Schwartz and Bent Sofus Tranøy note in their meta-analysis of the CPE's research agenda, 'VoC's supply-side focus explained how different national subsystems brought different goods to market, not how those goods found sufficient monetary demand on the other side of the transaction.'[59] By doing so, VoC moved away from the Regulation approach's macro-focus on accumulation regimes as patterns of production *and* consumption: in the Fordist wage-led growth model, wages grew in line with labour productivity, and household consumption and corporate investment were the primary drivers of aggregate demand. The wage-led growth model, which was institutionally underpinned by Keynesian macroeconomic policies and collective bargaining, collapsed due to inflationary pressures associated with intensified industrial conflict in the 1970s and with longer-term secular trends of globalization, deindustrialization and financialization. Governments and firms in the advanced capitalist world have had to respond to the challenges and opportunities created by these trends: 'At the top of their list of challenges was to find a replacement for the wage-led growth model, one that could deliver prosperity in the highly globalised and interconnected post-Fordist world.'[60]

Scholars working in the VoC tradition – David Soskice and Torben Iversen in particular – have increasingly acknowledged the importance of aggregate demand in the formation of national growth models since the 1980s: they have developed a sectoral perspective that emphasizes the deep inter-twinement between growth models and varieties of capitalism, with CMEs and LMEs pursuing export-led and consumption-led growth, respectively.[61] The basic premise of the VoC perspective on these growth models is that 'national governments … are deeply concerned with promoting the high value-added sectors of their economies, in which they enjoy comparative institutional advantage'. Since these sectors vary across countries, 'govern-ments want to control the detailed operations of regulatory systems in their own environments'.[62] In LMEs like the United States and the United Kingdom, governments privileged the interests of their 'innovative and high-risk' financial sector by deregulating financial markets and liberalizing regula-tions in ways that facilitated the access of households to banking credit and supported their consumption. In CMEs like Germany, on the other hand, governments promoted the interests of their high-value-added and export-oriented manufacturing sectors. Economic globalization was conducive to the formation of these two 'knowledge-intensive' growth models: 'globalization is not capitalism unleashed but the choice of advanced national governments in response to the collapse of Fordism as a competitive organizational technology and the onset of the information technology revolution'.[63]

The VoC perspective on growth models shares some of the shortcomings of the original VoC framework. It remains an overly functionalist interpretation that continues to downplay the central role of class conflict in the emergence of post-Fordist national growth models since the 1980s, which has been unrelated to the rise in income inequality according to the most recent models of VoC. In fact, Soskice and Iversen have argued in their 2019 book *Democracy and Prosperity* that median income groups have been 'exceptionally successful in keeping up with the overall growth of income'; and to the extent that rising inequality is driven by the transition to the knowledge economy, 'the middle and upper middle classes have benefited, either directly through the market or indirectly through the tax-financed welfare state'.[64] Their claim does not stand up to the scrutiny of recent empirical studies that have revealed a 'squeeze' of the middle classes.[65] They also hold a remarkably sanguine view on a key distributional shift associated with neoliberalization: financialization – that is, 'the increasing role of financial motives, financial markets, financial actors and financial institutions in the operation of the domestic and international economies'.[66] Rather than reflecting the power of capital and the interests of wealthy people, financialization is seen as 'a necessary part of the knowledge economy, and it is indirectly supported by a majority in the electorate for this reason': 'Because of the implied volatility in income, access to credit markets serves an increasingly important income-smoothing function that is not adequately addressed by the social protection system.'[67]

Other scholars, like Lucio Baccaro, Jonas Pontusson, Engelbert Stockhammer, Özlem Onaran and Eckhard Hein, have tried to avoid these functionalist defects by developing a post-Keynesian growth model perspective that highlights the role of working-class restructuring in the context of neoliberalization and financialization since the 1980s.[68] Their starting point is that neoliberalization (and resulting financialization) can be seen as a political project to weaken the organizational power of labour and restore the power of capital: 'In the Anglo-Saxon countries neoliberalism came with an outright attack on organized labour ... In continental Europe the organisational strength of labour was eroded by two decades of high unemployment, welfare state retrenchment and globalization.'[69] The resulting rise in income inequality and the fall in the labour income share have constrained economic growth in the advanced capitalist economies by depressing consumption (chapter 1). As a result, governments and firms had to find a solution 'to the problem of finding a replacement for the faltering "wage driver"' of aggregate demand and economic growth.[70] More specifically, 'advanced capitalist political economies

Table 2.3 Indicators of growth models, 1995–2007, and income inequality, 1980–2007

	Average annual contribution to GDP growth in percentage points (1995–2007)			Change in income inequality in percentage points (1980–2007)	
	Private consumption	Public consumption	Exports	Top 1% income share	Labour income share of GDP
LMEs					
UK	2.17	0.50	1.36	12.6	-2
US	2.37	0.26	0.59	9.2	-4
CMEs					
AT	1.01	0.34	2.89	1.2	NA
BE	0.84	0.35	3.54	-0.7	-7
DM	0.96	0.48	2.27	2.	-5
FI	1.77	0.42	3.04	3.0	-10
DE	0.53	0.24	2.37	4.3	-11
NL	1.28	0.63	3.67	1.5	-10
SE	1.32	0.18	2.90	3.2	-8
MMEs					
FR	1.27	0.31	1.45	3.5	-13
GR	2.46	0.67	1.55	1.1	6
IT	0.96	0.24	0.85	2.8	-13
PT	1.66	0.52	1.54	2.2	-4
ES	2.29	0.76	1.63	8.3	-11

Source: OECD, World Inequality Database

AT = Austria; BE = Belgium; DE = Germany; DM = Denmark; ES = Spain; FI = Finland; FR = France; GR = Greece; IT = Italy; NL = Netherlands; PT = Portugal; SE = Sweden; UK = United Kingdom; US = United States.

have responded to the insufficiency of aggregate demand associated with distributional shifts in favour of capital owners in essentially two ways: increasing reliance on credit as a source of household consumption (and investment) and increasing reliance on external demand'.[71] These debt-led and export-led growth models are also seen as intrinsically unstable and not rooted in the kinds of institutional equilibria analysed in the VoC literature.

Table 2.3 presents some data that cast light on these two opposing perspectives. In line with the VoC analysis, there appears to be a clear connection between growth models and varieties of capitalism: exports contributed much more to economic growth between 1995 and 2007 in the CMEs than in the LMEs or MMEs, whereas private consumption was particularly important for the LMEs (and in some MMEs like Greece and Spain). However, it is clear that the CMEs exhibit significant *intra-model* variety, as Baccaro and Pontusson have pointed out.[72] In line with a post-Keynesian growth model perspective, there seems to be a link between growth models and income inequality, which – apart from in Greece – rose in all the selected advanced economies between 1980 and 2007. However, as noted by Jan Behringer and Till van Treeck in a key contribution to the debate, CMEs and LMEs have witnessed different 'varieties of income inequality': in the LMEs the top 1 per cent income share rose much more than in the CMEs, while the labour income share of GDP fell much more in the latter economies than in the former.[73]

The growth model perspective elaborated in the following chapters belongs broadly to the post-Keynesian tradition for two reasons. First of all, we will clarify the linkages between the rise in inequality and the formation of these growth models by examining how neoliberal shifts in macroeconomic policy, labour market institutions, corporate governance and financial policy have weakened the bargaining power of labour and shaped aggregate demand in different varieties of capitalism since the 1980s (see chapters 3–6). Second, the resulting debt-led and export-led growth models are 'dysfunctional' in the sense that they cannot be seen as sustainable replacements of the Fordist wage-led growth model. Not only did economic growth during the neoliberal era remain far below growth during the Keynesian era, but these two growth models fuelled widening macroeconomic imbalances that eventually culminated in the global financial crisis of 2008 (see chapter 7).

3

Macroeconomic Policy: From 'Full Employment' to 'Sound Money'

In the previous chapter we have seen that Keynesian social democracy obtained a dominant influence over the organization of Western political economies and societies in the industrialized world after World War II. Politicians and citizens across different classes and political parties had become convinced that the government and the state had to play an active and central role in the economy – through the active management of business cycles, the promotion of collective bargaining and the expansion of a state-funded social security system. During the 1930s, experiments with activist monetary and fiscal policies had shown that governments had a number of effective tools at their disposal to boost economic growth and employment during economic recessions; these experiments led to the abandonment of the classical-liberal paradigm and to the emergence of a Keynesian macroeconomic policy regime. The central feature of macroeconomic policy was that the government and central bank had to adopt fiscal and monetary policies geared towards the attainment of 'full employment' in the economy. Full employment became the principal target of the government's macroeconomic policy because incumbent political parties and their politicians deemed strong economic growth and low unemployment a precondition for being re-elected. As Anthony Crossland, a leading politician of the UK Labour Party, wrote in 1956, 'The voters, now convinced that full employment, generous welfare services and social stability can quite well be preserved, will certainly not relinquish them. Any government which tampered with the basic structure of the full-employment Welfare State would meet with a sharp reverse at the polls.'[1]

The Keynesian macroeconomic policy regime did not last, however. During the 1970s its tools appeared to be ineffective in containing the stagflation crisis that plagued the industrialized world throughout this decade – a period of high unemployment, high inflation and economic stagnation. The stagflation crisis undermined the credibility of Keynesianism, which had postulated an inverse relationship, known as the Phillips curve, between the unemployment and inflation rates. The crisis set the stage for a neoliberal macroeconomic policy regime in which 'sound money' became the principal policy target. First, monetary policy was delegated to central banks that became 'politically independent' from the government and were instructed to target a low and stable level of inflation (instead of full employment). Second, increasing government spending to alleviate economic downturns went out of vogue: balanced annual budgets and reducing the public debt level became the principal targets for fiscal policy, ushering in an age of permanent austerity.[2]

How can we explain this transition? The shift towards a neoliberal macro-economic policy regime was legitimized by new economic ideas about the ineffectiveness of Keynesian macroeconomic policies in boosting economic growth and employment on a long-term basis; according to these ideas, expansionary monetary and fiscal policies would only disrupt the economy in the long term by fuelling inflation. These ideas informed and justified macro-economic policymakers in pursuing restrictive monetary and fiscal policies: governments and central banks fought inflation by showing that they were prepared to allow unemployment to rise to very high levels in order to pursue low and stable levels of inflation. The growing acceptance of these ideas during the 1980s and 1990s fundamentally transformed the government's role and responsibility in the economy.

The shift in the target of macroeconomic policymaking from full employment to price stability cannot be explained merely by new insights among econo-mists about the long-term ineffectiveness of monetary and fiscal policy. More important was the fact that the transition towards the neoliberal anti-inflation paradigm was actively promoted by capitalist employers, who had become increasingly disgruntled since the late 1960s about the negative effects of Keynesian full employment policies on their profitability: low unemployment levels during the 1950s and 1960s had strengthened the bargaining power of workers and labour unions vis-à-vis employers, eventually leading to 'excessive' wage demands that came at the expense of deteriorating profit levels for firms and their capitalist owners. In this regard, the shift towards restrictive monetary and fiscal policies should also be seen as a strategy to fight inflation by creating unemployment and weakening the power of workers and labour unions. Moreover, the lowering of inflation benefited wealthy owners of capital by upholding the real value of their financial investments as well as reducing the tax burden on these investments.

These distributional implications had important sectoral dimensions that reveal the key role of the neoliberal transition in macroeconomic policymaking in the formation of debt-led and export-led growth models. In the North European CMEs, restrictive macroeconomic policies helped to strengthen the competitiveness of export-oriented firms in the manufacturing sectors by containing labour costs in these sectors at the expense of depressing domestic demand and wage growth in the domestically oriented service sectors of the economy. The lowering of inflation also allowed a gradual decline in nominal long-term interest rates, which encouraged poor and middle-class households in Anglo-Saxon LMEs to accumulate debt in order either to purchase houses or to finance their consumption in the face of stagnating real wages. As such, the neoliberal shift in macroeconomic policy has been supported by divergent cross-class and sectoral coalitions undergirding these growth models.

Macroeconomic policy during the Keynesian era

A key pillar of the Keynesian macroeconomic policy paradigm is that policy-makers face a trade-off between boosting employment and keeping the general price level (i.e. inflation) low: the more they focus on reducing the level of unemployment, the higher inflation will be; the more they focus on reducing the inflation rate, the higher the unemployment rate will be. Underlying this Phillips curve relationship are both demand-side and supply-side mechanisms. From a demand-side perspective, lowering the level of unemployment in the economy will raise total labour income as more people have a job, thereby increasing aggregate demand in the economy in ways that push up the general price level. From a supply-side perspective, lowering the level of unemployment allows workers to ask for higher incomes by strengthening their bargaining position, leading firms to raise the price of their goods and services in order to maintain their profit margins. During the post-war era, it was evident that macroeconomic policymakers had to prioritize the attainment of full employment, even if this would lead to higher inflation. Full employment played a central role in the Fordist wage-led growth model, which linked wage growth to labour productivity growth as a way to enable mass consumption and support aggregate demand in the economy (chapter 2).

Within the Keynesian macroeconomic policy paradigm, the government's most effective instrument to stabilize aggregate demand and maintain economic growth was fiscal policy – the manipulation of government spending and taxation. When economic growth faltered and unemployment increased, the government had to increase its spending on goods and services (without increasing taxes). A reduction in income taxes (without a reduction in government spending) would accomplish the same thing because it would cause households and firms to spend more at any given price level. When the economy was booming, the government had to slow down the economy by running annual budget surpluses and build fiscal reserves that could be used to fund future spending programmes when it became necessary. Hence, Keynesianism advocated a *counter-cyclical* macroeconomic policy. When the private economy grew too much and excessive inflationary pressures arose, government spending had to be reduced or taxes increased: these restrictive policies would reduce aggregate demand in the economy and ease these pressures. Indeed, 'Keynes was opposed to [long-lasting] fiscal profligacy; and his critics misunderstood the fact that in Keynes's analysis, austerity was the necessary counterpart to stimulus – to be applied during the boom as a means of averting inflation or the risk of financial collapse.'[3]

A key reason why Keynesian economists believed in the effectiveness of fiscal policy was that they assumed that the *fiscal multiplier* is greater than one, especially during economic recessions. The fiscal multiplier is a central concept in Keynesian macroeconomic thinking, as it refers to the total increase in aggregate spending in the economy resulting from the government's fiscal stimulus (see box 3.1). If the government decides to spend €100 billion on public infrastructure and aggregate demand eventually increases by €150 billion, the fiscal multiplier amounts to 1.5 (€150 billion/€100 billion). The fact that the fiscal multiplier is greater than one had important implications for the long-term sustainability of expansionary fiscal policies based on deficit spending in economic downturns. It implied that the boost in economic activity resulting from an increase in government spending would be greater than the amount of money the government had to borrow to finance that spending. As a result, the public debt-to-GDP ratio – that is, the size of the public debt burden *relative* to the size of the economy, which is the predominant measure of public debt sustainability – would decrease even in the face of a deficit spending programme that increased the *absolute* public debt burden. Assume, for instance, that the public debt burden is 100 per cent of GDP, amounting to €100 billion, and that the government engages in a debt-financed stimulus programme of €10 billion (=10 per cent of GDP). When the fiscal multiplier is greater than one (e.g. 1.5), the economy will receive a boost of €15 billion (= €10 billion × 1.5). As a result, the debt-to-GDP ratio will decline to less than 96 per cent (= €110 billion/€115 billion) *even though* the absolute public debt burden increases to €110 billion.[4]

Box 3.1 The fiscal multiplier

In order to understand the fiscal multiplier, let us assume that the US government wants to fight an economic recession by implementing a fiscal stimulus programme that contains a US$20 billion order for new fighter planes with Boeing (the large aircraft manufacturer). By placing that order, the US government raises the demand for the output produced by Boeing and induces the company to hire more workers and increase production. Because Boeing is part of the US economy, the increase in the demand for Boeing jets implies an increase in aggregate demand by US$20 billion. If the fiscal multiplier is greater than one, aggregate demand in the US economy will ultimately increase by more than that US$20 billion. The only condition is that the MPC – that is, the fraction of extra income that a household consumes rather than saves – is greater than zero. So when the US government places an order of US$20 billion with Boeing, Boeing's shareholders and workers decide to spend some of the extra income they receive from the order. This will increase demand for goods and services that are produced by other companies in the US economy, which will raise the income of the shareholders and workers of these companies and induce them to spend more as well. As such, there is a positive feedback loop, as higher demand resulting from the initial fiscal stimulus leads to higher income, which subsequently leads to even higher demand. Once all these effects are added together, the total impact on aggregate demand can be much larger than the initial impulse from higher government spending.[5]

How much larger? The size of the fiscal multiplier depends on the MPC: of the extra income that households receive from the stimulus, the greater the part that is consumed, the greater the fiscal multiplier. There is an easy formula to calculate the total increase in aggregate demand: fiscal multiplier $= 1/(1 - MPC)$. So when the average MPC in the US economy is 0.75 (meaning that US households consume, on average, US$0.75 and save US$0.25 of every additional dollar they receive), the fiscal multiplier equals $1/(1 - 0.75) = 4$. In this case, the US$20 billion of government spending generates US$80 billion of demand for goods and services.

Evidently, the average MPC in an economy hides large variation across households, which differ in their income and wealth and in the credit constraints they face. Most households have little income and wealth, and even in rich countries many households are credit-constrained – that is, they cannot easily get a loan from the bank to finance ongoing consumption. So both for households that are credit-constrained and for those that are unable to save ahead of anticipated declines in income, consumption tracks income closely: the MPC for this group is closer to 1. For the small fraction of households who hold the majority of wealth, on the other hand, current income plays a very small role in determining consumption: their MPC is closer to zero. This means that for rich households, an increase in current income of US$1 would raise their consumption by just a few cents. A corollary is that fiscal stimulus programmes that particularly raise the income of poor households with a large MPC will be more effective than those that boost the income of rich households with a low MPC. More generally, fiscal redistribution of income from rich to poor households increases aggregate demand in the economy.

The emphasis on fiscal policy does not mean that monetary policy was unimportant during the Keynesian era: it certainly was important in shaping financial conditions in the economy and influencing borrowing costs via its effect on interest rates. As summarized in box 3.2, the central bank's power to create money enables it to influence macroeconomic conditions through a variety of channels, the most important of which is its effect on interest rates in the economy. Interest rates are extremely important variables that influence the spending decisions of firms and households by affecting borrowing costs: lower (higher) interest rates translate into lower (higher) borrowing costs, inducing households and firms to borrow more (less) money and spend more (less). Monetary policy was particularly important from a Keynesian perspective in helping to reduce the borrowing costs of the government: without the helping hand of the central bank's expansionary monetary policy, the government's ability to engage in deficit spending could be significantly constrained by rising interest rate costs.

Box 3.2 Instruments of the central bank

Central banks are public institutions responsible for managing state-issued money – that is, the money we use as a 'means for settlement' to pay for goods and services, receive wages or other kinds of income, get a loan from the bank, etc. The key objectives and responsibilities of central banks and the main instruments they use to achieve these objectives have evolved over time. Generally, a central bank's monetary policy can have the following goals: full employment; price stability; exchange rate stability; financial stability. The central bank is able to influence these variables through its control over the *supply of money* in the economy and its effect on interest rates. In most cases, a central bank does not directly set interest rates for loans such as mortgages or corporate loans. However, it does have certain tools at its disposal to push interest rates towards desired levels. Which instruments does the central bank have in controlling the money supply?

- *Credit facilities*: The central bank can create new money and lend it to private banks, which then use the money to lend to firms, households and governments. But in theory, the central bank can also directly lend money to firms, households and governments.
- *Open market operations*: The central bank can change the money supply by buying or selling government bonds. If it wants to increase the money supply, it can buy government bonds from private banks. Conversely, selling government bonds to private banks reduces the money supply, as the money the central bank receives for the bonds is out of circulation.
- *Reserve requirements*: A central bank can influence the money supply with reserve requirements, which are regulations on the minimum amount of reserves that private banks must hold against deposits. When the central bank wants more money circulating in the economy, it can reduce the reserve requirement and allow private banks to lend out more money. If it wants to reduce the amount of money in the economy, it can raise the reserve requirement to make sure private banks have less money to lend out.
- *Influencing interest rates*: The central bank holds the key to the policy rate – that is, the rate at which private banks can borrow from the central bank. When private banks can borrow from the central bank at a lower rate, they pass these savings on by reducing the cost of loans to their customers. Lower interest rates tend to increase borrowing in the economy, and this means the quantity of money in circulation increases.

From the 1930s to the 1970s, co-operation between governments and central banks was therefore the order of the day: central banks' monetary policy was ultimately controlled by the government. Monetary policy played a secondary role to fiscal policy in the economy: Keynesian *fiscal dominance* followed from the fact that government spending became a significant contributor to aggregate demand in many countries, which had to be enabled by highly accommodating policies from central banks. Indeed, central banks were subordinated to ministries of finance and had a wide range of goals, including the maintenance of historically low interest rates on government debt.[6] So when the government decided that it was necessary to increase spending in response to an economic recession, it could always instruct the central bank to lower interest rates and make it cheaper for the government to borrow and finance its spending. In this period, central banks sometimes even directly funded expansionary government spending by monetary financing – that is, the direct funding of public spending by central banks through the purchase and holding of sovereign bonds. The establishment of central banks during the first half of the twentieth century was closely linked to the government's need to finance its war efforts, as well as to the financial system's need to support private banking interests through its 'lender of last resort' function.[7] From a Keynesian perspective, the desire for greater monetary sovereignty through monetary financing was at least as important. Central banks played an important role in reflating their economies following the Great Depression and financing the war effort. After World War II, strengthening the government's borrowing capacity continued to be a crucial part of the central bank's tasks.[8]

Figure 3.1 offers some empirical evidence of fiscal–monetary policy coordination in the 1930s to 1970s. Both central banks and (often state-owned) commercial banks were required to purchase government debt to support fiscal policy objectives, including economic growth and debt sustainability: 'for a 30-year period following World War II to the late 1970s, between 40–50% of government debt was directly or indirectly funded by domestic

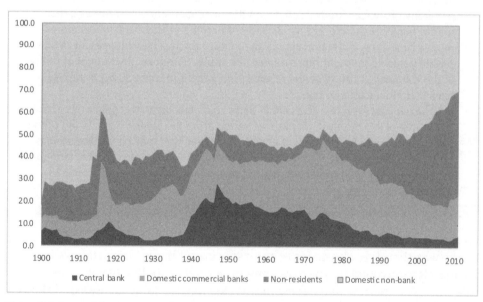

Figure 3.1 Ownership structure of government debt in twelve OECD countries, 1900–2011

Source: Abbas et al. 2014

Countries include Austria, Belgium, Canada, France, Germany, Ireland, Italy, Japan, Netherlands, Spain, Sweden, United Kingdom and United States.

monetary institutions rather than non-monetary agents (domestic market or non-resident investors)'.[9] Since the 1980s, the proportion of domestic monetary financing has been steadily declining: a growing part of government debt has been financed by non-residents (mostly foreign private banks and institutional investors) in the face of financial globalization, which increasingly constrained national governments in pursuing Keynesian reflationary macroeconomic policies, and put pressure on them to adopt neoliberal monetary and fiscal policies – as we will see below.

Neoliberal macroeconomic policy: towards 'sound money'

From the stagflation crisis of the 1970s to the fiscal crisis of the welfare state

The stagflation crisis ended the virtuous circle of the post-war accord between labour and capital during the Golden Age. By doing so, it undermined the legitimacy and attractiveness of the Keynesian macroeconomic policy paradigm. Despite galloping inflation, governments adopted expansionary monetary and fiscal policies during the 1970s to fight rising unemployment and mitigate intensifying social and political conflict. Rather than reducing unemployment, these Keynesian attempts to pump-prime the economy fuelled additional inflation. Eventually, inflation was brought down only by pursuing highly restrictive monetary policies. The first major country to do so was the United States, where the governor of the US Federal Reserve, Paul Volcker, decided to raise the federal funds rate from 4.6 per cent in 1977 to almost 20 per cent in 1981, and to allow unemployment to rise to whatever level was needed to bring inflation back down to acceptable levels – a policy move that became known as the *Volcker Shock*. Ultimately, unemployment in the US economy rose to more than 10 per cent – the highest level since the Great Depression. Deflationary monetary conditions in the US economy were subsequently exported to the rest of the advanced capitalist world: almost everywhere, a sharp rise in unemployment was needed to lower inflation (figure 3.2).

In the early 1980s, rising unemployment increased demands on social security systems. The sharply growing public debt burden since the 1980s seems to reveal that the successful fight against inflation came at the expense of a new type of crisis: the fiscal crisis of the KWS. The public debt ratio among the OECD countries roughly doubled from between 20 to 35 per cent of GDP in the 1970s to between 65 and 80 per cent of GDP in the first half of the 1990s (figure 3.3). The rising public debt burden mostly ensued from so-called automatic stabilizers rather than discretionary spending programmes: these automatic stabilizers are central features of the tax and transfer system of the KWS, which have the effect of *automatically* offsetting a contraction of the economy via the government's fiscal balance. Because wages and profits fell during the economic downturn of 1975–85, governments collected less personal income tax, payroll tax and corporate income tax. At the same time, government spending increased in response to soaring unemployment, which led a growing number of people to apply for unemployment benefits and other forms of income support. Rising interest rates in the wake of central banks' restrictive

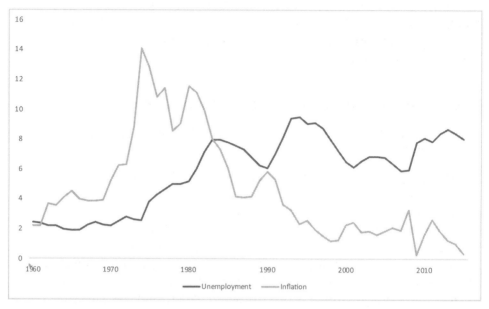

Figure 3.2 Unemployment and inflation rates in advanced economies, 1960–2015

Source: https://www.core-econ.org/

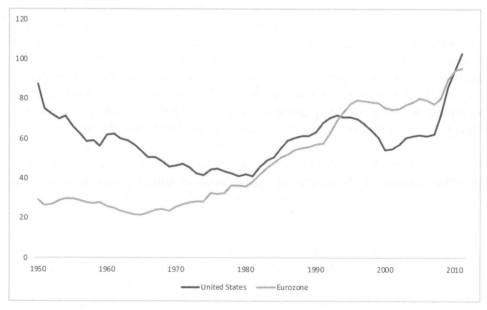

Figure 3.3 Public debt in selected regions and countries (in percentage of GDP), 1950–2011

Source: IMF

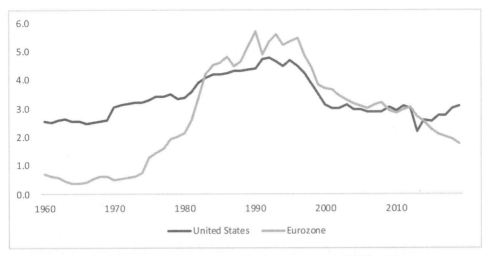

Figure 3.4 Net government debt interest payments (in percentage of GDP), 1960–2019
Source: OECD

monetary policies were another reason why government expenses increased significantly from the second half of the 1990s. As figure 3.4 shows, interest payments by governments soared as a percentage of GDP from 1975 to 1995.

Despite the key role of restrictive monetary policy in raising government borrowing costs, surging interest payments fed the perception among economists and policymakers that the amount of government spending in relation to the GDP and the accumulation of fiscal deficits had become excessive and unsustainable. If the stagflation crisis of the 1970s undermined the belief in the long-term Phillips trade-off between unemployment and inflation, the rise in the public debt burden in the 1980s dealt the final blow to the Keynesian macroeconomic paradigm. Governments and central banks abandoned the full employment target and replaced it with a macroeconomic policy regime oriented towards low inflation and low public deficits: 'A growing disillusionment with the impracticality of Keynesian reflationary macroeconomic prescriptions in a context of increasing international capital mobility became prevalent across the G7 countries and a convergence on the priority of sound money in macroeconomic policy followed.'[10] The neoliberal macroeconomic policy consensus turned the Keynesian Phillips curve on its head: governments and central banks could only reduce unemployment by fighting inflation and lowering public debt levels, which was deemed necessary to restore the confidence of firms and private investors and bring the economy back onto a trajectory of sustainable economic growth.

Depoliticization of macroeconomic policy

The shift from full employment towards sound money as the principal target of macroeconomic policymaking was legitimized by new economic ideas about the ineffectiveness of monetary and fiscal policy to boost economic growth and employment on a long-term basis. The stagflation crisis and the growth in public debt undermined the credibility of Keynesian macroeconomic policy, allowing new macroeconomic theories to emerge that seemed to offer a better explanation of what was happening and provided completely opposite policy prescriptions. As policymakers increasingly accepted these theories about the long-term ineffectiveness of macroeconomic policy in raising growth and employment, it made sense to make low inflation and balanced budgets the respective targets of monetary and fiscal policy (see box 3.3).

Box 3.3 The 'policy ineffectiveness' thesis: from monetarism to New Keynesianism

The stagflation crisis provided an ideal context for Milton Friedman's 'monetarist' views on monetary policy to gain growing acceptance among policymakers in the advanced capitalist world. In 1968 Friedman had published a paper in which he criticized the Keynesian Phillips curve.[11] In particular, Friedman argued that there is no reason to believe that the rate of inflation would, *in the long run*, be related to the rate of unemployment in the economy: *the long-term Phillips curve was vertical*. Expansionary monetary policy would only create higher inflation in the long term, just as seemed to have happened during the stagflation crisis of the 1970s. Only in the very short term can the central bank influence the rate of unemployment. Friedman assumed firms and their workers have *adaptive* expectations about the future inflation rate: in the long term they would expect higher inflation, leading to a wage–price spiral that would bring the unemployment level back to its 'natural' rate.

Neoclassical theories based on the assumption of *rational expectations* also criticized Keynesian belief in the effectiveness of fiscal policy to boost aggregate demand. In these theories, rational agents use the uniquely correct economic model and take into account all available information when forming expectations. A corollary of this assumption is that any discretionary increases in government spending or tax cuts would remain ineffective in bolstering private spending. The reason is that households and firms form rational expectations about the future: they are forward-looking and hence 'internalize' the budget constraint the government faces in the longer term; they assume that any increase in government debt would not boost long-term growth and would have to be followed by higher taxes in the future. When a government engages in debt-financed deficit spending, households and firms anticipate higher future taxes to repay the government debt. As a result, they will cut current consumption and investment spending in order to accumulate the savings needed to cover the increase in taxation they expect.[12]

Apart from this Ricardian equivalence hypothesis, rising interest rates in the 1980s seemed to offer empirical confirmation of the classical theory that rising government spending would crowd out private investment in the economy by raising interest rates. The 'crowding out' hypothesis follows from loanable funds theory, which states that market interest rates result from the interaction between the supply of savings (called 'loanable funds' because they can be lent out) and the demand for these savings: government borrowing increases the demand for savings that cannot be used to finance other private investments, which pushes up the equilibrium interest rate as it makes savings scarcer in the private sector. This, in turn, would harm the economy's long-term growth potential, which from a neoclassical perspective depends on private investment.

These ideas were also integrated into the New Keynesian school of macroeconomics, which embraced the rational expectations hypothesis and fully endorsed the view that macroeconomic policy cannot have any influence on the long-term economic growth and 'natural' employment level. New Keynesian economics and neoclassical economics are very similar in their framing and methodological commitment: according to New Keynesian economists, long-term growth is entirely determined by supply-side factors, politically independent central banks should be responsible for stabilizing the business cycle in the short term without endangering price stability, and governments should focus on balanced budgets and 'sound finance'.[13] A *New Consensus in Macroeconomics* was established in the 1990s within mainstream academic and policy circles and disseminated through various international policy fora.[14]

According to the neoliberal 'public choice' theory of political business cycles, governments would be inclined to instruct the central bank to pursue an expansionary monetary policy as a way to increase its chances for re-election: since the central bank can only provide a temporary boost to the economy, according to neoclassical theories, voters would be misled into believing that higher economic growth and lower unemployment are sustainable; in the longer term, after re-election, the monetary policy expansion would only have fuelled inflation. Since governments were believed to have policy preferences that were inconsistent with the needs of the economy, they could not be trusted to deliver appropriate monetary policy and had to make a pre-commitment to low inflation that is independent of political competition. Legislators did so by delegating monetary policy to a conservative central bank mandated to make the preservation of price stability its priority. But for this solution to be perceived as credible, the central bank also had to be made *politically independent* – that is, able to resist pressures from electorally motivated officials.[15] Since the 1990s, a rising number of central banks thus became politically independent from governments and were given a new mandate to maintain low inflation: price stability became the primary (or only) target of monetary policy.

Similar reasoning was applied to fiscal policy: according to one of the intellectual fathers of neoliberal public choice theory, 'the explicit Keynesian destruction of the rigid balanced budget rule produced a political bias [towards excessive public spending and debt] in the conduct of economic policy in a democratic society'.[16] So to overcome the fiscal crisis of the KWS, public finances had to be shielded from democratically generated pressure and demands by introducing rules that impose 'fiscal discipline' on democratically elected governments.[17] Keynesian fiscal dominance had to be replaced with a new regime of monetary dominance: the government's fiscal policy had to be subordinated to the price stability target of the central bank. Again, delegating monetary policy to independent central banks – combined with explicit or implicit rules that prohibited monetary financing of government deficits – was crucial for this aim, as one of the leaders of the rational expectations revolution clarifies: 'if the monetary authority could successfully stick to its guns and forever refuse to monetize any government debt, then eventually the arithmetic of the government's budget constraint would compel the fiscal authority to back down and to swing its budget into balance'.[18] Legislators in the industrialized world introduced new rules that impose 'fiscal discipline' upon democratically elected governments. In 1992 member states of the European Union signed the Stability and Growth Pact (SGP), which prohibited governments from running fiscal deficits higher than 3 per cent of GDP, and imposed a quasi-permanent austerity regime by obliging them to lower public debt levels to below 60 per cent of GDP.

These rules reflect what Marxist political economist Stephen Gill has called 'New Constitutionalism' – that is, 'the politico-legal dimension of the wider discourse of disciplinary neoliberalism', which 'seeks to separate economic policies from broad political accountability in order to make governments more responsive to the discipline of market forces and correspondingly less responsive to popular-democratic forces and processes'.[19] The key objective of these neoliberal rules was to depoliticize macroeconomic policymaking and force central banks and ministries of finance to pursue monetary and fiscal policies that are deemed 'credible' by financial market actors. As Andrew Baker rightly observes, these rules sought 'to represent and institutionalize the collective priorities of financial markets in domestic macroeconomic policy-making arrangements, while circumventing and largely ignoring the preferences of a broader range of domestic societal interests'. Policymakers set sound money targets for macroeconomic policy 'as a means of signifying their good intentions to international investors'.[20]

Financial globalization and 'market discipline'

Baker argues that 'inflation mandates for independent central banks and fiscal policy frameworks that set limits to budget deficits represent policymakers' attempts to communicate symbolically with financial markets and indicate their commitment to following finance-friendly macroeconomic policies, so as to inspire confidence and credibility in the world of finance'.[21] The concept of policy credibility played a key role in reconstructing macroeconomic policies along neoliberal lines, given that it is central, as Ilene Grabel has shown in her work, 'to the broader task of elevating the market as the principal means of directing economic affairs and the effort to place severe constraints on state manipulation of economic policy toward particularist aims'.[22] From a neoliberal perspective, governments can only ensure access to international financial markets if they adopt 'sound' macroeconomic policies that target low inflation and low fiscal deficits. The disciplinary effects of market integration were a key reason why neoliberals advocated financial liberalization, as Eric Helleiner argues: 'Neoliberals were not committed to the Keynesian welfare state but instead applauded international financial markets because they would discipline governments and prompt states to pursue more "sound" fiscal and monetary programs.'[23]

Financial globalization and open markets conferred *exit power* on private investors, who could dump sovereign bonds on secondary markets whenever they disapproved of the economic policies of the government (see box 3.4 for an explanation of a negative demand shock in a sovereign bond market). By increasing interest rates on newly issued public debt and raising borrowing costs, selling sovereign bonds could put pressure on the government to withdraw what international investors perceive as 'irresponsible' policies. The ministries of finance and central bankers of the Group of Seven (G7) leading industrial nations were fully convinced of the benefits of open markets and their disciplinary effects: 'if markets conclude that a country is pursuing poor economic policy they are likely to take their money elsewhere'.[24] In turn, 'good' policies would be rewarded by lowering the government's borrowing costs. The upshot is that in the face of cross-border capital mobility, governments were held hostage to the expectations and perceptions of domestic and foreign bond investors. Governments were only to be considered 'credible' by international financial markets if they pursued policies according to what markets believe to be sound: decisions by governments to adopt expansionary macroeconomic policies and other measures designed to respond to domestic democratic and societal demands were likely to result in the flight of domestic and foreign savings, to countries with governments providing a climate more 'hospitable' to international investors.

Box 3.4 Negative demand shock in sovereign bond markets

The internationalization of sovereign bond markets played a central role in imposing 'market discipline' on governments. As we saw in figure 3.1 above, governments have increasingly relied on foreign private banks and institutional investors to fund their fiscal deficits: on average, about 50 per cent of the public debt of OECD governments is currently owned by non-residents. Fiscal deficits are financed by issuing and selling sovereign bonds that can be traded on financial markets. These sovereign bonds are a type of loan from an investor to the government. The investor receives small cash payments at a fixed interest rate every year until the loan matures; when the loan matures the investor gets back all the money lent to the government. The owners of sovereign bonds can get their money back before the bonds mature by selling them to other investors in secondary markets. Since bonds are traded on markets, they have a price determined by the law of supply and demand (see box 1.1 in chapter 1): the lower the demand for any given supply of government bonds, the lower their price will be; in turn, the price of a bond is inversely related to the interest rate of the bond, so a lower price of bond implies that the government will need to pay higher interest rates on newly issued bonds. Figure 3.5 shows what happens when a market of sovereign bonds is affected by a negative demand shock from D_1 to D_2: the government's borrowing cost increases sharply, as the price of newly issued bonds falls and the interest rate on these bonds shoots up from R_1 to R_2.

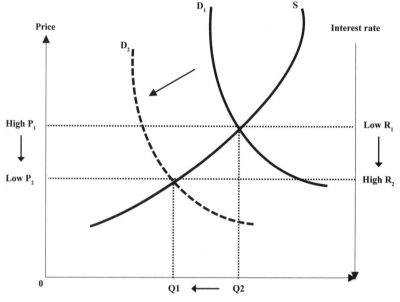

Figure 3.5 Negative demand shock in a sovereign bond market

A corollary is that leftist governments announcing supposedly 'unsound' spending programmes could face higher interest rates and be forced to withdraw these programmes. One of the best-known illustrations of the disciplinary effects of financial markets is the U-turn the French socialist François Mitterand had to make after his election as president in 1981. Confronted with rising unemployment, growing inflationary pressures and stagnant business activity, Mitterand came to power with a promise to take drastic measures to revive the French economy: he proposed a left-wing economic programme based on several nationalizations, a 10 per cent increase in the minimum wage, an increase in social benefits, a reduction in labour time and a tax on wealth. After being confronted with escalating capital flight that caused a spike in French interest rates and a collapse of the French currency, Mitterand chose the path of capitulation by pursuing austerity to restore the confidence of international investors – a move to the right that 'precipitated the long-term process of privatization and neoliberal restructuring in French capitalism'.[25] Mitterand's U-turn fed the following perception: if a government tries to pursue full employment and redistributive fiscal policies, it will be 'punished' by financial markets through capital flight with punitively high interest rates and a collapsing currency. Was France's experience unique or the initial manifestation of a more general trend?

There is a large literature in international and comparative political economy that has tried to assess the extent to which financial globalization has put new constraints on left-wing governments pursuing reflationary and redistributive macroeconomic policies. While substantial cross-national *diversity* continues to exist in social security, in organization of the labour market, in corporate governance and in the distribution of income (see chapters 4 and 5), Layna Mosley has shown that the internationalization of sovereign bond markets fostered cross-national *similarity* in terms of monetary and fiscal policies: 'Economic globalization appears related to substantial convergence on overall fiscal (the size of public deficits) and monetary policy (the inflation rate) outcomes.'[26] Based on numerous interviews she did with investors in sovereign bond markets, Mosley came to the following conclusion:

> a lack of concern for default risk implies that market participants rely on a set of macropolicy outcomes as decision-making criteria – the government deficit/GDP ratio, the rate of inflation, and (sometimes) the foreign exchange rate and the government debt/GDP ratio. Market participants have well-defined preferences regarding these indicators: they want inflation rates of less than 2 percent, and they want relatively small (that is, less than 3 percent) budget deficit/GDP ratios.[27]

In other words, there is evidence that international investors came to expect macroeconomic policies focused on public debt reduction and low inflation. On this basis, governments pursuing a left-wing reflationary programme have been more likely to be distrusted by sovereign bond investors and international financial markets more generally.[28]

The growing influence of credit rating agencies (CRAs) like Standard and Poor's (S&P), Moody's and Fitch also constrained governments from pursuing policies deviating from neoliberal 'sound money' principles. These American CRAs play a key role in international financial markets by 'rating' government bonds – ranging from AAA (prime) to C (at high risk of default) – and giving international investors information about their perception of the 'creditworthiness' of governments. Many investors rely on these ratings as they do not have adequate expertise or time to investigate the creditworthiness of governments and firms themselves. Because ratings by the CRAs are widely used by international investors to assess the creditworthiness of governments, they have a great influence over the perception of risk in international financial markets: governments with a 'good' rating will be perceived as less risky and hence be able to borrow at lower interest rates, whereas those with a 'bad' rating will be considered risky and have to pay higher interest rates on their debt.[29] These ratings do not reflect some objective truth about the alleged inappropriateness of Keynesian macroeconomic policies, and they often contain a neoliberal normative bias. Since good ratings by the two dominant US CRAs imply lower risk premiums and interest rates in sovereign bond markets, governments had a strong incentive to bring policies closer to the neoliberal norms of sound money.[30]

Low inflation and distributive conflict

Unsound macroeconomics of sound money

What are the consequences of the disciplinary effects of international financial markets? From a neoliberal perspective, imposing low inflation and austerity on policymakers will support long-term economic growth by 'crowding in' private investment. Remember that neoliberal economists argue that budget deficits lead to a higher interest rate and lower private investment. Budget surpluses work just the opposite of budget deficits, from their point of view:

> When government collects more in tax revenue than it spends, its saves the difference by retiring some of the outstanding government debt. This budget surplus, or public saving, contributes to national saving. Thus, a budget surplus increases the supply of loanable funds, reduces the interest rate and stimulates investment. Higher investment, in turn, means greater capital accumulation and more rapid economic growth.[31]

Hence, neoliberals endorse the idea of expansionary fiscal consolidation– that is, the idea that reductions in public debt levels would support rather than hinder growth. As public debt can be reduced by either raising taxes or cutting spending, it should be no surprise that neoliberal economists believe that only spending cuts, 'concentrated on government wages and transfers', can deliver the expansionary effects of fiscal consolidation.[32]

Keynesian-oriented political economists denounce these neoliberal views for their failure to correctly predict the depressing effects of austerity on industrialized economies.[33] Disinflationary macroeconomic policies did not

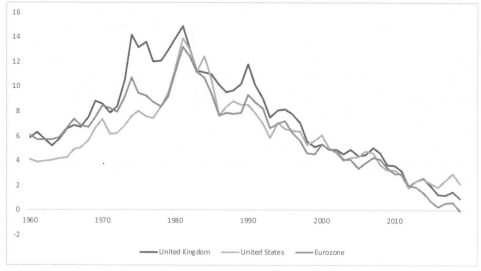

Figure 3.6 Long-term nominal interest rates, 1960–2019

Source: OECD

'Eurozone' refers to the unweighted average of France and Germany.

bring increased private investment and stronger economic growth, despite the decline in long-term nominal interest rates since the 1990s (depicted in figure 3.6): productivity growth was significantly higher and unemployment much lower during the Keynesian era than during the post-1980s neoliberal era, as shown earlier by figure 3.2 in this chapter and figure 2.3 in chapter 2. Empirical studies similarly failed to provide evidence for neoliberal economic theory's predictions about the negative long-term consequences of moderate inflation (less than 10 per cent) on economic growth and employment.[34] As Jonathan Kirshner concludes from a review of these studies: 'The evidence overwhelmingly supports the view that inflation rates at low or moderate levels have very little effect on the performance of the aggregate economy', casting 'new light on the long-held understanding that … low inflation and perhaps more importantly the macroeconomic policies designed to assure that it remains very low benefit some groups in society at the expense of others'.[35]

In short, it is much easier to identify the distributional effects of neoliberal macroeconomic policy than it is to empirically detect its positive effects on long-term economic growth and employment. Central bank independence and restrictive fiscal rules created a depoliticized context for macroeconomic policymakers, yet simultaneously have 'identifiable distributional effects and thus remain resolutely political and therefore partisanal institutions'.[36] The costs of austerity are usually distributed asymmetrically across different income groups: those at the bottom of the income distribution lose more than those at the top, for the simple reason that citizens in the middle or bottom half of the income distribution rely more on government services, both indirectly (tax breaks and subsidies) and directly (transfers, public transport, public education, health care).[37] It can be argued that advanced capitalist states actively tried to achieve such distributional objectives by internationalizing their sovereign bond markets. Sahil Dutta rightly cautions against 'casting the state as a passive recipient of creditor agendas when it raises public finance', as 'global financial markets also present opportunities for states to shape and improve the terms by which they obtain finance.'[38] The adoption of anti-inflationary monetary and fiscal policies was pivotal in this regard but had important regressive effects on the distribution of national income and wealth.

There is a broad consensus in the political economy literature that the holders of capital have been the key beneficiaries of the transition towards neoliberal macroeconomic policy. First, anti-inflationary macroeconomic policy weakened the bargaining power of workers and labour unions by creating higher levels of unemployment; the resulting repression of real wage growth allowed firms (and their capitalist owners) to restore their profitability. Second, the lowering of inflation benefited 'rentier interests' by redistributing income and wealth from debtors to creditors.

Rising unemployment and the weakening of labour power

The fight against inflation occurred primarily by allowing unemployment to rise to levels that were previously seen as unacceptable during the Keynesian period. Rising inflation made it more difficult for workers and unions to demand higher wages, which mitigates rising inflation by allowing firms to restore their profitability without resorting to price hikes. As Walter Korpi explains from a power resources perspective (see also chapters 2 and 4),

> the inverse statistical association found between unemployment and wages clearly indicates that an increase of unemployment is likely to affect the bargaining positions of employees and employers in opposite directions, reducing the bargaining power and aspirations of employees while increasing those of employers. Ceteris paribus, economic policies that work via variations in levels of unemployment to ensure that inflation remains stable are thus likely to have distributive consequences.[39]

While both employers and employees can improve their outcomes by co-operating in the production processes, the distribution of the revenues of production between profits and wages generates an inherent conflict of interest between capital and labour:

> The distributive process is … characterized by bargaining and manifest conflicts, the outcomes of which are affected by the resources that employers and employees have at their disposal for safeguarding their interests. Since variations in unemployment affect relations of power between employers and employees, these variations are likely to be reflected in distributive outcomes.[40]

Michal Kalecki, a Polish heterodox economist, had argued something similar back in 1943 in a famous paper called 'Political Aspects of Full Employment'.[41] While he was a strong advocate of the Keynesian macroeconomic policy regime, Kalecki doubted whether a situation of full employment could be politically sustainable. More specifically, he believed that the reduction in unemployment and the resulting scarcity of labour would ultimately strengthen the position of workers and labour unions to such an extent that they would become increasingly assertive in their wage demands. As a result, wage growth would exceed productivity growth and start eating into the profits of firms and their capitalist owners. In this vein, Kalecki argued that 'the assumption that a government will maintain full employment in a capitalist economy if it only knows how to do it is fallacious':

> Under a regime of permanent full employment, the 'sack' would cease to play its role as a disciplinary device. The social position of the boss would be undermined, and the self-assurance and class consciousness of the working class would grow. Strikes for wage increases and improvements in conditions of work create political tensions.[42]

Growing tensions between capital and labour regarding the distribution of profits since the end of the 1960s seemed to confirm Kalecki's predictions. In a historical perspective, the post-war Bretton Woods years stand out as a period during which the position of workers in distributive conflicts was stronger than ever before in the industrialized world, due to their increased organizational capacity via political parties and unions, as well as to the generally high demand for labour.[43] Accordingly, industrial disputes escalated in the late 1960s and the 1970s. These industrial conflicts greatly intensified after the first oil shock, when workers sought to secure their living standards by pushing through higher wages:

> The high unemployment rates after 1973 partly reflect attempts by business and conservative interests to reshape relations of power and patterns of redistribution prevailing during the full employment era into more favourable ones from their point of view. Instead of being the major problem, unemployment came to be seen as a solution to other problems now considered more serious.

– that is, preventing excessive wage inflation from eroding away capitalists' profits.[44]

The explanation that links the establishment of the neoliberal macroeconomic policy regime to an explicit desire in the capitalist class to break the power of labour unions has an obvious Marxist flavour to it. Indeed, Marx had argued long before that the unemployed 'reserve army of labour' plays a key function in the capitalist system by disciplining workers' wage demands and allowing capitalists to sustain their profits and extract surplus value from their workers. That is why Nicholas Kaldor (a famous post-Keynesian economist)

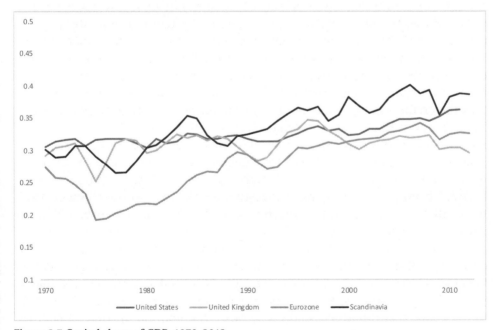

Figure 3.7 Capital share of GDP, 1970–2012
Source: OECD

called Margaret Thatcher, after her election as British prime minister in 1979, 'our first Marxist Prime Minister': 'They have managed to create a pool – or a "reserve army" as Marx would have called it – of 3 million unemployed ... the British working classes have been thoroughly cowed and frightened.'[45] The disinflation policies of the Thatcher government allowed British firms to restructure and restore their profitability.

This was a universal trend in the industrialized world: the labour income share has fallen in all of the advanced economies since the end of the 1970s and the capital income share has increased accordingly, reflecting a decline in the bargaining power of labour vis-à-vis the owners of capital (figure 3.7). Nevertheless, not all fractions of capital and economic sectors have benefited equally from the rise in the capital income share since the 1980s. Disinflation furthered the interests of firms in the manufacturing sectors by helping them to contain labour costs and strengthen their competitiveness, which clarifies why restrictive macroeconomic policies were most eagerly embraced by the export-led CMEs, as we will see below. Disinflation also greatly benefited financial capital and the financial sector by privileging the interests of creditors over those of debtors, as we will see in the next subsection.

Anti-inflation and rentier interests

The lowering of inflation benefited the holders of capital by redistributing income from debtors to creditors. To understand why this is the case, a clarification of the difference between *nominal* and *real* income or value is needed. For creditors, the only variable that counts is the real interest rate they can earn on their loans and investments and the real value of these investments. The nominal interest rate is the money a creditor receives from his or her debtors or the money an investor earns on his or her financial assets. The real interest rate corrects the nominal interest rate for the effect of inflation and tells the creditor or investor the true *purchasing power* of that money. The real interest rate (value) is the nominal interest rate (value) minus the inflation rate: *Real* interest rate (value) = *Nominal* interest rate (value) – Inflation rate.

Keeping inflation low therefore benefits the creditor and investor by maintaining the real value and purchasing power of the nominal income received from his or her loans or investments. Debtors, in turn, benefit from high inflation, which reduces the real value of the nominal payments they need to make to their creditor(s) every year: because the real payments of debtors are equal to the real revenues of creditors, they have opposite preferences regarding the optimal level of inflation. The reason why high inflation benefits debtors is maybe a little more difficult to understand than the reason why it harms creditors, but can be made more comprehensible if we take into account that inflation usually also raises the nominal income of debtors. In normal macroeconomic conditions, workers typically demand and receive higher (nominal) wages to protect their real purchasing power; in some countries, such as Belgium, workers' wages are even legally protected by an automatic wage indexation system that links wage increases to the consumer price index (CPI) inflation rate. So while inflation increases the nominal income of debtors, the real value of their liabilities (and in many cases their monthly down payment) remains the same – which is why we say inflation reduces the real debt burden of debtors.

Inflation is also especially harmful for investors in that it increases the tax burden. One example is the tax treatment of capital gains – that is, the profits made by selling an asset for more than its purchase price. Suppose that in 1980 an investor bought a stock from Apple for US$10 and that in 2010 she sold the stock for US$100. According to the tax law in the United States, the investors earned a capital gain of US$90. But suppose the overall price level quadrupled from 1980 to 2010. In this case, the US$10 invested in 1980 is equivalent (in terms of purchasing power) to US$40 in 2010. When the investor sells the stock for US$100, she has a real gain of only US$50. As the US tax code imposes a tax on a gain of US$90, inflation exaggerates the size of capital gains and raises the tax burden on this type of income.

Another example is the tax treatment of interest income. Income tax treats the nominal interest earned on savings as income, even though part of the nominal interest rate merely compensates for inflation. To see the effects of this policy, consider the numerical example in table 3.1. The table compares two economies, both of which tax interest income at a rate of 25 per cent. In Economy 1, inflation is zero and the nominal and real interest rates are both 4 per cent. In this case, the 25 per cent tax on interest income reduces the real interest rate from 4 per cent to 3 per cent. In Economy 2, the real interest rate is again 4 per cent, but the inflation rate is 8 per cent and the nominal interest rate is 12 per cent. Because the income tax treats this entire 12 per cent interest as income, the government takes 25 per cent of it (i.e. 3 per cent). So compared to the economy with zero inflation, the 25 per cent tax on interest income reduces the real interest rate from 4 per cent to 1 per cent for any saver and investor in the economy with an inflation rate of 8 per cent.[46]

Since only the richest households are creditors with a significant amount of *net* financial wealth – that is, with financial assets (e.g. savings deposits and stock market investments) that are worth substantially more than their liabilities (e.g. mortgage debt) – the lowering of inflation primarily benefited the most affluent classes; lower-income households, on the other hand, own no significant net wealth and in many cases they are net debtors – that is, they have more liabilities than assets – so they are either indifferent to or in favour of high inflation. There is also a generational component to this distributional effect, as 'the elderly are more inflation averse because they are more indifferent to unemployment than the rest of the population, being outside of the labour market, but are concerned about the real value of their savings and pensions'.[47] However, one should not overstate the importance of this generational dimension in the distribution of net financial wealth: 'intergenerational

Table 3.1 How inflation influences the tax treatment of interest income

	Economy 1 (price stability)	Economy 2 (inflation)
Real interest rate	4 per cent	4 per cent
Inflation	0 per cent	8 per cent
Nominal interest rate	4 per cent	12 per cent
Reduced interest rate due to tax rate of 25 per cent	1 per cent	3 per cent
After-tax nominal interest rate	3 per cent	9 per cent
After-tax real interest rate	3 per cent	1 per cent

inequalities emerge largely *through* structural, and especially class-based, inequalities, and are therefore best understood as a kind of epiphenomenal manifestation thereof'.[48] But is certainly the case that a growing number of middle-class people – especially from the older generations – self-identify as members of the asset-owning class, either through direct holdings of securities or through indirect investment in the form of mutual funds and private pension plans (see also chapter 4).

These observations have led political economists from the post-Keynesian tradition to conclude that the shift towards inflation-fighting independent central banks predominantly reflected the interests of the rentier class – that is, wealthy people who get most of their incomes from owning financial assets (savings accounts, stocks, bonds, etc.) rather than from selling labour (and earning wage income) or from owning productive assets (factories, natural resources, etc.) in the real economy.[49] For this reason, the transition also advanced the interests of the key sector that serves the rentier class by managing its assets: the financial sector. As Wynne Godley notes with respect to the ECB, 'it took a group largely composed of bankers (the Delors Committee) to reach the conclusion that an independent central bank was the only supra-national institution necessary to run an integrated, supra-national Europe'.[50] In a widely cited empirical analysis, Adam Posen has shown that there is a positive correlation between the strength of the financial sector and the degree of central bank independence in a country: central bank independence was promoted by the financial sector 'as a long-run means to price stability' and cannot be sustained 'without that group's ongoing protection of its counter-inflationary activities'.[51]

Neoliberal macroeconomic policy increased the share of national income going to the rentier class. 'Rentier income' typically denotes income that accrues from activity in the financial sector and the ownership of financial assets rather than activity in the 'real' sector or the holding of 'real' assets such as real estate or capital equipment used in the non-financial sector. As table

Table 3.2 Real rentier fraction of national income, selected countries, 1970s–1990s

	1970s	1980s	1990s	Difference 1990s – 1970s	Difference 1990s – 1980s
Australia	0.1	5.6	10.2	10.1	4.6
Belgium		7.8	9.0		1.2
Finland	-0.2	1.4	6.2	6.4	4.8
France	-0.4	5.6	14.3	14.7	8.7
Germany	3.1	6.6	6.9	3.8	0.3
United Kingdom	-4.2	4.9	8.6	12.8	3.7
Italy	0.4	4.2	9.6	9.2	5.4
Japan	-0.6	8.1	8.7	9.3	0.6
Netherlands	7.5	11.9	13.8	6.3	1.9
Norway	5.4	6.3	8.1	2.7	1.8
Portugal	-11.4	3.5	10.6	22.0	7.1
Spain		3.3	9.3		6.0
United States	1.8	9.7	10.2	8.4	0.5

Source: Epstein and Jayadev 2005

3.2 reveals, rentier returns – calculated as the profits earned by the financial sector plus interest income realized by the rest of the private economy (but excluding capital gains) – increased significantly as a share of national income in most advanced economies from the 1970s and 1980s. From a post-Keynesian perspective, this seems to suggest that central banks 'internalised the financial motives of private investors and creditors through inflation targeting, aimed at preserving the value of financial investments, which would be eroded with

Table 3.3 Keynesian and neoliberal macroeconomic regimes compared

Keynesian macroeconomic regime (1944–73)	Neoliberal macroeconomic regime (1974–2007)
Policy target	*Policy target*
Full employment	Price stability
Policy outcomes	*Policy outcomes*
Positive inflation	Secular disinflation
Strong labour unions	Weak labour unions
Finance weak and immobile	Finance strong and mobile
Markets mostly national	Markets globalized
Central banks weak and politicized	Central banks strong and independent
Labour share of GDP at historic high	Capital share of GDP at historic high
Inequality low	Inequality high

Source: Blyth and Matthijs 2017

stronger increases in the price level'.[52] For this reason, Mark Blyth and Matthias Matthijs have recently called the neoliberal macroeconomic regime a *creditor's paradise*. Its principal features are summed up in table 3.3 and contrasted with the Keynesian macroeconomic regime in which the interests of the rentier class and financial sector were subordinated. However, the common neoliberal macroeconomic regime took a distinctive shape in different models of capitalism and resulted in different growth models, as we will see in the next and final section of this chapter.

Macroeconomic policy and growth models

While all the advanced economies have prioritized the pursuit of price stability over the pursuit of full employment, there has never been a complete convergence in macroeconomic policy institutions. Member states of the Economic and Monetary Union (EMU) in Europe went furthest in drawing up highly restrictive monetary and fiscal policy institutions that almost completely eliminated their macroeconomic policy autonomy. When European nations agreed to establish the EMU in the Maastricht Treaty of 1992, it was decided that the new European currency would be governed by a highly restrictive macroeconomic policy regime with a one-dimensional focus on maintaining price stability in the region. Monetary policy was delegated to the ECB, which became the most independent central bank in the world due to a number of restrictive stipulations embodied in the Maastricht Treaty: the ECB would be prohibited from bailing out insolvent member states ('no-bail-out-clause', Article 125 of the Maastricht Treaty) or from monetary financing of their fiscal deficits (Article 123). In addition, the SGP had to contain inflationary fiscal profligacy of EMU member states by giving them the legal obligation to uphold conservative budgetary targets. Advanced economies outside the EMU and the European Union never adopted a similar set of self-constraining macroeconomic policy rules and institutions. Most illustrative is the United States, where the Federal Reserve has a 'dual mandate' to pursue both long-term price stability and 'maximum employment'. More generally, advanced economies outside the EMU have adopted more countercyclical fiscal policies: 'European countries, whose monetary policies are governed by the strongly independent European Central Bank, practice much more conservative fiscal policy than the United States, where the Fed has much more leeway.'[53]

While the rise of neoliberalism certainly played a role, it is important not to exaggerate the extent to which France and the Mediterranean countries fully endorsed these neoliberal macroeconomic policy views: low inflation particularly was a preference of Germany and the other CMEs, which insisted on establishing a highly restrictive macroeconomic policy regime as a precondition for joining the EMU. From a VoC perspective, there are several reasons why CMEs tend to pursue more restrictive macroeconomic policies than the

MMEs and LMEs. CMEs have larger welfare states and stronger automatic stabilizers, which increase government spending on unemployment benefits during economic recessions and make discretionary stimulus measures less expedient. Unemployed workers can also rely upon more generous unemployment benefits and for a more extended – in some countries like Belgium even unlimited – period of time than in the LMEs (and than Southern MMEs), so governments are typically under less political pressure to boost economic growth and fight unemployment. But the most important reason why CMEs have more restrictive macroeconomic policies is that these policies privilege the interests of employers in the manufacturing sectors by sharpening trade unions' incentives for wage restraint: unions are sufficiently coordinated in the CMEs to internalize the effects of macroeconomic policy, which enables a conservative central bank to deter 'excessive' wage hikes with threats to tighten monetary policy; to avoid neutralizing these threats, fiscal policy also 'must eschew an aggregate demand role' and be restrictive.[54]

The establishment of a restrictive macroeconomic policy regime was more pivotal in suppressing wage growth for workers in the domestically oriented service sectors than it was indispensable in encouraging wage restraint among unions in the export-oriented manufacturing sectors, given that '[i]nternational exposure provides incentives for mercantilism, irrespective of the growth context'.[55] Because these service sectors are 'sheltered' from international competition and mostly depend on *domestic* aggregate demand, they tend to have distinctive macroeconomic requirements and preferences regarding the appropriate *level* and *growth* of wages, as Baccaro and Pontusson have pointed out: 'each company individually would like to reduce costs by paying lower wages than their competitors, but the aggregation of individual choices would reduce demand for all companies, since wages are the most important component of household income.' The same logic does not apply to the export-oriented manufacturing sectors, where 'individual and collective rationality are better aligned in that, all else being equal, a reduction of wages relative to international competitors leads to greater demand for the industry as a whole as well as for individual firms'.[56] These distinctive sectoral requirements and preferences clarify why governments in the domestic demand-led MMEs traditionally tend to be more in favour of relatively more expansionary macroeconomic policies, which advance the interests of their dominant domestically oriented services sectors.[57]

All this suggests that a less functionalist interpretation of the role of restrictive macroeconomic policy in the formation of the export-led growth model of the CMEs is needed. CMEs had adopted a more balanced growth model during the Fordist era, when all private sources of aggregate demand – household consumption, corporate investment and exports – played a role in bolstering growth. Only after the stagflation crisis, which was itself the outcome of intensifying class conflict associated with the Keynesian full employment macroeconomic policy regime, did the CMEs become decidedly more export-oriented in their quest to find alternative sources of aggregate demand. The adoption of anti-inflationary monetary and fiscal policies served not merely to weaken the power of labour vis-à-vis capital, but especially to privilege the interests of the export-oriented manufacturing sectors over those of the domestically oriented sheltered sectors. Relatively high taxes on consumption and low taxes on savings also inhibited wage inflation in the sheltered sectors by actively depressing domestic demand. Especially in Germany, the interests of the manufacturing sectors prevailed as the transition towards a neoliberal macroeconomic policy regime coincided with an increasingly dualized labour market, as we will see in the next chapter. These developments depressed wage growth and prices in service sectors, which provided necessary inputs for firms in the export-oriented sectors and allowed these firms to reinforce their international competitiveness by reducing their production costs.[58] To some extent, this also furthered the interest of core workers in the manufacturing sectors by securing relatively well-protected jobs in these sectors.

LMEs have a stronger incentive to pursue macroeconomic policies that stabilize domestic demand if these policies do not undermine price stability.[59] Governments in LMEs are under more political pressure to pursue countercyclical policies during recessions in order to boost employment, as unemployed workers cannot rely on generous unemployment benefits and other kinds of income support. Furthermore, their growth model became increasingly dependent on the expansion of domestic demand. The structurally weak bargaining power of workers following far-reaching labour market flexibilization and low union density rates – to be discussed in the following chapter – have also tempered the 'risk' that expansionary monetary and fiscal monetary policies would result in excessive wage inflation and undermine price stability. Nevertheless, central banks in the LMEs continued to prioritize low inflation by withdrawing stimulus measures as soon as possible, to prevent labour markets from 'overheating' and keep a close lid on any 'excessive' wage inflation. Even the Federal Reserve's dual mandate only every so often produced inflation rates higher than 2 per cent to compensate for below-target periods. Based on an analysis of Federal Open Market Committee (FOMC) transcripts from 1960 to 2010, one study found that FOMC discussions increasingly emphasized inflation relative to unemployment from the 1980s, even as inflation itself fell eventually below 2 per cent.[60]

Inflation-targeting central banks provided institutional support for debt-led growth in Anglo-Saxon LMEs by enabling a fall in long-term nominal interest rates and indirectly fuelling asset price inflation. The lowering of inflation (figure 3.6) 'created an environment in which a sustained drop in interest rates could take place, reducing the cost of borrowing for consumers and creating a powerful incentive to accumulate assets in the housing market through mortgage credit'.[61] In the United States, the Federal Reserve under the chairmanship of Alan Greenspan (1987–2006) came to be seen as an institutional guarantor of asset price inflation by financial market participants due to its asymmetric approach to asset price movements, whereby the US central bank refrains from raising interest rates to prevent asset price bubbles but cuts interest rates swiftly and sharply to contain asset price busts. This policy stance, which came to be known as the 'Greenspan put', became a key ingredient of financialized growth from the 1990s. The principal motivation for the Federal Reserve's asymmetric policy stance was its recognition of the growing importance of asset prices in supporting household consumption via wealth effects and collateralized borrowing, which in the context of rising housing prices became an increasingly significant source of debt-led growth (see chapters 6 and 7). As Greenspan observed after the collapse of the 1990s stock market bubble and the concurrent boom of the housing market, '[n] o matter how one differentiates the effects on consumer spending of capital gains on stock market and housing wealth, it is clear that the massive increase in capital values over the past five years had a profound impact on output and income'.[62] Governments and central banks in the other LMEs have increasingly acted upon a new premise of 'sectorally differentiated' inflationary prefer- ences – that is, the idea that asset price inflation is good while consumer price inflation is bad.[63]

In sum, the shift to neoliberal macroeconomic policy resulted in divergent growth models that have been undergirded by distinctive cross-class and sectoral coalitions. In the following three chapters we will further dissect these coalitions by examining key institutional transformations in social policy, corporate governance and financial policy.

4

Social Policy: Globalization, Deindustrialization and Liberalization

By the standards of the golden post-war era, economic growth in the advanced capitalist world has been quite sluggish since the 1980s. At the same time, unemployment levels have increased. The stagflation crisis of the 1970s also heralded the crisis of the Fordist wage-led growth model that characterized the Keynesian period. During that period, a variety of institutional mechanisms ensured that average wage growth tracked productivity growth in the economy and aggregate demand grew in tandem with aggregate supply. This regime unravelled when the 1970s crisis induced governments and central banks to open up their markets and adopt anti-inflationary fiscal and monetary policies. By abandoning their responsibility for the active management and support of aggregate demand, governments increasingly attempted to boost long-term economic growth and employment by resorting to supply-side 'structural reforms' like the decentralization of collective bargaining institutions, the flexibilization of labour markets and the downsizing of state-funded social security. Faced with persistently high levels of unemployment and sluggish economic growth, even social-democratic parties of the more egalitarian CMEs discarded their faith in the effectiveness of Keynesian macroeconomic management in the context of financial globalization, and accepted the desirability of these structural reforms. As one social-democratic minister observed at the end of the 1990s:

> Due to the deregulation and explosion of the financial markets, nation states' macroeconomic policies have become increasingly dependent on approval or disapproval from international financial markets they do not control. National governments have accepted this new situation and they now have pinned their faith on boosting the microeconomic competitiveness of their firms rather than on the traditional [Keynesian] macroeconomic management of the economy.[1]

The abandonment of Keynesian macroeconomic management and the shift towards restrictive monetary and fiscal policies led to a sharp increase in unemployment during the 1980s, putting pressure on the advanced capitalist countries to deregulate labour markets and engage in welfare state retrenchment. These supply-side reforms were legitimized by neoliberal beliefs about the existence of a trade-off between equality and efficiency: neoliberal economists and policymakers argued that centralized bargaining and generous welfare states fostered a more equal income distribution only at the expense of raising labour costs for firms and reducing their ability to create jobs. From a neoliberal perspective, governments had to prioritize raising employment over egalitarian goals by decentralizing wage-setting, flexibilizing labour markets and reducing the generosity and eligibility of social security benefits – which are all measures to reduce labour costs and support firms' demand for labour. These views gained growing currency in the context of economic globalization, which intensified international competition and urged manufacturing firms to cut labour costs. In this chapter we will see how this neoliberal interpretation can be challenged on both conceptual and empirical grounds: equality-promoting institutions like centralized wage-setting can be 'beneficial constraints' pushing firms to invest in more efficient technologies and raise labour productivity, as more productive and capital-intensive firms can more easily bear the burden of high labour costs. It is, therefore, no coincidence that firms in the CMEs are, on average, more productive and more export-oriented than firms in the less egalitarian LMEs.

If equality-promoting institutions do not necessarily undermine the efficiency of manufacturing firms most open to international trade and investment, then why do we notice a universal trend towards liberalization? Scholars of the VoC school have argued that this trend has been caused not by economic globalization but by deindustrialization – that is, the declining share of the manufacturing sectors in aggregate employment and the rising share of private and public services sectors. According to VoC scholars, employers in the manufacturing sectors of CMEs have traditionally been ardent supporters of relatively strong welfare states and collective bargaining institutions, which support their international competitiveness by offering incentives for skills investments. The VoC analysis delivers a strong critique of the neoliberal claim that labour market flexibilization and welfare state retrenchment of CMEs strengthen the competitiveness of firms most open to international trade and investment. Deindustrialization rather than globalization is the central reason why CMEs are under pressure to liberalize their social model. Because services are typically much less prone to productivity-enhancing technologies, employers in the services sectors face comparatively high labour costs in the context of centralized wage-setting systems and generous welfare regimes. LMEs have thus been less constrained in expanding jobs in the services sectors of the economy than more egalitarian CMEs, which have responded to the employment challenge associated with deindustrialization through a variety of liberalization measures supported by various cross-class coalitions.

VoC approaches point to sectoral conflict instead of class conflict as the ultimate source of liberalization. 'Power resources' approaches have criticized the VoC interpretation for overstating the support of manufacturing employers in the formation of centralized bargaining structures and welfare regimes in CMEs, as well as for exaggerating the extent to which they have striven to defend these institutions. From a power resources perspective, the faith of equality-promoting institutions in social policy depends on the presence of a strong labour movement consisting of powerful trade unions and left-wing, working-class-oriented political parties. Globalization, deindustrialization and the transition towards anti-inflationary macroeconomic policies have fundamentally weakened the power resources of low-skilled and medium-skilled workers, not only in the domestically oriented services sectors of the economy but also in the more productive manufacturing sectors. Power resources approaches have pointed to the fact that even manufacturing employers have actively pushed for more liberalization, which was also supported by social-democratic parties that moved towards the political centre and increasingly endorsed supply-side reform programmes to deal with problems of persistent unemployment. The inability of (particularly low- and medium-skilled) workers in the manufacturing sectors to reap the benefits of productivity growth reveals the persistent relevance of class conflict as a driver of liberalization.

There is a clear link between, on the one hand, how advanced market economies reformed their labour markets and welfare regimes, and, on the other hand, the formation of distinctive debt-led growth models of the LMEs and export-led growth models of the CMEs, discussed in previous chapters. Labour market flexibilization and welfare state retrenchment definitely went furthest in the LMEs, moving these economies towards credit-based forms of social policy. While different trajectories of liberalization made all the CMEs more export-oriented by depressing wage-led growth, particularly countries like Germany privileged the interests of the manufacturing sectors by opting for an increasingly dualized labour market. The Nordic CMEs adopted a more balanced version of the export-led growth model in which the interests of workers in the services sectors have been better represented.

Industrial relations and social policy during the Keynesian era

As we saw in chapter 2, different varieties of the Keynesian welfare state emerged after World War II: countries diverged in terms of how they organized both their industrial relations and their social security systems. In terms of industrial relations, a key dimension of differentiation was the degree and level of collective bargaining. In all the advanced economies, the unionization level was higher than it is today: the share of workers represented by labour unions during the Keynesian period ranged from about 30 per cent of non-agricultural workers in the United States to more than 70 per cent in Nordic countries like Sweden. Unions bargained with employers to reach a collective agreement over diverse issues such as the setting of wages, working hours and conditions, vocational training, etc. What distinguished – and continues to distinguish – CMEs from the other models is that these agreements were reached at a centralized level – either national or sectoral (see box 4.1). Other models, which would later be identified as LMEs and MMEs by the comparative capitalism literature, lacked similar national-level or cross-sectoral bargaining structures.

Box 4.1 Centralized wage-setting: principles

In cases of a *national-level* agreement, all firms had to abide by the settlements of the agreement; in cases of a *sectoral-level* agreement, only firms belonging to that particular sector had to implement the deal. Nordic countries with peak-level union confederations – representing blue- and white-collar workers employed in different sectors of the economy – negotiated national-level wage agreements with national employer organizations, sometimes entering into additional agreements in which the government set wage guidelines. Sweden's Rehn–Meidner bargaining model in particular reflected this national-level macro-corporatism. In other CMEs like Germany, sectoral-level bargaining prevailed, but with collective agreements reached by the manufacturing sectors of the economy subsequently extended to the other sectors.

Centralized wage-setting fulfilled two central functions. First, unions agreed to 'restrain' their wage demands to make sure that average wage growth in the economy did not exceed average labour productivity growth. This would allow firms to contain their unit labour costs (see below), which was especially important for maintaining the competitiveness of firms in the export-oriented manufacturing sectors of the economy. In peak-level bargaining systems, unions look at average labour productivity in the economy. But even in sector-level systems of bargaining like Germany, unions in the manufacturing sectors (either the metal-working sectors or the chemical sectors) focused upon average labour productivity growth in the aggregate economy rather than the typically higher productivity growth in their manufacturing sector.

Second, centralization facilitated wage compression between high-skilled workers and low-skilled workers as well as between workers employed in high-productivity sectors or firms and those employed in low-productivity sectors or firms.[2] Centralized wage-setting strengthened the bargaining power particularly of low-wage/low-skilled workers: '[C]entralised bargaining – in the extreme, a single settlement for all wage earners – renders wage differentials more transparent and thus politicizes wage-distributive outcomes. By this logic, centralization not only empowers low-wage [and low-skilled] earners but also makes them more likely to demand redistributive measures.'[3] National-level wage agreements also compressed *inter-firm* and *inter-sectoral* wage differentials, as more firms and sectors were included in a single wage settlement: workers doing similar jobs earned similar-level wages or enjoyed similar annual wage increases across different firms and sectors (the 'equal pay for equal work' principle).

Apart from compressing wage differentials, centralized wage-setting had beneficial effects on overall macroeconomic performance by bolstering productivity growth. It is well established in the neocorporatist literature that centralized wage-setting fostered innovation at the company level, because 'it prevents enterprises from trying to obtain competitive advantages primarily by way of reducing their labour costs'.[4] Conversely, low-productivity firms could only survive in centralized wage-setting systems if they improved their productivity and profitability. As such, centralized wage and solidaristic wage-setting functioned as a 'productivity whip': 'Equal remuneration for identical jobs establishes cost pressure on low-productivity firms, requiring them to increase productive efficiency or die. The closure of inefficient firms enhances average productivity, both directly and indirectly, by freeing resources for the expansion of more dynamic firms.'[5] The realization of these benefits hinged on the existence of influential unions with high mobilization capacity at different bargaining levels of the economy. At the company level, unions were represented in work councils that encouraged the direct participation of workers in strategic managerial decision-making and established local productivity coalitions. However, these productivity gains could only be achieved if collective agreements put sufficient pressure on local firms, implying that these agreements had to be either reached at the national level or coordinated across sectors.

In countries that lacked these institutions for national or cross-sectoral collective bargaining, wages were set either at the industry level or at the company level. Although the United Kingdom's industrial relations system during the 1950s rested upon industry-level bargaining with limited formal regulatory institutions at the company level, it was decentralized to the level of the firm and the workplace over subsequent decades. Nevertheless, its industrial relations featured a powerful labour movement. Labour unions were less powerful in the United States, where collective bargaining predominantly occurred at the company level. In MMEs like France and Italy, the fragmentation and organizational weakness of labour unions inhibited the effectiveness and attractiveness of collective bargaining and gave the government a key mediating role in wage-setting and the organization of the labour market.[6] Industrial relations were more antagonistic in countries that lacked the more consensus-oriented corporatist structures of the CMEs, but firms were similarly forced to distribute productivity gains to their workers in the form of higher real wages. Indeed, by the 1970s, virtually all the advanced capitalist countries had adopted some version of a Fordist wage-led growth model.[7]

The organization of industrial relations did not take place in an institutional vacuum. For one thing, CMEs and MMEs both had stringent employment protection regulations, making it hard and costly for firms to dismiss their workers. Moreover, unions agreed to pursue wage restraint – that is, they agreed to avoid wage growth exceeding average productivity growth – in exchange for expanding social security programmes. These kind of political exchanges were especially prevalent in the Scandinavian CMEs with a strong tradition of macro-corporatist coordination, which is a key reason why these

Table 4.1 Three worlds of welfare capitalism

	Liberal	**Conservative**	**Social-democratic**
Organizational principle	Residual: means-tested assistance	Insurance: contribution-based assistance	Universal: social rights
De-commodification	Low	Medium	High
Social stratification	High	Medium	Low

Source: Esping-Andersen 1990

countries also developed the most generous social security systems. So just as national wage-setting systems had already diverged during the Keynesian era, organizational principles of national social security systems differed as well. Since the publication of his book *The Three Worlds of Welfare Capitalism* in 1990, Gosta Esping-Andersen's analysis of diversity in social security systems has become a standard reference in the literature. In his book, Esping-Andersen identified three types of welfare regimes, which he differentiated in terms of 'de-commodification' – that is, the degree to which a citizen is able to maintain his or her livelihood without relying on the market – and 'social stratification' – that is, the degree to which the welfare state differentiates between different social groups. See table 4.1.

The Anglo-Saxon liberal welfare regime had – and continues to have – the lowest degree of de-commodification and social stratification. This regime features 'means-tested assistance, modest universal transfers, or modest social-insurance plans'. Within these regimes, 'the progress of social reforms has been severely circumscribed by traditional, liberal work-ethic norms'.[8] Mostly excluded from state-funded social security programmes in the LMEs, middle- and upper-income classes have/had to seek compensation for health risks and pensions in the form of *private* insurance programmes. The conservative-corporatist welfare regime occupied the medium position in terms of de-commodification and social stratification. This regime was shaped by the historical legacy of Christian-Democratic social policy and a neocorporatist tradition of industry-level collective bargaining. Furthermore, labour market participation by married women was strongly discouraged at least until the 1980s, as the corporatist regime was committed to the preservation of traditional family structures (the classic male-breadwinner model). As a result, 'social insurance typically excludes non-working wives; day care, and similar family services, are conspicuously underdeveloped'.[9] In the 'social-democratic' welfare regime the level of de-commodification is the highest and the degree of social stratification the lowest. State-provided social insurance is directed towards achieving a system of generous, universal and highly distributive benefits that are independent of individual contributions. Social policy in the social-democratic regimes aimed at maximizing the capabilities of individual independence through labour market participation. Women were encouraged to participate in the labour market, especially in the public sector. This welfare regime was most dedicated to full employment in order to support the welfare state, for instance by offering state-provided child care in order to allow women to choose work rather than the household:

> On the one side, the right to work has equal status to the right of income. On the other side, the enormous costs of maintaining a solidaristic, universalistic, and de-commodifying welfare system means [sic] that it must minimize social problems and maximize revenue income. This is obviously done best with most people working, and the fewest possible living off of social transfers.[10]

Esping-Andersen did not include Southern European countries in his classification: in subsequent work these countries have been identified as belonging to a fourth world of welfare capitalism, which resembles the conservative regime but typically has less generous social security, more stringent employment regulation and generally less efficient welfare institutions. In these countries the family is the primary locus of solidarity in both social (provision of care and support) and productive terms (creation of family businesses), with the male breadwinner enjoying high employment protection and job stability and other labour force groups (women, young people, migrants) suffering from high unemployment and/or condemned to unprotected low-wage employment in the informal sectors of the economy.[11] We will mainly focus on the CMEs and LMEs in this chapter and return to the model of the Southern European countries in our discussion of the Eurozone crisis in chapters 6 and 7.

Neoliberalism, labour markets and social policy

From the 1970s onwards a number of developments started to undermine the wage-led growth models of the advanced capitalist economies, creating pressures on governments to liberalize labour markets and restructure their welfare states. The stagflation crisis had exposed the inflationary tendencies of wage-led growth, as in a context of full employment workers pushed for wage increases that started to outstrip productivity growth. This revealed the intrinsic tension between the role of wages as a source of aggregate household consumption and as firms' production costs (see box 1.3 in chapter 1): while stimulating aggregate demand by supporting household consumption, 'wages that were too high and profits that were too low per unit of output reduced capitalists' incentive to invest'.[12] The problem of 'excessive wage growth' was especially noticeable in countries that lacked national-level or cross-sectoral collective bargaining institutions that stimulated labour unions to enact wage restraint. To contain excessive inflation, these countries had to resort to politically fraught and often ineffective income policies, whereby the government mandated that wages could not grow above specific targets by imposing economy-wide wage ceilings. Ultimately, inflation could only be defeated by the neoliberal shift towards restrictive macroeconomic policies (chapter 3).

Economic globalization also intensified international competition, putting pressure on firms to reduce labour costs. In the neocorporatist literature of the 1980s, scholars argued that countries with collective bargaining institutions like those in Northern Europe would fare comparatively well in adjusting to this new international context, as trade unions engaged in various agreements with employer organizations and governments to mitigate their wage demands and support the competitiveness of manufacturing firms, in exchange for higher levels of social spending.[13] These agreements were crucial for minimizing social conflict and maintaining societal support for globalization, as advocates of the compensation thesis argue: that is, governments and firms in open economies preferred to retain some social protection

Table 4.2 Unemployment rate and contribution of exports to GDP growth (in percentages), 1960–2010

	Unemployment rate			Annual contribution of exports to GDP growth (1990–2010)
	1960–80	1980–90	1990–2010	
CMEs				
Austria	1.38	3.15	4.53	2.31
Belgium	3.18	9.54	8.16	2.84
Denmark	2.38	6.67	5.83	1.72
Finland	2.78	4.79	10.36	2.13
Germany	NA	NA	8.46	1.64
Netherlands	2.55	8.35	5.31	3.01
Sweden	2.22	3.26	7.83	2.39
LMEs				
Australia	NA	7.1	7.30	0.96
Canada	NA	NA	8.10	1.33
United Kingdom	2.69	9.45	6.74	1.10
United States	4.95	7.4	6.10	0.56
MMEs				
France	2.51	7.64	9.13	1.11
Greece	3.67	6.06	9.71	1.06
Italy	5.46	8.39	9.04	0.48
Portugal	3.77	8.21	7.44	1.18
Spain	3.84	16.28	14.79	1.24

Source: OECD; AMECO

mechanisms to cushion citizens and employees from the destabilizing effects of globalization to minimize the risk of social instability and political discontent.[14] The importance of compensation and social protection against the whims of globalization explains why West European countries most open to international trade and investment were also the ones that developed the most generous welfare regimes.

Social-democratic CMEs with encompassing national-level labour unions and employer organizations were better able to contain the growth in unemployment than conservative CMEs like Belgium and the Netherlands. Yet unemployment rose to unacceptable levels in practically all the continental European countries in the first half of the 1990s and remained – with exceptions like Austria, Denmark and the Netherlands – at levels above those in the LMEs during the 1990s and the 2000s (table 4.2). Persistently high levels of unemployment were widely seen by neoliberal economists and policymakers as an indication of growing 'Eurosclerosis', which could be attributed to continental Europe's overly 'rigid' labour markets and bloated welfare states.

One of the mainstays of neoliberalism and neoclassical economics more broadly is the idea that policymakers face a trade-off between equality and efficiency – an idea particularly associated with Arthur Okun (see also chapter 1).[15] According to Okun's trade-off, governments and unions may create a more equal distribution of income only at the expense of distorting market forces and diminishing long-term economic growth and employment. Neoliberal economists posit several reasons for such a trade-off with regard to labour market organization and social policy. Centralized wage-setting systems and overly generous unemployment benefits were criticized for creating disincentives among low-skilled workers and unemployed workers to respectively acquire skills or look for a job: by compressing wage differentials between low-skilled and high-skilled workers, centralized wage-setting systems supposedly made people less inclined to acquire skills that are in short supply in the labour market. By increasing the reservation wage – that is, the lowest wage at which workers would be willing to accept a particular job – generous unemployment benefits allegedly made unemployed people more reluctant to take on a job.

Apart from reducing the *supply* of labour, these equality-promoting institutions were also believed to underline *demand* for labour. Countries with centralized wage-setting, high minimum wages, stringent employment regulation and generous welfare states tend to have high labour costs. As we have seen above, collective bargaining and centralized wage-setting raise the wages of low-skilled workers, making them more expensive for firms. From a neoclassical perspective, a worker's wage should reflect his or her marginal product of labour (chapter 1), which is more likely in a decentralized wage-setting system in which wages are set at the individual or company level: low-skilled workers should earn less than high-skilled workers because they contribute less to the firm's profits; in turn, low-productivity firms should be able to pay lower wages to their workers than high-productivity firms. So

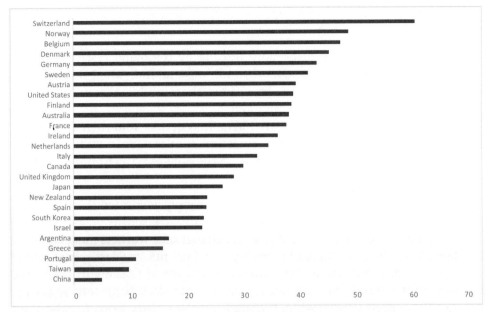

Figure 4.1 Hourly compensation costs (in US dollars): manufacturing sector, 2016

Source: Conference Board International Labor Comparisons program

while increasing income inequality, decentralized wage-setting systems were seen as more efficient in bolstering the employment of low-skilled workers. Moreover, social security is usually funded by relatively high payroll taxes levied on employees and employers. Consequently, countries with more generous welfare regimes tend to have *generally* higher labour costs (measured in terms of hourly compensation costs), as figure 4.1 shows. A central assumption of neoliberal theory is that these higher labour costs undermine the competitiveness of firms, making countries with centralized labour markets and expensive welfare states less attractive locations for manufacturing production.

These neoliberal arguments found a willing ear when the level of unemployment rose in the 1970s and remained stubbornly high in the 1980s (see chapter 3). Faced with high levels of unemployment, politicians of both left and right political parties became convinced that only 'structural reforms' – that is, liberalization of labour markets and restructuring of unemployment benefit programmes – could solve the problem. The insistent advice of international organizations like the OECD, the IMF and the European Commission via reports and surveillance activities helped forge a consensus about the benefits of these structural reforms in terms of employment and economic growth. The OECD's *Jobs Study/Strategy* especially played an important role in this regard.[16] In response to the sharp increase in unemployment levels in the 1980s, the OECD directed its Economic Secretariat to conduct a study and make substantive proposals for policy reform. The resulting *Jobs Study* (1994) made – amongst others – the following recommendations, which also formed the basis for its *Jobs Strategy*:

1 'Make wage and labour costs more flexible by removing restrictions that prevent wages from reflecting local conditions and individual skill levels';
2 'Reform employment security provisions that inhibit the expansion of employment in the private sector'; and
3 'Reform unemployment and related benefit systems – and their interaction with the tax system – such that societies' fundamental equity goals are achieved in ways that impinge far less on the efficient functioning of labour markets.'[17]

The IMF and the European Commission also strongly advocated these reforms, arguing that – in the words of one critic of this consensus – 'as firms are confronted by increasingly competitive, global markets, workers must adjust by accepting lower wages, stingier unemployment benefits, and less secure jobs'.[18]

There are, however, both conceptual and empirical reasons to doubt the neoliberal interpretation. As noted above, a centralized wage-setting system functions as a productivity whip, forcing low-productivity firms to raise their productivity by investing in labour-saving technologies. In the longer term, these investments boost the average labour productivity in the economy, rendering the average firm *more* rather than *less* efficient. The presence of centralized wage-setting systems helps explain why CMEs generally perform better in terms of average labour productivity (figure 4.2). This also sheds a different light on their comparatively high labour costs measured in terms

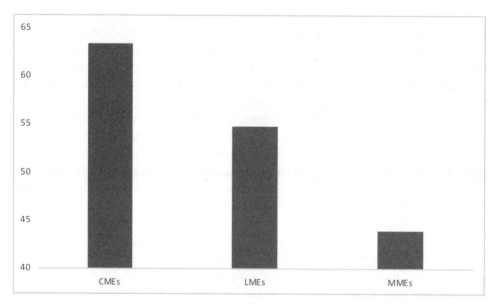

Figure 4.2 Average per hour worked(in current purchasing power parity (PPP) dollars), 2000–18
Source: OECD

of hourly compensation – observed in figure 4.1 above. To compare labour costs between different countries, it is important to look at *both* compensation and productivity levels. What matters for a firm is the average labour cost per unit of production (that is, *unit labour costs*), since high wage costs can be compensated for by high labour productivity. This is especially important for internationally exposed, capital-intensive manufacturing sectors, where the introduction of machinery and technologies tremendously increased labour productivity. For the same reason, firms in CMEs are better able to pay higher wages and bear the burden of high payroll taxes and labour costs because productivity is higher there.[19] High-productivity manufacturing firms are also not burdened by centralized wage-setting, which even allows them to trim their unit labour costs: wages in centralized wage-setting systems track average productivity growth, which is an average of typically higher productivity growth in the manufacturing sectors and typically lower productivity growth in the services sectors of the economy.[20]

For all these reasons, high labour costs are not necessarily problematic for highly productive firms in capital-intensive manufacturing sectors that are most exposed to international trade and investment. As such, the neoliberal claim that labour market decentralization and welfare state retrenchment are required to contain the labour of these firms and strengthen their competitiveness should be questioned: it is certainly no coincidence that the more egalitarian CMEs are more export-oriented than the more equal LMEs and MMEs, as the final column of table 4.2 shows. The key challenge for the CMEs is not to preserve the competitiveness of their manufacturing firms but to create jobs for low-skilled workers in the less productive services sectors of the economy: labour costs of workers in these sectors are pushed by centralized wage-setting systems that track average productivity growth in the economy as well by payroll taxes used to finance their more generous welfare states; these equality-promoting institutions might have made CMEs less effective in enhancing the employability of these low-skilled workers in less-productive service sectors in the economy. That is indeed the main argument of the VoC approach, as we elaborate in the next section.

Deindustrialization, social policy and varieties of capitalism

Social policy and sectoral conflict

Firm-centred VoC perspectives on labour market organization and welfare state development mostly focus on sectoral differences to identify the sources of employers' social policy preferences. They highlight differences in interests between internationally exposed manufacturing and domestically oriented service sectors and between high-skill and low-skill sectors. According to these accounts, social reforms are usually the product of cross-class alliances that result from sectoral conflict and cleavages. To the extent that CMEs have been under pressure to liberalize their labour markets and/or downsize their social security systems, liberal reforms should be linked to deindustrialization and the ensuing need to create jobs in the domestically oriented 'sheltered' services sector. A key argument of VoC perspectives is that demands for liberalization can be found in these sheltered sectors rather than in manufacturing sectors exposed to international competition.

The core argument of the VoC approaches is that firms in the manufacturing sectors of CMEs should have a keen interest in preserving centralized wage-setting institutions and relatively generous welfare regimes, which create incentives for firms and workers to invest in *industry-specific and/or firm-specific skills*. Due to these skills investments, firms in the CMEs tend to perform very well in terms of incremental innovation and quality differentiation – that is, continuous but small-scale improvements to existing product lines and production processes in order to improve and upscale the quality of existing products (see also next chapter). Incremental innovation tends to be important for maintaining competitiveness in established industries like automobiles, machine tools and factory equipment, consumer durables, engines, specialized transport equipment, etc. In these industries, 'the problem is to maintain the high quality of an established product line, to devise incremental improvements to it that attract consumer loyalty, and to secure continuous improvements in the production process in order to improve quality control and hold down costs'.[21] While radical innovation in more rapidly changing industries like ICT requires general skills that are transferable between firms and sectors, incremental innovation requires a deeper knowledge of the firm's production processes and the industry's market developments – that is, knowledge and skills that cannot be transferred and used across different firms and sectors.

Why do centralized wage-setting and welfare spending create incentives for firms and workers to invest in firm- and sector-specific skills? From the *employer's perspective*, centralized wage-setting institutions minimize the risk of poaching, which is one of the fundamental problems associated with sector-specific skills investment and training: if a firm invests in the sector-specific skills of its workers, there is a risk that another firm in the sector will attempt to 'poach' and hire these workers by offering higher wages in order to capture the returns on the first firm's skills investments; the consequence is that firms would avoid making these investments even if industry-specific skills are an important source of innovation and competitiveness. Centralized wage-setting mitigates this problem by inducing firms to pay similar wages for similar jobs and inhibiting them from offering higher wages to attract workers. Moreover, centralized wage-setting acts as a beneficial constraint: not only does it force firms to invest in low-skilled workers, who have to be paid wages similar to higher-skilled workers, but also the compression of wages makes investment in these skills more profitable for firms, as the wages of skilled workers would be higher in a decentralized setting.

From the *employee's perspective*, centralized wage-setting creates political demand for welfare state spending and stringent employment protection. One potential problem of centralized and solidaristic wage-setting is that it reduces the incentives of workers to acquire skills: 'If wages of skilled workers decline, so will the private incentive to acquire skills, and that in turn leads to skill shortages and pressure by skilled workers and their employers to break out of the centralized system.'[22] Stringent employment regulation and social protection benefits minimize the risk of unemployment associated with acquiring firm- or industry-specific skills: it is always possible that firms go bankrupt or are hit by industry-specific shocks, so workers will be unable to use their firm- and industry-specific skills in other firms or sectors; as a result, they could face long-term unemployment in a way that makes acquiring such skills a risky undertaking. Stringent job protection laws and various forms of social protection mitigate these risks.[23]

For VoC approaches, the upshot of these observations is that centralized labour markets and generous social insurance systems have bolstered the international competitiveness of firms in the advanced manufacturing sectors of the CMEs: 'the core institutions of social protection found in both the conservative and social democratic welfare states [are] complementary to the functioning of the advanced sectors of the economy ... [T]he political institutions that have promoted redistribution are also conducive to both business and union interests.'[24] While these observations lead to the conclusion that globalization will not force the CMEs to overhaul their social model, VoC approaches believe that these countries do face considerable pressure for liberalization. According to VoC approaches, the key challenge faced by egalitarian CMEs since the 1960s is not the deepening of economic globalization but 'the transition from an economy dominated by (exposed) manufacturing production to one dominated by (sheltered) services production'.[25] Deindustrialization reduced employment in those sectors of the economy that have had a key interest in preserving the centralized labour markets and institutions of social protection. This has resulted in new sectoral cleavages, pitching the interests of the exposed manufacturing sectors against those of the exposed services sectors.

Why has that been the case? At first sight, the transition from a predominantly industrial economy to a service economy resembles the shift in sectoral employment that accompanied the transformation of the agrarian economy to an industrial economy at the end of the nineteenth and the beginning of the twentieth century. There is one critical difference, however: unlike the golden era of manufacturing, most employment creation since the 1970s took place in service sectors that are inherently less conducive to productivity growth: 'Teachers can serve more students, nurses more patients, and waiters more customers, but this is not easily achieved without a decline in the quality of the service.'[26] Deindustrialization therefore has important implications for the wage structure in the economy, as high-productivity and capital-intensive manufacturing sectors can more easily bear the burden of high labour costs than low-productivity and labour-intensive service sectors without undermining their profitability.

In the advanced economies there is a general tendency for wages in the low-productivity services sectors to track those in the high-productivity manufacturing sectors; as a result, services have become comparatively more expensive than manufactured goods since the early 1980s – a phenomenon known as 'Baumol's cost disease'.[27] Yet growing sectoral differences in productivity levels and productivity growth are especially problematic for countries with centralized wage-setting systems that compress wage differentials between workers in high- and low-productivity sectors. When wages are tightly coupled between these sectors, workers and employees in low-productive service sectors can become too expensive and employment expansion might slow down, as Torben Iversen and Anne Wren explain: 'Whereas solidaristic wage policies in the *industrial* economy tended to shift production to the most efficient sectors where the scope of productivity increases was the greatest, solidaristic wage policies in the *service* economy tend to squeeze out the least productive workers without creating a compensating expansion in the overall level of activity.' Deindustrialization therefore reversed the effect of wage compression on job creation: 'in the past it promoted employment because it kept down relative wages in highly dynamic sectors; in the present it inhibits employment because relative wages are kept high in the least dynamic sectors'.[28]

Consequently, high growth in market-provided services – which is needed to compensate for declining manufacturing employment – presupposes a more *inegalitarian* wage structure. That is why decentralized labour markets in the LMEs have been more conducive to an expansion of service sector employment from the 1960s to the 1990s. Generous welfare regimes, which raise labour costs if they are financed by high payroll taxes, additionally constrain the capacity of CMEs to create jobs in low-skilled service sectors. These so-called 'rigidities' associated with centralized labour markets and lavish welfare states were seen by many as central components in the 'Eurosclerosis' of 1990 to 2005, exemplified by relatively weak employment growth and high unemployment, particularly among low-skilled workers in CMEs.

A counter-narrative to the supposedly superior labour market performance of LMEs is that the creation of jobs in the LMEs mostly consisted of so-called McJobs – low-paid, dead-end jobs in sectors like food, retail and catering services with low prospects of career opportunities. Nevertheless, if we look at the 'star pupil' among the LMEs – the United States – in terms of employment creation during this period, these kind of jobs were certainly not the only ones created in the service economy: a large amount of job expansion occurred in the top tier of the employment structure, with many high-paid managerial and professional jobs created in the finance, insurance and real estate (FIRE) and high-tech services sectors of the economy. Given that technological innovation destroyed many medium-skilled manufacturing and administrative jobs, this polarized structure of employment growth has been a key source of the growth in income inequality in the US economy.[29]

The fact that comparatively many jobs were created in high-skilled service sectors of the economy of LMEs suggests another potential source of conflict between firms in manufacturing and service sectors: most service sector firms thrive more on *general* skills – whether at the high end (e.g. software engineering, which involves broad technical training) or at the low end (e.g. retail and hospitality industries, where there is a premium on social and communication skills). High-end manufacturing, on the other hand, flourishes in an environment of centralized wage-setting and employment stability, allowing firms and workers to amortize investment in firm- or industry-specific skills. In high-end services, labour mobility often plays a crucial role in promoting skill acquisition – among other things, by providing a mechanism to ensure that the general skills in which a worker invests will be valued at full marginal product. But at the low-skill end of the spectrum as well, 'a high-quality public [state] school system that provides foundational general skills is arguably better equipped than traditional firm-sponsored apprenticeship training to generate the kind of social and communication skills that lower-level service-sector jobs demand'.[30] As such, differences in educational systems also contributed to differences in employment patterns between the LMEs and CMEs:

> Where wages are highly dispersed and students face tuition fees to repay, graduates are likely to enter dynamic private sector services, like the FIRE sector. Thus, partially private systems are likely to coincide with high levels of wage dispersion and dynamic service sector employment. In contrast, where wages are highly compressed and students have no university-related debts, they may choose to enter lower-paying careers that have greater non-pecuniary benefits or higher job stability: for example, non-dynamic services like the public sector or high-end manufacturing. Thus mass public higher education systems should be associated with higher wage compression and non-dynamic service sector employment.[31]

In sum, both centralized wage-setting systems and institutions for skill formation intensified cleavages between market-oriented service sectors and manufacturing sectors in ways that created pressures on the CMEs to overhaul and liberalize their social model. How did CMEs respond to these pressures?

Deindustrialization, liberalization and social investment

Advanced capitalist countries responded differently to these challenges. Kathleen Thelen distinguishes three 'varieties of liberalization':

1 'deregulation', which involves 'the active political dismantling of coordinating capacities (on one or both sides of the class divide) and declining coverage – and with that a marked individualization of risk';

2 'embedded flexibilization', which involves 'the introduction of new forms of flexibility within the context of a continued strong and encompassing framework that collectivizes risk'; and

3 'dualization', which involves 'continued strong coordination on the employer side but in the context of a distinct narrowing in the number of firms and workers covered under the resulting arrangements'.[32]

According to Thelen, outright deregulation of labour markets is mostly associated with LMEs, where labour unions are traditionally too weak to resist change.

The Nordic countries (as well as the Netherlands to some extent) engaged in embedded flexibilization: they combined market-promoting labour-market policies with social programmes designed to ease the adaptation of weaker segments of society to changes in the market (also known as 'flexicurity'). This typically involved a decentralization of national-level collective bargaining towards the sectoral level, combined with 'active labour market policies' to promote employment and labour mobility between different sectors. Although institutions of social protection remain strong in both the manufacturing and service sectors, these institutions revolve more than before around facilitating the successful (re)integration of workers and employees into the labour market (i.e., less about their 'protection' but more about their 'activation'). Hence, employment protection became significantly more flexible. Nordic CMEs also employed a comparatively high number of people in the public sector, which offered many new jobs in expanding social services, education and health care. In these countries, 'a well-organized public sector emerged as an important second pillar within the organized labour movement, and one that represented a very different constituency from traditional male-dominated manufacturing unions'.[33] Embedded flexibilization consists of a more egalitarian mitigation of the sectoral cleavage: it consists of a collectivization of risk 'by focusing resources on enabling society's most vulnerable to get and keep a good job' and 'frequently involves a functional conversion of existing institutions – whether collective bargaining institutions or labour market institutions – to new goals, and one that is based on a significantly reconfigured social coalition'.[34]

In conservative-corporatist CMEs, by contrast, public and private service sectors remained much smaller and the interests of manufacturing sectors dominate public policy. In these countries, the structure of union membership continues to be heavily concentrated among male blue-collar workers. The trajectory of liberalization in these countries took the form of an increasing 'dualization' of the labour market: manufacturing firms and their workers have been able to jointly defend traditional collective bargaining institutions and practices for themselves, whereas in the services sectors less co-operative, more flexible and less secure patterns of employment have emerged. In these cases, 'manufacturing employers will not necessarily be at the forefront of demands for deregulation, but neither can they be expected to oppose duali-zation, since export-oriented firms benefit doubly from the growth of a more flexible periphery – both through lower service prices and through lower taxes'. Traditional arrangements for 'labour-market insiders' are maintained under dualization 'even as an unorganized and unregulated periphery is allowed to grow outside their ambit, one that is characterized by inferior status and protections for labour-market outsiders'.[35] Regular workers in the 'core' manufacturing sectors of the economy remain protected by strong employment regulation and collective bargaining agreements, while a growing number of 'irregular' workers became employed in jobs in the services sectors that were more precarious, less protected and not covered. Dualization is widely identified as an important source of the growth in income inequality in the conservative-corporatist CMEs over the last decades. Germany is especially associated with this model (see box 4.2). [36]

Box 4.2 Hartz reforms and labour market dualization in Germany

Germany's labour market reforms in the first half of the 2000s – the Hartz reforms – provide the clearest illustration of how dualization promoted the interest of both employers and workers in the manufacturing sectors. The reforms, which were enacted by the red–green coalition government led by the social-democratic chancellor Gerhard Schröder, limited social transfers to the long-term unemployed: unemployment benefits were generally restricted to twelve months, after which long-term unemployed job seekers were forced to have recourse to much lower social assistance benefits (*Sozialhilfe*).[37] Furthermore, employment protection for 'irregular' contracts (fixed term, agency and marginal work) was diminished in order to reduce wage and non-wage labour costs for employers in the service sectors: in 2010 only about 10 per cent of marginal employment was in manufacturing, while more than 80 per cent was in service sector jobs – many of them so-called part-time 'mini-jobs'. Dualization was therefore a mechanism to mitigate cleavages between manufacturing and service sector firms.

Although service-sector firms also benefited from the change in policy, manufacturing industries depended on these firms to cut costs and remain profitable. Over time, service wages fell relative to manufacturing wages even though these sectors were sheltered from international competition.[38] Both employers and labour unions from the manufacturing sectors accepted and often even welcomed Hartz labour reforms. As manufacturing firms need to make use of different kind of services (e.g. catering, transport, cleaning etc.), these reforms indirectly cut their production costs and bolstered their profitability and competitiveness. This also secured job opportunities for high-skilled and well-paid manufacturing workers.[39]

One of the main conclusions of the VoC analysis of labour market liberalization is that class-based conflict is superseded by sectoral conflict: economic globali-zation and deindustrialization deepened the polarization of labour markets between well-paid, high-skilled workers and low-paid, low-skilled workers, giving rise to new cross-class coalitions. Figure 4.3 shows the most recent available evidence on job polarization across the OECD, which is exemplified by a fall in the share of middle-skill jobs relative to both high-skill and low-skill jobs from 1995 to 2016. A similar constellation of cross-class coalitions under-pinned shifts in welfare state spending away from 'public consumption' – that is, state expenditures that help people cope with a loss of income (due to unemployment, illness or retirement) – to issues of 'social investment' – that is, expenditures to 'empower people to earn a living in the labour market with policies classified under the rubrics of education, child care, labour market activation, research and development, and public infrastructure'.[40] A key impli-cation of these structural labour market shifts is that high-skilled workers have developed different preferences regarding welfare state spending from those of low-skilled workers. A recent study exploiting data on public opinion in eight European countries found that 'supporting coalitions for social investment reforms and more traditional social policies are distinct, hinting at potential trade-offs, political struggles and conflicts over the transformation of existing

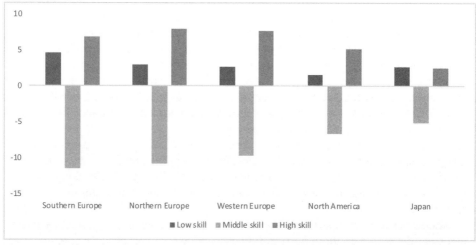

Figure 4.3 Change in employment shares of low-, middle- and high-skill jobs (in percentage points), 1995–2016

Source: OECD

High-skill occupations include jobs classified under the International Standard Classification of Occupations (ISCO-88) major groups 1, 2 and 3: legislators, senior officials and managers (group 1), professionals (group 2), and technicians and associate professionals (group 3). Middle-skill occupations include jobs classified under the ISCO-88 major groups 4, 7 and 8: clerks (group 4), craft and related trades workers (group 7), and plant and machine operators and assemblers (group 8). Low-skill occupations include jobs classified under the ISCO-88 major groups 5 and 9: service workers and shop and market sales workers (group 5) and elementary occupations (group 9). Southern Europe contains Spain, Greece, Italy and Portugal. Northern Europe contains Denmark, Finland, Norway and Sweden. Western Europe contains Austria, Belgium, Germany, France, Ireland, the Netherlands, Switzerland and the United Kingdom. North America contains Canada and the United States. Change is in percentage points.

welfare states': while social investment policies have become the most popular dimension of welfare state spending and find support among both high-skilled middle-class people and richer individuals, passive transfer policies continue to be most supported by low-income and low-skilled people.[41]

Globalization, social policy and power resources

Social policy and class conflict

VoC approaches maintain that employers in manufacturing sectors of CMEs do not push for deregulation of labour markets and retrenchment of welfare state spending, which preserve their international competitiveness by facilitating the investment in firm- and industry-specific skills. This core claim has been contested by power resources theorists, who argue that employers in *all* sectors of the economy strive to deregulate labour markets and roll back welfare spending in order to maximize their profits.[42] The central claim of these theorists is that 'because of differences in the ways that socio-economic class is related to types of power resources controlled by citizens as well as to patterns of life-course risks among individuals differently positioned within

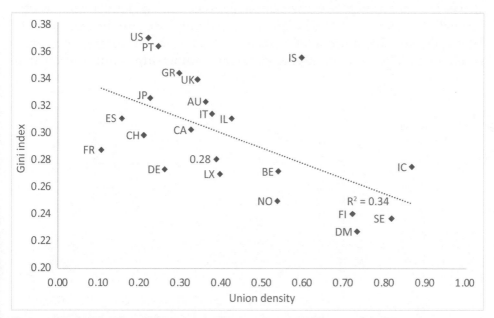

Figure 4.4 Union density and income equality in selected OECD countries, 1980–2010

Source: OECD

AT = Austria; AU = Australia; BE = Belgium; CA = Canada; CH = Switzerland; DE = Germany; DM = Denmark; ES = Spain; FI = Finland; FR = France; GR = Greece; IC = Iceland; IL = Ireland; ISR = Israel; IT = Italy; JP = Japan; LX = Luxembourg; NL = Netherlands; NO = Norway; NZ = New Zealand; PT = Portugal; SE = Sweden; UK = United Kingdom; US = United States.

socio-economic structures, welfare state development is likely to reflect class-related distributive conflict and partisan politics'.[43] Employers and employees have fundamentally conflicting interests and preferences with regard to the organization of the labour market and the generosity of the welfare regime:

> Employers and other interest groups disposing major economic resources are likely to prefer to situate distributive processes in the context of markets, where economic assets constitute strategic resources and, because of their concentration, tend to outflank labour power. Employees, especially categories with limited economic resources, are therefore expected to organize for collective action in political parties and unions to modify conditions for and outcomes of market distribution.[44]

As such, the principal reason why CMEs have centralized labour markets and generous social security systems is the historical success of working-class organization and mobilization in these countries. As we saw in chapter 2, a series of political and economic events in major economies eventually empowered labour movements during the interwar years, as the Great Depression discredited the policies and continuing power of the political establishment. CMEs developed higher levels of unionization – that is, a comparatively high number of employed workers were union members. Union density is especially high in the Nordic CMEs and Belgium. Figure 4.4 shows a strongly negative correlation between union density and income inequality: countries with the highest union density are also the ones with the largest income distribution (after taxes and transfers). In most conservative-corporatist CMEs (Belgium excluded) union membership is much lower than

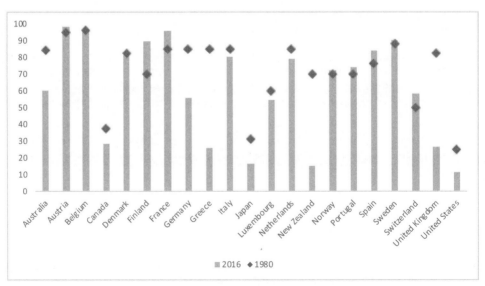

Figure 4.5 Bargaining coverage in percentage of employees, 1980 and 2016
Source: OECD

in the social-democratic CMEs, yet unions play a very important role in the organization of the labour market in these countries, and bargaining coverage – the degree to which the terms of workers' employment are determined by a collective agreement – is comparatively high (figure 4.5). Unions traditionally favour income redistribution not only through collective bargaining, but also through a state-provided and publicly funded social security system. The reason, from a power resources perspective, is fairly simple: labour unions' bargaining power vis-à-vis employer organization is stronger in the presence of a generous welfare regime that raises the reservation wage; employers are less able to threaten dismissals when there is a strong social safety net to protect the unemployed.[45]

A second reason why labour movements in the CMEs became stronger than elsewhere is that national working-class-oriented political parties became dominant political players in these countries. During the interwar years, mass enfranchisement and universal suffrage enabled working-class, left-wing parties to be elected on the basis of a platform consisting of egalitarian income redistribution, the recognition of collective bargaining rights, and state-provided social insurance and education. In the Scandinavian countries social-democratic parties with close ties to unions became dominant. In the conservative-corporatist CMEs, on the other hand, Christian-Democratic confessional political parties and unions, which used religion as a cleavage to compete with socialist parties for working-class voters, were established and became leading parties. These confessional parties have had an explicit cross-class basis, including workers, salaried employees, the self-employed and employers as organizational members. To be credible these confessional parties had to place some limits on employers, as a way to attract workers' votes, giving these parties a middling position along the left–right continuum. In any case, proportional electoral systems of CMEs made it almost impossible during most of the second half of the twentieth century to form coalition governments without the participation of either social-democratic or confessional political parties claiming to represent working-class interests.[46]

Power resources theorists tend to be less optimistic about the ability of CMEs to maintain centralized labour markets and generous social security systems in the context of globalization than VoC theorists. The reason is not because these equality-promoting institutions have made exposed firms somehow less efficient and competitive, but simply because even highly productive firms are primarily interested in easy profits and only secondarily in productivity, as Wolfgang Streeck astutely observed: 'if the latter comes at the expense of the former, capitalists are quite willing to do without it. Low growth is fine with capitalists as long as it is accompanied by a declining wage share and rising profits.'[47] Even the industrial segments of the capitalist class are therefore unlikely to defend these institutions in the face of a structurally weakened labour movement.

Globalization, social policy and the weakening of labour power

A key assumption of power resources approaches is that globalization and the ensuing mobility of capital have weakened the bargaining power of labour unions vis-à-vis firms and employer organizations. The basic idea is that most firms are not in favour of maintaining elaborate collective bargaining arrangements and generous welfare regimes, which increase their labour costs and reduce their profits compared to firms producing in countries with decentralized wage-setting, flexible labour laws and limited welfare spending. More intense international competition thus put more pressure on firms to cut production costs and flexibilize their production strategies, making internationally exposed firms increasingly vocal campaigners for the deregulation of labour markets and dismantling of welfare regimes. Moreover, globalization increased the structural power of capital by enabling firms to threaten labour unions and left-wing political parties with the 'exit option'. As a result, labour unions and left-wing political parties have been forced to accept an incremental decentralization of the labour market and a retrenchment of the welfare state.

There are three developments that point to a weakening of labour power and growing employer discretion in industrial relations.[48] First, most countries in the advanced capitalist world experienced a gradual decline in union density. The decline in unionization has been especially prominent in the LMEs, but the other models have not escaped the trend of de-unionization (figure 4.6). A number of cross-national studies have shown that the rise in income inequality can be linked to the decline in union membership.[49] This correlation is unsurprising from a power resources perspective, as strong unions typically induce

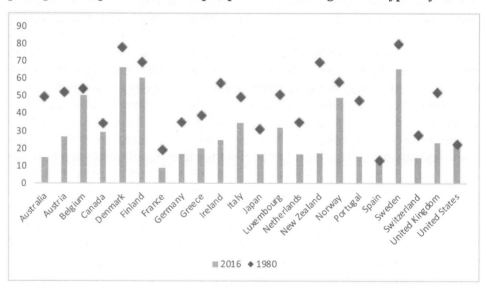

Figure 4.6 Trade union density in percentage of total labour force, 1980 and 2016
Source: OECD

politicians to engage in more redistribution by mobilizing workers to vote for parties that promise to redistribute income. Moreover, unions play a key role in the redistribution of income through their support of collective bargaining and the reduction of wage differentials between low-skilled and high-skilled workers. In this regard, lower union density also tends to raise top income shares, which are mechanically influenced by what happens in the lower part of the income distribution:

1 de-unionization weakens earnings for middle- and low-income workers, increasing the income share of corporate managers' pay and shareholder returns;
2 the weakening of unions diminishes the bargaining power of workers relative to capital owners, increasing the share of capital income – which is more concentrated at the top than wages and salaries; and
3 weaker unions reduce workers' influence on corporate decisions that benefit top earners, such as the size and structure of top executive compensation (see also chapter 5).

Second, declining union membership went hand in hand with a decentralization in collective bargaining to lower levels where workers have less bargaining power: 'In many (not all) countries industry or sector bargaining has taken the place of national (cross-industry) bargaining where it existed, and local or enterprise bargaining has gained more prominence either replacing sector bargaining or as an additional layer.'[50] What is more, there has been a steep decline in collective bargaining coverage in many countries either formally or informally. Formal bargaining coverage fell particularly in LMEs, but also in conservative CMEs like Germany and the Netherlands (figure 4.5) – an indication of growing labour market dualization in these countries. However, of even greater importance than the fall in formal coverage of collective bargaining is the growing prevalence of practices that permit – either legally or illegally – a decentralization of collective bargaining to the firm level – such as 'a simple failure to honour sectoral agreements, concessionary agreements at the firm level with the works council ... and the growing recourse to "opening clauses" within sectoral agreements that permit firms to modify the terms of the agreement'.[51] Opening clauses are closely connected with setting aside the 'legal favourability' principle, which has been a cornerstone of collective labour law in most countries by guaranteeing that lower-level agreements can only deviate from higher-level agreements in ways that are *more* favourable for workers. By contrast, opening clauses allow lower-level agreements with *less* favourable terms and conditions than those stipulated in higher-level agreements. In Germany, 22 per cent of workplaces took advantage of such clauses in 1999–2000, compared to 75 per cent in 2004–5.[52]

Third, trade unions became more responsive to the needs of employers to maintain competitiveness in globalized markets: collective wage bargaining increasingly focused on the 'supply-side' effects of labour costs on the international competitiveness of firms, with trade in the exposed sectors endorsing pay formulas aimed at keeping labour costs at levels that improved competitiveness in relation to foreign firms. This shift towards 'competitive corporatism' or 'supply-side corporatism' is closely related to the shift towards the neoliberal macroeconomic policy regime, which weakened the bargaining power of labour by abandoning Keynesian demand management and full employment policies (see chapter 3).[53] Greg Albo has called this development 'competitive austerity', whereby CMEs have depressed domestic demand in order to adopt 'an export-oriented strategy of dumping its surplus production, for which there are fewer consumers in its national economy given the decrease in workers' living standards and productivity gains all going to the capitalists, in the world market'.[54] Competitive corporatism and austerity coincided with a marked decline in industrial conflict (measured by the number of days not worked due to strikes and lockouts). Through combinations of concessions, wage restraint and fewer strikes, unions tried to protect well-paid jobs in the manufacturing sectors as much as possible. Fearing the loss of all political power, many labour movements accepted social pacts and coordinated decentralization, with the expectation that wage restraint would contain inflation and restore the competitiveness of internationally exposed firms.[55]

Importantly, power resources theorists have noted that labour market liberalization was not confined to the 'peripheral' service sectors of the CMEs but also extended to the 'core' manufacturing sectors of the economy. This is the argument Lucio Baccaro and Chris Howell vehemently defended in their book *Trajectories of Neoliberal Transformation* (2017). In Germany, industry-level collective bargaining coverage has shown a steep and uniform decline across sectors: in 1995 collective bargaining covered 72 per cent of workers in the economy as whole, 80 per cent in manufacturing, 92 per cent in manufacturing establishments with more than 250 employees and 72 per cent in services; in 2013 the coverage rates were 49, 50, 67 and 45 per cent, respectively. This decline in industry-level bargaining coverage has not been compensated for by more company-level agreements, as work councils have found it increasingly difficult to enforce collective agreements because of the diffusion of opening clauses, the increase in agency work and the growing use of subcontracting relationships.[56] In Scandinavian CMEs like Sweden, Baccaro and Howell observe a similar trend towards increasing employer discretion at the company level:

> The agreements that are the focus of coordinated bargaining are now minimalist framework agreements, establishing procedures for bargaining, sometimes setting some limited wage targets, but permitting wide discretion at the firm level ... A focus upon the bargaining institutions themselves misses the manner in which these institutions have come to function as mechanisms for permitting local variation.[57]

Finally, it is difficult to decouple deindustrialization from globalization as VoC scholars tend to do. Lower-cost competition from newly industrializing and

Central and Eastern European countries forced producers in high-cost CMEs to automate production or specialize in upmarket industrial products and highly productive services: employment in internationally exposed sectors of the economy can be maintained only through continuous product and process innovations and increases in labour productivity, thereby inhibiting job growth in these competitive sectors. The ensuing pressures are felt not only in the manufacturing sectors of the economy, 'but also in sheltered branches supplying local goods and services to internationally exposed firms, as well as in capital-intensive branches providing services that are locally produced and consumed'.[58] Furthermore, manufacturing firms in the CMEs have not been entirely absolved from the shareholder revolution in corporate governance, as we will see in the next chapter. Firms responded to cost pressure from international markets by *outsourcing* many lower value added activities – that is, by hiring external firms (both local and abroad) to produce at a lower cost goods and services that previously were produced in-house by the firm's own employees and staff. As a result, the value chains of big manufacturing companies became increasingly disintegrated and fragmented, thus contributing to the dualization of labour markets and putting downward pressures on the wages of low-skilled workers in outsourced jobs.[59]

Figure 4.7 suggests that workers in the manufacturing sectors have been unable to reap the benefits of labour productivity growth in the CMEs from 1980 to 2010: unit labour costs fell significantly in these sectors during this period, as wages failed to grow in line with productivity. If the decentralization of collective bargaining and wage-setting to the sectoral level and the concomitant flexibilization of labour markets for services sector workers would have been the outcome of a process whereby unions and employers in

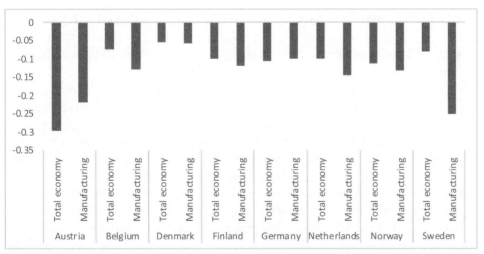

Figure 4.7 Fall in labour share in total economy and manufacturing in the CMEs (in percentage points), 1980–2010

Source: OECD

the manufacturing sectors bargained on an equal footing, it is hard to understand such a sharp fall in unit labour costs in the sectors. While manufacturing workers were unable to get their share of productivity gains, the gains they did receive predominantly went to high-skilled workers: IMF research revealed that the decline in the labour share was heavily concentrated among low- and medium-skilled workers, stemming from the rise of part-time employment and a decline in unionization rates.[60] These observations offer strong support for the claim that labour market liberalization was driven primarily by weakened labour power, particularly among low- and medium-skilled workers.

Social policy and growth models

LMEs and CMEs pursued distinctive growth models in response to the crisis of the Fordist wage-led growth model during the 1970s: economic growth in the LMEs since the 1980s has been mostly based on an expansion of private household consumption, whereas economic growth in the CMEs has been predominantly based on an expansion of exports. These different growth models can be linked to the growing income inequality associated with the liberalization of labour markets in the LMEs and the CMEs. The liberalization of industrial relations created the conditions for the emergence of a new set of post-Fordist growth models with the following common features:

> industrial relations were no longer of paramount importance in the regulatory architecture of capitalism; labour markets were much closer to being competitively regulated than ever before in the post-war period; and the resulting growth models were all unbalanced because they lacked an institutional mechanism ensuring that aggregate demand would grow in tandem with aggregate supply.[61]

In the Fordist growth model, wages rose with average productivity in the advanced capitalist economies, and governments saw it as their responsibility to support aggregate demand by pursuing countercyclical Keynesian macroeconomic policies.

These conventions unravelled in the 1970s, after which wages failed to keep up with productivity and governments began to emphasize fighting inflation instead of unemployment. The liberalization of industrial relations further undermined the wage-led growth model by weakening the bargaining position of workers vis-à-vis employers. As we have seen in this chapter, there continues to be academic disagreement about the extensiveness of labour power weakening, with VoC approaches arguing that the liberalization of industrial relations and welfare state retrenchment particularly forced workers in the service sectors into precarious and low-paid jobs, and power resources theorists arguing that these developments have also weakened the position of workers in the manufacturing sectors of the economy.

In any case, different varieties of liberalization in industrial relations and social policy led to different patterns in the evolution of personal income distribution. Particularly in the LMEs, liberalization took the form of outright labour market deregulation and a frontal assault on the power of labour unions. Far-reaching decentralization of wage-setting and flexibilization of labour markets help to explain why the real incomes of the bottom 50 per cent have barely increased since the 1980s, as table 1.1 (in chapter 1) revealed for the United States and Canada. Rising income inequality associated with labour market polarization was bound to create problems for economic growth in the LMEs, which have traditionally been consumption-led: governments had to find a replacement for the faltering wage driver of aggregate demand and economic growth, which they eventually did by deregulating the banking system and facilitating the access of lower- and middle-income households to cheap credit (see chapters 6 and 7). In LMEs like the United States and the United Kingdom, debt-led growth was bolstered by an 'asset-based welfare regime' that encouraged households to accumulate debt-financed housing wealth as an antidote to the retrenchment of the welfare state.[62] In these countries, governments and legislators actively promoted the expansion of household credit as a substitute for traditional social policy schemes. Thus, asset-based welfare enabled credit-based social policy: 'faced with stagnant wages and a falling real value of pensions, health insurance coverage, and other buffers against risk, households increasingly used credit and in particular housing-based credit as substitute buffer'.[63]

Wage inequality rose less fast in the CMEs, where the income of lower-skilled workers was protected by collective bargaining institutions, employee-friendly labour market regulations and more generous welfare state provisions. But the power resources of the working class weakened in these countries as well in the face of dwindling union membership rates and declining left-wing political parties. Globalization, deindustrialization and technological change put pressure on governments in CMEs to partially deregulate labour markets by giving employers more discretionary control over industrial relations. The differentiated response of CMEs to these challenges gave rise to distinctive growth models: while all the CMEs became decidedly more export-oriented in their quest to find alternative sources of aggregate demand, the interests of the export-oriented manufacturing sectors prevailed particularly in countries like Germany, where the dualization of the labour market was the selected response. In Germany, the share of low-wage jobs grew markedly from less than 19 per cent of total employment in 1995 to almost 25 per cent in 2011.[64] The repression of wage growth in both the services and manufacturing sectors depressed domestic consumption and made the growth of the German economy increasingly reliant on exports. Countries that opted for embedded flexibilization pursued a more balanced growth model, combining strong export growth with more robust consumption growth (chapter 7).

5

Corporate Governance: The Rise of Shareholder Capitalism

What is the ultimate goal of a capitalist firm? The evident answer is that it has to make profits to survive. Nevertheless, as we will elaborate in this chapter, there are different conceptions of how a firm can or should achieve this. These different conceptions are the ultimate topic of corporate governance – the system of rules, practices and processes by which a company is directed and controlled. Corporate governance essentially involves balancing the interests of a firm's many stakeholders, such as its shareholders, managers, employees, customers, the government or sometimes even the community. Two opposing models in corporate governance can be found in the advanced capitalist world. According to the shareholder model, the sole objective of the firm is to maximize short-term profits and returns for the owners of the firm – that is, its shareholders. In this model, total shareholder return becomes the key metric of corporate performance: firms have to boost their stock market valuation year on year and distribute as much profit as possible to the shareholders to attract investors or avoid hostile takeovers. According to the stakeholder model, on the other hand, firms have to balance the shareholders' financial interests against the interests of other stakeholders such as employees, customers and the local community. The fundamental distinction is that the stakeholder model recommends that the interests of all stakeholders have to be considered even if it reduces a firm's short-term profitability.

Over the past four decades the shareholder model has become increasingly dominant in the advanced capitalist world, but especially so in the LMEs. The rise of the shareholder model was closely intertwined with developments in the US economy, where since the 1970s large US companies adjusted their strategies in response to the stagflation crisis and growing foreign competition – especially from Japanese and German firms. Until the 1970s large US firms were almost always vertically integrated, in the sense that they controlled and operated many different stages of the production process. Although vertical integration benefited US labour by requiring large US firms to retain and reinvest their profits, one of the key problems is that they became too large to remain efficient. Many US firms switched to new business strategies from the 1980s onwards, whereby the maximization of shareholder value became the principal objective. The most effective way to achieve this was by outsourcing less profitable activities and parts of the production process in order to concentrate on core activities with the most value added. These new business strategies were legitimized by new neoliberal theories of corporate governance, arguing for the introduction of new incentive structures that had to align the interests and preferences of managers with those of the firm's shareholders. One key incentive was manager compensation: to make sure that CEOs and other managers of the firm would engage in business strategies focused on maximizing shareholder returns, an increasing part of the remuneration became linked to the stock market performance of the firms. As such, the rise of the shareholder model in corporate governance is a very important cause of the rise in the income share of the top 0.01 per cent (which mostly consists of CEOs and managers) in the US economy.[1]

As we have seen in chapter 1, the income share of the top 0.01 per cent did not increase as sharply in Europe as it did in North America. In this chapter we will see that the more confined growth of inequality at the top end of the income distribution can be explained by the fact that firms in continental Europe were more reluctant to adopt the shareholder model of corporate governance. How can we explain the divergence in corporate governance? The VoC literature addresses this question by pointing to the presence of distinctive sets of institutional complementarities – that is, mutually reinforcing relations between different institutional domains.

One of the most important complementarities, according to this literature, is that between corporate finance institutions and labour market organization. LMEs have *capital market-dominated* financial systems: firms predominantly obtain external funding by selling stocks or bonds (see box 1.2 in chapter 1); CMEs, on the other hand, have *bank-dominated* financial systems, whereby firms receive external funding by bank credit. A central claim of the VoC literature is that these different types of financial systems encouraged Anglo-Saxon and continental European firms to pursue different kinds of business strategies that rely on different types of labour markets: whereas Anglo-Saxon firms dependent on capital market funding were pushed to maximize shareholder returns by focusing on cost-cutting restructuring and shedding workers in flexible labour markets, European firms obtained 'patient' long-term capital from banks that allowed them to engage in strategic coordination with labour unions and invest in the non-transferable skills of their workers. These institutional divergences in corporate governance and financial systems clarify why firms in Anglo-American and European firms have developed different innovation strategies, with European firms performing particularly well in terms of 'incremental innovation' in more established industries (such as automobiles, chemistry and machinery) and Anglo-Saxon firms – especially US firms – excelling in 'radical innovation' in new high-tech industries like ICT.

It is important not to overstate the beneficial effects of the shareholder model on innovation, however: there are various indications that the shareholder model constrains long-term innovation by pushing firms to pursue short-termist strategies, like cutting costs wherever possible and using internal funds to pay out dividends and/or engage in share buybacks, instead of investing in research and development (R&D). According to a more critical reading, the shareholder model of corporate governance reflects the growing influence of institutional investors in globalized financial markets, not only over Anglo-Saxon firms but increasingly also over large publicly listed firms in continental Europe. By ignoring the transnational sources and effects of financialization, the VoC literature has downplayed the amount of pressure on continental European firms to pursue short-termist strategies that maximize immediate returns. The common outcome of the growing financialization of non-financial corporations in both the Anglo-Saxon and continental European economies is a decline in corporate investment and fixed capital formation – that is, the accumulation of tangible assets like plants and equipment required for production. The resulting depression of aggregate demand is another reason why advanced capitalist countries became increasingly reliant on either debt-led growth or export-led growth.

Corporate business strategies during the Keynesian era

Towards the end of the 1990s the Business Roundtable – a group of CEOs from the largest and most powerful US corporations – made the following mission statement: 'The paramount duty of management and of boards of directors is to serve the corporation's stockholders; the interests of other stakeholders are relevant as a derivative of the duty to stockholders.'[2] In the Anglo-Saxon economies the exclusive focus of corporations on shareholder value is a relatively recent phenomenon, rising to prominence in the 1980s as part and parcel of the neoliberal revolution.[3]

Until the 1980s a relatively small number of giant corporations, employing tens or even hundreds of thousands of people, dominated the economy of the United States. These giant corporations allocated their revenues according to a corporate governance principle that William Lazonick has called 'retain and reinvest': 'These corporations tended to retain both the money that they earned and the people whom they employed, and they reinvested in physical capital and complementary human resources.'[4] Retain-and-reinvest business strategies were associated with vertically integrated firms – that is, firms that owned and controlled many different steps in the production process (e.g. extraction of commodities, production and assemblage of components, R&D, marketing and retail sales). The large, vertically integrated firm was the main template for business organization during the Keynesian era. By inventing the assembly-line US car company, Ford took vertical integration to an organizational extreme:

> All major decisions were taken centrally and the departments were functional departments ... Ford owned and controlled the production and distribution of all materials and parts necessary to the production of cars. He bought steelworks, glassworks and rubber plantations, and owned railways to transport the needed supplies and to distribute the finished cars.[5]

By doing everything in-house and achieving economies of scale, Ford significantly cut production costs. The superiority of this model persuaded other companies and industries to adopt similar strategies, albeit with more decentralized organizational structures that could more adequately satisfy the ever-growing and increasingly diversified demand for consumer goods.

The heyday of the vertically integrated firm coincided with social-democratic reformism of the New Deal and the rise of the Keynesian welfare state, which provided firms with a range of incentives to retain profits for corporate reinvestment. As Adolf Berle and Gardiner Means wrote in their groundbreaking and influential work on corporate governance in the 1930s, if capitalism were to survive, 'the control of the great corporations should develop into a purely neutral technocracy, balancing a variety of claims by various groups in the community and assigning to each a portion of income stream on the basis of public policy rather than private cupidity'.[6] The retain-and-reinvestment business strategies of vertically integrated firms resembled centralized and technocratic bureaucracies, and had positive effects on the distribution of income. These strategies advanced the interests of US workers by expanding the productive capacities in the US economy and increasing demand for labour: the reinvestment of profits nurtured the expansion of output, leading to an exponential increase in demand for medium-skilled blue-collar and white-collar workers in the manufacturing sectors of the economy. The resulting changes in the structure of employment greatly compressed income inequality: although the automation of handling operations and a considerable number of processing tasks diminished the need for unskilled workers, 'it raised the demand for semiskilled workers capable of repairing and devising machine tools'.[7] Furthermore, 'by encouraging the formation of large corporations, it led to the expansion of new layers of white-collar, relatively well paid jobs – from accounting departments to car dealerships'.[8] Finally, vertical integration implied that the profits of these large firms were shared by a highly heterogeneous workforce:

> Real wages more than doubled in the era 1939 to 1973; wage inequalities between working-class occupations declined, internal labour markets, often with formal systems of seniority promotion, became highly validated ... The pay gap between executives and line workers shrank, but of equal import, so too did the distance between the incomes of janitors and office workers, between garment workers and auto workers, and between retail clerks and truck drivers.[9]

Retain-and-reinvestment business strategies were based on the principle that share ownership should be separated from manager control: corporate managers had to have sufficient autonomy to pursue goals other than short-term profit maximization, including the expansion of market share, the infiltration of new businesses and the prestige that came from producing high-quality products of advanced technology. Alfred Chandler has famously referred to this epoch as 'managerial capitalism', whereby in the entire industrialized world firms clustered in much the same types of industries and grew in much the same manner: 'In nearly all cases they became large, first, by integrating forward (that is, investing in marketing and distribution facilities and personnel); then, by moving backward into purchasing and control of raw and semi-finished material; and sometimes, though much less often, by investing in research and development.'[10]

By the end of the 1960s and during the 1970s, however, the principle of retain and reinvest began running into problems for two interrelated reasons. First, US firms were much larger and more numerous than those in other countries and many of them had grown too large to remain efficient:

> Through internal growth and through merger and acquisition, corporations grew too big with too many divisions in too many different types of businesses. The central offices of these corporations were too far from the actual processes that developed and utilized productive resources to make informed investment decisions about how corporate resources and returns should be allocated to enable strategies based on 'retain and reinvest' to succeed.[11]

Second, growing foreign competition put a squeeze on the oligopolistic profit margins of US firms: for instance, 'there were no longer three car companies with an oligopolistic grip on one continental market, but nearly a dozen global competitors in this key industry, thus for the first time in decades subjecting the once insular managers at Ford and General Motors to real competitive pressures and an insecure hold on power'.[12] This made it more difficult to maintain a model of internalized employment relations – based on the existence of mid-level jobs via internal labour markets in vertically integrated firms and the payment of relatively high wages indexed to productivity – which was made possible 'by the structural context of an oligopolistic, nationally-bound market, which allowed competitive pressures to be subordinated to progressive employment relations'.[13]

Japanese and German competition, especially, forced US companies to rethink their business strategy. Japanese and German firms were particularly strong in the mass-production industries of automobiles and consumer electronics and in the machinery and tools sectors that supplied capital goods to these consumer durable industries. US companies had previously been the world leaders in these sectors, which had been central to the growth in prosperity of the US economy since the 1920s. Japan and Germany were able to challenge the United States in these industries because their manufacturing firms innovated through the development and utilization of integrated skill bases that were broader and deeper than those in which their American competitors had invested, as the work of Lazonick has shown. US industrial development during the twentieth century relied almost exclusively on the managerial organization of new productive capabilities. Compared with US practice, shop-floor workers in Germany and Japan were more involved in strategies of organization learning. The German economy also developed a core of manufacturing firms that were largely Fordist and vertically integrated but in certain respects more flexible than their US counterparts. German firms put a stronger emphasis on technical learning and vocational training, especially since unions were represented in work councils that offered co-determination rights (*Mittbestimmung*) to shop-floor workers on company boards.[14]

Japanese skill bases similarly integrated the capabilities of people with a broader array of functional specialties and a deeper array of hierarchical responsibilities into processes of organizational learning: 'The hierarchical integration of Japanese skill bases extended from the managerial organization to shop-floor production workers and subsidiary firms that served as suppliers and distributors.'[15] 'Fordism' in Japan took a distinctive and more flexible form that is often labelled as 'Toyotism', which reflected a new system of corporate organization and management that was able to produce high-quality goods – especially in the automobile sector – at much lower costs. Japanese firms derived major cost advantages from the organization of the supply process, which was based on the 'just-in-time' principle: frequent deliveries, directly at the place of use (the assembly plant), in order to avoid the investment of capital in large inventories and storage facilities and reduce the personnel costs of transportation within the plant.[16] Shop-floor workers had more responsibilities and autonomy under Toyotism than their counterparts within large US corporations organized on Fordist principles: Japanese workers were expected to assume a multiplicity of tasks as needed, carrying out production, inspection and repair functions themselves. Through the formation of quality circles, groups of employees engaged not only in production but also in the development and design of new products as well as the quality improvement of existing products. In contrast,

> US companies tended to use their managerial organizations to develop and utilize technologies that would enable them to dispense with shop-floor skills in order to prevent production workers from exercising control over the conditions of work and pay. US companies also tended to favour suppliers and distributors who would provide goods and services at the lowest price today, even if it meant that they were not engaged in innovation for tomorrow.[17]

The rise of the shareholder model in the US economy

From retain-and-reinvest to downsize-and-distribute

Struggling with these problems of excessive centralization and innovative competition during the 1970s, major manufacturing US corporations gradually changed their business strategies from retain-and-reinvest towards downsize-and-distribute: 'Under the new regime, top managers downsize the corporations they control, with a particular emphasis on cutting the size of the labour forces they employ, in an attempt to increase the return on equity.'[18]

The underlying idea is that firms had to refocus their business strategy on the most profitable activities with the most added value, and outsource all other, less profitable parts of the production process to suppliers and subcontractors. By shedding and outsourcing the production of high-cost but low-added-value goods and services to these peripheral firms, the core corporation would be able to maximize the return on its assets in order to 'distribute' as much value and income to its shareholders as possible (in the form of dividend and a higher market price for the firms' stocks). From a shareholder perspective, one of the main problems associated with vertical integration and retain-and-reinvestment was that these business strategies were not particularly effective in boosting firms' return on assets (RoA), which equals the net income (profit) of the firm divided by the value of its assets (administrative building, factories, and intangible assets like international property rights). In many cases, the accumulation of assets did not result in a parallel increase in profits, eroding firms' RoA and hence reducing the key metric of shareholder returns: return on equity (RoE) – which is positively correlated with their RoA.[19] By refocusing on the most profitable activities of the firm with the highest value added and outsourcing all other, less profitable activities, downsize-and-distribute business strategies helped to raise firms' RoE by boosting their RoA. As such, the downsize-and-distribute business model was based on what Neil Fligstein has called the 'portfolio approach to the firm', in which the firm was increasingly conceived as 'a collection of assets earning different rates of return'.[20]

The ascent of this model among US corporations was supported by the decline in transportation and ICT costs and the liberalization of trade, which made it much cheaper and more feasible to split the different stages of the production process between units and firms across different countries within integrated global value chains. It became especially profitable for firms to shift the labour-intensive stages of the production process – for example, assembly – to subcontractors in low-wage counties, which reduced labour costs tremendously for the core corporation. As such, downsize-and-distribute business strategies fostered 'factoryless manufacturing' or 'factoryless good producing' firms – that is, 'firms that perform all preproduction activities (such as design and engineering) in their headquarters' country while conducting all their production activities abroad (directly or through purchases of contract manufacturing services)'.[21] While factoryless manufacturing had already emerged in the US apparel sector in the 1950s, it spread much more widely into other sectors in the wake of the ICT revolution a few decades later. The shareholder value strategy emphasizes reducing the footprint of labour and physical assets inside a company:

> Put simply, if what matters to financial markets is return on assets, then dividing a large numerator (monopoly profits) over a small denominator (the costs of labour and physical assets) produces the biggest financial market bang for the buck ... Financial markets thus press firms to contract out physical-asset-heavy production and contract out labour-intensive services when those things are not a core activity for the firm.[22]

Apple Inc. offers a perfect illustration of this model (box 5.1).

Box 5.1 Apple's business strategy

A typical illustration of the rise of the shareholder model is the most profitable company so far of the twenty-first century: Apple Inc. Apple has been able to maintain its market dominance in part through high investments in product innovation and design and the use of state-backed intellectual property rights (IPRs) to protect these innovations. When in the second half of the 1990s Apple's Steve Jobs returned to the company he founded, he set out to revamp Apple's business model, focusing on 'own the consumer' strategies based on high-quality/high-margin technology products like the iPhone and the iPad, which 'lock in' customers with integrated hardware and software components. 'In combining high margins with spectacular revenue growth, Apple raked in 92 percent of mobile smartphone profits in 2015 with merely a 20

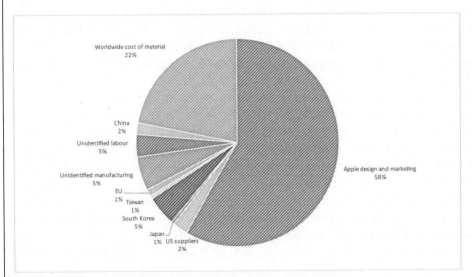

Figure 5.1 Profit distribution in Apple iPhone's global value chain

Source: Kraemer et al. 2011

percent market share.' This has resulted in a phenomenal growth in Apple's stock price, which increased from less than US$2 per share in the beginning of the 2000s to more than US$200 in 2019.[23]

The restructuring of Apple was based on an offshoring strategy that aimed to minimize costs and amplify profits (and hence maximize Apple's share price). Today, the operations of Apple Inc. are organized geographically, with its business activities in the Americas headquartered in Cupertino (California, United States), and its operations in the rest of the world headquartered in Cork (Ireland). R&D is conducted in the United States, while components for Apple products are sourced globally from other companies. Finally, the assembly of Apple products is outsourced to third-party manufacturers in China, and the distribution of these products is again organized via Apple headquarters in the United States and Ireland.

In this way, Apple has been able to minimize its workforce and labour costs. Apple's employee headcount is about 90,000, but 60,000 of these are contract workers in its retail stores. In contrast, the Taiwanese company Foxconn, which is the principal assembler of Apple products, employs 1.4 million workers in China alone. But because the assemblage of different components into final products is a labour-intensive process with low value added, Apple has been able to capture most profits within its global value chains. Figure 5.1 shows the distribution of profits linked to the production and sale of one of the first iPhones.

Agency theory: neoliberalism and corporate governance

The neoliberal interpretation of the decline in US manufacturing competitiveness vis-à-vis Germany and Japan was that large and vertically integrated firms had given rise to an excessive divergence of interests between managers and shareholders. A group of American financial economists thus developed a neoliberal approach to corporate governance known as agency theory, which is based on the assumption that the market is always superior to organizations in the efficient allocation of resources.[24] Agency theory posited that shareholders were the principals and managers were their agents in the governance of the corporation. Since corporate managers were not disciplined by the market mechanism, agency theory argues that they would opportunistically use their control over the allocation of corporate resources and pursue objectives that were contrary to the interests of shareholders. Given that shareholders advance capital to the company and are its residual claimants – that is, they are the lead risk takers, with no guaranteed return – managers are supposed to spend corporate funds only in ways that have been authorized by the shareholders – and that is to maximize profits and shareholder returns. Indeed, as Milton Friedman wrote in what seems to be an early formulation of agency theory: 'There is one and only one social responsibility of business – to use its resources and engage in activities designed to increase its profits so long as it … engages in open and free competition, without deception or fraud.'[25]

Which solutions did agency theory propose to address the principal–agent problem? The first way to align manager and shareholder interests was by developing capital markets that would function as markets for corporate control. Since the 1980s, US stock exchanges have increasingly started to facilitate company takeovers: if managers wanted to avoid being taken over by other companies, they had to make sure that their company performed relatively well in capital markets (see box 5.2 for an explanation of capital markets): in that case the company would have a higher stock price, making a potential takeover by other companies too expensive to be attractive; firms that underperformed on the stock market would have a low stock market valuation and a takeover would be cheap. US economist Henry G. Manne was one of the first to defend the role of equity markets as markets for corporate control: 'The lower the stock price, relative to what it could be with more efficient management, the more attractive the take-over becomes to those who believe that they can manage the company more efficiently. And the potential return from the successful takeover and revitalization of a poorly run company can be enormous.'[26] As such, the conduct of takeovers by companies in that market and the accompanying threat of takeover were seen as external control mechanisms that could solve the agency problem and induce managers to pursue business strategies that maximize the firm's stock market value.[27]

Box 5.2 Capital markets

Capital markets consist of both bond markets and stock markets and allow the firm to directly get capital from the public.[28] Corporate bonds are a certificate of indebtedness that specifies the obligations of the corporation to the holder of the bond: it identifies the time at which the loan will be repaid – that is, the date of maturity – and the rate of interest that will be paid periodically until the loan matures. The buyer of a bond gives his or her money to a company in exchange for this promise of interest and eventual repayment of the amount borrowed (called the principal). The buyer can hold the bond until maturity or can sell the bond at an earlier date to someone else in the corporate bond market. One important feature of a corporate bond is credit risk – the probability that the borrower will fail to pay some of the interest or principal: firms might default on their loans by declaring bankruptcy. When bond buyers perceive that the probability of default is high, they demand a higher interest rate to compensate them for this risk: financially shaky corporations, for instance, raise money by issuing *junk bonds*, which pay very high interest rates.

Corporate bonds tend to be less risky for investors than corporate stocks (or shares), which represent ownership ('equity') in a firm and are therefore a claim to the profits that the firm makes. For example, if a firm has issued a total of 1,000,000 shares, each share represents an ownership claim on 1/1,000,000 of its net asset value (assets minus liabilities). Stocks and bonds are very different types of financial assets: stocks offer investors both higher risk and potentially higher return. If the firm is very profitable, its profits can be distributed to its shareholders. But if the company runs into financial troubles, the bondholders are paid before shareholders receive anything at all.

A company 'goes public' after an initial public offering (IPO), which is the first time that the stock of a private company is offered to the public. After a corporation becomes a public or publicly listed company, these shares are traded between investors on organized stock exchanges. The most important US stock exchanges are the New York Stock Exchange and NASDAQ (National Association of Securities Dealers Automated Quotation system). While large non-US firms are often listed on these major US stock exchanges, most of the world's countries have their own stock exchanges on which the shares of local companies can be traded. The prices at which shares are traded on stock exchanges are determined by the supply and demand for these shares. Since stock represents an ownership claim on a firm, the demand for a firm's outstanding stocks reflects investors' assessment of its future profitability: if these investors are optimistic about a firm's future, they raise their demand for its stock and thereby bid up the price of a share of stock. When investors expect a firm to make little profit or even losses, there will be less demand for its stock and the market price of its shares will fall.

During the 1970s, development of stock markets and markets for corporate control found support from a new source in the US economy – the institutional investor: 'The transfer of stockholding from individual households to institutions such as mutual funds, pension funds and life insurance companies made possible the takeovers advocated by agency theorists and gave shareholders much more collective power to influence the yields and market values of the corporate stocks they held.'[29] A mutual fund is a financial institution that sells shares to small investors and uses the proceeds to buy a selection of various types of stocks and bonds – its portfolio. A key benefit of mutual funds, according to neoclassical and neoliberal theory, is that they allowed people with small amounts of money to diversify:

> people who hold a diverse portfolio of stocks and bonds face less risk because they have only a small stake in each company. Mutual funds make this diversification easy: with only a few hundred dollars, a person can buy shares in a mutual fund and, indirectly, become the part owner or creditor of hundreds of major companies.[30]

Pension funds collect the savings of middle-class and wealthy households to invest in highly rated corporate equity and bonds, making the savers' retirement income increasingly dependent on the overall performance of capital markets. It was widely claimed that mutual funds and pension funds would contribute to the 'democratization of finance' by giving lower- and middle-class households a stake in corporate capitalism. Mutual fund companies, for instance, allegedly give ordinary people access to the skills of professional money managers, who would buy only 'the stock of those companies that they view as having a profitable future and sell the stock of companies with less promising prospects'.[31] Corporations increasingly shifted employees from defined benefit pensions, which guaranteed an income in retirement, to defined contribution plans that were overwhelmingly invested in the stock market: by 2000 more than half of US households owned shares, compared to just one in five two decades earlier.[32] These developments gave rise to what Adam Harmes called a 'mass investment culture' that served to 'reinforce neoliberal ideology by creating the appearance of a material link between the interests of workers and those of financial capital'.[33]

Performance-related manager compensation based on stock options was the second mechanism through which agency theory proposed addressing the principal–agent problem between shareholders and managers. Advocates of agency theory believed it was highly problematic that the remuneration of managers and CEOs had become detached from the firm's stock market performance: 'In most publicly held companies, the compensation of top executives is virtually independent of performance. On average, corporate America pays its most important leaders like bureaucrats. Is it any wonder then that so many CEOs act like bureaucrats rather than the value-maximizing entrepreneurs companies need to enhance their standing in world markets?'[34] The solution they proposed was a bonus system based on stock options. A stock option is a privilege that gives the holder the right to buy a stock at an agreed price within a certain period of time. Stock options were increasingly seen as an effective way to incentivize top managers to pursue shareholder maximization. If a significant part of the CEO's salary were performance-based in the form of stock options of its firms, she or he would have a clear incentive to engage in business strategies that would increase the firm's stock market price; if the stock price in the market rose significantly above the price agreed in the stock option agreement, the CEO could exercise the options by buying the stocks and selling them for a profit at a higher price in the market.

Table 5.1 Average CEO compensation in the US economy, 1973–2013

	CEO annual compensation	Stock market indices		CEO/worker income ratio
	(US$ thousand)	S&P 500	Dow Jones	
1973	1,054	496	4,268	22.3
1978	1,442	310	2,652	29.9
1989	2,685	578	4,488	58.7
1995	5,684	810	6,731	122.6
2000	19,880	1,903	14,298	383.4
2007	18,274	1,636	14,593	351.3
2010	12,286	1,200	11,235	227.9
2011	12,484	1,294	12,206	231.8
2012	14,074	1,379	12,965	278.2
2013	15,175	1,644	15,010	295.9

Source: Bivens and Mishel 2013; Davis and Mishel 2014

While the practice of giving stock options as part of managers' compensation schemes already existed in the 1950s and 1960s, it started booming in the 1980s and – especially – in the 1990s. Until 1991, the 1934 Securities Exchange Act – which was part of the stringent financial regulations that came with the New Deal – required that top executives had to wait at least six months before selling the acquired stocks; in this way, top executives were prevented from reaping short-swing profits – that is, short-term profits at the expense of their firm – when they exercised their stock options. In 1991, the US Securities and Exchange Commission determined that henceforth the six-month waiting period would begin at the grant date – not the exercise date. Since the option grant date is always at least one year before the option exercise date, 'top executives, as company insiders, can sell the shares acquired from stock options immediately upon exercise and keep what would have previously been short-swing gains'.[35] Due to the growing use of stock options in remuneration schemes, the average income of US CEOs grew exponentially from 1980 to 2000 and became increasingly connected to the dynamics of the US stock market (table 5.1). As a result, the CEO-to-worker compensation ratio skyrocketed from about 25 in the 1970s to almost 400 in 2000.

Rent-seeking and managerial power

Samuel Knafo and Sahil Dutta have recently called the shareholder revolution a myth that 'has led scholars to lend too much power to shareholders and underestimate the role of corporate managers as the agents of the financialization of corporate governance'.[36] The rise in executive pay seems related to a broader shift in structures of corporate governance towards what Peter Gourevitch and James Shinn call 'managerism', in which opportunities for well-positioned elites to extract resources increase.[37] Rather than addressing the principal–agent problem and realigning the interests between managers and shareholders, a countervailing hypothesis is that CEO compensation based on stock options reflects the growing capacity of managers to engage in such extraction.

There are some indications that managerial power and rents have played an important part in the rise of CEO pay. First, CEO compensation arrangements do not seem to reward relative performance, as the work of Lucian Bebchuk and Jesse Fried has shown.[38] A well-designed contract for executive pay should offer rewards based on performance relative to competitors in the same industry: executives should be rewarded if their company performs less badly than other companies in an industry where stock prices are down across the board, yet should not be rewarded if their company's stock price rises less than that of rival firms in an industry in which there is a general stock market boom. Compensation arrangements for CEOs and top executives are usually 'camouflaged' to look like the result of contractual arrangements that reward relative performance: 'managers will prefer compensation practices that obscure the total amount of compensation, that appear to be more performance-based than they actually are, and that package pay in ways that make it easier to justify and defend'.[39] A principal example of such camouflage is the construction of stock options that largely reward the luck of whether the stock market rises or falls in response to changes in macroeconomic conditions rather than to the specific performance of the firm. For instance, the stock price of an oil-producing firm may increase due to a rise in the world oil price, rewarding its executives for reasons that are beyond their managerial control.

Second, CEOs often have a disproportionate influence over the composition of company boards, which are responsible for decisions on CEO compensation schemes. Top management usually plays a role in selecting directors, who are often paid hundreds of thousands of US dollars to attend six to ten meetings a year. To safeguard their lucrative position, company board directors are more likely to approve than to reject exorbitant CEO pay packages:

> It is extremely rare for directors to be removed because they allowed the company's CEO to be overpaid. By contrast, if a director were to make a point of objecting to a pay increase to which her colleagues assented, ... she could jeopardize her future as a director. With this asymmetry in incentives, it should not be surprising that directors are generally happy to go along with high CEO pay.[40]

Shareholders find it more difficult to contest these decisions in the context of dispersed ownership: because dispersed shareholders can be expected to be rationally apathetic, managers will be relatively unconstrained in their action. Although the rise of institutional investors led to an increasing concentration of ownership in the US economy (see below), the managers of these institutional investors manage other people's money and therefore have little interest in the running of the company or avoiding exorbitant pay packages.

Finally, CEO pay is on average more than three times as high in the United States as in the rest of the advanced capitalist world, as table 5.2. shows. Existing cultural norms about the ideal CEO-to-worker compensation ratio cannot easily account for this observation: in all countries the actual ratio is much higher than the ideal one, and the ideal US ratio does not differ very much from the ideal ratio in countries (like Germany and France) where the actual ratio is much lower than in the United States. Another possible explanation is that CEO compensation in the United States is based more on equity performance than in most other advanced capitalist countries. In the 2000s, an average of 57 per cent of the total remuneration of US top executives was paid out in equity (and another 20 per cent as bonuses). In most other advanced economies, the usage of equity-based pay is significantly lower than in the United States, although it is clear that equity-based remuneration tends to be much more prominent in the Anglo-Saxon countries than in continental European countries. In other words, 'the comparative evidence of American (or at least Anglo) exceptionalism with regard to executive pay suggests that there is nothing about the structure of modern capitalism that makes such

Table 5.2 CEO-to-worker compensation ratio in selected countries: actual vs ideal, 2012

	Average compensation (US$)		Ratio	
	CEO	Worker	Actual	Ideal
Australia	4,183,419	44,993	93	8.3
Austria	1,567,908	43,555	36	5.0
Denmark	2,186,880	45,560	48	2.0
France	3,965,312	39,132	101	6.7
Germany	5,912,781	40,223	147	6.3
Japan	2,353,591	35,143	67	6.0
Norway	2,551,420	43,990	58	2.3
Portugal	1,205,326	22,742	53	5.0
Spain	4,399,915	34,387	128	3.0
Sweden	3,358,326	37,734	89	2.2
Switzerland	7,435,816	50,242	148	5.0
United Kingdom	3,758,412	44,743	84	5.3
United States	12,259,894	34,654	354	6.7

Source: Harvard Business Review

extraordinary increases in executive salaries inevitable or even likely'.[41] This suggests that there is a link between CEO compensation, corporate governance and varieties of capitalism.

Shareholder vs stakeholder models in varieties of capitalism

Market-based vs bank-based corporate finance

The main tradition in comparative political economy attributes differences between national varieties of capitalism to differences in corporate governance and the differentiated role equity markets play in corporate finance. US political economist John Zysman drew, among others, a distinction between 'market-based' and 'bank-based' systems of corporate finance.[42] As we will see in this section, these different types of financial system have been associated with, respectively, the shareholder capitalism of the LMEs and the stakeholder capitalism of other varieties.

There is broad consensus in the CPE and IPE literature that the prominence of markets for corporate equity distinguishes the historical experience of Anglo-Saxon capitalism. In the continental European countries and Japan, bank credit played a more important role than stock markets in offering funding for industrialization and corporate investment. Banks held long-term relationships with industrial firms by offering patient capital – that is, long-term capital that is not withdrawn in the face of short-term oscillations of capital markets or temporary falls in corporate profitability or cash flows.[43] Apart from the more prominent role of bank credit in financing industry, ownership of firms tends to be more concentrated in the CMEs and – to a lesser extent – in the MMEs than in the LMEs. With limited exit options, owners of large equity stakes can be expected to behave quite differently from portfolio investors or small shareholders operating in highly liquid markets. The conventional wisdom holds that strategic investors like banks offer management the luxury of pursuing long-termist strategies.

The first numerical column of table 5.3 reports on the relative importance of stock markets and banking in fourteen OECD countries during the 1990s and 2000s. The data reported in this column were obtained by dividing the average total stock market valuation of publicly listed firms from 1990 to 2010 by the average value of bank credits to the private sector during the 2000s. Any ratio of less than one means that the total value of outstanding bank credit to the private sector exceeded the total value of tradable corporate stocks. By this measure, the LMEs clearly stand out as far more dependent on stock markets than other economies. US firms have also relied heavily on bond markets for funding, so the American system of corporate finance would look even more on capital markets based in comparison to other LMEs as well as to CMEs if we take into account the role of bonds as a source of corporate finance.[44]

Ownership structures of firms in CMEs differ considerably from those in LMEs.[45] German law allowed commercial banks to own corporate equity, so the large commercial banks traditionally held significant equity stakes in many companies with which they maintained long-term relationships.[46] Another important source of ownership concentration in Germany and other CMEs is family ownership and cross-shareholding among non-financial firms. The second and third numerical columns of table 5.3 illustrate the differences between liberal and coordinated market economies in this respect: more than 60 per cent of the largest twenty firms in the LMEs are 'widely held' – here defined as the absence of any owner that controls more than 20 per cent of the shareholder votes in the firm in question. The contrast between LMEs and CMEs in terms of ownership concentration is even more pronounced for smaller firms. The dominance of 'insider systems' of corporate governance is also revealed by the final column of table 5.3, which reports the index of minority shareholder protection (MSP) – ranging from zero to 100 – based on formal and informal rules determining the rights of minority shareholders who are not represented on the board. Higher scores on this index indicate that 'insiders' represented on boards of directors (management, large shareholders and banks with long-term stakes) are more constrained by 'outsiders' (minority shareholders) without any special relationship to the company in question. Large shareholders tend to behave differently from portfolio investors or small shareholders, as they can less easily sell ('liquidate') their large equity stake. The conventional VoC interpretation is that these sources of patient capital have offered firms more opportunities to pursue long-term business strategies.

Table 5.3 Selected measures of corporate finance ownership, 1990–2010

	Equity relative to bank credit[a]	Widely held firms percentage of total[b]		Minority shareholder protection
		Large firms	Small firms	
Nordic CMEs	*0.78*	*31*	*20*	*43*
Denmark	0.28	40	30	36
Norway	0.31	25	20	48
Sweden	0.78	25	10	46
Continental CMEs	*0.69*	*30*	*18*	*33*
Austria	0.25	5	0	30
Belgium	0.88	5	20	34
Germany	0.41	50	10	33
Netherlands	0.77	30	10	36
LMEs	*1.46*	*67*	*60*	*94*
Australia	0.86	65	30	71
Canada	1.69	60	60	83
United Kingdom	1.23	100	60	97
United States	2.05	80	90	97
Other	*0.73*	*57*	*10*	*35*
France	0.81	60	0	47
Italy	0.65	20	0	24
Japan	0.70	90	30	37

Source: World Bank; Bank of International Settlements; Pontusson 2005; Gourevitch and Shinn 2005

[a] Average stock market capitalization (in per cent of GDP) divided by the average value of outstanding bank credits to the private sector (in per cent of GDP), 1990–2010.

[b] Percentage of publicly traded firms without an ultimate owner (individual or family) who controls at least 20 per cent of shareholder votes. Large firms are defined as the twenty largest firms in each country, based on market capitalization at the end of 1995.

Corporate governance and institutional complementarities

The divergence between the LMEs and CMEs in terms of financial systems is not a coincidence. For a number of reasons, market-based financial systems work well in the context of flexible and decentralized labour markets, while bank-based financial systems are more compatible with centralized labour markets. A central assumption of the VoC framework is that LMEs and CMEs each have their own institutional complementarities: that is, institutions in one domain are strongly supported and reinforced by institutions in other domains. VoC approaches have identified such complementarities between five interdependent institutional domains: (1) the financial system; (2) corporate governance; (3) industrial relations between employers and employees; (4) the skills system; and (5) innovation.[47]

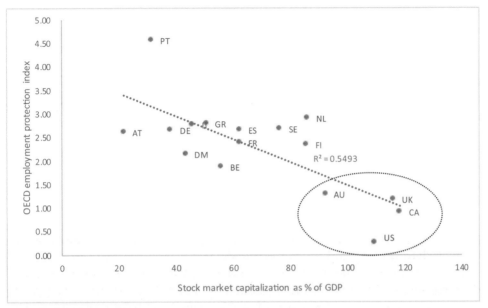

Figure 5.2 Employment protection and stock market capitalization

Source: World Bank; OECD

AT = Austria; AU = Australia; BE = Belgium; CA = Canada; DE = Germany; DM = Denmark; ES = Spain; FI = Finland; FR = France; GR = Greece; IT = Italy; NL = Netherlands; PT = Portugal; SE = Sweden; UK = United Kingdom; US = United States.

R—[54] is the square of the correlation and measures the extent to which the variation in one variable can be attributed to the variation in another variable. The correlation is meaningful if R—[54] > 0.35.

According to the original VoC framework, national models of capitalism would cluster around two ideal types – the LMEs and CMEs – each of which is associated with distinctive institutional complementarities. LMEs have capital market-based financial systems that require shareholder models of corporate governance and educational systems that encourage investment in general and transferable general skills through the school system. As firms in these countries rely on arm's-length and dispersed equity markets and risk being victims of hostile takeovers, flexible labour markets are needed to allow their managers to focus on current profitability and short-term stock price evaluation: '[L]abour markets allowing for high levels of labour turnover and competitive wage-setting will be more efficient, because they enable managers to reduce staffing levels quickly or to hold down wages in response to fluctuations in current profitability.'[48] In contrast, CMEs have bank-dominated financial systems that are institutionally complementary to regulated labour and product markets, stakeholder models of corporate governance and educational systems stimulating investment in industry- and firm-specific skills: 'firms that do not have to sustain current profitability [and take into account short-term stock market fluctuations] are better placed to make long-term commitments to their employees about wages and jobs, and therefore to realize the gains available from deploying production regimes based on such commitments'.[49] As an illustration of these institutional complementarities, figure 5.2 shows a negative correlation between a country's total stock market capitalization – which measures the total market value of its publicly listed firms and is the most often used indicator of stock market development – and the degree of legal employment protection.

While top income dynamics received only scant attention in the original VoC framework, the institutional dynamics it describes are relevant and useful to an understanding of differences between the Anglo-Saxon countries and the rest of the advanced capitalist world. LMEs dominate the group of countries with higher top incomes shares, whilst CMEs tend to have lower shares (chapter 1). Since firms in CMEs rely to a greater extent on bank lending and concentrated ownership structures, top managers have less bargaining power vis-à-vis shareholders and other stakeholders.

Most specifically, labour representatives have strong incentives to resist the introduction of US-style remuneration practices.[50] Exorbitant management compensation reduces the share of profits that can be distributed to the company's workers in the form of wages or expansion of jobs, while equity-based remuneration schemes are linked to downsize-and-distribute business strategies that involve labour-shedding. Furthermore, unions and workers can have a direct influence over corporate decisions regarding the size and structure of top executive compensation. In most CMEs, workers have a legal right to be represented in medium and large firms' decision-making processes through work councils. Co-determination is deeply rooted in Germany's tradition of corporate governance, which has an explicit social dimension: co-determination on the company level is meant to introduce equal participation of shareholders and employees in a firm's decision-making. Co-determination and worker representation promote 'equality of work and capital' – which 'requires companies not only to consider the interests of the shareholders but also those of the employees' – and long-term business strategies: 'In works councils and supervisory boards the employees, just like the employer, need to keep an eye on the long term development of the company. This is why all of the laws on co-determination are directed towards enabling fruitful co-operation between both sides and creating a productive balance of interests.'[51]

These differences in labour representation in corporate governance are also connected to the differences in the skill systems of LMEs and CMEs.[52] In the previous chapter we have seen that firms in the LMEs rely more on transferable general skills, whereas firms in the CMEs – especially those in the export-oriented manufacturing sectors – primarily depend on non-transferable firm- and industry-specific skills. When employee skills are portable across firms or investments in skills are low, employees may favour exit over voice in response to grievances – that is, they might prefer to switch jobs instead of trying to change managerial decisions. Conversely, when employees and workers have firm-specific skills, their greater dependence on the firm makes the option to exit more difficult. Thus, 'investments in firm-specific skills create incentives to exercise voice in how those skills are formed and deployed. In particular, employees may have a long-term vested interest in safeguarding the organization and their job security. Therefore, skills influence the degree to which employees have a "stake" in the firm.'[53] In LMEs, vacancies are more likely to be filled through external labour markets (hiring from outside the firm): 'In these labour markets, managers and employees tend to develop transferable skills, reflecting a culture of generalist management and strong financial orientation.'[54] To recruit outside managers and retain them, remuneration schemes must incorporate performance-based incentives with a high proportion of variable pay in the form of bonuses and stock options. The university system also reflects the need for portable managerial skills: a full quarter of American graduate students earn a Master of Business Administration degree (MBA).[55]

Varieties of innovation and business strategies

The different sets of institutional complementarities that can be found in LMEs and CMEs encourage firms to pursue different kinds of innovation strategies: whereas firms in the CMEs perform best in incremental innovation, the institutional infrastructure of the LMEs favours radical innovation. In his bestselling book *The Competitive Advantage of Nations* (1990), Michael Porter made the important observation that nations have developed different patterns of innovation because of country-specific institutional environments in which their firms operate: he showed that the strengths of the United Kingdom and the United States were in areas of radical innovation and rapidly changing technologies, stressing the key role of the financial system in determining these outcomes. More specifically, he argued that nations with financial systems dominated by capital markets excelled at funding and promoting radical technological innovation because they were able to provide risk capital.[56]

VoC approaches have sought to elaborate on Porter's basic distinction in order to better define the institutional preconditions for different sorts of innovation. A crucial point is that national variants of capitalism will have differential innovation performance across sectors and may tend to further specialize around these particular areas of production. CMEs – but also countries like Japan – 'often prove better able to generate the collective inputs necessary to foster incremental innovations within stable organizational settings'. Bank-dominated financial systems bolster long-term capital investments, which together with highly skilled manual workers and co-operative labour relations 'all help foster innovations depending on incremental improvement of process or product design'.[57] Incremental innovation is particularly important in well-established industrial sectors. This explains why countries such as Germany and Japan have a comparative advantage in the production of durable consumption goods (cars, electronics) and capital goods (machinery, tools, engines).

By contrast, competitive labour markets and market-oriented financial systems are better able to generate the labour mobility and venture capital necessary to pursue radical innovation. Venture capital offers funds to start-ups – that is, small, early-stage, emerging firms that are deemed to have high growth potential. Venture capital funds invest in these early-stage companies in exchange for an ownership stake in them. As such, these funds take on the risk of financing risky start-ups in the hope that some of the firms they support will become successful, allowing venture capitalists to sell their stake at a high profit when these firms are publicly listed. For example, Peter Thiel, a famous US venture capitalist, sold a large part his 10.2 per cent stake in Facebook, for which he had paid US$500,000 in 2005, for more than US$1 billion after Facebook went public in 2012. Well-developed capital markets thus enhance the supply of high-risk capital by giving venture capitalists an exit mechanism to sell on successful start-ups during their IPO. Start-ups are usually based on an innovative technology or business model and are normally from the high-technology industries, such as ICT or biotechnology, which is why the United States and the United Kingdom have a comparative advantage in these industries (see also chapter 4). The presence of highly developed capital markets and the prevalence of MBAs in university programmes have also underpinned these countries' competitive advantage in financial services.

The comparative advantage of the United States in ICT and financial services illuminates why the shareholder model of corporate governance and the associated downsize-and-distribute business strategy became so dominant there. Recall that this strategy involves concentrating on the most profitable activities and outsourcing all other activities to domestic and foreign suppliers and contractors. IPRs – patents, copyrights, trademarks, etc. – are a key source of profits in ICT industries. IPRs give firms the exclusive right to exploit and benefit from their creations and the right to exclude others from the use of their creations. IPRs are state-backed monopoly rights of exploitation and give rise to state-backed monopoly profits. The shareholder model of corporate governance induces large US firms to concentrate on the production of these intangible assets. The profitability of large firms in the ICT and high-tech industries increasingly stems from their control over intangible assets, as Herman Schwartz argues: 'The biggest firms in terms of market capitalization and profitability are those controlling the most valuable patent and IPR portfolios. In a significant change in industrial organization, these firms largely subcontract everything not related to the direct production of their IPRs, shrinking their employee base to the absolute minimum.'[58]

In their recent book *Capitalism Without Capital*, Jonathan Haskel and Stian Westlake have shown that, while all advanced capitalist economies have started to invest more in intangible assets – IPRs linked to product design, branding,

R&D – than in tangible assets like machinery, buildings and computers, the rise of the intangible economy is particularly a US phenomenon. In contrast to the vertically integrated firms of the mid-twentieth century whose profitability depended on their control over physical capital, the market value of contemporary US firms – especially those in ICT sectors of the 'new economy' – increasingly relies on their intangible assets. For instance, 'The traditional assets of plant and equipment were only US$3bn, a trifling 4 percent of Microsoft's assets and 1 percent of its market value.'[59] The IPR phenomenon has not been limited to high-tech firms in the ICT sectors. Rather, the distinguishing features of the intangible economy are the adoption of a profit strategy based on IPR production and outsourcing. This combination extends all the way from high-tech firms (e.g. Apple) to decidedly low-tech firms that control brands (e.g. Nike) and/or sell franchising rights (e.g. McDonald's), that is, rights that allow local firms to use the franchisor's business model and brands. In the 1960s, *tangible* assets such as plant and equipment constituted 80 per cent of the stock market capitalization of the S&P 500 – the 500 largest publicly listed US companies. By 2005, *intangible* assets constituted 80 per cent of the market capitalization of the S&P 500.[60]

Financialization of non-financial corporations

While the presence of well-developed capital markets and the abundant supply of venture capital might have supported the capacity of US firms to excel in radical innovation in ICT, it is more questionable whether the shareholder model of corporate governance also fosters innovation and productivity growth in the long term. The growing shareholder-value orientation of firms has been associated with an excessive short-termism in their business strategies, leading to a long-term decline in productive investment and productivity growth.[61]

Two mechanisms can account for the negative relationship between real investment and what is usually called the *financialization of the non-financial corporate sector* in the literature. First, non-financial corporations have increasingly started to accumulate financial assets rather than investing in the expansion of their productive capacities. Greta Krippner has shown in her work that returns on financial investments assume a growing share of non-financial corporate profits in the US economy: the ratio of portfolio income to corporate cash flow increased exponentially among non-financial firms, from less than 10 per cent in the 1950s and 1960s to more than 40 per cent in the 1990s.[62] Depending on one's particular business model and relative success, financialization of corporations can take two distinctive forms. For firms like Apple, profits ensuing from production structurally dwarf returns from financial investments; these firms amass profits and reserves far beyond their capacity to reinvest them in productive capacities (i.e. the 'real' economy), so they increasingly invest their reserves in financial assets and come to resemble large financial investors.[63] For other firms, returns from financial activities have equalled or even exceeded returns from productive activities. A classic example here is General Electric, which set up GE Capital to provide a variety of financial services – ranging from extending consumer credit to selling leasing contracts – to its customers.

Second, shareholder capitalism has been associated with increased payments to financial markets, which impede real investment by decreasing available internal funds as well as by shortening the planning horizon of the firm's management. More specifically, financialization of non-financial corporations has featured 'increased financial pay-out ratios in the form of interest payments, dividend payments and stock buybacks'.[64] The practice of share buybacks especially is often criticized for wasting firms' internal funds to the benefit of shareholders and top managers. Using these funds to buy back some of the company's traded shares is an effective way to boost its stock price, as future profits will need to be distributed among a smaller group of shareholders. This common practice calls into question the role of stock markets in funding corporate investment. While conventional wisdom holds that the role of the stock market is to enable businesses to raise capital for investment in productive capacity, 'the historical evidence shows that only in periods of speculative fervour such as the late 1920s, the late 1950s, and the late 1990s has the stock market provided significant amounts of funding to companies'.[65]

To boost their stock market valuation, publicly listed US corporations have increasingly used their internal funds for share buybacks. Over the decade 2004–13, 454 companies that were in the S&P 500 in March 2014 and that were publicly listed over the ten years spent US$3.4 trillion in stock buybacks. In fact, net issuance of stocks was *negative* over these years: the number of stocks that were repurchased by corporations exceeded the number of new stocks that were issued and sold to the public. J. W. Mason argues that these developments reflect a 'rentier-dominated' corporate governance regime, in which 'corporate finance is no longer a system for getting funds into firms, but is instead a system for getting funds out of them'.[66]

These observations cast strong doubts on the effectiveness of capital market-based financial systems and the shareholder model of corporate governance to promote long-term innovation and productivity growth. Another potential constraint on long-term investment indirectly linked to the shareholder model is the increasing concentration of capital:

> IPRs give some US firms monopoly or near monopoly power in the global (and local) commodity chains they construct. The extension of US IPR law through various trade treaties … allows US IPR firms to capture a disproportionate share of global profits via that monopoly power. This shifts claims on value added towards those firms, concentrating profits into a small number of US firms.[67]

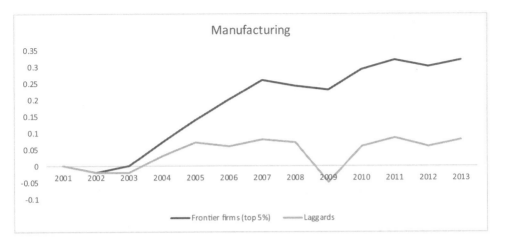

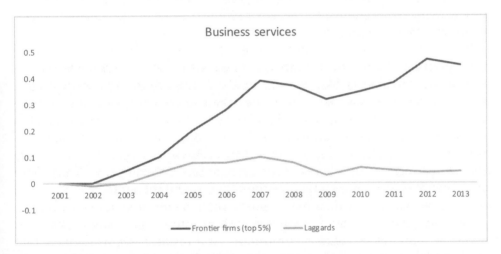

Figure 5.3 Widening productivity gap between global frontier firms and other firms, 2001–13
(a) Manufacturing
(b) Business services

Source: Andrews et al. 2016

The global frontier is measured by the average of log labour productivity for the top 5 per cent of companies with the highest productivity levels within each industry. Laggards capture the average log productivity of all the other firms. Unweighted averages across 2-digit industries are shown for manufacturing and services, normalized to 0 in the starting year. The vertical axes represent log differences from the starting year: for instance, the frontier in manufacturing has a value of about 0.3 in the final year, which corresponds to approximately 30 per cent higher in productivity in 2013 than in 2001.

From 2006 to 2018, US firms accounted for a disproportionate 33.9 per cent of cumulative profits generated by all firms appearing on the Forbes Global 2000 list – the world's largest 2,000 firms by market capitalization – and firms in IPR-intensive sectors were responsible for a disproportionate 26.6 per cent of those profits.[68] An influential study from the OECD has shown that there has been a growing divergence between the leading 'top 5 per cent' firms (the global frontier firms) and 'laggard' firms in terms of productivity levels (figure 5.3) – a manifestation of the 'winner-take-all' dynamics that are especially strong among ICT services (e.g. computer programming, software engineering, data storage, etc).[69] The rise in inter-firm inequality is a direct outcome of downsize-and-distribute business strategies, which have limited the scope for improving productivity in those firms where work has been outsourced. The low productivity performance of these laggard firms results from their focus on the production of low added value goods and services that the leading firms have outsourced.[70] It also depressed *aggregate* productivity growth: aggregate productivity was significantly weaker in industries where productivity divergence was more pronounced.[71]

Parallel to the growing concentration of corporate power is the growing concentration of stock ownership associated with *asset manager capitalism*: the rise of asset managers like pension funds, mutual funds and, increasingly, exchange traded funds 'has transformed the United States from a dispersed-ownership economy with weak shareholders into a concentrated-ownership economy with strong shareholders'.[72] The 'Big Three' asset managers – BlackRock, Vanguard and State Street Global Advisors – together hold more than 20 per cent of the shares of the average S&P 500 company. While these asset managers do not directly own these shares and therefore have less 'skin in the game' than individual shareholders, their clients predominantly consist of wealthy investors who *do* have a persistent interest in business strategies aimed at shareholder value maximization. As a result, it seems unlikely that they will use their voting power to divert publicly listed firms away from these strategies. One study, for example, found that the Big Three asset managers side with company management in more than 90 per cent of votes, echoing 'increasing concerns of various stakeholders about the lacking response of investment funds on critical corporate governance issues such as executive pay'.[73] So given the highly unequal distribution of wealth, the growing importance of these asset managers as stock market investors should be expected to consolidate the shareholder model of corporate governance at the expense of deepening the financialization of the non-financial corporate sector and further weakening the power of labour.

Corporate governance and growth models

The financialization of the non-financial sector in the LMEs played a central role in their quest to find a replacement for their Fordist wage-led growth model. Robert Boyer was one of the first critical scholars to ask from a Regulationist perspective whether the rise of the shareholder model would create a new 'finance-led growth regime' in which 'the financial regime plays the central role that used to be attributed to the wage-labour nexus under Fordism':[74]

> Many giant mergers, capital mobility between countries, pressures on corporate governance, diffusion of equity among a larger fraction of population; all these transformations [could] lead to a totally novel regulation mode, currently labelled 'the new economy' ... [which] would combine labour-market flexibility, price stability, developing high tech sectors, booming stock market and credit to sustain the rapid growth of consumption, and permanent optimism of expectations in firms.[75]

A key problem of financialized growth is that the increasing stock market orientation of Anglo-Saxon firms depressed aggregate demand by leading to a decline in long-term productive investment and fixed capital formation. The financialization of these firms also required flexibilized labour markets, which had the effect of depressing the consumption capacity of the lower- and middle-class workers by dampening wage growth. Yet economic growth in the LMEs was driven by an expansion of consumption, as we have seen in previous chapters: in the United States, for instance, the share of consumption in GDP grew from about 65 per cent in the 1960s to more than 70 per cent in the 2000s. The fact that rising income inequality coincided with a rising share of consumption in GDP points to trickle-down consumption, whereby growing income and consumption at the top end of the income distribution induced households on lower tiers of the distribution to save less and consume more. The steep increase of the income share of the top 1 per cent helps explain why households just below the top of the income distributions reduced their savings and accumulated debt in the 1990s and 2000s. The explanation, based on the idea that household expenditure decisions are to a large extent directed at maintaining or achieving a high social status – Thorstein Veblen's 'conspicuous consumption'[76] – is that the skyrocketing incomes of the top 1 per cent, and the exorbitant lifestyles enabled by these incomes, put social pressure on those below the top of the income distribution to emulate the consumption patterns of the top 1 per cent by saving less and spending in excess of income.[77]

The expansion of consumption in the US economy in the face of rising income inequality reflects the increasing impact of asset markets on the consumption behaviour of US households through so-called wealth effects. Sufficient stocks of private property (equity, real estate) are concentrated in the United States to allow households to raise consumption based on rising asset prices and enhanced access to credit. Although the distribution of US equity ownership remains heavily skewed towards the richest households – with the top 10 per cent owning about 90 per cent of publicly traded shares – increasing shareholdership made the returns to savings of a growing group of US households – and their consumption – dependent on the performance of the stock market.[78] The growing importance of stock markets in bolstering household consumption through wealth effects is a key reason why central banks in the LMEs have adopted relatively expansionary monetary policies that put a floor on these markets and prevented market slumps from developing into market meltdowns (chapter 3). Another possible reason is the increasing alignment of large industrial and financial firms in the US economy, described in this chapter, which led, according to Gerald Epstein, 'to a greater emphasis by Alan Greenspan and the US Federal Reserve on financial asset appreciation as a goal of monetary policy'.[79]

While the VoC literature rightly points to persistent cross-national differences in corporate governance, continental European firms and economies have not been entirely absolved from financialization. National banking systems and capital markets in the Eurozone have undergone substantial institutional changes under the pressure of European financial integration. Developing integrated European financial markets has always been a priority for European policymakers, who have traditionally envied the alleged effectiveness of the United States' deep capital markets in channelling the savings of millions of households to the most profitable companies. However, the integration of European financial markets was plagued from the start by a battle of financial systems, in which the bank-based models of the continental European countries had to compete with the capital market-based model of the United Kingdom. Given the liberalization bias of EU regulation, it is unsurprising that European financial integration privileged the capital market-based model over the bank-based models.[80] Critical political economists have argued that European financial and monetary integration was 'part of a broader strategy to revitalize the European economy by creating a strong European base within a transnational finance-led regime of accumulation'.[81] European business elites and policymakers hoped that integrated stock markets would improve investment conditions and unleash high-risk capital in ways that would make European firms more competitive in the high-tech sectors of the new economy.[82]

At the same time, soaring public debt levels put pressure on European governments to promote private defined-contribution pension schemes, as the ageing of the population and slowdown of economic growth cast doubt on the fiscal sustainability of publicly guaranteed defined-benefit schemes. Most continental and Southern European countries still overwhelmingly rely on public social insurance, yet there has been a gradual replacement of defined-benefit pensions schemes by defined-contribution ones in almost all OECD countries. CMEs like the Netherlands, Denmark, Sweden and Switzerland introduced mandatory or quasi-mandatory private pension provision, leading to a massive expansion in the size of assets held by private pension funds.

The inflow of pension savings turned corporations into 'corporate rentiers who increasingly face an incentive structure that rewards equity investments – for portfolio-building reasons, for reasons of mergers and acquisitions, or as equity buybacks – and punishes, relatively, productive investment'.[83] As such, 'the rise of institutional investors – such as private pension funds – pushing for shareholder value maximisation' could pose 'the greatest threat for the resilience of CMEs and their encompassing welfare states'.[84]

What are the implications of the capital market bias of European financial integration? Although banks remain the principal source of external finance for non-financial corporations in CMEs and MMEs, it is clear that stock markets have grown strongly over the past few decades. As figure 5.4 shows, stock market capitalization of publicly listed firms grew from less than 20 per cent of GDP in these countries to more than 70 per cent in the 2000s. Large firms in continental Europe increasingly depend on stock and bond markets for external funding, leading to a more internationalized investor base that has promoted a stronger shareholder orientation. At the same time, banks reduced the size of their equity stakes in individual non-financial firms and loosened their long-term relationship with these firms, restraining their access to patient capital. The growing dependence of large publicly listed firms on capital market funding increased their shareholder orientation, which had a fundamentally negative impact on investment by European firms in the

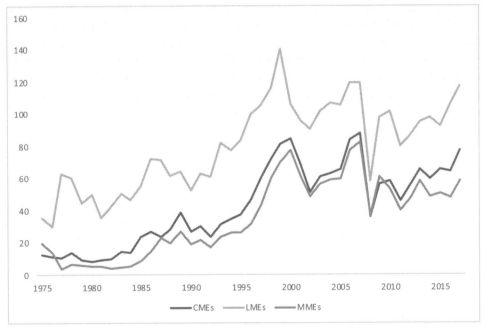

Figure 5.4 Stock market capitalization of publicly listed firms (in percentage of GDP), 1975–2017

Source: OECD

last few decades, and contributed to the fall in the labour income share in continental European economies.[85] Manufacturing firms in the CMEs have increasingly outsourced less profitable activities and made use of non-standard employment, externalizing risks to low value added suppliers, service providers and peripheral workforces in ways that contributed to increasingly segmented and polarized labour markets (chapter 4).[86] These developments depressed domestic demand in the CMEs and made their growth more reliant on exports.

On the other hand, banks continue to play a dominant role in the allocation of credit in continental Europe. While large German firms have increasingly turned to international securities markets – from 1993 to 2005, international corporate debt of large firms rose from 0.3 to 3 per cent of German GDP – there has been no clear, long-term structural shift from bank loans to securities in Germany.[87] In France, equity market capitalization increased much more strongly in real terms to reach 105.5 per cent of GDP in 2007, so the country might be best described as having an equity-dependent but still largely bank-based financial system.[88] Nevertheless, large European banks responded to the shareholder revolution by moving increasingly towards a model of market-based banking, whereby banks' lending capacity has become more and more determined by conditions in capital markets. As we will see in the next chapter, both Anglo-Saxon and continental European banks have massively expanded their balance sheets since the 1990s by borrowing from other banks and financial institutions on the wholesale market – that is, by issuing bonds, engaging in repurchase agreements or borrowing from the interbank market – and using these market-based liabilities to finance the acquisition of market-based assets such as equities, bonds and asset-backed securities. The rise of market-based banking led to a sharp and ultimately unsustainable rise in household debt in the advanced capitalist world, as well as an unparalleled entanglement between US and European banks, eventually culminating in the global financial crisis.

6
Financial Policy: Market-Based Banking and the Global Financial Crisis

At the beginning of the twenty-first century, banking sectors and financial markets of the advanced capitalist world were more integrated than ever before. The liberalization of capital controls since the 1970s had combined with technological innovation in ICT to deepen financial globalization in an unprecedented way. The globalization of banks and financial markets marked a fundamental break with the Keynesian post-war era, when banks and the financial sector were subject to new kinds of stringent regulations and international financial integration remained subdued in the face of capital controls. The gradual liberalization of these regulations since the 1970s had unshackled banks from their national territory, encouraging a shift towards market-based banking.

Market-based banking blurred the boundaries between national financial systems dominated by capital market funding and those predominantly reliant upon banking credit. While in the traditional banking model of financial intermediation during the Keynesian era, banking credit was predominantly funded by retail deposits, market-based banks increasingly rely on wholesale funding markets to finance their lending and investment activities. In these wholesale funding markets, banks borrow short-term cash from each other by engaging in market-based sources of financing like repurchase agreements and selling debt securities. Large banks increasingly accumulated such market-based liabilities to invest in market-based assets like stocks, bonds and other marketable securities. At the same time, banks – especially those from the United States and the United Kingdom – also developed a new business model called 'originate-and-distribute', whereby they increasingly extended loans with the intention not of keeping them on their own balance sheets but of selling them to other financial market actors via new securitization techniques.

The rise of market-based banking encouraged a massive expansion of household credit in many advanced capitalist economies, which proved to be unsustainable in countries like the United States and the United Kingdom. How can we explain the rise of market-based banking and the exponential growth in banks' balance sheets that were at the heart of the global financial crisis? As we will see in this chapter, it was widely believed that the securitization of mortgage and other forms of household credit – that is, the bundling of loans into marketable securities that could be sold to a large group of investors in international financial markets – would spread and minimize risks associated with these loans in ways that would enable banks to lend money even to low-income households that previously could not have access to credit. These techniques were praised for promoting a *democratization of credit* and informed by a strong belief in the efficiency of financial markets, yet excessive lending fuelled housing bubbles that were the proximate cause of the global financial crisis of 2008. This occurred particularly in Anglo-Saxon economies like the United States and the United Kingdom, where banks created and traded highly complex securitized financial assets that were backed by mortgages and other kinds of loans to households. The transition towards an originate-and-distribute banking model buttressed their asset-based welfare regimes based on privatized Keynesianism, whereby the management of aggregate demand and the fulfilment of social needs became increasingly dependent on rising asset prices and expansion of household credit.

Large banks from continental Europe were also deeply implicated in the global financial crisis, as they massively invested in the complex securitized assets produced by US financial institutions, and funded these investments by borrowing dollars in short-term US and UK money markets. When the housing bubbles collapsed and the value of these mortgage-backed securities crashed in 2007 and 2008, numerous large Anglo-Saxon and European banks had to be saved and bailed out by their governments. These events pushed market-based banks of the 'core' Eurozone countries to withdraw their funding from the 'peripheral' member states in the region, precipitating a sovereign debt crisis in these countries. The deep entanglement of US and European market-based banks, and their role in the global financial crisis of 2008 and the Eurozone crisis of 2010, suggest that the conventional distinction of the CPE literature between the market-based financial systems of the Anglo-Saxon countries and bank-based financial systems of the continental European countries has become increasingly untenable.

The fiscal and social costs of the global financial crisis were dramatic, raising the question of why banks were allowed to take excessive risks in order to maximize their short-term profits. One important explanation is the structural power enjoyed by large market-banks in the United States and Europe because of the central role they play in both the debt-led growth models of the LMEs and MMEs and the export-led growth models of the CMEs. The rise in household debt and growing homeownership was certainly not merely an Anglo-Saxon phenomenon but occurred in many continental European countries as well: households in most advanced capitalist countries have become dependent on market-based banks for the accumulation of financial and housing wealth. But while the accumulation of credit-financed assets played a key role in supporting the consumption capacity of lower- and middle-income households in the Anglo-Saxon economies, the sharp rise in household debt (and associated wealth accumulation) in the Nordic countries was made possible by the fact that their more generous welfare states and egalitarian income distribution have created a large pool of creditworthy middle-class borrowers. Together with their distinctive social policy approach, discussed in chapter 4, the Nordic countries' relatively liberal financial policy clarifies why domestic demand played a greater role in their export-led growth model than in more financially restrictive CMEs like Germany.

Banks and financial intermediation during the Keynesian era

A primer on banks, financial intermediation and bailouts

In order to understand how banks work and make profits, as well as to comprehend the transition from the typical banking model of the Keynesian era to the market-based banking model of the modern era, we should first have a closer look at the bank balance sheet depicted in figure 6.1. The balance sheet consists of the liabilities and assets of banks and clarifies their role in financial intermediation, which is the process through which banks channel savings from deposit holders to those who need to borrow money: the principal job of banks is to take in deposits from people who have surplus savings and extend loans to people who want to borrow. By doing so, banks make profits, since the returns they receive on their assets (e.g. the interest rate they ask for loans) are higher than the interest rate they need to pay on their deposits. The loans banks make to households and firms are usually long-term, whereas the deposits they take are short-term: banks have short-term liabilities and long-term assets. By taking deposits and making loans, banks engage in maturity transformation: bank depositors can withdraw their money from the bank without notice, but banks lend over a fixed time span on which the loan will be repaid and cannot require the borrower to repay sooner. As the length of a loan is called its maturity, this is called *maturity transformation*: banks turn short-term liabilities into long-term assets by engaging in short-term borrowing and long-term lending. This process is also often called *liquidity transformation*, as the banks' liabilities are liquid – that is, they can easily be turned into cash by deposit holders – while banks' assets are difficult to sell and turn into cash.

It is easy to see that, by engaging in maturity and liquidity transformation, banking is an intrinsically risky business. On the *liabilities side* of the banks' balance sheet, the main risk is that deposit holders withdraw their money at the same time because they fear that their bank risks becoming insolvent and unable to repay their deposits. In normal times, banks allow deposit holders to withdraw their money by keeping cash holdings – that is, reserves – at the

Figure 6.1 Balance sheet of a traditional bank: an illustration

Assets	%	Liabilities	%
1. Loans to firms and households	60	1. Deposit	80
2. Financial assets	15	2. Borrowing from other banks and financial institutions	10
3. Cash reserve balances at central bank	10		
4. Loans to other banks	10		
5. Fixed assets such as office buildings and equipment	5	*Total liabilities*	*90*
Total assets	*100*	*Net worth = Equity*	*10*

central bank. These reserves only cover a small fraction of the deposit liabilities of banks, based on the assumption that their clients will not withdraw all their deposits at the same time. When banks temporarily face more withdrawals than expected, they can borrow short-term cash from other banks and financial institutions. However, banks are in trouble if their reserves are insufficient to meet their clients' desire to withdraw money or if they are unable to borrow from other financial institutions – a danger that is particularly acute during periods of financial crisis. During the Great Depression of the 1930s, many American and European banks failed because of massive *bank runs* – that is, joint deposit withdrawals that caused banks to run out of money and therefore created self-fulfilling dynamics: as more and more deposit holders withdrew their money, the risk of default increased, prompting even more people to withdraw their deposits.[1] But why would deposit holders withdraw their money in the first place? Usually, bank runs start with the fear that one or several banks risk bankruptcy because of losses accumulated on the *asset side* of their balance sheet – either because they have too many *non-performing loans* that cannot be repaid by borrowers, or because they have made financial investments that went bad. Banks are insolvent when these losses exceed their *net worth* – that is, the equity or capital invested by their shareholders.

Why is bank failure so problematic? The failure and elimination of low-performing and non-efficient firms normally allow more innovative firms to thrive and are a key source of the dynamism of the capitalist system. However, the failure of a large bank does not have this beneficial effect. Unlike the failure of a non-financial firm, the bankruptcy of a large bank can bring down the financial system as a whole and endanger the livelihoods of people throughout the entire economy. Governments are often forced to bail out their banks, as bank failure can have a domino effect: if one bank fails, there is a risk that it may spread to the entire banking system. Depositors of other private banks may believe that the failure of one bank will also affect their own bank; if they withdrew their money en masse, the ensuing bank runs would trigger the systemic banking crisis they feared. The economic consequences of such a crisis would be devastating, given the crucial role the banking system plays in the allocation of credit and the management of savings.

For these reasons, large private banks are typically considered to be 'too big to fail' by their government, which will prevent such failures by bailing out these banks. A *bank bailout* refers to the provision of funds to a bankrupt or nearly bankrupt bank in order to prevent the bankruptcy of the financial institution. Generally, bailouts are made by the central bank and the government. In the case where a bank only temporarily runs into liquidity problems (cash problems) and is unable to borrow from other private financial institutions, the central bank can act as a *lender of last resort*. In a severe financial crisis, banks that have extended too many non-performing bad loans or made too many bad financial investments might face solvency problems, which could lead to bankruptcy without government intervention. Solvency problems can only be resolved by injecting taxpayer money into the failing bank in order to strengthen its equity position or even temporarily nationalize the bank.

Banking crises and bailouts have several problematic side effects. If large banks know they are 'too big to fail', they may be encouraged to take on more risk than is optimal – a problem that is known as *moral hazard*: banks receive all the benefits from the risk taking (in the form of higher profits), while the government is forced to bear the cost of failure by bailing out the bank using taxpayer money; in this way, it is often said that banks can *privatize the profits and socialize the losses*.[2] A severe banking crisis also has disruptive effects on public finances. On the one hand, bank bailouts have a directly devastating effect on the fiscal balance by forcing the government to inject money into the ailing banking system. On the other hand, banks and financial institutions will typically push back their lending, making it more difficult for households and firms to get a loan to finance their consumption and investment spending. The resulting fall in economic growth will then diminish the government's tax returns (as there is less economic activity to tax) and raise its spending (e.g. on unemployment benefits and/or on a discretionary fiscal stimulus programme to support growth and employment).

Based on their investigation of a unique dataset of financial crises going back to 1800, Carmen Reinhart and Kenneth Rogoff have shown that banking crises almost invariably lead to sharp declines in tax revenues as well as large increases in government spending: 'On average, government debt rises by 86 percent during the three years following a banking crisis.'[3] Moritz Schularick similarly demonstrated that the budgetary costs of financial crises are large and have increased greatly in the course of the past 140 years: whereas ratios of public debt to GDP were by and large unaffected by financial crises prior to World War II, public debt ratios typically rose by one third or about 20 percentage points of GDP in the five years after a systemic financial crisis.[4]

These findings add an important new element to conventional narratives of public debt dynamics in the twentieth century: while historically public debt dynamics in the Western world have reflected the fiscal costs of fighting major wars, the debt build-up in the second half of the twentieth century stands out as the first marked increase of public sector debt ratios in peacetime. The rising fiscal costs of financial crises have played a key role in this development, as Schularick explains:

> In many countries, major financial crises were key factors behind the worsening of public debt trajectories. In this respect, the rise in the level of public debt in the last decades of the twentieth century is not solely a reflection of generous welfare programs or costly economic policies by spendthrift governments. The spectacular growth of the financial sector and the increasingly large fiscal costs of financial crises played an important, and in some cases a dominant role.[5]

Banking regulation and '3-6-3 banking' during the Keynesian era

In order to avoid bank failures and the disruptive effects they have on public finances and the state of the economy, the government and the public have a clear interest in regulating the banking sector in ways that make bank runs and bank defaults less likely. Financial regulation usually involves the following three interlinked key components:[6]

1 The government provides depositors with some protection – up to a certain level – against the risk that they would lose their money in case their bank goes bankrupt, which is meant to avoid panic-stricken bank runs among deposit holders.
2 In return for its deposit protection, the government has the authority and responsibility to contain excessive risk taking by establishing financial rules and regulations. The most important form of regulation requires banks to restrict their leverage and hold a minimum amount of capital (equity) against their assets. As a result of these capital adequacy regulations, banks are better able to protect their balance sheet again financial losses. Moreover, the government can prohibit banks from investing in specific products and/or from lending to and investing money in foreign countries.
3 Financial supervision by a government agency is needed to ensure an effective implementation of these financial regulations. Financial supervisors are responsible for monitoring banks and guaranteeing that they comply with all financial regulations.

The financial structure of the post-war Keynesian period is sometimes referred to as '3-6-3' banking, as bankers allegedly gathered deposits at 3 per cent, lent them at 6 per cent, and were on the golf course by 3 o'clock in the afternoon. The implication of the 3-6-3 model is that the banking industry was a boring one, marked by a lack of aggressive competition. Tight regulation is thought to have limited competition and allowed the 3-6-3 model and the concept of bankers' hours to survive. The lack of competition also implied that banks did not need to take excessive risks to make profits.[7]

There are three types of financial regulations that limited competition in the banking system within the traditional 3-6-3 model of financial intermediation. First, there were regulations that restricted and even prohibited the entry of new firms into the banking industry, allowing incumbent banks to retain their profit opportunities. An important dimension of these bank entry regulations was capital controls and restrictions on international capital flows, which prevented foreign banks from setting up businesses in the domestic banking industry. Second, branching restrictions curbed the ability of banks to set up new offices in new locations, limiting the degree of competition between banks to attract new customers. Third, interest rate controls imposed restrictions on the payment of interest on deposit accounts and other types of bank deposits (e.g. savings accounts). These restrictions prevented potentially destructive competition between banks by constraining their ability to offer high interest rates as a way to attract customers. Because this would erode bank profits, the fear was that banks would respond by acquiring riskier assets with higher expected returns. Interest ceilings on deposits hence played an important role in thwarting financial speculation, encouraging banks to lend to local firms at relatively low interest rates.

These banking regulations offered the basis for a long post-war period of relative stability in domestic finance that coincided with the golden age of welfare state capitalism, invoking the metaphor in the United States of 'finance as servant': 'The possibility of a capital–labour accord [during the welfare state] rested on the construction of a financial sector that would not be disruptive and would promote growth by financing industrial production ... The New Deal constructed a regulated financial sector that was the hand maiden to industry.'[8] The other industrialized countries adopted similar banking relations. In Germany, the state's restrictive regulation of stock markets discouraged their development as a source of long-term capital for industry.[9] While long-term finance shifted from capital markets to banks, long-term credit agencies shifted their main focus to the general support of small and medium-sized businesses. This regulatory system supported a banking system that 'has been remarkably free of the speculative bubbles and credit crunches experienced in other industrialized countries'.[10] As in Germany, the pattern of long-term finance for industry in Japan shifted away from securities markets to the banking system: the proportion of external finance for industry accounted for by bank loans increased from about 50 per cent in the 1910s and 1920s to about 80 per cent in the 1960s and 1970s.[11] In most industrialized countries, a system of financial repression emerged from the more stringent banking regulations of the interwar period, involving a set of regulations constraining the development of capital markets and depressing interest rates in the economy to make credit cheaper for both non-financial corporations and the government.[12]

Financial liberalization and the rise of market-based banking

Financial liberalization from the 1970s and 1980s onwards promoted the rise of market-based banking and fundamentally altered the traditional model of banking regulation. A first key step was the liberalization of capital controls, allowing local banks and financial institutions to engage in international financial transactions – for example, borrowing money from foreign investors, extending loans to foreigners and investing in foreign securities, etc. – as well as allowing foreign banks and financial institutions to start business in local markets. Apart from opening up national financial systems, governments removed restrictions on banking competition by abandoning all interest rate controls and restrictions on credit creation: banks could henceforth engage in a wide range of financial activities, expanding credit particularly to households and other financial institutions. Gregory Fuller called this evolution the 'great debt transformation', which introduced banks 'to a far less friendly world: more freedom has also meant more competition'.[13]

One of the best illustrations of the intensified competition between banks is the depression of their net interest rate margin – that is, the difference between the interest rate banks earn on their assets (e.g. interest rate on loans) and the interest rate they pay on their liabilities (e.g. deposit rate). The removal of regulatory ceilings on deposit rates intensified competition between banks

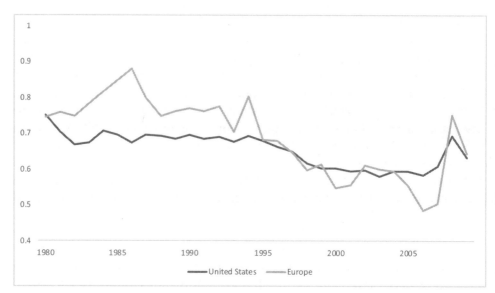

Figure 6.2 Share of net interest income in bank profits, 1980–2009

Source: OECD; author's calculations

'Europe' is a non-weighted average of Austria, Belgium, Denmark, Finland, France, Germany, the Netherlands and Sweden.

to attract deposits, pushing up interest rates on deposit accounts. At the same time, the removal of barriers to competition in lending markets pushed down interest rates that banks could charge on their loans. The ensuing decline in net interest margins is a key reason why the share of net interest rate income in bank profits has been falling since the 1980s, as figure 6.2 shows for the United States and Europe.

Banks responded to intensifying competition by engaging in mergers and acquisitions, expanding their balance sheets and pursuing financial innovation. Financial liberalization first of all prompted an explosion of bank mergers and acquisitions: 'By removing the regulatory barriers between different types of financial institutions, large firms could integrate all the various activities previously done by specialty finance houses. This allowed the creation of large universal banks offering one-stop shopping to their clients: the same bank could take consumer deposits, use those deposits for either lending or trading.'[14] Smaller banks that could not compete were either pushed out of business or purchased by the larger banks. As a result of bank failures, mergers and acquisitions, concentration in the banking sector increased significantly during the 1990s. Table 6.1 presents data on an often-used measure of industry concentration in the banking sector: the C5 ratio,

Table 6.1 Increasing banking concentration in the OECD: C5 ratio, 1985–99

	1985	1995	1999
Austria	35.9	39.2	50.4
Belgium	48.0	51.2	77.4
Denmark	61.0	72.0	77.0
Finland	38.0	70.6	74.3
France	46.0	41.3	42.7
Germany	-	16.7	19.0
Greece	80.6	75.7	76.6
Ireland	47.5	44.4	40.8
Italy	-	32.4	48.3
Luxembourg	26.8	21.2	26.1
Netherlands	72.9	76.1	82.3
Portugal	61.0	74.0	72.6
Spain	35.1	47.3	51.9
Sweden	80.8	86.5	88.2
United Kingdom	-	28.3	29.1
United States	10.0	19.0	31.0

Source: ECB 2000; Crotty 2008

For the United States the C3 ratio is given – that is, the bank assets of the largest three banks as a percentage of total bank assets retrieved from Crotty 2008.

which is the share of the five largest banks in the total value of all assets in the banking industry. While banking concentration grew in most OECD countries, the increase was especially prominent in the United States: at the end of the 1990s, the top three commercial banks owned just 10.5 per cent of industry assets; a manic merger process raised that figure to 31 per cent of industry assets by 2000. The largest seven commercial banks in the United States owned nearly 50 per cent of total industry assets in 2003.

Banks also responded to financial deregulation and intensifying competition by expanding their balance sheet and leverage: 'if the returns on individual transactions are compressed by competitive pressure, one obvious adjustment is to conduct more transactions. In effect, banks made up for shrinking margins with volume, transforming deposits, interbank borrowing, and bond issues into new assets on a massive scale'.[15] Increasing assets implied that bankers became less reluctant to lend to poorer households as well as more willing to accumulate riskier financial assets and engage in proprietary trading. As a result, banks' balance sheets exploded, as figure 6.3 shows: apart from in Japan, the total value of bank assets compared to GDP grew drastically in the OECD world between 1990 and 2007 – the start of the global financial crisis. The bank-asset-to-GDP ratio particularly skyrocketed in small countries with comparatively large banking sectors like Ireland, the Netherlands and Switzerland. But even in large economies like France, Germany and the United States, bank balance sheets inflated in relation to GDP. Because growth in deposits was insufficient to fund the expansion of their balance sheet, banks increasingly relied on borrowing from other banks and financial institutions

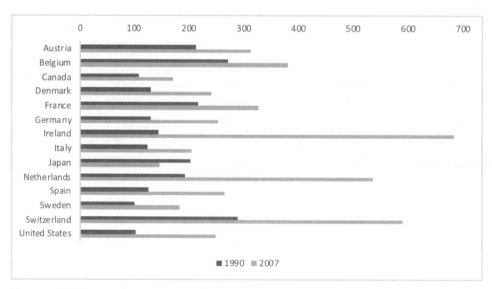

Figure 6.3 Bank assets (in percentage of GDP), 1990 and 2007
Source: OECD

in wholesale money markets. This increased reliance on wholesale market funding allowed banks to increase their leverage – that is, increase the size of their balance sheet relative to equity capital – as a way to boost their RoE and shareholder value. Maximizing RoE and shareholder returns became the ultimate metric of performance of large market-based banks in different varieties of capitalism, not only in the LMEs but also in CMEs like Germany and MMEs like France.[16]

Finally, banks engaged in financial innovation. On the asset side of the balance sheet, one of the key developments in banking since the 1980s and particularly 1990s has been the growth of loan securitization and the transition from the originate-and-retain model of banking towards the originate-and-distribute model. In the new model, loans are not kept on the asset side of the balance sheet but are increasingly bundled and repacked in the form of marketable asset-backed securities (ABSs) that can be sold to numerous other investors. On the liability side of the balance sheet, banks developed new techniques to reduce their reliance on deposit funding and borrow short-term liquidity from other banks and financial institutions. The most important new source of market-based funding was repo finance (repurchase agreements), whereby banks borrowed short-term cash in wholesale money markets by selling securities with a promise to buy them back shortly afterwards at a slightly higher price. The creation of off-balance-sheet structured investment vehicles (SIVs) was another innovation to free up liquidity: SIVs, which function as a kind of subsidiary of banks, issue a type of short-term liability known as asset-backed commercial paper (ABCP) to raise funds to purchase ABSs from the sponsoring bank. These developments gave rise to a shadow banking system, a term that refers to a plethora of market-based intermediation activities – aptly summarized by Perry Mehrling and his colleagues as 'money market funding of capital market lending' – that take place outside ('in the shadows of') the traditional, regulated banking system.[17]

To understand the key features of market-based banking, it is instructive to look at the changes in the composition of the balance sheet associated with the new model – depicted in figure 6.4. These features imply a blurring between

Figure 6.4 Balance sheet of a market-based bank: an illustration

Assets	%	Liabilities	%
Loans to households and firms	38	Deposits	56
Financial assets	30	Borrowing from other financial institutions	40
Securitized loans	30		
Fixed assets such as office buildings and equipment	2		
Total assets	*100*	*Total liabilities*	*96*
		Net worth = Equity	*4*

the capital-markets-dominated financial systems of the LMEs and the bank-based financial systems of the CMEs and MMEs. On the liability side, banks increasingly started to rely upon borrowing from other banks and financial institutions in short-term money markets to fund lending and financial investments. These market-based funding sources are typically much more skittish than the more 'sticky' deposit liabilities: other banks and financial institutions are usually much swifter in withdrawing their funding during a crisis than deposit holders, whose money is – after all – guaranteed by the government up to a certain limit. On the asset side of the balance sheet, banks increasingly started to invest in financial assets, whose prices and returns are determined by developments in volatile capital markets. Furthermore, loans to non-financial firms constitute a falling share of all bank credit in recent decades; banks' lending to the 'real economy' has increasingly consisted of household loans – especially mortgages.[18] These loans were increasingly securitized as ABSs that were sold to other investors, freeing up funds that can be lent out or reinvested. However, as we will see below, rather than distributing risk, securitization and the originate-and-distribute banking model encouraged excessive *opacity* and *concentration of risk* in the banking system.[19]

Market-based banking and transatlantic financial instability

Securitization, the democratization of credit and the US subprime crisis

Since its development at the end of the 1970s, the securitization of loans has been hailed as one of the most socially useful financial innovations of recent times:

> The securitization process has allowed Wall Street to more efficiently finance Main Street, bringing capital from securities markets to loan originators, relieving them of the need to finance and maintain loans on their balance sheets. Further, by effectively splitting the ownership of loans into many smaller units – through the sale of securities – the process was thought to diversify credit risk more widely across national and, indeed, global capital markets rather than concentrate that risk on the balance sheets of the institutions that originated the loans.[20]

As the IMF argued in a 2006 *Global Financial Stability Report*, 'rapid growth of derivative and structured credit markets in recent years, particularly among more complex products, has facilitated the dispersion of credit risk by banks to a broader and more diverse group of investors ... [which] has helped to make the banking and overall financial system more resilient and stable'.[21] In doing so, securitization encouraged banks to extend loans to borrowers who previously did not have access to cheap credit because they were considered to be too risky.

Here is an example of how securitization is supposed to work. Assume that there is a large real estate project that would cost about €800 million. When the project manager goes to the bank to receive an €800 million loan to finance the investment, most banks will not be very eager to extend it: there is an unwarranted risk that the bank's capital will be wiped out completely if the project manager goes bankrupt. The project would not be able to get funding and would remain dormant as long as the bank had to keep the €800 million loan on its balance sheet. Securitization changes the banks' risk calculation. Suppose that the bank could make 1,000 marketable securities of €800,000 out of the original loan and sell these securities to 1,000 different investors. In this way, risks associated with extending the €800 million loan would be dispersed over these 1,000 investors: if the project manager goes bankrupt, the 1,000 investors would 'only' lose their €800,000 each. That would be unpleasant but they would probably be able to absorb the loss without going bankrupt. So because securitization disperses risks over a large number of investors, it allows banks to expand credit to riskier borrowers.

The practice of securitization was practically invented by two government-sponsored enterprises – the Federal National Mortgage Association and the Federal Home Loan Mortgage Corporation, commonly known as Fannie Mae and Freddie Mac – in the US mortgage market at the end of the 1970s. Fannie Mae and Freddie Mac started to purchase mortgage loans from primary lenders and then issued mortgage-backed securities (MBSs) on the basis of these loans. It was believed that this process allowed for a diversification of risk, as the mortgages in the pool had been originated in many different parts of the country and reflected different risk profiles. Fannie Mae and Freddie Mac played a key role in the 'democratization of credit' in the United States. In 1977, the US Congress signed the Community Reinvestment Act and encouraged banks to help meet the needs of borrowers in all segments of their communities, including low- and moderate-income neighbourhoods. Fannie Mae and Freddie Mac reassured banks that they would securitize these riskier loans, thereby functioning as the 'pull' factor that complemented the 'push' factor of the Act. By embracing the Act as well by guaranteeing the solvency of Fannie Mae and Freddie Mac, the American state has been exceptionally involved in mortgage finance:

> For more than seven decades the American state has used its power and material resources to produce outcomes in mortgage lending that financial markets left to themselves would not have delivered. These outcomes have entailed more mortgage lending at cheaper rates of interest and more of that lending being directed to low-income households than would otherwise have been the case.[22]

The homeownership rate grew dramatically in the United States from less than 64 per cent in 1994 to almost 70 per cent in 2005. The number of homeowners in low- and moderate-income communities grew nearly twice as fast as the number of homeowners in high-income areas during the 1990s.

For its proponents, securitization increased the efficiency of financial markets to allocate credit where it is most needed.[23] Together with the privatization of public housing, private homeownership was actively promoted by the liberalization of financial markets, the deregulation of banking and the securitization of mortgage loans. In this regard, it is important to note that policy elites fully embraced these developments. For instance, Alan Greenspan – former governor of the US central bank – praised securitization for 'providing expanded access to credit for the vast majority of consumers, including those of limited means'.[24] For its critics, securitization and market-based banking intensified rather than dampened the tendency to engender periodic cycles of excessive credit creation. This left the banking system vulnerable to a crisis due to any one of a number of factors – for example, higher interest rates or a fall in house prices – that slowed economic growth and left highly indebted entities unable to pay down their financial obligations. This is what happened in 2007, when the housing boom in the US economy became a bubble that eventually burst: when housing prices started to stagnate and fall after 2006, it became clear that the regime of privatized Keynesianism and asset-based welfare was based on a financial house of cards.

In the traditional securitization model, banks issued mortgages to households and subsequently sold these loans to a government-sponsored entity like Fannie Mae and Freddie Mac. In order to be eligible for Fannie Mae- and Freddie Mac-backed mortgages, homebuyers had to meet certain minimum credit requirements – for instance, they had to make a minimum down payment and have a minimum credit score.[25] From the end of the 1990s, Wall Street commercial and investment banks like Goldman Sachs, Citibank, Merrill Lynch and Lehman Brothers increasingly purchased loans from borrowers who did not meet these minimum requirements and were therefore considered as subprime. Wall Street banks aggregated these subprime mortgages into large pools and then issued increasingly complex MBSs, whose yield was derived from the pass-through of payments of interest and principal from the underlying pool of mortgage debt. However, far from diversifying risk as proponents of the securitization and originate-and-distribute banking model intended, the participation of Wall Street banks fuelled excessive opacity and risk concentration in the financial system.[26]

The most prevalent of these new classes of engineered financial assets are known as collateralized debt obligations (CDOs), whose rapid growth between 2000 and 2006 lies at the root of the subprime crisis (box 6.1). The major US CRAs – Moody's, S&P and Fitch – shared in the vast profits of the boom at the cost of abandoning their supposed role of providing prudent monitoring and oversight of the quality of the underlying pools of mortgage debt. These CRAs played a crucial role in the originate-and-distribute banking model, as investors in MBSs and CDOs did not have sufficient information to assess the underlying risks of these financial products and therefore depended entirely on the agencies' rating. Remember from chapter 3 that ratings issued by the

CRAs provide information about the risk profile of financial investments such as sovereign bonds and other kinds of debt securities: because their ratings serve as a widely accepted, standardized scale of creditworthiness of firms, financial instruments and countries, CRAs are considered as gatekeepers in the international financial system. However, conflicts of interest led to an overvaluation of MBSs and CDOs, as CRAs advised issuers of these financial products on how to structure and prioritize the tranches of an MBS/CDO in order to help issuers squeeze profits from the MBS/CDO by maximizing the size of its highest rated 'premium' tranches. Because CRAs underestimated the complexity of those instruments, they gave a top rating to most securities backed by subprime mortgages and were too slow in downgrading these financial products when market conditions started to deteriorate.

Box 6.1 CDO, SIV and ABCP

A CDO is a highly complex derivative composed of a large number of MBSs, whereby the payment streams are carved up and distributed to various risk tranches that are distinguished according to their level of exposure to losses from defaults occurring in the underlying mortgage pool. The basic idea is that investors in CDOs can trade off protection from losses for returns: investors holding the lowest (often unrated) tranche with the highest return are the first to absorb losses; only when all the lower-rated tranches exhausted are losses applied to investors in the highest-rated (senior) tranche. Based on the assumption that a sufficient number of mortgage borrowers would never default on their loans, it was believed that the senior tranche could provide investors with full protection against losses.

By carving up payment streams into different risk tranches, investment banks and CRAs thought it was possible to create completely safe asset classes receiving AAA-grade credit rating out of underlying subprime mortgages. CDOs fulfilled an important need in the financial systems, allowing fund managers to more readily recalibrate the relative balance of risk and return in their portfolios.

SIVs served as off-balance-sheet funding vehicles for the creation and trading of CDOs. Remember that SIVs are a kind of subsidiary of banks that issues a type of short-term debt known as ABCP to raise funds in money markets. These funds allow the SIV to purchase collateralized obligations from the sponsoring bank. Using these SIVs, the sponsoring banks hoped to make easy profits by borrowing on short-term money markets at low interest rates and investing in high-yielding CDOs without having to set aside equity to comply with existing capital adequacy regulation rules. Given the enormous short-term profits being made, Wall Street banks were seemingly unconcerned about the fact that the growing volume of CDOs was being built upon a huge mass of mortgage debt that was unlikely to be fully repaid. Because in most cases banks retained explicit or implicit exposure to these entities, risk was much more concentrated than commonly assumed prior to the crisis: sponsoring banks had to absorb these SIVs back on to their balance sheet when US money and ABCP markets dried up in the wake of the subprime crisis, thereby reversing the main motive behind the originate-and-distribute banking model.[27]

Another reason why banks extended too much mortgage credit and took too much risk is the remuneration structure of the originate-and-distribute banking model. In the traditional model of financial intermediation in which banks retained the loans on their balance sheet, bank profits came from the spread between the interest rate charged on loans and the rate banks paid on deposits. In the new model in which loans are securitized and sold to investors, banks and other financial institutions realized profits on the fees they charged for services provided in underwriting the transactions – from 2003 to 2008 around US$2 trillion in fees from home sales and mortgage securitization went 'to banks and mortgage brokers who sold the loans, investment bankers who packaged the loans into securities, banks and specialized institutions who serviced the securities and rating agencies who gave them their seal of approval'.[28] Evidently, this created an incentive to extend as many loans as possible, as every new loan and MBS/CDO sold on the secondary market boosted banking fees. Moreover, excessive bonuses caused bankers to earn more in the short term but led to unsustainable risks that eventually materialized in the financial crisis.

As Wall Street's desire to issue and trade MBSs and CDOs grew, mortgage lenders began to extend loans to working-class households with low to moderate income and a prior history of credit problems – the so-called subprime mortgage market. Some of these loans were called NINJA loans, as they were extended to individuals with 'no income, no job and no assets'. To entice low-income households to take out these loans, banks issued mortgages with no down payment: even low-income households could borrow the full value of the house without having to make an initial up-front payment. Moreover, lenders allowed these households to delay loan repayments by extending interest-only mortgages, which only required them to pay interest charges and were often set at seductively low 'teaser' rates: these loans took the form of adjustable rate mortgages, which started with very low (even zero) interest rates that were set to increase sharply after a few years. Subprime borrowers were told not to worry about future higher interest rate payments: it was widely believed that they would be able to refinance their mortgage into a new loan with more attractive conditions. Refinancing a mortgage means paying off the existing loan and replacing it with a new one with lower interest rates. The reasoning was that a few years after the extension of the loan, subprime borrowers would become wealthier due to rising housing prices and be able to 'exploit' the extra housing wealth by getting a more attractive refinancing rate from their bank.

> ## Box 6.2 Mortgage equity withdrawal: an illustration
>
> Assume that a US household took a mortgage of US$190,000 to buy a house valued at US$200,000 in the year 2000. In this situation, the household only had US$10,000 in housing equity (which equals the market value of the house minus the value of the outstanding mortgage). If by 2005 the estimated market value of the house had risen to US$300,000 and US$40,000 of the mortgage has been paid off to the bank, the housing equity of the household would have grown to US160,000. Now assume that the household wants extra cash to the tune of US$100,000 in order to buy a new car and get a new bathroom and a new kitchen. It could then do a mortgage equity withdrawal (MEW) by using the additional housing wealth to get a new loan worth a total of US$250,000 from the bank (i.e. the US$150,000 still owed on the original mortgage plus the US$100,000 in cash). As a result, its housing equity would fall again to US$50,000.

The rise in the US homeownership rate during the 2000s was largely attributable to the rise of subprime mortgage borrowers: annual new subprime mortgage originations increased from US$34 billion in 1994 to about US$600 billion in 2004–6. The proliferation of subprime mortgage loans boosted demand for new homes, leading to skyrocketing housing prices between 1995 and 2007. This created new opportunities for existing homeowners, as rising housing prices enabled them to 'cash out' additional housing wealth via so-called mortgage equity withdrawals (MEWs). MEWs are a form of refinancing of an existing mortgage loan, where the new mortgage loan is for a larger amount than the existing mortgage loan and the borrower receives the difference between the two loans in cash (e.g. to purchase durable consumption goods or make home improvements) (see box 6.2 for an illustration). Easy mortgage refinancing and MEWs are typical features of Anglo-Saxon systems of housing finance, which have flexible rules that minimize the transaction costs involved in mortgage origination and refinancing.[29] In the United States, a total of US$1.45 trillion of the rise in household debt from 2002 to 2006 came from MEWs, which accounted for approximately 6 per cent of disposable income between 2001 and 2006 (figure 6.5).

In short, securitization and originate-and-distribute banking bolstered the formation of a consumption-oriented and debt-led growth model whose sustainability rested on persistently rising housing prices. The problem was that housing prices were bound to stagnate at some point, as Herman Schwartz explains:

> The essence of the subprime crisis is that banks and borrowers alike needed continued 10 percent annual housing price appreciation to bring their bets into the money. But the very arrival of subprime borrowers signalled the end of house price appreciation. The supply of creditworthy new and trade-up buyers was exhausted, which is why banks began offering loans to less creditworthy households. No new buyers meant that housing prices could not continue to rise indefinitely, yet the only available new buyers were people who could not actually afford their mortgages.[30]

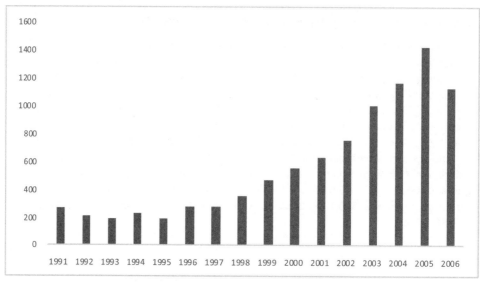

Figure 6.5 Total MEWs in the US economy (in billion US dollars), 1991–2006
Source: Greenspan and Kennedy 2008

When not enough new, creditworthy buyers entered the market and house prices began to stall, overstretched borrowers did not have sufficient housing equity and were unable to refinance into a conventional mortgage at lower interest rates. At the same time, the Federal Reserve's monetary tightening to thwart the inflationary pressures arising from the oil and commodity price boom raised short-term interest rates and further dampened housing prices. As a result, refinance was impossible and a growing number of subprime borrowers began to default. SIVs found it harder and harder to raise short-term cash to fund their investments in CDOs, as defaults compromised the value of their collateral. Banks became so worried about counterparty risk – that is, the risk that a bank that borrowed from them might default – that they stopped lending to other banks against nearly all kinds of collateral. This fear produced the massive credit crunches of August and November 2007 and March and July–October 2008.

From the subprime crisis to the Eurozone crisis

It would be wrong to conclude from all this that the rise of market-based banking and the resulting financial crisis were merely a US phenomenon. Since the originate-and-distribute banking model had promoted the securitization of mortgages into securities that were traded on a global basis, European banks were deeply invested in these securities: via the securitization process, European banks ensured the financing of the US housing bubble. European banks invested massively in CDOs by setting up off-balance-sheet vehicles like SIVs. Just like large US investment banks, they used SIVs to engage in a carry trade, borrowing short-term cash in US money markets via issuing ABCP at low interest rates to invest in higher-yielding CDOs (see box 6.1 for an explanation of these terms). European banks profited massively from the spread created by the apparent maturity difference between the long-term CDOs that they held and the short-term ABCP they issued to fund purchases of those CDOs. European investors held about 29 per cent of non-conforming high-risk MBSs and CDOs composed of mortgages not backed by Fannie Mae or Freddie Mac. At the height of the securitization boom in 2007, British and continental European banks backed a third of newly issued MBSs sold by US investment and commercial banks, while overall two thirds of ABCP had European sponsors. As Adam Tooze observed in his widely acclaimed book *Crashed* (2018), 'European banks operated just like their American counterparts. They borrowed dollars to lend dollars.'[31]

Before the crisis, European banks believed that the MBSs and CDOs they had bought could be easily sold to other investors. But when a growing number of subprime borrowers began to default and a major US investment bank (Lehman Brothers) went bankrupt, investor preferences massively shifted towards safer assets like sovereign bonds. As a result, European banks were shut off from US money markets and faced huge losses on their MBSs and CDOs, bringing the crisis across the Atlantic to Europe. The fact that European banks were deeply implicated in the US subprime crisis is a clear reflection of the rise of market-based banking on the European continent. The financial crisis revealed that it is the market that determines banks' capacity to lend. This stands in stark contrast with the concept of 'patient capital' that has been so central in the financial systems of European CMEs (chapter 5): central to patient capital is the view that banks have the power to resist market pressures; with market-based banking, this power has increasingly disappeared.[32]

The global financial crisis came at a huge fiscal cost. As the value of CDOs and other financial assets collapsed during the massive credit crunch in wholesale funding markets, many large banks had to be saved from bankruptcy and to be bailed out by their government and central bank. Bank bailouts consisted of the three mechanisms of government intervention: (1) the recapitalization

Table 6.2 Government support measures of financial institutions (in billion euros unless stated otherwise), October 2008–May 2010

	Capital injection	Liability guarantees	Asset support	Total commitment as % 2008 GDP
Eurozone	160.8 (231)	735.2 (1,694)	120.7 (238)	28
United Kingdom	37.5 (55)	157.2 (300)	217.8	25
United States	235.3 (580)	277.9 (464)	114.9 (1,148)	26

Source: Stolz and Wedow 2010

Numbers in parentheses show total commitments to each measure. Some of the measures may not have been used, even though they were announced.

of private banks by the state; (2) state guarantees for bank deposits and other liabilities; (3) public asset purchases to remove bad assets from private banks' balance sheet. Total government commitments to bank bailouts in the Eurozone, the United Kingdom and the United States amounted to, respectively, 28 per cent, 25 per cent and 26 per cent of GDP (see table 6.2 for details).

The global financial crisis had large repercussions for the sustainability of debt accumulated by governments and banks from the 'peripheral' Eurozone countries (Greece, Ireland, Italy, Portugal and Spain), which had borrowed on a massive scale from banks of the 'core' Eurozone countries (France and the northern member states) in the preceding decade. The latter banks took advantage of financial globalization and European financial and monetary integration by raising their leverage. After the introduction of the euro, a profitable strategy for these banks was to invest in peripheral sovereign bonds and lend money to peripheral banks. These peripheral sovereign bonds were also used by market-based banks in the core Eurozone countries as collateral to obtain funding in wholesale repo markets.[33] Local banks in several peripheral countries also became increasingly dependent on wholesale funding, as their deposit base was insufficiently large to finance the domestic credit boom. These banks carried the bulk of the risk of default by domestic borrowers in addition to carrying the risk of being shut off from the wholesale market. These risks were particularly pronounced for countries in which a sharp expansion of credit during the boom years had fuelled domestic housing bubbles – as in Spain. Spanish banks – the local politicized *cajas* in particular – had funded their heavy exposure to the property boom by borrowing on the wholesale market to more than 60 per cent of their balance sheet.[34]

The growing dependency of the peripheral countries on external funding from the core Eurozone banks made these countries increasingly vulnerable to capital flight. The US subprime crisis forced core Eurozone banks to repatriate funds to their home market and reassess their international exposure levels, given that they had bought massive amounts of US-originated securitized products that had become effectively worthless. This deleveraging process disproportionally affected those countries with the greatest reliance on their external funding.[35] More generally, local banks in the southern countries became increasingly fragile against the backdrop of weak economic growth prospects after the global financial crisis, which uncovered the sharp decline in the external competitiveness of their non-financial firms (see chapter 7). Because national fiscal authorities remained entirely responsible for bailing out their banks and supporting their economy, peripheral governments' fiscal deficits soared in ways that undermined investors' confidence in the sustainability of their public debt and led to spiralling interest rates on their sovereign bonds. The resulting sovereign debt crisis imposed a severe macroeconomic adjustment process on these countries, as we will see in the next chapter.

Market-based banking, regulatory capture and financialization

Many commentators and banking scholars have argued that regulatory capture of public agencies and public policy by leading banks was one of the main causal factors behind the financial crisis of 2007–9. This, it is claimed, resulted in a permissive regulatory environment that turned a blind eye to excessive risk taking by banks: 'government agencies have been frequently described as being at the mercy of the financial sector, often allowing financial interests to hijack political, regulatory and supervisory processes in order to favouring their own private interests over the public good'.[36] In the United States the political clout of financial lobbies has repeatedly been seen as an important source of the regulatory failures that were at the heart of the crisis: US financial industry groups were able to influence regulatory policies by using their financial resources to finance electoral campaigns. The Report by the Financial Crisis Inquiry Commission (FCIC) established by the US Congress to investigate the roots of the crisis found that: 'the financial industry itself played a key role in weakening regulatory constraints on institutions, markets, and products'.[37]

While lobbying and privileged access to financial policymakers enable banks to directly influence financial regulation and supervision in ways that reflect the banks' interests, they also have considerable structural power that is perhaps an even more important mechanism of regulatory capture. Business groups often have the ability to limit the choices available to policymakers in regulating their activities even without having to actively put pressure on policymakers. A key source of structural power commonly associated with the banking industry concerns the role the sector plays in controlling access to credit: 'Governments typically need to anticipate and seriously consider the demands of banks because bank lending is a critical determinant of overall levels of investment and economic performance.'[38] The structural power of banks and financial firms has been strengthened by the removal of capital controls since the 1970s and 1980s, which made it much easier for them to move profitable financial activities to jurisdictions with fewer regulations and lower taxes.[39]

Given the importance of banking credit for the overall functioning of the economy, politicians and regulators are often concerned about the negative externalities that excessively stringent regulations can impose on the cost and availability of credit (e.g. the imposition of higher capital requirements on banks). For this reason, the structural power of the banking industry in the Anglo-Saxon economies is constrained by the competition that these firms face from capital markets in providing capital and credit to businesses. Conversely, banks can be expected to enjoy greater structural power in the context of different European financial systems, where banks are responsible for most of the domestic credit intermediation and non-financial corporations are more reliant on bank credit as an external funding source. Furthermore, as European banks have been major purchasers of sovereign debt, the growth of public debt tied the interests of governments more closely to the well-being of the banking industry.[40]

Other dimensions of the financial sector's structural power can be found in both continental European and Anglo-Saxon economies. The financial sector has increased in size and centrality compared to other sectors in most industrialized economies since the 1970s. In this regard, the 'too big to fail' problem is a feature of both the European and Anglo-Saxon banking systems. In the United States, finance became the largest and fastest-growing sector in the economy from 1980 to 2002, growing from 14 per cent to 21 per cent of GDP; finance even accounted for 47 per cent of US corporate profits in 2007. But in many European countries' GDP, the size of the banking sector grew as well from the 1990s: bank assets grow exponentially as a share of GDP in both European and Anglo-Saxon economies (see figure 6.3 above). The financialization of the economy is not limited to the increased size and mobility of the financial industry but also extends to other actors in the economy. As we have seen in chapter 5, finance has come to play an increasingly central role in the day-to-day activities of non-financial firms. The financialization of the non-financial corporate sector, whereby firms' revenues increasingly rely on financial investment returns, heightened the impact of regulatory policies on the profitability of business firms. In fact, non-financial corporations have frequently mobilized against a number of regulatory reforms introduced in response to the crisis, directly or indirectly allying with key financial industry players.[41]

At the same time, the financialization of households strengthened the structural power of banks and financial industry firms by increasing public support for financial liberalization and deregulation. Using data from the American National Election Survey and the British Household Panel Survey, Ben Ansell has shown that homeowners experiencing house price inflation tend to be less supportive of government spending on social insurance, and lean to the right ideologically, because growing housing wealth acts as private insurance that makes them less dependent upon state-provided income support.[42] In a similar vein, individuals who have turned themselves into 'investor subjects' by putting their savings into financial markets can be expected to align their preferences more directly with those of financial industry: based on their analysis of the 2010 Cooperative Congressional Election Study Survey, Stefano Pagliari and his colleagues found that, all else being equal, support for more financial regulatory policies is lower among those individuals with higher levels of individual investment in tradable financial assets.[43] From this perspective, the financial sector's structural power increasingly stems from the growing dependency of middle-income households on booming financial and housing markets.[44]

In their recent book, Jeffrey Chwieroth and Andrew Walter refer to these developments as the 'wealth effect' – that is, 'the heightened demand by large segments of contemporary society – roughly, the middle class – for policies

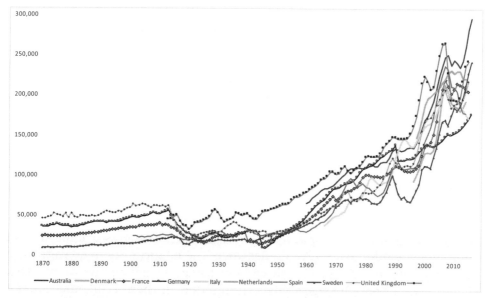

Figure 6.6 Net private real wealth per adult in advanced countries, 1870–2014

Source: World Inequality Database

Data in PPP exchange rates and constant 2016 US dollars.

that protect their wealth and incomes from the damage that banking crises can inflict'.[45] Figure 6.6 shows that net wealth per capita in the advanced capitalist world grew exponentially during the second half of the twentieth century, and especially so from the 1980s. Although national net wealth is distributed more unequally than national income, and wealth inequality has risen significantly since the 1980s (see chapter 1), many middle-class households have accumulated sufficient amounts of financial and housing wealth to self-identify with the interests of the most affluent classes. This growing alignment between wealthy elites and the wealth-owning middle classes had important policy implications: while during the Keynesian era governments were more strongly committed to the protection of employment income than to the protection of wealth, governments in the entire advanced capitalist world have become subject to a stronger pressure from a wider political coalition to pursue policies that protect these groups from wealth destruction – for example, by bailing out banks – and further promote financialization at the expense of inducing rising financial fragility.

Financial policy and growth models

The above analysis has mainly focused on the sharp rise in household debt in the United States, where politicians aimed to maintain support from the masses by deregulating the banking system and expanding credit to lower-income households in order to offset the negative distributional impact of the growth model. Other Anglo-Saxon economies adopted similar debt-led growth models fuelled by booming housing markets, reflecting the emergence of a new constellation that Colin Crouch suitably called 'privatized Keynesianism', as aggregate demand was increasingly held up by private borrowing rather than public spending.[46] This dependency on housing markets – by both individual, income-restrained households and the economy at large – is also referred to as *asset-based welfare*.[47] Before the rise of market-based banking, housing wealth tended to remain illiquid during people's lives: it remained locked up in the house until homeowners decided to sell it at a higher price. As restrictions on the terms of loans were loosened, the number of households that became eligible for mortgages increased and a variety of products to release housing equity emerged, allowing households to use their home as a kind of cash point: home equity loans gave homeowners the opportunity to convert their housing assets into available cash without having to sell and move out. This offered a vital boost for aggregate consumption in these economies, which would normally have faced depressed aggregate demand due to median wage stagnation and rising income inequality.

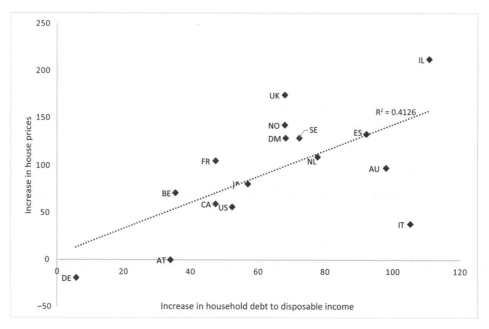

Figure 6.7 Increase in household debt and house prices in selected countries (in percentage), 1995–2008

Source: OECD; author's calculations

AT = Austria; AU = Australia; BE = Belgium; CA = Canada; DE = Germany; DM = Denmark; ES = Spain; FI = Finland; FR = France; IL = Ireland; IT = Italy; NL = Netherlands; NO = Norway; SE = Sweden; UK = United Kingdom; US = United States.

However, it is important to note that there has been an almost universal rise in household debt in the advanced capitalist world since the 1990s. Indeed, 'the notion of household debt finance both differentiating the liberal model from its coordinated economy foil, and providing the mechanism whereby ordinary voters' support for economic policy decisions is secured in liberal countries, has become accepted wisdom without even quite simple exposure to empirical scrutiny'.[48] As figure 6.7 shows, practically all advanced economies – even many CMEs – witnessed a combination of rising house prices and rising household debt from 1995 to 2008; the only CMEs where household debt levels (as a percentage of disposable income) did not budge or even declined a little were Austria and Germany. In the Netherlands and the Scandinavian CMEs, the increase in household debt was about as high as in the United Kingdom (although housing prices did not grow as fast). Belgium and Finland are somewhere in the middle. MMEs are homogeneous in terms of neither household debt nor price dynamics. Three questions arise from these observations. First, how can we explain these intra-model divergences in household debt? Second, why did the rise in household debt in the Nordic CMEs not culminate in a housing market collapse like that in the United States and the United Kingdom? And third, how did it affect their export-led growth model?

Cross-national differences in the evolution of household debt are to a considerable extent attributable to distinctive regulations and practices with regard to banking credit. In his work, Greg Fuller developed a composite index of different countries' systemic approach to credit during the 2000s based on five different dimensions of government policy that can affect the expansion of credit to households:[49]

1   interest rate restrictions on household borrowing;
2   capital gains rules on the transfer of household assets;
3   rules about the ratio of typical mortgage loans to the value of the property purchased;
4   mortgage subsidies; and
5   the size of a secondary market for household debt (as a measure of mortgage loan securitization.

Table 6.3 compares regulatory scores derived from existing rules in these five dimensions. It shows that the US government encouraged credit expansion more than any other government in the advanced democracies, and the LMEs were – on average – much more encouraging than the CMEs. Nevertheless, there have been major differences between the Netherlands and the Nordic CMEs on the one hand and continental CMEs like Germany and Austria on the other. There are several examples of regulations that encourage household credit more – or mitigate it less – in the former countries than in the latter. While the capital gains tax – that is, the tax that sellers must pay on the difference between the sale price of their home and the purchase price (less depreciation and maintenance costs) – is zero in the Netherlands

Table 6.3 National index of approach to credit, 2000s

LMEs		Nordic CMEs		Conservative CMEs		MMEs	
Canada	0	Denmark	0	Austria	-5	France	-2
	1	Finland	-1	Belgium	-3	Greece	-2
New Zealand	0	Iceland	1	Germany	-5	Italy	-5
United Kingdom	1	Sweden	-1	Luxembourg	-4	Portugal	0
United States	3	Norway	-1	Netherlands	2	Spain	1

Source: Fuller 2015

These scores were calculated by assigning and summing up the following values to the five regulatory dimensions: +3 for high credit encouragement, +2 for modest credit encouragement, +1 for limited credit encouragement, −1 for limited credit mitigation, −2 for modest credit mitigation and −3 for high credit mitigation. It should be noted that these scores are intrinsically meaningful only in a relative sense.

and Denmark on any home sale, capital gains in Austria and Germany are only fully waived on property that has been owned for ten years. On other regulatory dimensions, the Netherlands and Nordic CMEs like Denmark allow for a higher expansion of household credit as well. Major differences with regard to regulatory approaches to household credit can be observed in the group of MMEs too, with Spain especially having a lenient approach.

It remains something of a puzzle why rising household debt in CMEs with a more lenient regulatory environment did not result in a similar housing market collapse to that in the United Kingdom and the United States. Several explanations are plausible. First of all, the subprime segment of continental European housing markets (characterized by loan-to-value ratios close to or above 100 per cent, no-documentation/self-certified income loans and negative amortization contracts) was much more contained – even in countries like the Netherlands and Denmark. Furthermore, mortgages in the Eurozone countries are used to buy the primary house, for occupation by the owner, rather than as devices to extract home equity and support consumption spending: loans granted for the former purpose accounted for 70–90 per cent of all the housing mortgages granted in the region in 2007, according to a questionnaire put out by the ECB.[50] Because the diffusion of uncapped variable rate mortgages and home equity loans remained much more limited in the Eurozone countries than in the United States, mortgage borrowers were less vulnerable to rising interest rates and falling housing prices.

These observations suggest that household credit was less important in supporting household consumption. Indeed, one reason why household debt increased relatively sharply in the Nordic CMEs and the Netherlands is that the wages of lower- and medium-income households were relatively high and rose relatively fast, making mortgages more easily affordable.[51] As such, there are two distinctive linkages between demand for household credit and income inequality: in countries with sharply rising inequality – like the United States – household credit functioned for the bottom 50 per cent as a *substitute* for stagnating real wages by bolstering the consumption of lower- and middle-income households, whereas in countries with lower inequality, faster real wage growth for the bottom 50 per cent acted as a necessary *complement* to mortgage borrowing.[52] In the Nordic CMEs – as well as in the Netherlands – a generous welfare state, coordinated wage bargaining and worker-friendly labour market regulations have made large parts of the population creditworthy borrowers. Together with favourable tax regimes, 'a generous and universal welfare state characterised by a relatively equal income distribution creates a large pool of creditworthy potential buyers whose income, pension and healthcare security makes them willing and able to take on quite high debt levels. The demand for homeownership creates a vicious cycle of rising prices financed by ever larger mortgages.'[53] As such, *income equality* can be an important driver of *wealth inequality*, as housing becomes increasingly expensive for younger people who cannot rely on the 'bank of mum and dad'.[54] The sharp rise in household debt did not really affect the export-led growth model of the Nordic CMEs and the Netherlands, however, as household consumption – and overall wage inflation – continued to be constrained by their coordinated wage-setting institutions. As we saw in chapter 4, unions in the CMEs have a strong incentive to pursue wage restraint – that is, wages not exceeding average productivity growth – in order to maintain the export competitiveness of the core manufacturing sectors of the economy. These wage-setting institutions coordinated by export-led political coalitions enabled a countercyclical incomes policy that tamed the inflationary effects of sharp increases in mortgage debt.[55]

The more lenient approach to household credit helps to explain why the Nordic CMEs and the Netherlands had a more balanced growth model – with both household consumption and exports contributing more or less equally to GDP growth – than Germany. Household debt in Germany grew only slightly between 1995 and 2008 and remained below 70 per cent of GDP. German banks did not compensate for low household demand for mortgage credit by extending more corporate loans: because a combination of wage restraint and labour market flexibilization greatly reduced their unit labour costs and enhanced their profitability during this period, German non-financial corporations had more internal funds to finance their investment and became less dependent on German banks. German banks responded to tepid domestic credit demand with a combination of financialization and internationalization: they raised their leverage borrowing from each other and from foreign banks and financial institutions to engage in international market-based lending activities. The global financial crisis and its destabilizing effects on the Eurozone revealed the intrinsic risks associated with these activities, exposing the fundamental weakness of the German banking system.[56]

In the next chapter, we zoom in more closely on the political-economic anatomy of national growth models, how they gave rise to unsustainable macroeconomic imbalances in the decade preceding the global financial crisis, and a politically fraught adjustment process thereafter.

7

Macroeconomic Imbalances Before and After the Crisis

The global monetary system – the structure that governs financial relations between nations and their macroeconomic policies – plays an indispensable role in the smooth functioning of the world economy and even world politics. As Richard Cooper observed during the global monetary turmoil of the 1970s, '[w]hen monetary relations go well, other relations have a better chance of going well; when they go badly, other areas are likely to suffer too'.[1] The monetary volatility of the 1970s was linked to the breakup of the Bretton Woods regime and the shift from fixed but adjustable exchange rates towards flexible ones, which had loosened the constraints on national monetary policies. When the advanced market economies dismantled their capital controls during the 1970s and 1980s, the re-emergence and volatility of cross-border capital mobility and global finance further contributed to the idea that the global monetary system had transformed into an increasingly unstable 'non-system'.[2] Emerging markets and developing countries (EMDC) have been particularly vulnerable to the instabilities of global finance: during the 1980s Latin America and the developing world were plagued by an international debt crisis, whereas during the 1990s many emerging market economies experienced bank and balance-of-payments crises after having removed their capital controls. In the advanced capitalist countries, by contrast, there was a sense among government and central banks that the adoption of 'sound' monetary policies had ushered in an era of 'Great Moderation', with a steady decline in financial instability as well as in variability of output and of inflation from the 1990s.[3]

The global financial crisis and the Eurozone debt crisis were the latest manifestation of the dire state of the global monetary system, showing that the advanced capitalist world was only temporarily absolved from its instability. While the underlying dynamics of these crises were complex and multifaceted, many scholars and policymakers now believe that the unsustainable rise in global macroeconomic imbalances played a key role. In the years preceding the crisis, the United States had been running an increasing deficit on its trade balance. The unprecedented growth in the US trade deficit was increasingly financed – at least from the end of the 1990s – by borrowing from central banks in emerging markets and especially from East Asia, which ran increasing trade surpluses and accumulated an extraordinary amount of foreign exchange reserves that were mostly invested in US dollar assets. The rise in these global imbalances between the United States and the rest of the world, which is a reflection of the fact that the US economy had been increasingly living 'beyond its means', is now widely seen as an indirect macro-economic source of the crisis that erupted in 2007 in the US housing market.[4] A similar constellation of imbalances arose in the Eurozone, where the rising deficits of the peripheral countries were matched by the rising surpluses of the northern countries since the introduction of the euro. The growth of these regional imbalances is also recognized as having contributed to the banking and sovereign debt crisis.[5]

While the literature on macroeconomic imbalances used to be dominated by neoclassical economists, scholars of IPE and CPE have produced many insights that are crucial for understanding how these imbalances evolved before the financial crisis and continue to evolve after it. By reviewing the IPE and CPE literature, this chapter argues that the global imbalances and their evolution after the crisis resulted from the asymmetric capacity of the advanced market economies to maintain the growth model associated with their national variety of capitalism. Before the crisis, the escalation of global and European macroeconomic imbalances ensued from a temporary, symbiotic, yet ultimately unsustainable relationship between debt-financed, consumption-led growth models in deficit countries and export-led growth models in surplus countries. As we have seen in previous chapters, the formation of these debt-led or export-led growth models has been mediated by historically developed domestic institutions of distinctive national models of capitalism, which shaped the relative power of different classes and sectors in the domestic economic decision-making process. This explains why international macroeconomic coordination between deficit and surplus countries to readjust the imbalances in a growth-friendly way is so politically difficult; in this regard, macroeconomic imbalances are more structural than many neoclassical economists like to believe.

The adjustment of the imbalances after the crisis has been highly asymmetrical, with deficit countries – especially in the Eurozone – being forced to deleverage their economy – that is, paying off and reducing their debt by cutting back on consumption – and most surplus countries refusing to boost domestic demand. At the same time, the crisis forced overly indebted households in the United States and the United Kingdom to deleverage, constraining a restoration of finance-led growth. These problems of macroeconomic adjustment are a key reason why economic growth remained so fragile and stubbornly low in the advanced capitalist world, leading a resurgence of debates about secular stagnation. In this chapter, we will clarify how the resurfacing of secular stagnation can be linked to the asymmetric adjustment of macroeconomic imbalances after the crisis, and can be traced back to the domestic political constraints experienced by many advanced market economies in trying to revive their pre-crisis growth models.

Widening macroeconomic imbalances before the crises: empirics

As figure 7.1 shows, the world economy featured widening macroeconomic imbalances in the pre-crisis years, which were largely based upon a rising current account deficit in the US economy and a parallel surge of current account surpluses in the East Asian countries and oil-exporting countries (for the meaning of 'current account balance' and its distinction from 'trade balance', see box 7.1). Neoclassical accounts of these global imbalances accordingly focused on these players, generating two opposing camps that put the blame on either East Asia or the United States. The most dominant account is the 'global saving glut' view, which was put forward by Ben Bernanke, the former governor of the Federal Reserve, and attributes the growth in global imbalances to the hoarding of savings in oil-exporting countries and East Asia.[6] Oil-exporting countries saved more due to sharp oil price rises, but the bulk of the global saving glut originated in East Asia, where central banks started to accumulate massive foreign exchange reserves (mostly dollar-denominated assets). According to the Bretton Woods II hypothesis, the build-up of these dollar reserves ensued from their mercantilist exchange-rate interventions, which kept their currencies relatively undervalued against the US dollar to promote export-led growth.[7] Building reserves also followed from their precautionary desire to 'self-insure' against capital flight, which is an endemic risk for EMDC. Several studies found that self-insurance against financial crises was the main motivation for foreign exchange accumulation in these

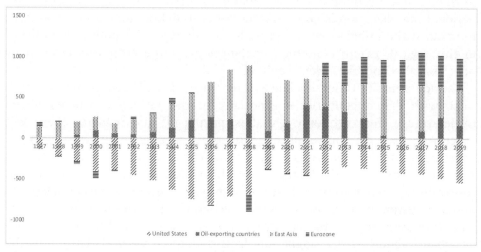

Figure 7.1 Global current account imbalances (in billion US dollars), 1997–2019

Source: IMF World Economic Outlook Database

countries.[8] This could explain why reserve accumulation mostly originated in East Asia, which was hit by a severe international financial crisis in 1997–8.

Box 7.1 The balance of payments

To understand the significance of the external imbalances and how they are linked to the global financial crisis, a brief explanation of the balance of payments (BoP) is required. The BoP is the annual record of all the transactions between the residents of a country – its households, firms and government – and the rest of the world. It consists of the current account and the capital account:

Balance of payments = Current account + Capital account

A country's current account records all revenues and payments linked to its international trade and its net international investment position (NIIP – that is, its foreign assets minus its foreign liabilities). It is the sum of its trade balance (i.e. exports of goods and services minus imports) and its income balance (i.e. income on foreign assets – such as dividends on foreign equities held by residents – minus payments on foreign liabilities – such as interest rate payments on sovereign bonds held by foreigners). For most countries, the trade balance is by far the largest component of the current account balance, which is why the two terms are often used interchangeably (although, technically, they are not the same).

  A country's capital account records all the flows of capital and finance between its residents and the rest of the world, including:

1 real foreign direct investment (FDI) – domestic firms establishing a manufacturing facility in foreign countries and/or acquiring a majority stake in foreign firms, and foreign firms setting up a factory in the domestic economy and/or acquiring a majority stake in domestic firms;
2 portfolio investment – domestic investors purchasing or selling foreign portfolio securities (equities, bonds), and foreign investors purchasing or selling domestic financial assets; and
3 reserve assets – foreign financial assets that are controlled by the central bank.

Given that a country's BoP should be in equilibrium, its current account balance should be equal and opposite to its capital account balance: so if the United States runs a current account deficit of US$700 billion (as it did in 2007), it has to run a surplus of US$700 billion on its capital account (or the other way around). Large and rising current account deficits can be a problem because ever-growing surpluses on the capital account are needed to finance these deficits, implying that foreigners need to be willing to invest an ever-growing amount of capital in that country. Another way to put this is that any country with rising current account deficits has to accumulate foreign liabilities or run down foreign assets – for example, by selling the central bank's foreign reserve assets – in order to fund these deficits.

  In general terms and in the absence of any valuation changes on its foreign assets and liabilities, a country's current account balance equals the change in its NIIP (i.e.

net foreign wealth): by definition, a country with a current account deficit (surplus) experiences a deterioration (improvement) of its NIIP. That is why countries with persistently large current account deficits are *net debtors* to the rest of the world, while countries with persistently large current account surplus are *net creditors*. For this reason, excessive current account deficits can easily be unsustainable, as a country's NIIP deteriorates to such a degree that foreigners start having doubts about the capacity of the country to meet its foreign liabilities, and become unwilling to finance the external deficits. If this happens, a deficit country can fall into a BoP crisis, which goes hand in hand with massive capital flight and – usually – a sharp fall in the value of its currency.

Other economists challenged Bernanke's global saving glut theory by claiming that the global imbalances were driven by the autonomous decisions of the US government and US households to reduce savings and increase borrowing.[9] A wide range of empirical studies have shown that the current account typically deteriorates in countries witnessing a domestic credit boom, which fuels imports by stimulating aggregate demand in the economy. The intrinsic connection between domestic credit booms and external deficits elucidates why it is not only the United States that has experienced a significant decline in its current account balance since the 1990s, but also other LMEs like the United Kingdom and Australia as well as most MMEs in the Eurozone (figure 7.2). The Eurozone ran a current account that was more or less in balance during this period and hence played a negligible role in the rise of the global imbalances, yet behind its balanced current account loomed widening imbalances between the northern and peripheral members of the region (figure 7.3). While CMEs like the Netherlands and especially Germany ran growing surpluses, Ireland and the southern Eurozone countries ran growing deficits.

These observations suggest that the widening of global and European imbalances reflected an interdependent yet ultimately unsustainable relationship between the debt-led growth models of the Anglo-Saxon LMEs and southern European MMEs on the one hand and the export-led growth models of CMEs on the other. In trade terms, debt-led growth in the LMEs and MMEs fuelled aggregate demand in these countries, a part of which 'leaked out' in the form of higher imports of manufacturing goods produced by the CMEs, and bolstered the latter countries' export-led growth models. In financial terms, CMEs with persistent current account surpluses accumulated excess savings that were reinvested in economies with debt-led growth models and helped them to finance their current account deficits: export-led CMEs have been net lenders to debt-led CMEs and MMEs.

In order to understand why countries with current account surpluses (deficits) have a surplus (shortage) of domestic savings, the Keynesian aggregate demand function we first encountered in chapter 1:

(a) LMEs

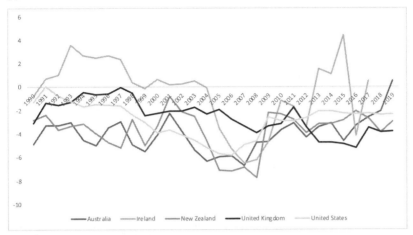

(b) MMEs

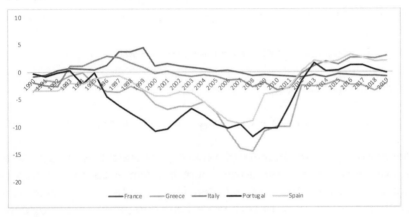

(c) CMEs

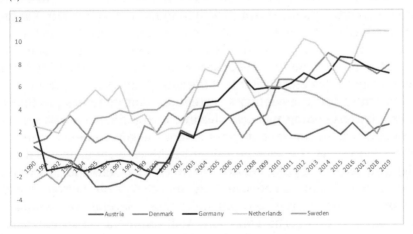

Figure 7.2 Current account balance (in percentage of GDP), 1990–2019

Source: IMF World Economic Outlook Database

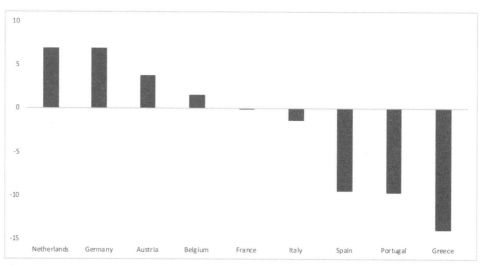

Figure 7.3 Current account balance of Eurozone countries (in percentage of GDP), 2007

Source: IMF World Economic Outlook Database

$$Y = C + I + (G - T) + (X - M)$$

can be rewritten as follows:

$$(X - M) = (Y - C) - I + (T - G) = (S - I) + (T - G)$$

In other words, the trade balance of a country is determined by the savings gap of the private sector and the government balance. A country with a current account deficit always has a savings deficiency in the private sector (S < I), in the public sector (T < G) or in both the private and public sector; by definition, a country with a current account surplus has a savings surplus in the private sector (S > I), in the public sector (T > G) or in both. If we further disaggregate the private sector into the household sector and the corporate sector, another way to put this is that a country's current account balance depends on the financial balances of the household sector, corporate sector and public sector – where 'financial balances' refer to differences between income and expenditures in each sector: if a country's current account increases (declines) there must be a corresponding increase (decline) in the financial balance(s) of the corporate sector, the household sector and/or the government sector.[10]

Table 7.1 presents the average values of these sectoral financial balances for eighteen selected OECD countries between 1995 and 2007, as well as the change in these balances between 1999 and 2007 – the period of widening global and regional current account imbalances. Several conclusions can be drawn from this table. The LMEs and MMEs show a consistent pattern of declining financial balances for the total economy, reflecting a deterioration of their current account balance throughout this period. Only Canada deviates

Table 7.1 Sectoral financial balances in selected OECD countries (in percentage of GDP), 1995–2007

	Total		Non-financial corporate sector		Household sector		Government sector	
	Δ(1999–2007)	μ(1995–2007)	Δ(1999–2007)	μ(1995–2007)	Δ(1999–2007)	μ(1995–2007)	Δ(1999–2007)	μ(1995–2007)
LMEs								
AU	-3.24	-4.78	-5.34	-3.57	NA	NA	-1.28	0.26
CA	0.37	0.81	2.62	2.53	NA	NA	0.16	0.16
IL	-9.17	-0.55	-2.43	1.28	-6.60	-6.30	-2.15	1.51
NZ	-2.13	-4.32	-4.05	1.04	-2.40	-4.45	4.46	2.53
UK	-3.02	-1.86	-2.76	-2.42	-5.45	2.78	-3.26	-1.95
US	-3.37	-3.69	-2.77	-4.29	-4.20	0.57	-3.50	-3.26
CMEs								
AT	6.64	0.09	2.69	-5.03	NA	NA	1.24	-2.76
BE	-3.43	3.99	-0.45	-1.11	-2.00	4.15	0.62	-1.25
DM	-0.20	2.46	-2.17	4.51	-1.80	-3.37	4.15	1.01
FI	-0.10	5.24	0.37	6.13	-2.20	-1.51	3.44	1.93
DE	7.54	1.42	6.08	-3.46	2.10	4.45	1.98	-3.11
NL	2.11	5.00	2.08	3.83	-1.80	-1.04	-0.35	-1.54
SE	4.85	5.02	0.27	1.85	2.40	1.65	2.60	-0.03
MMEs								
FR	-3.31	1.30	-4.02	-2.50	-0.50	2.74	-1.03	-2.97
IT	-2.29	0.46	-1.30	-4.67	-1.70	4.04	0.43	-3.52
GR	-8.64	-6.83	-0.26	-4.80	-5.8	-3.29	-0.91	-6.67
PT	-2.19	-6.48	-2.84	-9.22	0.00	2.02	0.02	-4.35
ES	-7.40	-4.48	-2.26	-4.73	-6.80	-1.10	3.25	-1.36

Source: AMECO; IMF World Economic Outlook Database; OECD

Δ(1999–2007) = Change between 1999 and 2007 in percentage points. μ(1995–2007) = Average balance in percentage of GDP between 1995 and 2007. AT = Austria; AU = Australia; BE = Belgium; CA = Canada; DE = Germany; DM = Denmark; ES = Spain; FI = Finland; FR = France; GR = Greece; IL = Ireland; IT = Italy; NL = Netherlands; NZ = New Zealand; PT = Portugal; SE = Sweden; UK = United Kingdom; US = United States.

from this pattern. In the case of the LMEs, falling financial balances of households were a common source of the decline in their current account balance. In the United States and the United Kingdom, rising fiscal deficits also played an important role. In the case of the MMEs, the picture is more mixed. France's and Italy's current account balance deteriorated less severely than those of the other MMEs and was, on average, in modest surplus. Spain and Greece especially experienced exponentially rising current account deficits, which mostly resulted from a sharp decline in the financial balances of their households. It is also noteworthy that all the MMEs had, on average, a significant fiscal deficit, although Spain's government balance improved markedly during this period. The CMEs, finally, all had significant surpluses on their current account balance, on average. Germany stands out as the country with the strongest improvement in its current account balance, which can be explained mostly by the sharp rise in financial surpluses in the non-financial corporate sector and – to a lesser extent – the household sector.

In the next section, we examine the linkages between these patterns and the formation of debt-led growth models in LMEs and MMEs on the one hand and export-led growth models in the CMEs on the other – two types of growth models that resulted from the changes in macroeconomic policy, social policy, corporate governance and financial policy we have discussed in the previous four chapters.

Macroeconomic imbalances and growth models before the crisis

In previous chapters, we have discussed key institutional transitions that have been central to the formation of debt-led growth models in LMEs like the United States and the United Kingdom – growth models that are often also called 'finance-led' because of their dependency on financial markets and financialization.[11] From a VoC perspective,

> the US and UK governments allowed a lax interpretation of financial regulations governing leverage, both in the valuation of the risky assets that highly-leveraged financial institutions owned and in the assessment of bank capital ... because they saw it as beneficial to one of the most important economic sectors in which the United States and the United Kingdom had comparative institutional advantage.[12]

As shown in figure 7.4, the share of the FIRE sector in GDP was, on average, significantly higher in the LMEs than in the CMEs and MMEs in the mid-1990s, and even increased moderately from then. What resulted was a dysfunctional growth model: the consequence of the centrality of the FIRE sector in the United States and the United Kingdom is that 'the functioning of the economy is no longer evaluated in terms of the production of employment or rising standards of living, but by the movements of the stock market, the realization of shareholder value, and the profits of the financial sector'.[13]

The growing centrality of the FIRE sector in the growth model of the LMEs

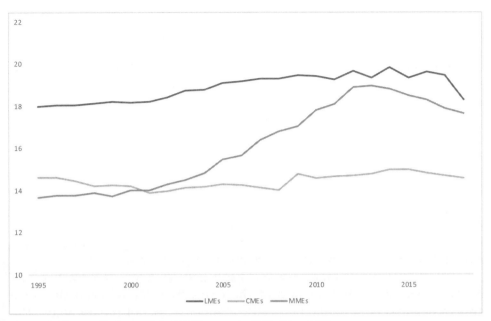

Figure 7.4 Share of value added of FIRE sector in GDP, 1995–2018

Source: OECD

was linked to institutional developments in other parts of the economy. As we have seen in chapter 4, the liberalization of labour markets in the Anglo-Saxon countries took the form of an outright assault on labour unions, resulting in a sharp decline in union density. These developments undermined the power resources of low- and medium-skilled workers and contributed to the rise in personal income inequality and the stagnation of real wages of the bottom 50 per cent of households. At the same time, the already relatively meagre, market-oriented welfare states of the LMEs underwent significant – often hidden – forms of retrenchment.[14] The (neo)liberalization of industrial relations and retrenchment of the welfare state made homeownership and the expansion of credit to lower-income households critical to supporting their consumption levels in the face of real wage stagnation, and to maintaining aggregate demand in the economy. The resulting asset-based welfare regime relied on growing – and ultimately unsustainable – homeownership rates, as homeowners increasingly depended on their capacity to tap housing wealth as a buffer against income shocks (chapter 6). The rise of the shareholder model of corporate governance also played a key role in the formation of a finance-led growth model by inflating stock prices and encouraging wealth effects: people were inclined to spend more money as they felt richer. While shareholder ownership remains heavily concentrated among the wealthiest households, booming stock markets also buttressed wealth accumulation among middle-class households particularly via their participation in defined-contribution private pension schemes. As such, consumption among a growing share of the population in the LMEs became increasingly dependent on an unsustainable rise in asset prices and debt accumulation.

As we have seen in chapter 3, the transition towards a low-inflation monetary policy and restrictive fiscal policy regime was universal in the advanced capitalist world, and was instrumental in weakening the power of labour and constraining the capacity of workers to demand higher wages. Nevertheless, LMEs have a stronger incentive to pursue relatively expansionary macroeconomic policies during economic recessions, given the facts that their growth model is so reliant on domestic demand and that their labour markets are sufficiently flexible to maintain price stability by thwarting wage growth among low- and medium-skilled workers. The more expansionary macroeconomic policy stance of LMEs manifests itself in two ways. On the one hand, governments in the United States – and to a lesser extent the United Kingdom – have run more lenient fiscal policies, exemplified by budgetary deficits that were significantly larger than those of the CMEs (table 7.1). On the other, inflation-targeting central banks provided institutional support for finance-led growth in LMEs by fuelling asset price inflation (chapter 3).

Relatively restrictive monetary and fiscal policies have played a key role in the export-led growth models of the CMEs by pushing down the wage growth of workers in the domestically oriented sectors of the economy. The principal objective of institutional organization is to preserve and support the competitiveness of the manufacturing sectors. Centralized wage bargaining, worker representation in company boards and generous welfare states acted as beneficial constraints that supported the incremental innovation strategies of firms in these sectors by pushing them to invest in the industry- and firm-specific skills of their workforce. CMEs also have bank-dominated financial systems, which have traditionally offered long-term 'patient' capital in ways that encourage manufacturing firms to invest in these skills through on-the-job vocational training. As a result of these institutional complementarities, manufacturing firms in the CMEs have a comparative institutional advantage in the production of high-value-added and quality-differentiated goods.

A number of developments since the 1980s made the growth model of CMEs more reliant on external demand. Economic globalization and the steady integration of low-wage developing countries like China created more export opportunities but also put more pressure on manufacturing firms to strengthen their cost competitiveness. Cutting labour costs was crucial in this regard. Centralized wage bargaining institutions had traditionally done the trick here, given that manufacturing firms typically enjoyed higher-than-average productivity growth. But firms in the domestically oriented services sectors of the economy were affected by rising unit labour costs (ULC), which either constrained job growth in these sectors or engendered higher prices. While economic globalization weakened the bargaining power of unions in the manufacturing sectors of the economy and encouraged them to engage in wage restraint in order to preserve as many jobs as possible, that is not necessarily the case for workers in the domestically oriented service sectors that are sheltered from international competition. In these sectors, unions do not face a market-imposed constraint on their wage demands, creating the risk of spiralling wage inflation and rising prices. The key problem is that rising ULC in these sectors can produce an 'inflationary squeeze' on firms in the export-oriented manufacturing sectors, which can be adversely affected by higher input prices of services produced by the sheltered sectors.[15] The flexibilization of labour markets in the services sectors and the pursuit of restrictive macroeconomic policies were key to preserving the cost competitiveness of the export-oriented manufacturing sectors by depressing wage growth in the sheltered sectors (chapter 4).

Some CMEs went further in this regard than others, however. Manufacturing interests prevailed particularly in Germany, reflected by the relatively low contribution of private and public consumption to GDP growth between 1995 and 2007 (see table 2.3 in chapter 2) as well as by the evolution in economy-wide nominal ULC depicted in figure 7.5. The 'golden wage rule' stipulates that nominal wages should grow at the full rate of labour productivity growth plus the inflation target of the central bank; only when ULC grow at 2 per cent can a central bank reach its inflation target at the same time as maintaining a stable functional income distribution and wage share of GDP. Figure 7.5 shows that the growth in nominal ULC from 1990 remained below the 2 per cent target in all the CMEs. However, Germany stands out as the country with the lowest growth in ULC: after experiencing a sharp rise in ULC in the first half of the 1990s in the wake of the reunification of West and East Germany – which created a strong political push for wage equalization between the richer western part and the poorer eastern part – nominal ULC basically remained flat between 1995 and 2008.

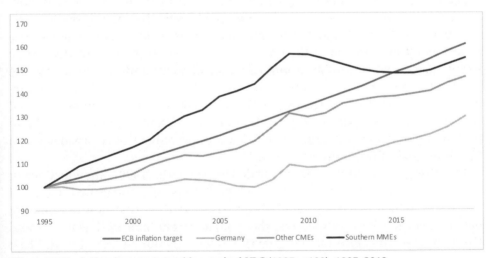

Figure 7.5 Evolution in economy-wide nominal ULC (1995 = 100), 1995–2019

Source: AMECO; author's calculations

'Southern MMEs' is a non-weighted average of Greece, Italy, Portugal and Spain; 'Other CMEs' is a non-weighted average of Austria, Belgium, Denmark, Finland, Sweden and the Netherlands.

Germany's outlier position is connected to the liberalization of industrial relations and wage-setting institutions especially in the labour-intensive services sectors, which has resulted in an increasingly dualized labour market (chapter 4).[16] Neoliberal labour market restructuring was deemed necessary not only to deal with the challenges of deindustrialization but also to redress the inflationary effects of German reunification. Germany's repressed wage and consumption growth can also be linked to weak public spending: Germany adopted more restrictive fiscal policies than the other CMEs.[17] Another feature distinguishing Germany from the Nordic CMEs is its comparatively low public sector employment. In the latter countries, 'large public sectors produce higher levels of demand by stimulating the economy with the multiplier effect and ... directly expand consumption by marginal groups, because state employment of low-skill workers tends to raise low-end employment and wages'.[18] Moreover, Germany's public sector employees underwent significant wage restraint caused by an increase in atypical employment contracts in the public sector and by a restrictive fiscal policy stance.[19] The repression of ULC – combined with corporate governance institutions that encourage firms to retain profits rather than distributing dividends to shareholders and paying out exorbitant salaries to top managers – clarifies the comparatively large increase in net corporate savings in the German economy (table 7.1).[20]

The Nordic countries also responded to the challenges of deindustrialization by liberalizing their labour market, but chose a different path: that of embedded flexibilization. Formal collective bargaining institutions underwent a consistent decentralization, but high levels of bargaining coverage and unionization were maintained across sectors and skill groups (chapter 4).[21] Together with more lenient regulatory approaches with regard to household credit (chapter 6), these countries have adopted a more balanced growth model that combined more robust consumption growth with strong exports. The export-led growth model of the CMEs has thus been supported by distinctive social blocs – that is, configurations of class and sectoral interests – as Baccaro and Pontusson argue: while unskilled workers have been increasingly marginalized and a class-based narrowing of the dominant social bloc can be observed in all the CMEs, the export-led growth model of the Nordic countries (and also of Belgium and the Netherlands) has been underpinned by a broader social bloc than that of Germany.[22]

The diverging trend in economy-wide ULC since the 1990s, shown above in figure 7.5, is a good starting point from which to portray the growth model of the MMEs, which has traditionally been based on the expansion of domestic demand. From a VoC perspective, the comparatively high ULC growth – and the associated consumption-led growth model – should be linked to the lack of collective bargaining institutions that promote wage restraint, especially in the sheltered sectors of the economy. In their seminal 2001 edited volume *Varieties of Capitalism*, Peter Hall and David Soskice suggested that the Southern European countries adopted a distinctive variety of capitalism featuring some capacities for coordination in the sphere of corporate governance and very limited capacities for strategic coordination in the sphere of industrial relations, but these authors had little to say about it beyond the observation that these political economies reflected a history of state intervention. MMEs generally lack the consensus-oriented labour market institutions that enable manufacturing firms and workers to negotiate wages and develop production strategies that are responsive to changes in external competitiveness. As Bob Hancké notes, MMEs 'can perhaps best be understood in a two-tiered framework, in which firms attempt to negotiate the production of collective goods among themselves, but are forced to rely on the state to compensate for the gaps in the institutional framework which precludes them to deliver autonomously'.[23] Unions are usually much weaker and industrial relations much more conflictive than in CMEs, giving the state a key mediating role in national wage-setting and labour market regulation.[24] French industrial relations, for instance, have traditionally featured strong competition between labour unions that do not make concessions as a way to attract members; as a result, wage formation evolves 'mainly via the disciplinary role of high unemployment, and not at all via the internalization by the social partners of the costs of poor job creation'.[25]

Governments in MMEs have traditionally adopted accommodating macro-economic policy regimes that strengthen domestic demand and (before adopting the euro) improve their international price competitiveness through occasional currency devaluations. Because the national central banks were controlled by the national ministries of finance, governments frequently used monetary creation in order to finance public debts. While inflationary levels in MMEs usually exceeded those in the CMEs, the nominal exchange rate was regularly devalued in the 1980s and 1990s to compensate for the loss in export competitiveness (table 7.2). However, exports for manufacturing firms were mostly seen as complements to sales to the domestic market; the growth model of MMEs was led by the dynamism of domestic consumption based on real wage growth – a growth model 'especially suitable for economies in which small and medium-sized businesses are responsible for a large portion of economic activity'.[26] European monetary integration had strong effects on the growth model of the MMEs: the introduction of the euro prevented their governments from compensating for the lack of responsiveness of their labour market institutions to developments in external cost competitiveness through sporadic exchange rate devaluations, which in the comparative capitalisms literature is generally seen as a key cause of the sovereign debt crisis in Eurozone by contributing to unsustainable current account imbalances.[27]

Unions and firms in the manufacturing sectors of the CMEs became more willing to exert wage restraint after the introduction of the euro: '[i]f trade partners cannot devalue, it becomes more likely that nominal wage restraint will actually result in the enhancement of price competitiveness not only in the short, but also in the medium run'.[28] While making wage restraint a

Table 7.2 Average annual change in nominal exchange rate and inflation, 1980s and 1990–8

	Average annual change in the nominal exchange rate		Average annual change in inflation	
	1980s	1990–8	1980s	1990–8
Austria	2.41	1.40	3.84	2.61
Belgium	-0.56	1.33	4.90	2.26
Finland	1.43	-1.27	7.32	2.24
Germany	2.89	2.00	2.90	2.73
Netherlands	1.84	1.32	3.00	2.60
Export-led average	*1.60*	*0.96*	*4.39*	*2.49*
Greece	-11.67	-4.83	19.50	12.05
Italy	-2.41	-1.45	11.20	4.38
Portugal	-8.83	-0.87	17.35	6.59
Spain	-2.34	-1.57	10.26	4.44
Demand-led average	*-6.31*	*-2.18*	*14.58*	*6.87*

Source: Johnston and Regan 2016

more rewarding strategy in CMEs, the adoption of the euro is believed to have reduced the MMEs' incentive to keep ULC in check. In the run-up period to the EMU during the 1990s, inflation across all member states of the European Monetary System (EMS) converged towards the low levels of Germany and the Deutschmark bloc (i.e. the bloc of countries that had pegged their currency against the Deutschmark during the 1980s). The ability of national central banks to thwart excessive wage inflation in the sheltered sectors – particularly in the public sectors where unions were often most powerful – through restrictive monetary policies was paramount in the ability of the southern MMEs to meet one of the Maastricht convergence criteria for adopting the euro: that is, an average inflation rate not more than 1.5 percentage points above the rate of the three best performing member states. A prevailing interpretation in the comparative capitalisms literature on the Eurozone crisis is that monetary union removed the constraints that national central banks in these MMEs were able to impose on excessive wage demands in the sheltered sectors:

> EMU lifted the hard monetary constraint by removing the strong disciplining capacity of the national central banks and replacing it with the much weaker disciplining capacity of the ECB ... Whereas national central banks could credibly threaten action against inflationary wages in one country, the ECB is constrained by its mandate to target an EMU-wide aggregate inflation rate. It cannot, therefore, punish individual unions who no longer play a disinflationary game. With the monetary constraint lifted, [unions in the sheltered sectors] went for higher wages – wages above what its (implied) productivity rate would permit.[29]

The ECB's 'one-size-fits-all' monetary policy fuelled consumption-led growth in southern MMEs by leading to relatively lower real interest rates and cheap credit. Since the ECB focuses on *region-wide average inflation*, its monetary policy was too restrictive for countries with lower-than-average inflation and too expansionary for countries with higher-than-average inflation. Recall from chapter 3 that only *real* interest rates, which adjust *nominal* interest rates for inflation, matter for borrowers or investors. A key problem for the EMU is that the nominal interest rate set by the ECB translates into different real interest rates in the member states when national inflation rates diverge. CMEs faced relatively high real interest rates that depressed domestic demand and bolstered the competitiveness of their manufacturing sectors by restraining wage growth in the sheltered sectors; MMEs, on the other hand, enjoyed relatively low real interest rates that fuelled a debt-led expansion of domestic demand at the expense of additional wage inflation and the declining export competitiveness of their manufacturing sectors.[30] The upshot is that European monetary integration put the southern Eurozone countries into a condition of 'dependent financialization': temporarily, 'the deteriorating export competitiveness in production after the introduction of the euro had been masked – more precisely: overcompensated – with regard to its negative effect on economic growth by an increasing private indebtedness and rising asset prices, fuelling booms in construction and consumption'.[31] The extraordinary rise in the GDP share of the FIRE sector (figure 7.4) was a clear manifestation of this condition.

Growth models and macroeconomic adjustment after the crisis

In November 2008 government and state leaders of the G20 – the Group of 20; that is, the world's twenty largest and most powerful countries – came together in Washington, DC, to formulate a coordinated macroeconomic policy response to the global financial crisis. To deal with the 'deteriorating economic conditions worldwide', the G20 leaders agreed at their first summit that 'a broader policy response is needed, based on closer macroeconomic cooperation'. They recognized 'the importance of monetary policy support, as deemed appropriate to domestic conditions' and recommended the use of 'fiscal measures to stimulate domestic demand to rapid effect, as appropriate, while maintaining a policy framework conducive to fiscal sustainability'.[32] At the same summit, the G20 leaders hinted that widening global macroeconomic imbalances had played a central role in the crisis: 'Major underlying factors to the current situation were, among others, inconsistent and insufficiently coordinated macroeconomic policies, inadequate structural reforms, which led to unsustainable global macroeconomic outcomes.'[33] At the Pittsburgh summit in September 2009 the G20 called for a 'Framework for Strong, Sustainable and Balanced Growth' as a way to redress these imbalances.

More specifically, countries with 'sustained, significant' external deficits pledged to 'undertake policies to support private savings and undertake fiscal consolidation', whereas those with sustained and significant surpluses would 'strengthen domestic sources of growth'.[34]

More than ten years after the announcement of this framework, it is clear that the G20's attempt to engage in the international coordination of macro-economic adjustment failed, as reflected by the persistence of global current account imbalances shown in figure 7.1. From a political economy perspective, this should not be surprising: macroeconomic adjustment has major distri-butional implications, which make it politically difficult for governments and central banks to pursue adjustment policies.[35] In surplus countries, governments and central banks are typically reluctant to accept a nominal appreciation of the currency or adopt reflationary macroeconomic policies that undermine the competitiveness of export-oriented sectors. In deficit countries, on the other hand, governments are usually unwilling to undertake a nominal exchange rate depreciation or pursue deflationary macroeconomic policies that are opposed by producers of non-tradable goods and services (such as local services, construction, real estate) and involve a reduction in the domestic purchasing power and standard of living of large swathes of the population. These macroeconomic adjustment policies clash in fundamental ways with the class and sectoral interests underpinning the pre-crisis growth models that we discussed in the previous section and chapters.

This observation does not suggest that there has been no macroeconomic adjustment at all nor that the main players of the global current account imbalances have remained the same. One of the most significant developments since the eruption of the global financial crisis is the rise of the Eurozone's aggregate current account surplus (see figure 7.1). This development is the outcome of a highly asymmetrical adjustment process *within* the region, as the current account deficits of the southern Eurozone countries have completely dissipated, whereas the current account surpluses of the northern countries persisted or even grew further (figure 7.6). The southern MMEs were forced to implement internal devaluation measures – that is, austerity and deregulation of labour markets – to reduce their ULC and restore competitiveness, whereas the northern CMEs were unwilling to boost domestic demand by pursuing expansionary fiscal policies or other types of internal revaluation measures (see below).

The experience of the southern MMEs might not seem very remarkable in light of the fact that countries with excessive external deficits usually face more pressure to adjust than countries with large surpluses. After all, current account deficits need to be financed by attracting foreign capital inflows – an external financing constraint that countries with surpluses by definition do not have. Recurrent international financial crises in EMDC during the 1980s and 1990s are a clear testimony to the severe macroeconomic adjustment process that countries with excessive external deficits can be subjected to

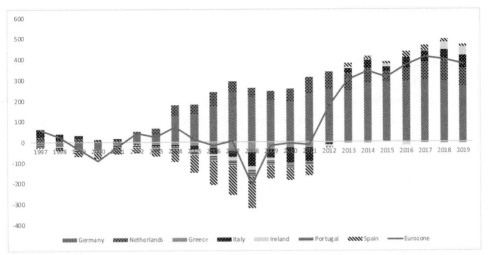

Figure 7.6 Current account balance of selected EMU countries (in billion US dollars), 1997–2019

Source: IMF World Economic Outlook Database

when massive capital flight makes these deficits unsustainable. The post-crisis experience of the United States and the United Kingdom reveals that not every country with large current account deficits faces these risks, however: by 2016, the US deficit in non-petroleum goods was almost as large as its pre-crisis peak, whereas the UK deficit in 2016 (5.2 per cent) even exceeded its pre-crisis peak (4.8 per cent in 2008).

How can the different external adjustment pressures on their finance-led growth models and the debt-led growth models of the southern MMEs be explained? The IPE literature has identified two mutually non-exclusive reasons. First, the United States and the United Kingdom host the world's two largest global financial centres with the most open and liquid capital markets, which have supported their structural capacity to delay the burden of macroeconomic adjustment by offering a magnet to foreign savings. The international monetary power of the United States is further bolstered by the international status of the US dollar, which gives the US economy the 'exorbitant privilege' of running balance-of-payments deficits 'without tears' – as the French economist Jacques Rueff famously remarked in the 1960s.[36] Second, the United States and the United Kingdom are both *monetarily sovereign* countries, as the bulk of their foreign debt is issued in a currency that they have fully under control. If debt is issued in the domestic currency, the central bank plays an essential role in preserving the safety of that debt through its capacity to create money and act as a lender of last resort: 'a central bank can make any domestic-currency debt asset safe by providing it with a "monetary backstop", i.e., by committing to provide the issuer with the currency required to repay the debt or to buy the asset itself at the no-default price'.[37] The ultimate market backed by the central bank's power to create money is the market for public debt, which is a key reason why it functions as a risk-free asset in the eyes of private investors: 'In its own domestic currency the national state is essentially always creditworthy, and default is impossible, since the central bank can always buy government bonds and monetize the debt.'[38]

The Eurozone countries have surrendered this ability by issuing debt in a currency that is controlled not by their national central bank but by the ECB, which was much more reluctant than the Federal Reserve and the Bank of England to engage in the large-scale asset purchase programmes known as QE. QE is the creation of money by central banks to buy financial assets – usually sovereign bonds – to reduce interest rates on these bonds. The ECB's reluctance to pursue QE offered the northern CMEs a mechanism to deflect the burden of macroeconomic adjustment onto the southern MMEs. In the United States and the United Kingdom, as we will see below, QE can be seen as an attempt to minimize the macroeconomic adjustment costs of the global financial crisis by restoring the key pillars of finance-led growth.

Macroeconomic adjustment in finance-led LMEs

The main concern of governments and central banks in the United States and the United Kingdom was to mitigate the fallout of the crisis on their finance-led economy, the growth of which was hampered by the deleveraging of the household and financial sector. The bursting of the housing bubble marked the beginning of a phase of financial retrenchment for the US economy: in 2008 the savings rate of US households rose from virtually zero to above 4 per cent, reducing the US current account deficit from more than 6 per cent of US GDP in 2006 to less than 5 per cent in 2008. Hence, after the bursting of the housing bubble, the US economy was plagued by a deficiency of aggregate demand: the debt overhang put pressure on US households to cut their debt levels in a way that depressed consumer spending and impeded the economic recovery. The one-third drop in national average home prices between mid-2006 and 2009 led to a sharp drop in households' consumption in order for them to pay back debt. Richard Koo has aptly called the Great Recession a 'balance-sheet recession' – a recession induced by the need for private sector deleveraging, whereby households and firms massively increase savings and pay down debt even though interest rates are at a record low.[39] As the pre-crisis debt-led growth model was based on the financialization of households, in terms of the increasing relevance of financial decisions in everyday life due to the democratization of finance (chapter 6), the debt-servicing capacity of a growing number of households started to depend on the value of their financial and – especially – real estate assets.

A plethora of empirical studies have shown that the collapse in housing prices left many households in Anglo-Saxon economies like the United States and the United Kingdom with high levels of debt relative to the value of their assets, creating a debt overhang that has depressed consumer spending.[40] Figure 7.7 suggests that there has been a negative correlation between household debt and deleveraging in the OECD world: countries with the largest increases in household debt before the crisis experienced the greatest falls in the level of consumption relative to estimates of pre-crisis trends. The diminished borrowing capacity was the counterpart of financial institutions' reduced willingness to lend – a development ensuing from the need to deleverage in the private banking sector as well in response to the bursting of the housing bubble. After all, housing price deflation and rising mortgage defaults directly translated into the downgrading of MBSs and CDOs, leading to a massive contraction in the markets for repos and ABCP that had funded the purchase of these securitized assets.

Macroeconomic policy expansion was required to deal with the fallout of these dynamics. In the face of such tremendous pressures on US households and financial institutions to deleverage their balance sheets, US authorities have attempted to mitigate the depression of domestic demand through unprecedented fiscal and monetary policy expansion. In autumn 2008 the US Treasury initiated the Troubled Asset Relief Program (TARP), which gave the US Treasury the authorization (without any strong accountability to the US Congress) to spend US$700 billion purchasing subprime mortgage assets from troubled US financial institutions, but which was subsequently used to inject capital into the US banking system. In addition, in 2009 the US Congress enacted an economic stimulus package – the American Recovery and Reinvestment Act – which injected US$787 billion into the US economy to boost GDP and employment. US fiscal policy expansion was accommodated

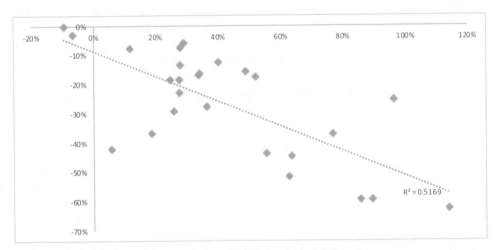

Figure 7.7 Cross-country falls in consumption and pre-crisis debt levels

Source: OECD; author's calculations

Countries included are Australia, Austria, Belgium, Canada, Czech Republic, Denmark, Finland, France, Germany, Greece, Hungary, Ireland, Italy, Japan, Luxembourg, Netherlands, Norway, Poland, Portugal, Slovak Republic, Slovenia, Spain, Sweden, Switzerland, United Kingdom, United States.

by exceptional monetary expansion by the Federal Reserve, which slashed the federal funds rate from 5.25 per cent to a range of 0–0.25 per cent and introduced an alphabet soup of lender-of-last-resort facilities and mechanisms to inject an extraordinary amount of liquidity into the financial system.[41] The most controversial measures taken by the Federal Reserve at the time were its QE programmes, through which it attempted to drive down long-term interest rates and borrowing rates by blowing up asset prices. The Fed increased its balance sheet by more than US$3,500 billion during three QE programmes between November 2008 and November 2014, mostly due to purchases of US Treasury bonds and MBSs. QE was also the primary instrument of macroeconomic stabilization in the United Kingdom, where the Bank of England bought a total of £370 billion in financial assets between 2009 and 2013.

QE became increasingly important for the recovery of finance-led growth after 2010 when the US and UK governments returned to fiscal austerity. At the 2010 summit in Toronto, stirred by the escalation of the sovereign debt crisis in the Eurozone (see below), the leaders of the G20 countries emphasized the need to coordinate around 'growth-friendly fiscal consolidation', with the argument that 'sound fiscal finances are essential to sustain recovery, provide flexibility to respond to new shocks, ensure the capacity to meet the challenges of aging populations, and avoid leaving future generations with a legacy of deficits and debt'.[42] The global financial crisis and the Great Recession generated a massive increase in public debt ratios, which became a source of growing concern among politicians and policymakers in the advanced capitalist world. The public-debt-to-GDP ratio skyrocketed from 65 per cent in the United States and 40 per cent in the United Kingdom in 2007 to, respectively, 105 per cent and 85 per cent in 2015 (see also figure 3.3 in chapter 3 for the evolution of public debt since 1950). Concerns about public debt were instigated by growing instability in the sovereign bond markets of the peripheral Eurozone countries throughout 2010–11 (see below). According to the G20's interpretation, the experience of these countries reflected the fact that 'concerns over large fiscal deficits and rising debt levels in some countries [had] become a source of uncertainty and financial market volatility'.[43] Hence, austerity was deemed necessary to restore 'confidence' in international financial markets, which would lead to stronger economic growth by reducing risk premiums on sovereign bonds and by lowering interest rates. The shift towards austerity made monetary policymaking the only game in town, as central bankers were forced to fill the void left by governments' retreat from fiscal policy to stabilize aggregate demand.[44]

The main problem faced by the Federal Reserve and the Bank of England was that their conventional instrument for increasing aggregate demand – that is, cutting short-term interest rates – quickly ran into its limits: the short-term nominal interest rate controlled by the central bank *cannot go below zero*. This is the *zero lower bound* on the nominal interest rate, which hinders the ability of central banks to stabilize growth in cases where a nominal interest rate of zero is not low enough to get the economy going again. As a result, the Fed and the Bank of England had to implement unconventional monetary policy instruments like QE to fuel growth. QE is supposed to affect the economy through changes in interest rates on long-term sovereign bonds, which act as a benchmark for loans to the private sectors. To have a significant impact on interest rates, central banks have to purchase sovereign bonds on a large scale: an increased demand for these securities raises their prices and lowers their yields (chapter 3). The Federal Reserve also intervened more directly in US mortgage markets by purchasing MBSs on a massive scale (US$1.7 trillion in total) in an effort to revive the US housing market.

For these reasons, it can be argued that QE was an explicit strategy to restore finance-led growth. In the US case, 'monetary stimulus for housing – supporting mortgage debt, homeownership, and housing wealth – ties in with the country's larger strategy of "mortgage Keynesianism" and privatised welfare'.[45] By 2019 real housing prices recovered to their pre-crisis peak in both the United States and the United Kingdom. However, the fruits of the housing recovery have been shared unequally across different income and wealth groups, making consumption growth more lacklustre than during the previous housing boom. In the United States, the share of the bottom 50 per cent in net national housing wealth – that is, the value of all real estate assets minus the outstanding value of all mortgage liabilities – remained relatively constant above 20 per cent from 2000 to 2007 (figure 7.8). Due to sharp deleveraging in the wake of the housing bust, the bottom 50 per cent increased its share to 27 per cent in 2012 when US housing prices flattened out. By 2019 its share had declined to 17 per cent, whereas the top 10 per cent raised its share from 23 per cent in 2012 to 33 per cent in 2019.

At the same time, rising housing prices and the QE-induced decline in mortgage borrowing costs did not improve US housing affordability. Within

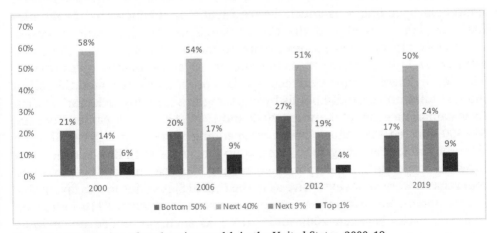

Figure 7.8 Distribution of net housing wealth in the United States, 2000–19

Source: Federal Reserve Flow of Funds

the bottom 50 per cent of income earners, the share of owning and renting households paying more than 30 per cent of disposable income on housing costs remained steady at 70 per cent. Notably, within the group of owners, that share increased from 57 per cent in 2012 to more than 59 per cent in 2018, according to survey data from the US Census Bureau. Similar observations can be made with respect to the UK.[46]

More generally, QE aimed to support economic growth by boosting asset prices and generating wealth effects among the holders of these assets. As Ben Bernanke observed in 2010: 'Lower mortgage rates will make housing more affordable and allow more homeowners to refinance. Lower corporate bond rates will encourage investment. And higher stock prices will boost consumer wealth and help increase confidence, which can also spur spending.'[47] As we have seen in the previous chapter, these wealth effects were especially important in bolstering the finance-led growth of the United States before the crisis, and Bernanke explicitly acknowledged that QE can be seen as a monetary strategy to rekindle these wealth effects: 'If people feel that their financial situation is better because their 401(k) looks better or for whatever reason – their house is worth more – they're more willing to go out and spend … That's going to provide the demand that firms need in order to be willing to hire and invest.'[48] The main channel through which QE is supposed to elevate the value of financial assets is the portfolio rebalancing mechanism: when the central bank buys sovereign bonds and other financial assets from private banks and financial institutions, these private investors will use the money to purchase riskier assets like corporate stocks and equities. QE contributed to the boom in US and UK stock markets: the S&P500 and the FTSE100 – the two most important stock market indices in the United States and the United Kingdom, respectively – doubled in value during the QE period.

While econometric studies have shown that QE was successful in boosting asset prices, its effect on the real economy – on corporate investment and household spending – is much less evident.[49] In financialized economies like the United States and the United Kingdom, the dominant corporate governance arrangement requires firms to maximize shareholder value and returns by linking manager compensation to stock market performance (chapter 4). There is some evidence that US corporations exploited the fall in interest rates on corporate bonds by engaging in share buybacks rather than fixed capital investment. Between 2007 and 2016, 436 US companies from the S&P500 boosted their stock prices by spending more than US$4 trillion on share buybacks, revealing that 'there is no longer a strong link between real investment spending and corporate borrowing'.[50] In the United Kingdom, share repurchases were not as extensive as in the United States, due to less favourable tax treatment, but even there companies spent more than £110 billion on share buybacks between 2009 and 2015.[51] As such, QE ended up 'helping managers [with stock options and other equity-linked incentives] to enrich themselves without necessarily improving the economic fundamentals'.[52]

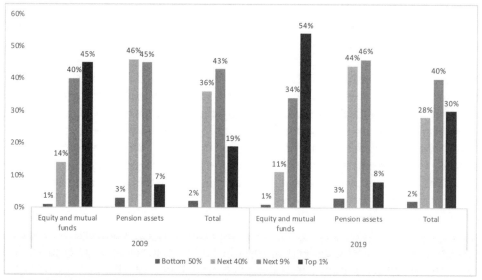

Figure 7.9 Distribution of financial wealth in the United States, 2009 and 2019

Source: Federal Reserve Flow of Funds

Hence, financialized firm behaviour hampered the transmission mechanism of QE, as contemporary 'stock markets … reward companies that favour dividends and buybacks and punish those that undertake more investment'.[53]

For the same reason, QE exacerbated already high levels of wealth inequality. As QE seeks to create an upward asset-price spiral in order to boost aggregate demand via the resulting wealth effects, it is 'a monetary policy approach that intentionally privileges members of society that hold assets, those who do not rely exclusively upon wages for increases in income and wealth'.[54] The ownership of financial assets is heavily concentrated within the top 10 per cent of wealthiest households, so QE measures provide disproportionate benefits to the wealthiest segment of society. Figure 7.9 shows that the top 10 per cent in the United States managed to raise its ownership share of equity and mutual funds from 85 per cent in 2009 to 88 per cent in 2019. Even after including indirect ownership of financial assets via private pension schemes, the picture does not change very much: the top 10 per cent increased its share from 62 per cent to 70 per cent during this period, suggesting that the benefits of the stock market recovery have been concentrated within this group. As such, monetary policy contributed to rising wealth inequality, which has been a key source of weak aggregate demand and a central reason why economic recovery remained so fragile, according to post-Keynesian economists.[55]

Macroeconomic adjustment in the Eurozone: export-led CMEs vs debt-led MMEs

The architects of the EMU believed that the creation of the euro would address the problem of current account imbalances by promoting the integration of European financial markets and facilitating the financial intermediation between surplus and deficit member states. There is ample evidence that the EMU deepened financial integration and lowered long-term borrowing costs and temporarily reduced the spread on sovereign bond yields between Germany and the peripheral Eurozone countries (figure 7.10).[56] In the previous chapter, we have seen that the peripheral Eurozone countries had financed their rising external deficits by borrowing from core Eurozone banks, which either bought peripheral sovereign bonds or extended loans to peripheral banks via integrated wholesale funding markets. When these wholesale funding markets collapsed in the wake of the global financial crisis, peripheral Eurozone countries faced massive capital flight that triggered liquidity crises for Italy and Spain and even solvency crises for Greece, Portugal and Ireland.[57]

The unwillingness of the ECB to act as lender of last resort to Eurozone governments was complicit in allowing these liquidity and solvency crises to spiral out of control, thereby deflecting the burden of macroeconomic adjustment onto the peripheral member states. The reluctance of the ECB to actively intervene in secondary markets for sovereign debt resulted in escalating yields on sovereign bonds issued by governments of member states with high country-specific vulnerabilities, such as external and public deficits and reduced competitiveness. The fact that these governments were not backstopped by a central bank willing to liquidate their sovereign bonds not only increased the yield on these bonds; it also led to a reassessment of risk among sovereign bond investors, who came to recognize that default had become a real possibility for governments that had lost control over monetary policy.[58]

The main problem was that the establishment of the EMU and the associated loss of monetary sovereignty deprived member states of crucial policy instruments to deal with sudden stops of capital inflows, making their sovereign bond markets vulnerable to movements in financial market sentiments, and creating a vicious cycle between rising capital outflows and sovereign debt spreads. Since they have lost their capacity to issue debt in a currency over which they have full control, countries with rising current account and fiscal deficits can therefore be forced into liquidity and solvency crises and find it impossible to use budgetary policies to stabilize their economies. In this regard, the Eurozone member states have been downgraded to the status of emerging market economies, which similarly issued excessive amounts of debt in foreign currencies over which they had no control.[59] This Eurozone version of 'original sin' was, of course, particularly a problem for the Eurozone's peripheral countries, which had relied excessively on foreign banks to fund their deficits.

It is important to note that this disadvantageous effect of EMU membership directly ensued from the EMU's orthodox macroeconomic governance regime, which prevented the ECB – through the no-bailout clause and the rule prohibiting monetary financing of government deficits – from supporting governments in fiscal distress by aggressively intervening in their sovereign

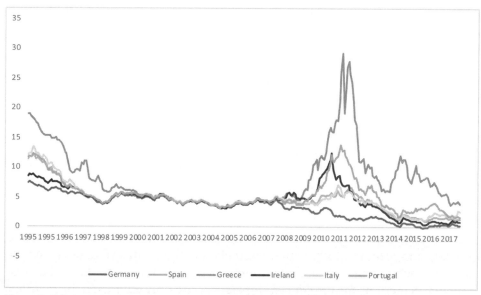

Figure 7.10 Interest rates on ten-year sovereign bonds of selected Eurozone countries, 1995–2018

Source: ECB

bond markets. As mentioned in chapter 3, these rules were a German precondition for joining the monetary union and a way to prevent inflationary fiscal profligacy by member states. As it turns out, the reluctance of the ECB was also a highly effective instrument for the CMEs to use in deflecting the burden of macroeconomic adjustment onto the other countries. The no-bailout clause had to be circumvented when the peripheral countries – beginning with Greece – were shut off from international financial markets and could not meet their international debt obligations. The bailout mechanism selected by the other Eurozone member states was the European Financial Stability Facility (EFSF), which bestowed on creditor countries the most blatant instrument for deflecting the burden of macroeconomic adjustment: conditionality. Crisis countries were offered emergency loans conditional on the implementation of highly stringent fiscal austerity programmes and structural reforms (usually of labour markets).

The reluctance of the ECB to buy more of the sovereign debt of deficit member states also left Italy and Spain at the mercy of financial speculation and forced them to pursue harsh austerity measures in order to meet growing interest payments.[60] Although the ECB bought €207.5 billion-worth of sovereign debt in an effort to curb the borrowing costs of distressed member states through its Securities Market Programme, its meagre support was made conditional on stringent reforms in the countries concerned. As one ECB official recognized, the resumption of new purchases of Spanish and Italian government bonds in 2011 only took place 'after the announcement of new fiscal and structural policy measures by the Italian and Spanish governments'.[61]

The main purpose of these measures is to restore the price competitiveness of these countries through internal devaluation, which – in the words of the European Commission – must 'mimic the effects of nominal devaluations by reducing the domestic prices'.[62] Since flexible labour markets are seen to be central to this inbuilt adjustment mechanism, they are instructed to implement various structural labour market reforms that are meant to remove downward wage rigidities – for example, changing 'the degree of centralization' of wage-setting agreements, abolishing 'indexation mechanisms' and ensuring that 'wages settlements in the public sector support the competitiveness efforts in the private sector'.[63] As a result of these adjustment pressures, southern MMEs have moved closer to a fragmented and decentralized model of collective bargaining.[64]

The emphasis on internal devaluation as the primary instrument of macroeconomic adjustment was reinforced by the introduction of the Macroeconomic Imbalance Procedure (MIP), which compels member states to take corrective measures when current account imbalances are found to have become excessive. Sanctions for unreduced imbalances are only envisaged for member states with excessive current account deficits, however. Moreover, the MIP introduced an asymmetry in the threshold for the definition of excessive imbalances: current account *surpluses* are considered excessive only if they are above 6 per cent of GDP, whereas *deficits* are defined as excessive if they surpass 4 per cent of GDP. In short, institutional reforms aimed to promote a structural adjustment of the models of capitalism of the MMEs, without putting a similar pressure on the CMEs to rebalance their export-led growth models by pursuing internal revaluation based on a more expansionary fiscal policy.

The asymmetrical distribution of the burden of macroeconomic adjustment threw the Eurozone into a deflationary spiral that eventually forced the ECB to start its own QE programme in March 2015 – almost seven years after the Federal Reserve began its first one. As figure 7.11 shows, core inflation in the region – which excludes energy and food prices from the Harmonized Index of Consumer Prices, as they tend to be very volatile and not under the control of the central bank – fell sharply from January 2012 to January 2015. The peripheral countries particularly slipped into deflationary territory because of the depressing effects of austerity and labour market reforms on wages and domestic demand. However, it is striking that core inflation rates fell even in the CMEs, where the fall in unemployment failed to translate into significant wage and ULC inflation.

A key reason why ULC failed to increase more strongly in the CMEs is that governments in these countries adopted fiscal consolidation programmes as well after 2010. Though the EU treaties and the newly established Fiscal Compact compelled CME governments to reduce their public deficits, restrictive fiscal policies also aimed to bolster the competitiveness of manufacturing sector firms by sharpening the incentives of wage restraint among trade unions, especially in the sheltered sectors. The overall outcome of these

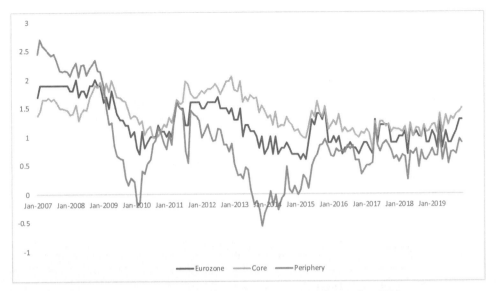

Figure 7.11 Core inflation rates in the Eurozone, January 2007–December 2019

Source: OECD

'Core' is the non-weighted average of Austria, Belgium, Finland, France, Germany and the Netherlands. 'Periphery' is the non-weighted average of Greece, Ireland, Italy, Portugal and Spain.

restrictive policies was the risk of region-wide deflation, which prompted the ECB to announce its Asset Purchase Programme (APP): the APP would consist of monthly purchases of €60 billion (later extended to €80 billion) of financial assets (mostly sovereign bonds) until March 2017, after which these purchases were gradually 'tapered' and finally ended in December 2018.

The transmission mechanisms of the ECB's QE programme operated differently in the Eurozone countries and in finance-led LMEs like the United States and the United Kingdom. In the less financialized economies of the Eurozone, non-financial corporations felt less urge to exploit the reduction in borrowing rates by engaging in debt-financed share buybacks. The portfolio rebalancing mechanism of the ECB's QE worked primarily through the depreciation of the euro, which allowed manufacturing firms in the region to reorient exports from the weaker intra-Eurozone market towards the rest of the world. This did not result in a viable recovery strategy, however. Exports became increasingly important drivers of GDP growth in southern economies, but their share in GDP remained too small to make the recovery strategy sufficiently strong and politically legitimate in the southern MMEs.[65] The Eurozone's macroeconomic adjustment strategy reflected – in Fritz Scharpf's words – 'a gigantic, and indeed hubristic, gamble of technocratic social engineering whose visionary goal is the creation of an integrated European economy that is fit for competition in the ever more contested global markets'.[66] While the lower nominal exchange rate of the euro and the depression of ULC improved the price competitiveness of manufacturing sectors from the southern MMEs in the short term, scholars of CPE have criticized the notion that far-reaching labour market liberalization will bring these countries onto a sustainable path of export-led growth in the longer term. These reforms will most likely result in a further hybridization of their variety of capitalism, undermining the very collective bargaining institutions that have proved vital for the export competitiveness of the CMEs:

> The labour market reforms prescribed to, and largely carried out, in Southern Europe have weakened labour unions, reducing their role in wage setting and damaging their legitimacy. They have thereby also undermined some of the institutional conditions typically associated with export-led growth in the Eurozone's core. In addition, export-led growth in the European core is also premised on strong investment by employers in worker training. Yet such a commitment by companies (as well as workers) is less likely when employment protections are eased and it is easier for companies to adjust to market conditions by firing workers.[67]

Macroeconomic imbalances and secular stagnation

In this chapter we have seen that the macroeconomic imbalances and their evolution after the crisis resulted from the asymmetric capacity of nations to maintain the growth model associated with their variety of capitalism. The pre-crisis escalation of global and regional imbalances centred on the consumption-led growth models of the Anglo-Saxon and peripheral Eurozone countries, fuelling the export-led growth models of the northern Eurozone countries. In the post-crisis era, deflationary deleveraging and macroeconomic adjustment in the consumption-led countries have not been sufficiently complemented by reflationary adjustment in the export-led countries. This partial and asymmetric global adjustment process has resulted in persistently weak and fragile world economic growth.[68]

In 2013, Lawrence Summers, former US Treasury Secretary under the Clinton administration and director of the National Economic Council for President Obama, for the first time advanced the claim that the advanced capitalist world faces a long period of low growth due to persistent demand-side weaknesses – a situation referred to as secular stagnation:

> Most observers expected the unusually deep recession to be followed by an unusually rapid recovery, with output and employment returning to trend levels relatively quickly. Yet even with the US Federal Reserve's aggressive monetary policies, the recovery (both in the United States and around the globe) has fallen significantly short of predictions and has been far weaker than its predecessors.[69]

As figure 7.12 shows, there has been a clearly downward trend in economic growth in the United States, the Eurozone and the United Kingdom since the

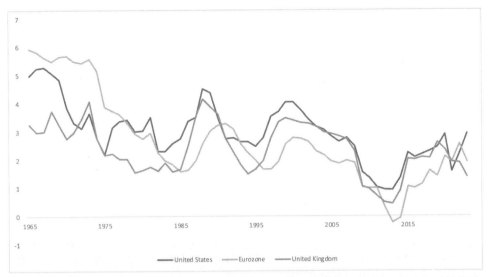

Figure 7.12 Five-year moving average of GDP growth in the United States, Eurozone and United Kingdom, 1965–2018

Source: World Bank

stagflation crisis of the 1970s, and this downward trend was only reinforced by the global financial crisis and the euro crisis.[70]

The core of Summers' theory is that 'changes in the structure of the economy have led to a significant shift in the natural balance between savings and investment, causing a decline in the equilibrium or normal real rate of interest that is associated with full employment'.[71] Rising income inequality is a key source of the increasing propensity to save: because richer households typically save a much larger part of their income than poorer households (whose income is usually entirely consumed), a less equal income redistribution increases the aggregate of money that is saved and reduces the aggregate of money that is consumed in the economy (chapters 1 and 3). Demographic changes like the increase in life expectancy have also pushed households to save more to offset the need for increased retirement income. The decreasing propensity of firms to invest, in turn, can be linked to the rise of the shareholder value model of corporate governance, which – as we saw in chapter 5 – is especially prevalent in high-tech sectors that flourish by accumulating intangible assets like intellectual property rather than investing in tangible assets like new plants and production capacities: 'Apple and Google, for example, are the two largest US companies and are eager to push the frontiers of technology forward, yet both are awash in cash and are under pressure to distribute more of it to their shareholders.'[72]

According to Summers, secular stagnation is not merely a post-crisis phenomenon but a structural condition, whose macroeconomic effects in the 1990s and 2000s were temporarily concealed by the explosion of private debt and the development of financial bubbles. The real interest rate consistent with full employment has declined since the second half of the 1980s, giving rise to financial bubbles that provided a short-lived yet unsustainable push to consumer and investment spending in many advanced market economies. Nevertheless, it is important to note that economic growth during that period has been below the average growth of the pre-1980s era even in the face of a massive housing bubble in the United States: 'Capacity utilization wasn't under any great pressure. Unemployment wasn't under any remarkably low level. Inflation was entirely quiescent. So somehow, even a great bubble wasn't enough to produce any excess in aggregate demand.'[73] After the global financial crisis and the ensuing deleveraging process, the 'natural' real interest rate even fell below zero. This explains why central banks were forced to engage in large-scale asset purchase programmes to revive growth. But recovery remained very weak even in the face of aggressive monetary stimulus by central banks, which have undershot their inflation target of 2 per cent for most of the time since the crisis.

Summers' secular stagnation theory provides clear ammunition for heterodox theories that have fewer problems in explaining the fall in economic growth during the neoliberal period since the 1980s. In the Marxist analysis, economic stagnation is an entirely expectable outcome of the inherent contradictions in capitalist accumulation and the conflictive role of wages as sources of both production costs and aggregate demand. Globalization intensified capitalist competition, which induced firms to maximize profits by repressing wage costs, either by switching to labour-shedding technologies or by offshoring the labour-intensive parts of the production process to low-wage countries. The resulting repression of the wages of low- and medium-skilled workers in the advanced market economies boosted company profits in the short to medium term, but removed an important source of aggregate demand in the longer term. So while wage repression in the short run enhanced capitalist profits by reducing production costs, it hindered the accumulation of capital in the long run by creating tendencies of underconsumption and constraining the *realization* of these profits (chapter 1). According to Marxist scholars, financialization temporarily alleviated these contradictions of capitalist accumulation by allowing workers to engage in debt-financed consumption. At the same time, the increasing concentration of capital and market power among the largest firms drove down the investment rate (and productivity growth) in the real economy. While there is a striking similarity between the Marxist interpretation of the problem of stagnation and the mainstream interpretation, Marxist theory offers a more structural interpretation of the changes that have created the imbalance between savings and investment and its connection to the expansion of finance.[74]

For post-Keynesian scholars, the transition from the Keynesian 'full employment' macroeconomic policy regime towards the neoliberal 'sound money' regime was responsible for many of these changes.[75] The establishment of an anti-inflation macroeconomic regime, which was itself promoted by deepening financial globalization, has lowered the share of national income going to wages in most advanced market economies over the past few decades by weakening the bargaining power of trade unions (chapter 3). Being constrained in the use of expansionary monetary and fiscal policy, governments attempted to raise employment by flexibilizing and deregulating labour markets in ways that also increased personal income inequality between low-skilled and high-skilled workers. At the same time, the financialization of non-financial firms depressed corporate investment. From a post-Keynesian perspective, advanced capitalist economies developed debt-led and export-led growth models in order to find new sources of aggregate demand in a world of rising income inequality. Financial globalization was conducive to the formation of these two growth models by 'ironically' increasing 'the room for different developments across countries', as '[c]urrent account imbalances can be maintained for longest – essentially as long as markets trust the situation'.[76]

The asymmetric macroeconomic adjustment of these two growth models in the wake of the global financial crisis goes a long way in explaining the very weak recovery, as we have seen in this chapter. The dynamics of global imbalances after the crisis and secular stagnation have common political and institutional roots, namely the difficulty experienced by advanced capitalist economies in reviving their growth models and finding new sources of aggregate demand that do not clash with dominant social classes and economic sectors in their model of capitalism. In the next and final chapter, we assess the prospects of these growth models and probe the future of egalitarian capitalism in the face of secular stagnation and a couple of other key challenges.

8

The Future of
Egalitarian Capitalism

Rising inequality, growth models and crisis

In this book we have examined the linkages between rising inequality and rising financial instability in the advanced capitalist world from a growth model perspective. The global financial crisis can be traced back to an interdependent but unsustainable relationship between debt-financed, consumption-led growth models in LMEs and MMEs, and export-led growth models in CMEs, which temporarily alleviated secular stagnation by blowing financial and real estate bubbles in debt-led economies in ways that supported aggregate demand and economic growth in the export-led economies. These two growth models arose as a differentiated outcome of an anti-inflation macroeconomic policy regime, in response to the stagflation crisis of the 1970s, and accompanied by a deregulation of international capital mobility and a weakening of labour power.

While rising inequality since the 1980s has been a universal phenomenon, we have observed major cross-national differences between different varieties of capitalism in their patterns of inequality. Personal income inequality rose faster and stranded at much higher levels in the LMEs, yet the fall in the labour share of GDP and shift in the functional distribution of income towards capital was more pronounced in the CMEs and MMEs. Figures 8.1 and 8.2 summarize these differences. While the United States and Western Europe had similar levels of income inequality in 1980, 'today they are in radically different situations'.[1] In the United States, as figure 8.1 shows, the national income share of the top 1 per cent almost doubled, from a bit less than 11 per cent in 1980 to more than 20 per cent in the 2010s, and the bottom 50 per cent's share fell from more than 20 per cent in 1980 to 13 per cent in 2016. Income inequality rose less drastically in Western Europe, if we look at the evolution of the national income shares of the bottom 50 per cent and the top 1 per cent: the share of the bottom 50 per cent fell by less than 3 percentage points whereas the share of the top 1 per cent rose by only 3.5 percentage points. The evolution of labour's share of GDP – shown in figure 8.2 – paints a different

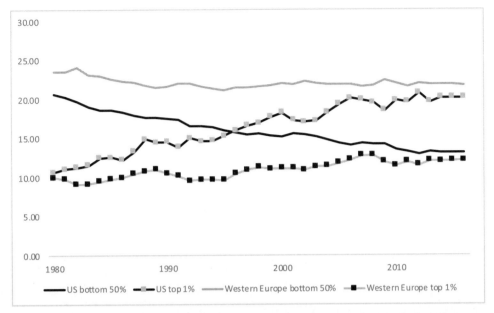

Figure 8.1 Top 1 per cent vs bottom 50 per cent national income shares: United States vs Western Europe, 1980–2016

Source: Alvaredo et al. 2018

picture: the fall in the labour share was much deeper in the CMEs and MMEs than in the LMEs.

Neoclassical models have failed to provide a satisfying explanation for these *varieties of inequality*. SBTC and economic globalization have certainly played a role in the rise in income inequality in the advanced capitalist world, but these developments cannot account for the observation that personal income inequality rose less in Western Europe than in the United States, despite being subject to similar levels of technological change and being exposed to even higher levels of economic integration. Nor can the fall in the labour income share be explained by these models, which expected average wages in the economy to grow in tandem with average labour productivity. It is certainly true that more recent neoclassical models have claimed that the latest wave of technological changes, like digitization and robotization, tend to be 'capital-biased' and primarily benefit the owners of capital instead of skilled workers.[2] But technological change has always been both capital-biased *and* skill-biased, so it is difficult to clarify why the labour share of GDP rose in the post-war Keynesian era – a period of extremely rapid technological innovation – and started to fall from the 1980s.

According to the political economy perspective elaborated in this book, the effects of technological change and globalization on the distribution of income and wealth in the advanced economies have been mediated by various institutions that both shape and reflect the distribution of bargaining power between labour and capital, on the one hand, and between non-skilled and

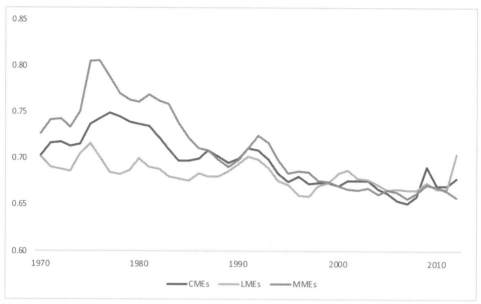

Figure 8.2 Labour income share: CMEs, MMEs vs LMEs, 1970–2012
Source: OECD

skilled workers, on the other. During the post-war Keynesian era of egalitarian capitalism, both the personal and the functional income distribution
improved because of a combination of expansionary macroeconomic policies,
steered towards maintaining full employment, and solidaristic collective
bargaining institutions, aimed at compressing wages between skilled and
non-skilled workers and translating productivity growth into overall wage
growth. Large manufacturing firms were vertically integrated and retained
profits for reinvestment, allowing profits to be redistributed among a highly
diverse workforce consisting of low- and medium-skilled blue-collar workers
and high-skilled white-collar employees. The financial sector was subject to
stringent regulations that reduced borrowing costs for the government and the
manufacturing sectors. These equality-promoting institutions were supported
by a historical compromise between the working classes – a coalition of
manufacturing and public sector workers – and the industrial segments of
the capitalist class, as well as by a cross-party ideological consensus about the
desirability of state intervention and income distribution. Strong Keynesian
welfare states emerged particularly in CMEs, with encompassing unions and
employer organizations and strong worker-oriented political parties. But some
version of wage-led growth emerged in practically all the advanced capitalist
economies during the post-war era.

The stagflation crisis of the 1970s undermined the legitimacy of the
Keynesian full employment macroeconomic regime and destabilized the pillars
of wage-led growth. A negative supply shock resulting from skyrocketing oil

prices was the proximate cause of the crisis, yet the wage-led growth models already faced rising problems in some countries, like the United States and the United Kingdom, at the end of the 1960s. From a Kaleckian perspective, full employment had strengthened the bargaining power of the working classes to such an extent that their wage demands started to exceed productivity growth and erode capitalist profits.[3] Rising inflation therefore reflected intensifying struggles about the distribution of productivity gains between employers and workers. The stagflation crisis provided a window of opportunity for businesses and conservative political parties to prioritize the fight against inflation over the fight against unemployment, and provided a justification for a shift in monetary policy away from full employment towards price stability. The sharp rise in unemployment following the Volcker Shock at the end of the 1970s served to weaken the bargaining power of unions and thwart their wage demands. Soaring nominal interest rates raised the borrowing costs of governments during the 1980s and made the containment of fiscal deficits increasingly compelling, leading to an era of permanent austerity and welfare state restructuring. Together with deepening economic globalization and deindustrialization, which raised calls for labour market liberalization to trim labour costs, these developments have fundamentally weakened the working classes in ways that fuelled inequality in income and in wealth.

The neoliberal era certainly did not result in an institutional convergence of CMEs to become LMEs, as the VoC literature has rightly indicated. The VoC literature developed sophisticated arguments that clarify why employers in the manufacturing sectors should be in favour of preserving collective bargaining institutions and generous welfare regimes, which bolster their international competitiveness by facilitating the acquirement of industry- and firm-specific skills. Pressures for liberalization should be linked to deindustrialization rather than globalization: centralized wage-setting and generous welfare states inhibited job creation in the services sectors by raising the labour costs of unskilled workers, which clarifies why services sector employment growth in many CMEs lagged behind that of the LMEs. In a seminal contribution to the debate, Thelen has argued that varieties of capitalism responded to these challenges through 'varieties of liberalization': outright labour market deregulation in the LMEs, embedded flexibilization in the Nordic countries (and the Netherlands) and dualization in Germany.[4] Persistent differences in social policy are the principal reason why the national income share of the bottom 50 per cent fell much less in Western Europe than in the United States, yet liberalization amplified disposable income differentials between high-skilled and low-skilled workers in most CMEs as well. The extraordinary rise in the national income share of the top 1 per cent in the United States – and to a lesser degree the other LMEs – can to a great extent be attributed to the rise of the shareholder model of corporate governance, which large US firms adopted more eagerly in the context of well-developed capital markets and flexible labour markets.

One of the main conclusions of the VoC perspective is that sectoral conflict superseded class conflict in the advanced capitalist world. In terms of labour market organization, deindustrialization intensified sectoral conflict and contributed to class fragmentation, with the interests of manufacturing firms and their high-skilled workers increasingly pitted against those of services firms and their low-skilled workers. At the same time, high-skilled workers are in favour of shifting welfare state spending away from income support towards various issues of social investment (e.g. education, child care, labour market activation, R&D and public infrastructure). In the latest book of the two most prominent scholars in the VoC tradition, outsourcing and vertical disintegration are believed to reflect 'an across-the-board decentralization of decision-making in terms of both corporate strategy and employee autonomy, permitting the opening-up of product markets across the advanced world in response to the radical geographical specialization of goods and services'.[5] Financialization and banking deregulation are seen as necessary responses to 'the radical destandardization of careers and of company organization and decision-making (decentralized competition) and the increase in uncertainty which has accompanied this shift', which required 'a transformation of the financial sector, and also the insurance sector, from one which provided standardized financial products to individuals and companies to one capable of generating complex, customized, risk- bearing and risk-insuring assets'.[6]

Developments discussed in this book point to the persistent relevance of class conflict, however. The manifest drop in the labour income share in the CMEs suggests that rising income inequality goes beyond high-skilled workers enjoying stronger wage growth than low-skilled workers: *average* labour income growth has lagged behind productivity growth since the 1980s, implying a shift in the balance of class power away from wage earners to the owners of capital. One of the principal benefits of this book's extensive scope is that it has covered institutional changes in four separate policy domains that show a general trend towards neoliberalization and the associated weakening and fragmentation of labour power. These dynamics are broadly in line with the expectations of power resources theory, which 'is largely built on the assumption that the first-order priority of employers is liberalization, with only the capacity of labour to resist standing in their way'.[7] Economic and financial globalization and the transition towards an anti-inflation macroeconomic policy regime in the wake of the stagflation crisis of the 1970s primarily reflect the interests of the owners of capital, and strengthened their power to demand more liberalization in labour markets, social policy, corporate governance and financial policy. While wealth-owning and high-skilled middle-class workers might have increasingly internalized the preferences of the wealthy owners of capital, it is difficult to escape the verdict that the gains of technological innovation, economic globalization and financialization have been heavily skewed towards the latter.

The central claim developed throughout this book is that governments in the advanced capitalist economies had to find new sources of aggregate demand in the wake of the stagflation crisis of the 1970s, which was widely interpreted as a crisis of the wage-led growth model of the post-war era.[8] From a post-Keynesian perspective, rising personal income inequality and a falling labour share of GDP have depressing effects on long-term economic growth by reducing the total level of consumption in the economy, given that wealthy households have a higher marginal propensity to save than poorer households and the MPC out of capital is lower than out of labour. Advanced capitalist countries temporarily avoided these effects by adopting distinctive growth models that were shaped by pre-existing institutions and distributions of power resources. The growth of the Anglo-Saxon countries and several Southern European countries became dependent on debt-financed household consumption: the deregulation of banking credit allowed households to finance their consumption in the face of stagnating real wages and rising inequality. The economic growth of the Northern European countries, on the other hand, increasingly came to rely on external demand via increased exports: a combination of wage restraint and labour market flexibilization depressed household consumption but also strengthened the competitiveness of the export-oriented manufacturing firms by decreasing their labour costs.

These two growth models have been dysfunctional in the sense that they were unable to provide a sustainable replacement for the more egalitarian wage-led growth model of the post-war era. In the debt-led economies, the expansion of consumption became dependent on an unsustainable expansion of banking credit to households, as well as – particularly in LMEs like the United States and the United Kingdom – on an unsustainable inflation of asset prices. The collapse of real estate bubbles since 2006 has also undermined the growth of the export-led CMEs, which are 'domestically only weakly financialized themselves but rely on the financialization of their trading partners'.[9] Private market-based banks in the CMEs also became heavily exposed to debt-led economies like the United States and the peripheral Eurozone countries, as the outbreak of the global financial crisis and the European sovereign debt crisis revealed. Macroeconomic adjustment of these imbalances in the decade after the crisis has been partial and asymmetrical, which has been a key cause of the resurfacing of secular stagnation.

What are the prospects of egalitarian capitalism in the face of the intrinsic instability of debt-led and export-led growth models, secular stagnation, and other future challenges like global warming and the rise of radical-right populist parties? Below, we argue that macroeconomic policy reform will be central to each of these challenges, and briefly assess whether the mitigation of the economic fallout of the coronavirus crisis offers a political window of opportunity for such reform.

Secular stagnation and macroeconomic policy reform

As we have seen in the last chapter, according to Summers' New Keynesian interpretation, the structural cause of secular stagnation is an imbalance in the advanced capitalist economies between the propensity of households to save and the propensity of firms to invest. Because the effectiveness of monetary policy is constrained by the zero lower bound on nominal interest rates, and persistently low real interest rates risk blowing new financial bubbles, Summers argues that an expansionary fiscal policy, based upon increased public investment spending, is likely to be more effective in tackling the problem of secular stagnation in a way that ensures both full employment and financial stability:

> An expansionary fiscal policy can reduce national savings, raise neutral real interest rates, and stimulate growth. Fiscal policy has other virtues as well, particularly when pursued through public investment. A time of low real interest rates, low materials prices, and high construction unemployment is the ideal moment for a large public investment program. It is tragic, therefore, that in the United States today, federal infrastructure investment, net of depreciation, is running close to zero, and net government investment is lower than at any time in nearly six decades.[10]

Summers' theory of secular stagnation prompts a fundamental revision of the anti-inflationary macroeconomic policy framework based on politically independent central banks and balanced government budgets. Despite differences between heterodox and mainstream economists on the sources of secular stagnation, they all agree that the phenomenon requires a fundamental reform of the neoliberal macroeconomic policy framework.

First of all, there is a consensus that monetary policy will fail to redress the imbalance between savings and investment, which will necessitate permanently higher levels of public spending. The QE programmes adopted by the major central banks of the advanced capitalist world were unable to bolster aggregate demand sufficiently to raise inflation levels to their official target of 2 per cent. QE contributed to rising wealth inequality by inflating asset prices, as studies by central banks' research staff have acknowledged.[11] While central banks have legitimized their QE programmes by claiming that they have had positive effects on income inequality through their positive effects on employment and wage inflation, their failure to reach their inflation target suggests that they have not been so successful in this regard.[12] The role of the financial sector in QE's transmission is generally seen as the weak spot of this monetary strategy, which is based on the assumption that low interest rates are enough to encourage banks and their potential clients to lend and borrow. Many households and firms do not wish to take out any more loans; they believe their debt levels are already too high. When the private sector refuses to increase its borrowing, monetary policy cannot do much to increase spending in the economy.[13]

Second, there is growing agreement between heterodox economists and mainstream economists – at least among those of the New Keynesian school – that the neoliberal macroeconomic policy framework has prevented a more effective coordination between monetary and fiscal policy. Governments responded to the fall in long-term interest rates and borrowing costs by engaging in austerity rather than fiscal expansion. Austerity, in turn, put more pressure on central banks to further loosen their monetary policies to mitigate the deflationary effects of public spending cuts. The outcome has been a 'self-defeating' and 'economically irrational' macroeconomic policy mix, as the expansionary effects of QE are offset by the contractionary effects of austerity.[14] Central bankers have been aware of the self-defeating nature of the macroeconomic policy mix at least since 2013. The then Chairman of the Federal Reserve, Ben Bernanke, noted in Congressional testimony in 2013 that 'although monetary policy is working to promote a more robust recovery, it cannot carry the entire burden of ensuring a speedier return to economic health', urging the US Congress and the Obama administration 'to put the federal budget on a sustainable long-run path that promotes economic growth and stability without unnecessarily impeding the current recovery'.[15] More than a year later, Mario Draghi, in his capacity as governor of the ECB, similarly asked governments from the northern Eurozone countries 'to exploit the available fiscal space, so that fiscal policy can work with rather than against monetary policy in supporting aggregate demand'.[16]

The occurrence of this counterproductive macroeconomic policy mix has significant implications for our understanding of the politics of central bank independence. Recall that the main motivation for delegating monetary policy to politically independent central banks was to prevent governments from pursuing overly expansionary policies, which would merely result in higher inflation, according to neoliberal economic theories (chapter 3). So although one of the key justifications of central bank independence was that it would keep a check on the intrinsic and inflationary *deficit bias* of democratically elected governments, fiscal policy after the crisis was marked instead by a deflationary *surplus bias* that hindered a more balanced macroeconomic policy mix. Three years after ending his mandate at the Fed, even Bernanke had to admit that 'the inflation-centric rationale for central bank independence looks a bit outdated in a world in which inflation and nominal interest rates are too low, rather than too high; and in which politicians have criticized central banks for being too expansionary rather than not expansionary enough'. Although Bernanke did not go as far as calling for the abolition of central bank independence, he continued that 'the same logic that holds that central bank independence is necessary to avoid excess inflation can be turned on its head, to imply that central bank independence is a barrier to the fiscal-monetary coordination needed to combat deflation'.[17] In this regard, the combination of QE and austerity seems to reflect the institutional logic of the pre-crisis macroeconomic governance regime: central bank independence and fiscal policy rules constrained elected politicians' discretion in advanced capitalist countries, placing monetary policy at the centre of macroeconomic governance.[18]

There is thus a growing consensus in the community of academic macro-economists that increased public spending has to play a much more important role in macroeconomic governance more generally, and in addressing the problem of secular stagnation in particular. In his last presidential lecture at the American Economic Association in 2019, Olivier Blanchard made a key intervention that revealed how much mainstream macroeconomic consensus has shifted: he argued that governments should not be concerned about rising public deficits and debt as long as the interest rate they pay on sovereign bonds is lower than the growth rate of the economy.[19] Blanchard's analysis offered a final blow to the mainstream consensus – exemplified by Carmen Reinhart and Kenneth Rogoff's much-cited 2010 working paper *Growth in a Time of Debt* – that public debt above a critical threshold of 90 per cent of GDP becomes a substantial drag on the economy.[20] Yet a critical distinction between heterodox economists and 'converted' mainstream economists like Blanchard is that the former call for additional measures to revive aggregate demand. Debt-financed public spending encounters two problems. First, public debt is regressive since ownership of government bonds is heavily concentrated among the wealthiest households, as research by Sandy Hager has shown with respect to US public debt and research by Toby Arbogast with respect to Italian public debt.[21] Second, if public spending is successful in raising economic growth and inflation, 'it could eventually lead to substantially higher interest rates and create debt-servicing difficulties'.[22]

For these reasons, heterodox economists maintain that the government's public spending capacity should be supported by (1) a more progressive tax base and (2) a more subordinate and expansionary central bank. A more progressive tax structure supports aggregate demand by redistributing income from households and individuals with a high marginal propensity to save to those with a high MPC. This would also help to correct market-generated inequalities, which would be particularly desirable in countries like the United States and the United Kingdom where the distribution of income and wealth has been skewed most towards the top 1 per cent. But the most radical proposal to support the public spending capacity of the government is to force the central bank to create money and hand it over either to the government or directly to citizens – a policy proposal known as 'QE for the people'. This proposal comes in two variants. The first variant proposes that central banks should hand consumers cash directly: 'In practice, this policy could take the form of giving central banks the ability to hand their countries' tax-paying households a certain amount of money.'[23] The other variant of QE for the people boils down to monetary financing of government spending by the central bank: rather than transferring cash directly to households, the central bank could create money and transfer to it the government, which would use it to fund public spending programmes that would support long-term economic growth.[24] The difference between existing QE and monetary financing is that the government would not have to create an increased future public debt burden, and that the central bank would actively have to co-operate with the government in financing the stimulus programme.

From a growth model perspective, such a more progressive macroeconomic policy mix would not only have led to a stronger economic recovery and higher inflation; it would also have promoted a rebalancing of the debt-led and export-led economies: 'fiscal policy can be a tool for tackling the problems of rising inequality not just through its distributional function, but also through its effect on sectoral allocation and the rebalancing of national growth models'.[25] The key question, of course, is whether these proposals have any chance of being adopted in the current political context. Although QE reflects the limits of the pre-crisis monetary policy framework, politicians and governments have shown a remarkable reluctance to exploit the levers of fiscal policy to address the deficiency in aggregate demand. The political reluctance to use fiscal policy is especially strong in the Eurozone, but even the Obama administration in the United States, and particularly the Cameron administration in the United Kingdom, gave priority to fiscal consolidation. How can the failure of macroeconomic policy to minimize the risk of secular stagnation be explained? Three compatible explanations are worth considering:

- Advanced economies are generally characterized by the decreasing power of labour and the increasing power of (financial) capital, so one possibility is that '[t]he weakness of workers' unions and parties does not allow them to carry out their past political function as the main supporters of counter-cyclical fiscal expansions'.[26] As we saw in chapter 2, governments are reluctant to pursue expansionary policies that might be punished by international financial markets. These disciplinary effects of financial markets are reinforced by the 'New Constitutionalism' – that is, restrictive fiscal and monetary rules that have removed macroeconomic policymaking from the democratic decision-making process (e.g. the SGP in the European Union, which was further strengthened after the crisis through the Fiscal Compact). In this regard, maintaining a restrictive and anti-inflationary macroeconomic policy regime is key to (1) preserving the short-term profitability of capital via the weakening of labour unions' bargaining strength, and (2) advancing the creditor interests of the rentier classes. From a class-based perspective, therefore, the preference for QE as the primary instrument of macroeconomic stabilization can be seen 'as an expression of the growing influence of affluent citizens and financial interests in democratic politics': 'elected politicians delegated expansionary policy to central banks because they want to minimize compensatory redistribution and to avoid ratchet effects commonly associated with fiscal stimulus (i.e., spending increases during down-turns follow by tax increases during upturns)'.[27]

- From a growth model perspective, a more prominent role for fiscal policy would clash with the interests of the cross-class coalitions underlying the debt-led growth model of the LMEs and the export-led growth model of the CMEs. In export-led CMEs, expansionary fiscal policy would fuel higher wage inflation in the sheltered sectors in ways that could undermine the price competitiveness of manufacturing firms and reduce the purchasing power of manufacturing workers (as sheltered services would become more expensive). Expansionary fiscal policy would be especially important for public sector workers, whose bargaining position is to a great extent determined by the government's fiscal policy stance. But an expansionary fiscal policy is equally essential for workers in the services sectors, where wage growth is more dependent on the tightness of the (often more flexible) labour market. In a similar vein, an expansionary fiscal policy would serve to reconfigure the cross-class and sectoral underpinnings of the debt-led growth models of the LMEs. A growing body of scholarship has argued that asset ownership and asset prices systematically affect citizens' preferences for redistributive fiscal policies and social spending: rising housing wealth acts as 'private insurance' for homeowners, who become less dependent on state-provided income support and more opposed to redistributive taxes.[28] Asset price inflation – at least partly induced by QE – therefore generates what Ben Ansell has aptly called an 'anti-redistributive cycle' in debt-led LMEs: 'low redistribution creates demand for credit in response to inequality, but this then produces asset booms that themselves reduce the demand for redistribution'.[29]
- A fundamental rethink of macroeconomic policy faces strong ideological contestation. Conservative politicians have strongly criticized central banks for supposedly exceeding their mandates by adopting 'quasi-fiscal' measures that might undermine the political independence of central banks in the longer term. As one economist summarizes this view: 'The unprecedented size of the central bank balance sheets … has far-reaching implications for the financial dimension of central bank independence by the monetary financing of government debt undermining the credibility and independence of the central banks.'[30] From a conservative perspective, QE already consists of 'monetary financing' of fiscal deficits: governments have increasingly relied on central banks' QE programmes to fund their deficits, rather than selling sovereign bonds to private investors in international financial markets. This has distorted interest rates and the prices of these bonds, so the argument goes: governments have been able to profit from 'artificially' low interest rates that have weakened the 'disciplinary' effect of financial markets on government finances. Moreover, lower debt-servicing costs have allegedly reduced the pressure on governments to pursue structural reforms like flexibilizing the labour market and downsizing the welfare state, which are seen as necessary to bolster longer-term economic growth and employment in the economy. These supply-side views continue to hold sway over conservative politicians and parties.

The rise of populism and the decline of social democracy

The failure to redress secular stagnation will have a profound impact on European politics, as Erik Jones has argued:

> It will lower opportunities for each successive generation while at the same time increasing pressure on (European) governments to curtail the welfare state. It will make it easy for populist political movements (and political entrepreneurs) to rally opposition to traditional political parties, governing elites, and national constitutional arrangements. It will heighten antagonism between Europe's 'indigenous' peoples and its more recent immigrants.[31]

As shown in figure 8.3, authoritarian-populist parties are on the rise in Europe: their mean vote share doubled from about 10 per cent in the 1990s to more than 20 per cent in the 2010s – a surge in popularity that is almost entirely due to the rise of radical right populism. Authoritarian populism has established itself as the third ideological force in European politics, behind conservatism/ Christian Democracy and social democracy. The election of Donald Trump in 2016 as president of the United States suggests that the rise in populism is not confined to the European continent. Populism remains a contested concept, however. Beyond the lack of scholarly agreement on the definition of populism, there is a fairly broad consensus that both right-wing and left-wing populism include some kind of appeal to 'the people' and the denunciation of 'the elites'. An often-used definition of populism, articulated by Cas Mudde, defines it as 'a thin-centred ideology that considers society to be ultimately separated into two homogeneous and antagonistic camps, "the pure people" versus "the corrupt elite," and which argues that politics should be an expression of the

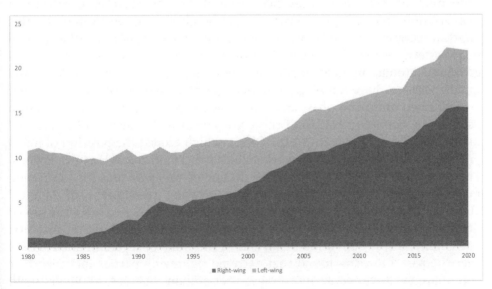

Figure 8.3 Mean vote share of right-wing and left-wing populist parties, 1980–2020

Source: Timbro Authoritarian Populism Index

volonté générale (general will) of the people'.[32] Jan-Werner Müller emphasizes its anti-pluralism, specifying that 'populism inevitably involves a claim to a moral monopoly of representing the supposedly real people – and also inevitably results in *exclusionary identity politics*'.[33] The latter description suggests that populism comes most naturally in its right-wing variant, and is often equated with 'democratic illiberalism' for its rejection of both rule of law and respect for minority rights.[34]

How can we understand the rise in populism in the advanced capitalist world? One major strand in the populism literature emphasizes the increasing role of cultural issues in Western politics, especially the backlash against immigration.[35] Western nations have seen a large influx of immigrants with different cultural and religious backgrounds in recent decades. This might explain the growing appeal of, in particular, radical-right populism in Europe, which received the largest share of international migrants (76 million out of a total 250 million international migrants in 2015). But the two major shocks to the international liberal order – Brexit and the election of Donald Trump as president of the United States – are also often represented as 'unprecedented electoral victories' of 'anti-establishment parties and candidates … casting themselves as defenders of their nations against the twin threats posed by foreigners and a corrupt elite'.[36] The refugee crisis and the spree of jihadist terrorist attacks since 2015 have only exacerbated fears among white voters across the West that their cultures and identities are under threat. Many of these voters are also believed to rally against post-materialist 'cosmopolitan' values like environmentalism, gender equality and respect for minority rights.

Another prominent strand in the literature on populism links it to the deepening of economic grievances caused by the disruptive effects of globalization, technological change and neoliberalism. According to this political-economic interpretation, 'increasing trade openness, the rise of non-Western economic powers, diminished government regulation, and growing automation have made life more insecure for the working and middle classes, have privileged highly educated and urban dwellers over less-educated and rural ones, and have made capitalism more of a zero-sum game'.[37] An important source of these grievances is the decline of traditional manufacturing employment in the OECD, which eroded the position of many previously well-paid industrial workers in North America and Western Europe. The stagnation of real wages and the decline of well-paid jobs for lower- and medium-skilled workers translated into growing resentment of political elites, so the argument goes. Their resentment only increased after the global financial crisis, which deepened social divisions and economic uncertainty: one empirical study of voting behaviour in the wake of severe financial crises over the past 140 years found that extreme right-wing parties increase their vote share by 30 per cent, on average, after a financial crisis, as 'voters seem to be particularly attracted to the political rhetoric of the extreme right, which often attributes blame to minorities or foreigners'.[38]

It is not easy to disentangle the role of economic and cultural factors, given that particularly lower-educated white voters faced with declining economic security tend to feel threatened by immigration and the spread of post-materialist values. A third strand of the literature therefore looks at the interaction between economic and cultural change in the rise of populism. Ronald Inglehart and Pippa Norris argue that long-term social structural developments in post-industrial societies – such as growing prosperity and rising access to college education – produced a generational shift towards socially liberal and post-materialist values during the post-war era, which in turn provoked a reaction among more materialist voters that has become increasingly explosive since the fallout of the global financial crisis: 'Cultural backlash explains why given individuals support Populist Authoritarian movements. Declining existential security explains why support for these movements is greater now than it was thirty years ago.'[39] Other scholars, like Noam Gidron and Peter Hall, brought together economic and cultural explanations for populism by understanding support for parties of the radical right and left as a problem of social integration: 'long-term economic and cultural developments have increased feelings of social marginalization among people with low levels of income or skills', who are 'more likely than people with higher levels of subjective social status to be alienated from mainstream politics, to abstain from voting and to vote for parties of the radical right or left'.[40]

These developments have pushed white low-skilled workers increasingly towards far-right parties that 'explicitly acknowledge and address the widespread anxieties among the shrinking middle and thereby gain their support – despite the virtual absence of concrete policy remedies'.[41] Many European right-wing populist parties moved from a neoliberal position on socio-economic issues towards a pro-welfare state position – albeit a 'welfare-chauvinist' one that aims to restrict social benefits to 'deserving' natives.[42] In one of the first systematic comparative studies of the impact of populist radical right parties (PRRPs) on redistributive (i.e. social spending and welfare generosity) and regulatory (i.e. market-making) economic policies in Western Europe, Leonce Röth and his colleagues found that centre-right governments with PRRP participation (formal or informal) show less political will to retrench welfare benefits than other centre-right governments, but significantly more inclination to deregulate the economy.[43] The working-class constituency of PRRPs makes them less enthused to support welfare retrenchment, which would directly affect many of their voters – particularly when it comes to traditional social insurance schemes like pensions. The political agendas of centre-right parties and PRRPs find more common ground in the deregulation of the economy, especially in areas that are dominated by labour unions. PRRPs are traditionally hostile towards unions, which can mobilize their members to vote for left-wing political parties. In a recent study of how unionization shaped voting behaviour in the period 2001–15, Line Rennwald and Jonas Pontusson found that union membership decreased the probability that voters who 'left the mainstream left' voted for the radical right in subsequent elections, and increased the likelihood they voted for the radical left.[44]

How will mainstream left political parties respond to the challenges posed by the rise of the populist radical right? The answer to this question will have significant implications for the future of democratic capitalism, given how important social-democratic parties have been for the ascent and evolution of the welfare state. A prevailing interpretation in the literature is that the 'neoliberalization' of social-democratic parties has played a key role in the growing appeal of right-wing populism among working-class voters.[45] Mainstream left and mainstream right political parties have increasingly converged since the 1990s 'on a policy agenda that supports the relatively free movement of goods, capital, and people, particularly within an enlarging European region'.[46] These 'catch-all' parties of the post-war era engaged in three survival strategies in response to the crisis of wage-led growth in the 1970s, as Jonathan Hopkin and Mark Blyth have recently argued: (1) the expectations of voters by proclaiming their devotion to free markets and the global economy; (2) externalizing their policy commitments through the delegation of monetary policy to independent central banks and the introduction of constraining fiscal policy rules; and (3) using extensive political marketing to sell political leaders to voters on the basis of personal charisma and technocratic competence. According to this analysis, populist parties 'emerged and grew on the back of a critique of the establishment and a commitment to replace it with a different form of governance based more explicitly on the popular will': 'populism is a predictable reaction to the increasingly undifferentiated policy positions of the mainstream parties and the growing detachment of elected politicians from civil society'.[47]

There is no consensus in the literature as to which electoral strategies social-democratic parties should pursue to win back voters and diminish the appeal of PRRPs. A number of prominent scholars have argued that social-democratic parties should adopt a left-wing version of populism. In her recent book *For a Left Populism* (2018), Chantal Mouffe argues that the contemporary 'populist moment' represents an opportunity for democratic reinvigoration, if the left combats right populism with a left version that is more 'inclusive' and moves significantly away from the conventional technocratic solutions endorsed by most social-democratic parties.[48] According to Wolfgang Streeck, the basic reason behind the left's demise is 'the seemingly total absence of a realistic anti-capitalist, or at least anti-neoliberal, left-wing political strategy related to the European Union'.[49] In his view, social-democratic parties can only survive in the long term by listening to the concerns of the less-well-educated working classes and by 'reclaiming the nation state' through a return to patriotism, traditional working-class values and a defence of 'really existing democracy, i.e., nation-state democracy, against its "cosmopolitan" replacement with castle-in-the-sky supranational democracy'.[50] Advocates of the 'social investment' paradigm, on the other hand, argue that social-democratic parties should recognize that their constituencies have increasingly and permanently shifted from culturally traditional, blue-collar, working-class voters with lower levels of education towards culturally cosmopolitan, middle-class voters in the service sectors of the economy with higher levels of education. From their perspective, social-democratic parties can only be electorally successful in the long term if they appeal to the latter voters by (1) promoting investment-oriented policies aimed at individual skill development instead of direct social transfers and (2) taking open and progressive positions on cultural issues such as gender equality, European integration and immigration.[51]

It seems implausible that a reconciliation of these two perspectives is impossible. While social investment advocates might be right that taking an explicit anti-immigration position will not be a successful electoral strategy, many social-democratic parties have endorsed – either implicitly or explicitly – austerity policies after the crisis in ways that have most likely alienated voters with lower levels of education.[52] Their endorsement of restrictive policies has been based on a persistent belief in what Björn Bremer and Sean McDaniel have called 'supply-side' Keynesianism, which has the following three dimensions:

1 downplaying the possibility of persistent deficiencies in aggregate demand;
2 prioritizing monetary over fiscal policy as the main instrument of macroeconomic stabilization; and
3 using the state to generate long-run growth and more equitable outcomes by investing in human capital formation, alongside a belief that the state's fiscal capacity must be protected to ensure this.[53]

These beliefs seem outdated in the face of the challenges posed by secular stagnation and the difficulties in reviving pre-crisis growth models. It is hard to contemplate a revival of social democracy – and a more egalitarian form of democratic capitalism – without explicitly turning one's back on austerity. In any case, as Sheri Berman – an internationally renowned expert on social democracy – concludes: 'If centre-left parties are unable to offer voters distinctive and attractive solutions to contemporary challenges, their decline will continue, populism will flourish, and democracy will continue to decay.'[54] The climate crisis and coronavirus crisis offer social democrats a window of opportunity to reconsider their outdated macroeconomic policy views, as we will see in the final two sections.

Climate change and the decarbonization of the economy

Perhaps the most existential challenge for mankind and democratic capitalism in particular is to find a solution to the potential environmental, social and economic impacts of global warming. While there is still scientific debate over the likely scale of climate change and its potential consequences, there is a consensus among climate scientists – reflected in the reports of the United

Nations Intergovernmental Panel on Climate Change (IPCC) – that (1) global average temperatures have risen over the last 150 years by almost 1°C (and continue to rise by about 0.2°C per decade) and (2) the anthropogenic emission and accumulation of greenhouse gases since the Industrial Revolution are the primary cause of this evolution.[55] The IPCC's reports, which offer a comprehensive summary of the scientific knowledge of the causes and effects of climate change, involve a periodic reminder that urgent and wide-ranging action is required to contain global warming. According to the most optimistic scenario, the IPCC expects the global surface temperature increase to exceed 1.5°C relative to the period 1850–1900 by the end of the twenty-first century, but more pessimistic scenarios predict global temperatures rising by as much as 4.8°C. The economic and social implications of such high temperature rises could be daunting: the influential *Stern Review* on *The Economics of Climate Change*, which was published by the UK Treasury in 2007, estimated that the overall costs and risks of climate change would be equivalent to losing at least 5 per cent of global GDP each year – an estimate of damage that could rise to 20 per cent of GDP if a wider range of risks and impacts is taken into account.[56]

The IPCC's Fifth Assessment Report provided the scientific input to the 2015 international Paris Agreement, which 'aims to strengthen the global response to the threat of climate change by holding the increase in the global average temperature to well below 2°C above pre-industrial levels and to pursue efforts to limit the temperature increase to 1.5°C above pre-industrial levels'.[57] Achieving these objectives will require radical changes in how the economy and daily life are organized. The changes needed are captured by the term 'decarbonization', which refers to 'the process of taking the carbon out of the energy we use to run the economy' and should result in what Peter Newell

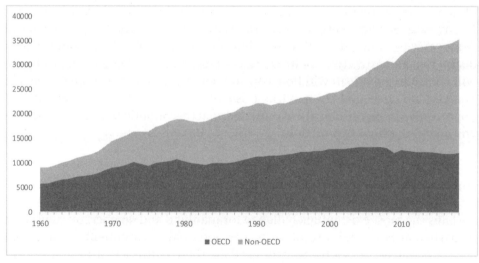

Figure 8.4 Greenhouse gas emissions (in gigatonnes), 1960–2018
Source: globalcarbonatlas.org

calls 'climate capitalism' – that is, 'a model which squares capitalism's need for continual economic growth with substantial shifts away from carbon-based industrial development'.[58] Reducing greenhouse gas emissions sufficiently to meet the targets of the Paris Agreement will be a major technical and political undertaking, given that approximately 80 per cent of the world's energy consumption comes from the combustion of fossil fuels. Hence, it will come with wide-ranging social implications, raising a number of practical as well as normative challenges for modern welfare states and social wellbeing at different levels of governance.[59]

Figure 8.4 illustrates the scale of the challenge: it shows the greenhouse gas emissions in gigatonnes in the world since the 1960s and the contribution of OECD versus non-OECD countries. While the OECD countries have in aggregate slightly reduced their emissions since the middle of the 2000s, these emission cuts pale in comparison with the additional cuts that are needed to meet the targets of the Paris Agreement: scenarios looked at by the IPCC in 2018 required between 100 and 1,000 gigatonnes of CO_2 – which is the primary greenhouse gas emitted through human activities – to be removed from the atmosphere by the end of the century. The European Union's current goal is to cut its CO_2 emissions by 40 per cent by 2030 compared to 1990 levels, but the European Parliament would like to go further and reduce emissions by 50 per cent by 2030 and become entirely 'climate neutral' by 2050. These aims reflect Europe's ambition 'to lead in global climate action and to present a vision that can lead to achieving net-zero greenhouse gas emissions by 2050 through a socially-fair transition in a cost-efficient manner'.[60]

What will be the impact of decarbonization on the distribution of income and wealth? This key question will be central to debates on the political economy of climate change policy and the evolution of advanced capitalism in the twenty-first century. The distributional effects of decarbonization will be contingent on the following two factors: (1) the distribution of costs and (2) the effects on economic growth. The first factor will be particularly important in the short to medium term. Decarbonization will require higher taxes on energy consumption that are most likely regressive in their distributive impact, given that lower-income households spend a larger share of their budget on electricity, and that demand for energy is relatively price-inelastic. It is highly plausible that such regressive climate change policies will not be considered as fair and equitable by a large part of the electorate, creating a risk that decarbonization strategies will face political backlash. The uprisings organized by the Yellow Vests (*Gilets Jaunes*) from the autumn of 2018 started as a protest against the French government's announcement that it would raise fuel taxes as part of its plan to fight climate change. The French experience with spontaneous outbursts of popular revolt suggests that governments and politicians would be well advised to develop inclusive decarbonization strategies that (1) minimize adverse distributional consequences by taking measures that primarily affect the rich, and/or (2) compensate lower-income households for any adverse effects of climate policies. Since it will be difficult – if not impossible – to decarbonize the economy merely by taking measures that affect the rich, introducing various compensation mechanisms for lower-income households will be a crucial part of any inclusive climate change plan.[61]

This brings us to the second factor that will determine the distributional impact of decarbonization – that is, its effects on long-term economic growth, which will shape governments' fiscal capacity to finance additional compensation mechanisms. Some observers have argued from an ecological perspective that decarbonization and economic growth are mutually exclusive policy objectives. The common starting point here is that the ecological crisis is a basic feature of high-consumption capitalism, which needs to be re-embedded into planetary limits by abandoning the goal of economic growth altogether, and moving towards a 'steady-state' economy that 'aims to keep the throughput of material and energy in production and consumption processes at sustainable levels and as low as possible'.[62] In order to make sufficient room for peoples in developing countries to raise their living standards, these observers argue that advanced capitalist countries should 'turn their backs on the expansionary economic model that has so far provided the economic foundation for the welfare state' and even aim for a *contraction* of economic activity (de-growth).[63] However, the steady-state economy and de-growth are incompatible with the accumulation drive of capitalism and hence require a completely different system of economic organization: advocates of these objectives call for the abandonment of capitalist principles through the intro- duction of far-reaching restrictions on consumption and highly redistributive policies – such as imposing maximum limits on income and wealth – that do not seem politically viable in the current political context:

> For nearly forty years now, the gains from economic growth have persistently favoured the rich. Nevertheless, the prospects for reversing inequality in all countries will be far greater when the overall economy is growing than when the rich are fighting everyone else for shares of a shrinking pie. ... In political terms, the attempt to implement a de-growth agenda would render the global clean-energy project utterly unrealistic.[64]

The dominant discourse is that decarbonization and economic growth are mutually compatible: climate change policies should aim at 'greening' economic growth, which is a project that is more consistent with 'the basic requirement of all states in capitalist societies to secure and promote the conditions for capital accumulation'.[65] This discourse is especially prominent in the European Union, where the European Commission regards decarboni- zation as an opportunity for the EU to step up its action to show leadership and reap the benefits of first mover advantage. More specifically, the decar- bonization strategy of the European Commission seeks to ensure that the transition 'is socially fair – not leaving any EU citizens or regions behind – and enhances the competitiveness of EU economy and industry on global markets, securing high quality jobs and sustainable growth in Europe'.[66] While there seems to be broad political support for this policy discourse, critics have drawn attention to the shortcomings of its market-oriented approach: the primary policy instrument through which the European Union has aimed to achieve its targets is the EU Emissions Trading Scheme (EU ETS), whereby companies are allocated permits to emit greenhouse gas emissions and must either stay within these limits or buy additional permits from other companies that have reduced their own emissions below their limits and have surplus permits to sell. As far too many emission permits were initially handed out for free – notably to carbon-intensive sectors claiming that they would otherwise face a competitive disadvantage – the market price for these permits is generally seen as being much too low to have any effect at all on curbing emissions.[67]

Since it is increasingly clear that reaching the targets of the Paris Agreement will be impossible via market-based emission trading schemes alone, the 'green growth' discourse recently shifted towards a stronger emphasis on state intervention. Central to this shift is the idea of a Green New Deal (GND), which figures prominently as a 'post-neoliberal imaginary' that many hope could formulate a solution to the problems of both secular stagnation and global warming. The United Nations was one of the first international organizations to call for a GND in response to the global financial crisis as a way to stimulate economic recovery and at the same time improve the sustainability of the world economy via a massive allocation of stimulus funding to green sectors.[68] Ten years later the European Commission, led by its president Ursula von der Leyen, also jumped on this train by calling for a European Green New Deal. Apart from the extension of the EU ETS to carbon-intensive sectors such as transport and agriculture, this includes the introduction of a Carbon Border Tax and Sustainable Europe Investment Plan that will support €1 trillion of investment from 2020 to 2030 'in every corner of the EU'.[69] The GND also gained political traction in the United States, where Democratic members of Congress Alexandria Ocasio-Cortez (also known by her initials, AOC) and Edward Markey called for a GND 'to create millions of good, high-wage jobs and ensure prosperity and economic security for all people of the United States' through a ten-year mobilization plan based on massive public investment and a job guarantee (to compensate workers and communities whose livelihoods depend on fossil fuel industries).[70] In the United Kingdom, Jeremy Corbyn similarly endorsed a GND during the (highly unsuccessful) 2019 election campaign as leader of the Labour Party.

An effective GND would cost a lot of money. AOC projected that it would require spending at least US$10 trillion.[71] The global transition towards a carbon-neutral economy would require a worldwide programme to invest between 1.5 and 2 per cent of global GDP every year to raise energy efficiency standards and expand clean renewable energy supplies, according to one estimate by a GND advocate.[72] A major shift away from the 'sound money' consensus in macroeconomic policymaking would be needed to finance the GND. Massively increasing clean energy investments will not happen without strong industrial policies, including R&D support, preferential tax treatment and subsidies for clean energy investments, and price regulations. These policies will be likely to have a detrimental effect on governments' fiscal balance in ways that should compel them to abandon their austerity dogmas. At a minimum, the European GND would require the European Union to increase the flexibility of its fiscal rules to encourage member states to invest in the energy transition: 'the European fiscal rules should be reformed to deter countries from slashing public investment when they consolidate their public finances and to ensure that they are able to take advantage of favourable interest rates to invest in public goods'.[73]

Some go further, arguing that a GND should involve broadening central banks' objectives to include emission reduction targets set by governments. There are various ways by which monetary policy can help achieve these targets. The most radical way is depressing governments' borrowing costs by buying up long-term sovereign bonds and keeping these bonds on central banks' balance sheets, which would imply subordinating monetary policy to fiscal policy. Left-wing advocates of a GND, like AOC, have explicitly endorsed monetary financing of fiscal deficits as a way to fund public spending on climate change. Their inspiration is the controversial Modern Monetary Theory – a heterodox theory claiming that governments can never go bankrupt as long as they finance their public debt in a currency issued by their own central bank, which can set the interest rate at whatever level is required to stabilize the public debt ratio. A less radical way by which central banks can help governments reach their climate targets is removing 'brown' corporate bonds issued by fossil fuel industries from their large-scale asset purchase programmes, and giving 'green' assets issued by clean energy companies favourable treatment in their collateral frameworks. By greening their monetary policy via these measures, central banks could play a central and proactive role in the fight against global warming.[74]

In sum, just like addressing secular stagnation, decarbonizing the economy will need a fundamental rethink of the role of the state in macroeconomic governance. The coronavirus crisis has further demonstrated the necessity as well as the opportunity of such a rethink.

The coronavirus crisis and the future of egalitarian capitalism

At the time of writing (May 2020), the world economy was hit by a massive and simultaneous negative supply-and-demand shock resulting from coronavirus lockdown measures. With these measures extended to the entire industrialized world, production in most non-essential sectors requiring physical proximity between workers and/or customers came effectively to a halt. The crisis also represented a massive negative demand shock. Sectors dependent on outdoor consumption of leisure services especially – for example, airlines, tourism and entertainment (restaurants, bars, event organizers, hotel chains, shopping malls, etc.) – were directly affected by the initial stages of the lockdown. Businesses in these sectors had to close down and in some cases made their employees redundant. The destruction of income undermined the consumer confidence of households and the business confidence of firms that were largely unaffected by the crisis, creating a negative feedback loop between rising unemployment, dwindling household consumption and falling business investment.

The coronavirus crisis further revealed the weaknesses of advanced capitalist growth models. In particular, debt-led growth models reliant on a continuous expansion of consumption and asset price inflation were vulnerable to the effects of the lockdown measures, as Mark Blyth has argued: in the United States, 'the Federal Reserve and Congress can try to put a floor on asset prices by bailing out companies, but there is no bottom for the broader problem of consumption that occurs when a third of the labour market is laid off and the other two- thirds are locked at home for an extended period of time'.[75] But the crisis also exposed the intrinsic vulnerability of export-led growth models that are excessively reliant on external demand. Germany will not be able to export its way out of the crisis as it did after the global financial crisis and the Eurozone crisis: 'The global economy as a whole has been hit hard by the repercussions of coronavirus, and the partial interruption and questioning of global value chains will make an export-based recovery strategy more difficult to implement in the medium term as well.'[76]

Predictions about the ultimate impact of the crisis are mired in uncertainty, but we can already be certain that the 'Great Lockdown' will cause the worst global economic downturn since the Great Depression. According to IMF estimates in April 2020, GDP in the advanced economies will fall by 6.1 per cent in 2020. Income per capita is projected to shrink for over 170 countries.[77] These estimates even take into account the unprecedented macroeconomic policy expansion enacted by central banks and governments in the advanced capitalist countries.

The crisis forced governments to save businesses from bankruptcy by granting financial support and subsidies, and to assist workers by funding temporary unemployment schemes. As Mark Blyth and Eric Lonergan note, the crisis will deal the final blow to the conservative myth 'that the best way to deal with a collapse in spending by consumers and companies – such as we face as a result of the coronavirus pandemic – is to restore confidence by cutting government budgets'.[78]

In the United States, 'the economic effect of the novel coronavirus has turned conservatives who weeks ago were boasting about the shrinking of the US government into raving Keynesians, proclaiming the virtues of deficit-financed economic stimulus'.[79] On 25 March 2020, the US Congress agreed on a US$2,000 billion stimulus package, the largest stimulus in US history.[80] The deal included US$500 billion for a major corporate liquidity programme through the Federal Reserve, US$367 billion for a small business loan programme, US$100 billion for hospitals and US$150 billion for state and local governments. The stimulus also gave a one-time cheque for US$1,200 to Americans who make up to US$75,000 – and an additional US$500 for each child under the age of seventeen. The UK government unveiled a plan that included a scheme for the state to pay up to 80 per cent of employees' wages, as well as deferring £30 billion of value added tax payments by companies until the end of June, and offering cash grants to small businesses and help for the self-employed, renters and the jobless.[81] Even the German government abandoned its notorious fiscal conservatism and long-term aversion to debt by announcing that it would raise €356bn in new borrowing (10 per cent of GDP).[82]

Figure 8.5 shows the level of fiscal support as a percentage of GDP in the nine largest advanced market economies as of mid-April 2020. At a time of declining tax revenues, these fiscal support measures trigger a major surge in public debt ratios. According to IMF projections, the average public debt ratio in the advanced capitalist world will exceed 120 per cent of GDP.[83]

Skyrocketing fiscal deficits pose a number of pressing problems. First of all, they evoke disturbing memories of the global financial crisis, when governments responded to the extraordinary growth in public debt with

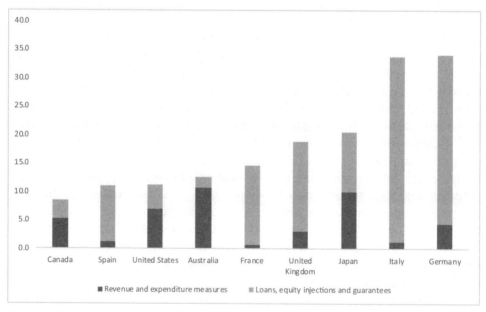

Figure 8.5 Fiscal support measures during the coronavirus crisis (in percentage of GDP), mid-April 2020

Source: IMF 2020

harsh austerity measures and drastic cuts in social spending that primarily affected low-income groups and the most vulnerable households: the costs of austerity are typically distributed unevenly across different income groups and exacerbate already high levels of income inequality, as citizens in the middle or bottom half of the income distribution rely more on public services (social transfers, public transport, public education, health care).[84] The revival of Keynesian deficit spending might prove to be short-lived as governments in the advanced capitalist countries return to austerity to reduce public debt levels as soon as their economy recovers. In the United States, the flood of pandemic-relief spending from the federal government rekindled concerns among Republican legislators about swelling fiscal deficits.[85] In the European Union, the European Commission activated the general escape clause of the SGP, allowing member states to temporarily depart from the SGP's budgetary requirements to undertake adequate fiscal support measures. But there are no indications that the stringent rules of the SGP will be loosed after the economic recovery.

Second, steeply rising fiscal deficits also risk turning the coronavirus crisis into a full-blown sovereign debt crisis. This risk is particularly acute in the Eurozone, whose member states are not monetarily sovereign, in the sense that they have surrendered their ability to issue public debt in a currency controlled by their national central bank (chapter 7). Most worrying to date has been Italy, where yields on ten-year sovereign bonds jumped from less than 1 per cent in January 2020 to almost 3 per cent in March 2020. Nine heads of government (led by France, Italy, Spain and Portugal) called for the introduction of a jointly issued public debt instrument ('coronabonds') to mitigate widening sovereign bond spreads and mutualize the fiscal cost of the crisis – a proposal that was quickly rejected by the region's 'frugal four' (Austria, Finland, Germany and the Netherlands). The lack of an adequate European-level fiscal recovery fund and burden sharing again put more pressure on the ECB to contain government borrowing costs. In March 2020 the ECB initiated a €750 billion Pandemic Emergency Purchase Programme (PEPP) and emphasized its commitment 'to increase the size of its asset purchase programmes and adjust their composition, by as much as necessary and for as long as needed'.[86] Most remarkably, the ECB even stressed it would revise the self-imposed limits on these purchases if needed. In its previous asset purchase programmes, the ECB decided that it would not buy more than 33 per cent of the public debt of a single member state – a decision that was made to reassure the conservative politicians of Germany and other northern Eurozone countries that the ECB would not implicitly engage in the monetary financing of national governments' fiscal deficits.

There are clear signs that rising public debt levels will make fiscal and monetary policy a central terrain of political contestation and social struggle for the foreseeable future. In terms of fiscal policy, the coronavirus crisis might strengthen political support for the introduction of more progressive taxation as an alternative – or in any case complement – to austerity. In a book published only a few months before the crisis, Emmanuel Saez and Gabriel Zucman have shown that the 50 per cent of Americans with the lowest incomes today pay higher tax rates than billionaires. In their book, these authors proposed a tax of 2 per cent on the wealth of 'ultra-millionaires' (and 3 per cent on that of billionaires) to tackle growing wealth concentration – a tax they claim would yield the federal government about 1.2 per cent of GDP.[87] Wealth tax proposals like these are likely to become more prominent in the United States and other advanced countries. As even an editorial in the *Financial Times* recognized, governments will have to accept a more active role in the economy: 'Redistribution will again be on the agenda; the privileges of the elderly and wealthy in question. Policies until recently considered eccentric, such as basic income and wealth taxes, will have to be in the mix.'[88]

In terms of monetary policy, the coronavirus crisis will further highlight the vital role of central banks in the management of public debt. An increasing number of (political) economists have argued that the current crisis provides a window of opportunity to at least remove the monetary financing prohibition and get rid of the neoliberal taboo that central banks should be made responsible for lowering governments' borrowing costs, as was the case during the post-war Keynesian era (chapter 3).[89] As Paul De Grauwe rightly notes, the benefit of this approach is that it spares national governments from having to issue new debt. 'Because all new debt would be monetized, the crisis would not increase government debt-to-GDP ratios. For those countries suffering the worst of the pandemic, the threat of a bondholder panic will have been removed from the equation.'[90] Central banks have already engaged in implicit monetary financing. The Bank of England will purchase £200 billion of British sovereign bonds and the ECB will buy up to €750 billion of Eurozone sovereign bonds. The US Federal Reserve even committed to buy 'unlimited' quantities of Treasury bonds. As such, 'central banks will end up providing monetary finance to fund fiscal deficits. The only question is whether they should make that explicit.'[91]

In sum, the coronavirus crisis will be likely to lead to a further contestation of the neoliberal macroeconomic policy regime that has played a key role in the transition towards a less egalitarian form of capitalism since the 1980s. This 'sound money' regime – that is, politically independent central banks maintaining low inflation and permanent austerity for governments focusing on public debt reduction – served the interests of the owners of capital very well by weakening the bargaining power of labour and preserving the real value of their own assets (chapter 3). Monetary financing of fiscal deficits would completely shatter the conservative myth that the government should always 'live within its means', possibly urging voters to fundamentally rethink the political priorities of macroeconomic policy and 'reclaim the state' as a vehicle for progressive change.[92] As Adam Tooze astutely observed ten years after the global financial crisis, 'the lesson of 2008 and afterwards is that if you have an activist central bank, you can do whatever the fuck you like in terms of fiscal policy'.[93] The coronavirus crisis has made this lesson doubly clear. It is far from certain whether the crisis will sufficiently shake up existing power structures to enable a return towards a more progressive macroeconomic policy regime. In any case, the political contestation of the neoliberal macroeconomic policy regime will need to be central to any transition towards a more egalitarian and more sustainable form of capitalism.

Notes

Introduction

1 Streeck 2014.
2 Alvaredo et al. 2018.
3 All abbreviations used in the text of this book are given with their full versions when they first appear, and are listed on pp. xi–xii.
4 Foa and Mounk 2016: 7.
5 Foa and Mounk 2016: 7.
6 Berman 2019; Broz et al. 2019; Hopkin and Blyth 2019; Rodrik 2017.
7 Petry 2016; Wade 2009.
8 Friedman 1953: 15.
9 Prescott 2016: 2.
10 Bernanke 2018: 251.
11 Mankiw 2013: 30–1.
12 Hacker and Pierson 2011.
13 See Harvey 2006 for an introduction to neoliberalism and Slobodian 2018 for an intellectual history.
14 Manduca 2019.

Chapter 1 Rising Inequality in Advanced Capitalism

1 Piketty 2014.
2 Ibid.
3 Kristal 2010.
4 Bengtsson and Ryner 2015: 411; Onaran 2012.
5 Bivens et al. 2014.
6 Piketty 2014.
7 OECD 2018: 52.
8 Goldin and Katz 2008: 7–8.
9 https://www.tutor2u.net/economics.
10 Heilbroner 1995: 57.
11 Autor et al. 2016.
12 OECD 2015a: 11.
13 Mankiw 2018: 5, 418.
14 For a review of the neoclassical literature on the relationship between inequality and growth and an empirical assessment of that relationship, see Barro 1999. In his study, Barro finds that, at least for the advanced countries, 'active income redistribution

appears to involve a trade-off between the benefits of greater equality and a reduction in overall economic growth' (1999: 32).

15 Piketty 2014: 314.

16 Hager 2018: 7.

17 An underlying assumption is that labour and capital shares are determined entirely by production technology, which increases the marginal product of capital and labour by the same amount. See Kristal 2010: 736–7 and Piketty 2014: 217–20 for a discussion.

18 Marsh 1983: 4.

19 Lindblom 1977.

20 Gill and Law 1989: 481; see also Cox 1987; Gill 1998; van Apeldoorn 2002; Overbeek and Jessop 2018.

21 Hacker and Pierson 2002: 282.

22 Korpi 1983; Esping-Andersen 1990; Huber and Stephens 2001; Stephens 1979.

23 Hall and Soskice 2001; Hancké et al. 2007.

24 Korpi 1983; Esping-Andersen 1990; Huber and Stephens 2001; Stephens 1979; Baccaro and Howell 2017.

25 Galbraith 2012; Onaran et al. 2011; Ostry et al. 2014; Stiglitz 2015; Stockhammer 2015. See Michell 2015 for a review.

26 Cingano 2014.

27 Cynamon and Fazzari 2016; Kumhof and Rancière 2010; Rajan 2010; Onaran et al. 2011; Stockhammer 2015; Stockhammer and Onaran 2013.

28 Mian et al. 2020; see also Goda and Lysandrou 2014; Goda et al. 2017.

29 Sweezy 1942. See Clarke 1994 for an overview of Marxist theories of crisis.

30 Marx 1967: 484.

31 Baccaro and Pontusson 2016; Behringer and van Treeck 2019; Onaran 2015; Stockhammer and Onaran 2013; Stochammer 2018; Stockhammer and Kohler 2019.

32 Ahlquist and Ansell 2017; Montgomerie and Büdenbender 2015; Schwartz 2012; Watson 2009.

Chapter 2 The Rise and Fall of Egalitarian Capitalism

1   Ingham 2008; Portes 2016.

2   Polanyi 1944: 146–7.

3   Piketty 2014: fig. 10.6.

4   For a classic account of the Wall Street crash and subsequent Great Depression, see Galbraith 1955.

5   Frieden 2006; Hiltzik 2011; Rauchway 2007.

6   Ruggie 1982: 393.

7   For scholarly works on the origins of the Bretton Woods system, see James 1996 and Steil 2013. For clear and concise summaries of the Bretton Woods order, see Frieden 2006: ch. 12; Helleiner 2008.

8   Helleiner 2008: 220.

9   Frieden 2006: 187–290.

10 Keynes quoted in Clift 2018: 18.

11 Harry Dexter White, US representative at the Bretton Woods conference, quoted in Helleiner 1994: 34.

12 Baccaro and Howell 2017: 209.

13 Jessop 1997: 523.

14 Aglietta 1979; Boyer and Saillard 2002; Jessop 1997; Lipietz 1987.

15 Tickell and Peck 1995: 360.

16 For several classical accounts of the Golden Age of capitalism, see Armstrong et al. 1991, Marglin and Schor 1990, and Frieden 2006: part III. It should be noted that not all scholars agree with this conventional account of the post-war boom. For a critical Marxist account, see Brenner 2006.

17 On social blocs, see Amable and Palombarini 2009 and Baccaro and Pontusson 2019.

18 Clift 2014: 124. See Hall 1997 and Blyth 2009 for a review of these three theoretical traditions.

19 Korpi 1983; Esping-Andersen 1990; Huber and Stephens 2001; Stephens 1979.

20 Przeworski 1986: 207. On the rise of social democracy, see Baldwin 1992; Berman 2006; Korpi 1983; Stephens 1979.

21 Frieden 2006: 244.

22 Mares 2003; Swenson 2002.

23 Swenson 2002; 2004.

24 Helleiner 1995: 318.

25 Korpi 1983: 48.

26 Van Apeldoorn 2002: 20.

27 Przeworski 1986: 36.

28 Blyth 2002.

29 Clift 2014: 161.

30 Rohlf 2010; Heilbroner 1995; Whapshott 2012.

31 Keynes 1936; see Rohlf 2010; Heilbroner 1995; Whapshott 2012 for an introduction to Keynesian economics.

32 Streeck 2010: 21. See also Martin and Swank 2010; Thelen 1994; Swenson 2002; Martin 2000; Mares 2003.

33 Martin and Swank 2010: 7. See also Thelen 1994; Swenson 2002; Mares 2003.

34 Lijphart 1999.

35 Iversen and Soskice 2006; 2009; Cusack et al. 2007.

36 Gowa 1983.

37 James 1996; Eichengreen 1996.

38 Helleiner 2008.

39 Glyn 2001: 7.

40 Harvey 2006: 2–3.

41 Frieden 2006: 385.

42 Taylor 2008: 1. On the rise of global value chains, see Baldwin 2016; Neilson et al. 2016; Gereffi 2018.

43 Helleiner 1994; 1995; 2008; see also Abdelal 2007; Chwieroth 2010.

44 Clift 2009: 201.

45 Cerny 1997; Jessop 2002; see Genschel and Seelkopf 2015 for a recent review of this literature.

46 See Genschel and Schwarz (2011) for a review of the effects of international tax competition.

47 Hall and Soskice 2001; Hancké et al. 2007.

48 Hall and Gingerich 2009.

49 Boyer 2005; Jackson and Deeg 2006; Peck and Theodore 2007.

50 Molina and Rhodes 2007.

51 Hall and Soskice 2001: 21.

52 Hassel 2014: 10.

53 Amable and Palombarini 2009; Streeck 2010.

54 As Mark Blyth (2009: 204) notes in a pointed critique: 'the works of generations of labor historians, and quite a few political scientists, are thrown into question in what is a rather apolitical reading of events where strikes, lockouts, shootings, revolts, Communist Party agitations, socialist Sunday schools, and hunger marches all become quite puzzling. After all, employers apparently wanted to give workers a welfare state, so what was all the trouble about?'

55 Streeck 2010: 22.

56 Howell 2003; Jackson and Deeg 2006; Mentz 2017.

57 This is a point most often made by Marxist critics. See, e.g., Bruff and Ebenau 2014; Panitch and Gindin 2012. In fact, as Coates (2006: 22) notes, 'the more orthodox the Marxist scholarship, the greater has been the propensity to treat the "varieties of capitalism" … as simply different versions of a common mode of production, and to see each model as equally prone as the rest to experience internal contradictions, and eventually decline and decay'.

58 Korpi 1983; Esping-Andersen 1990; Huber and Stephens 2001; Stephens 1979; Baccaro and Howell 2017.

59 Schwartz and Tranøy 2019: 45.

60 Hope 2016: 74.

61 Soskice 2007; Iversen and Soskice 2013; Hope and Soskice 2016; Hope 2016.

62 Iversen and Soskice 2013: 37.

63 Iversen and Soskice 2019: 50.

64 Iversen and Soskice 2019: 23, 42.

65 Nolan and Weisstanner 2020.

66 Epstein 2005: 3. See also Krippner 2012 and Van der Zwan 2014 for critical views on financialization.

67 Iversen and Soskice 2019: 150–1.

68 Baccaro and Pontusson 2016; 2018; Behringer and van Treeck 2019; Hein et al. 2020; Onaran 2015; Stockhammer and Onaran 2013; Stockhammer 2018; Stockhammer and Kohler 2019.

69 Stockhammer 2016: 368.

70 Baccaro and Pontusson 2016: 25. See also Baccaro and Pontusson 2018; Baccaro and Howell 2017.

71 Baccaro and Pontusson 2016: 25.

72 See, especially, Baccaro and Pontusson 2016.

73 Behringer and van Treeck 2019.

Chapter 3 Macroeconomic Policy

1 Quoted in Glyn 1995: 33.

2 Pierson 2001.

3 Konzelman 2014: 714.

4 Blyth 2013; Calgano 2012. In this example we do not take into account interest rate payments by the government on outstanding public debt.

5 Mankiw 2018: ch. 32.

6 Braun and Downey 2020.

7 Goodhart 1988; Capie et al. 1994.

8 Ryan-Collins and van Lerven 2018.

9 Ryan-Collins and van Lerven 2018: 9.
10 Baker 2006: 21.
11 Friedman 1968.
12 Barro 1974.
13 For a very good overview (and criticism) of the New Keynesian views on macroeconomic policy, see Mason and Jayadev 2013.
14 Baker 2006: 75.
15 Barro and Gordon 1983; Bernhard 1998; Bernhard et al. 2002. For an overview of political business cycle theory, see Drahokoupil 2007.
16 Buchanan et al. 1978: 79.
17 Alesina and Rosenthal 1989; Alesina and Roubini 1992.
18 Sargent 1985: 248; see also Burdekin and Laney 1988.
19 Gill 1998: 5; Gill and Cutler 2014.
20 Baker 2005: 93.
21 Baker 2006: 76.
22 Grabel 2003: 25. See also Grabel 2010.
23 Helleiner 1994: 116.
24 Halifax Communiqué, G7 Summit 1995, quoted in Baker 2006: 69.
25 Birch 2015. See also Andrews 1994.
26 Mosley 2005: 357; 2000.
27 Mosley 2000: 747.
28 For a recent empirical confirmation of this claim, see Sattler 2013. See also Rommerskirchen 2020, who finds that the market pressure on governments to pursue fiscal consolidation increases with the share of foreign bond holders.
29 Sinclair 2005; see also Paudyn 2013.
30 For a recent empirical assessment and confirmation of these dynamics, see Barta and Johnston 2018.
31 Mankiw 2018: 572.
32 Alesina et al. 1998: 198.
33 Blyth 2013; Dellepiane-Avellaneda 2014.
34 E.g. Barro 1995; 1996.
35 Kirshner 2000: 430, 432; see also Kirshner 1999.
36 McNamara 2002: 53.
37 Blyth 2013; Heimberger 2020b.
38 Dutta 2018: 4.
39 Korpi 2002: 397.
40 Korpi 2002: 373–4.
41 Kalecki 1943.
42 Kalecki 1943: 351.
43 Korpi 1991.
44 Korpi 2002: 397. See also Burdekin and Burkett 1996; Clarke 1988; Glyn 2007; Hung and Thompson 2016; Devine 2000; Rowthorn 1980; Blyth and Matthijs 2017.
45 Kaldor 1983: 15.
46 This example is taken from Mankiw 2018: ch. 29.
47 Vlandas 2018: 516.
48 Christophers 2018: 101.
49 Argitis 2008; Epstein 1992; Epstein and Jayadev 2005; Kirshner 1999; 2000.
50 Godley 2000: 174.
51 Posen 1995: 254.

52 Karwowski 2019: 1017.
53 Kalinowski and Hlasny 2017: 24.
54 Soskice 2007: 101.
55 Höpner and Lutter 2014: 19.
56 Baccaro and Pontusson 2019: 8.
57 Vermeiren 2017.
58 Dustmann et al. 2014; Hassel 2014.
59 Soskice 2007; Iversen and Soskice 2013; Kalinowski and Hlasny 2017.
60 Kaya et al. 2019. Shapiro and Wilson (2019) directly estimated the FOMC's loss function from a text analysis of the tone of the language used in FOMC transcripts, minutes and members' speeches, and found that the FOMC had an implicit inflation target of approximately 1.5 per cent from 2000 to 2013.
61 Lavery 2019: 26. Hay et al. 2006 were the first to make this case for the British growth model.
62 Greenspan 2001: 6.
63 For the UK economy, see Hay 2009; Watson 2009. For the Australian economy, see Adkins et al. 2019.

Chapter 4 Social Policy

1   Vandenbroucke 2000: 25. Author's own translation of following text in Dutch: 'Door de deregulering en explosie van de financiële markten, zijn de nationale staten in hun macro-economische beleid in toenemende mate afhankelijk geworden van de "goed- of afkeuring" door internationale financiële markten die zij niet controleren. De nationale regeringen hebben zich daarbij neergelegd, en in de plaats van het traditionele macro-economische beheer van de economie, verwachten zij nu alle heil van het micro-economische concurrentievermogen van hun bedrijven.'
2   Rueda and Pontusson 2000; Wallerstein 1999.
3   Rueda and Pontusson 2000: 361.
4   Schulten 2004: 5.
5   Erixon 2008: 369.
6   In France, for instance, the government extended sectoral agreements beyond the industry or region of the original signatories, making aggressive use of the minimum wages at the low end of the pay scale.
7   Baccaro and Howell 2017.
8   Esping-Andersen 1990: 26.
9   Esping-Andersen 1990: 27.
10 Esping-Andersen 1990: 28.
11 Karamessini 2007; 2008.
12 Baccaro and Howell 2017: 201.
13 See Katzenstein 1985 for a key reference in this tradition.
14 Cameron 1978; Garret 1998; Rodrik 1998.
15 Okun 1975.
16 Armingeon and Beyeler 2004; McBride and Williams 2001.
17 OECD 1994: 45.
18 Howell 2003: 3.
19 Storm and Naastepad 2009; Vergeer and Kleinknecht 2014.
20 A simple numerical example can illustrate why manufacturing firms with higher-than-average productivity growth benefit from a national-level wage-setting system.

Assume that an economy consists of two equally large sectors: one manufacturing sector with annual productivity growth of 10 per cent and one service sector with annual productivity growth of 2 per cent. In a national-level wage-setting system, unions and employers will agree that wages can grow annually by 6 per cent, which is significantly below the 10 per cent annual wage growth that workers in the manufacturing sector would get in the context of an industry-level wage-setting system.

21 Hall and Soskice 2001: 39.
22 Busemeyer and Iversen 2012: 208.
23 Estevez-Abe et al. 2001. Busemeyer 2009 points to varieties in skill formation systems based on firms' involvement in skill formation and the vocational specificity of the education system. On the basis of three case studies, he demonstrates the existence of three distinct skill regimes in non-liberal market economies: the segmentalist (firm-based) skill regime of Japan, the integrationist (school-based occupational) skill regime of Sweden and the differentiated (workplace-based occupational) skill regime of Germany.
24 Iversen and Soskice 2015: 18.
25 Iversen and Wren 1998: 508.
26 Iversen and Wren 1998: 511–12.
27 Baumol and Bowen 1966.
28 Iversen and Wren 1998: 512.
29 Acemoglu and Autor 2011; Autor 2010; Wright and Dwyer 2003.
30 Thelen 2012: 152–3.
31 Ansell and Gingrich 2013: 202. See also Wren et al. 2013.
32 Thelen 2014: 13–14.
33 Thelen 2012: 153.
34 Thelen 2014: 14.
35 Thelen 2014: 13. See also Rueda 2007 and Emmenegger et al. 2011.
36 Carlin and Soskice 2009; Emmenegger et al. 2011; Rueda 2007; Thelen 2014; Dustmann et al. 2014.
37 The level for a single person was initially €374 per month (known as the *Regelsatz*) and subsequently raised to €391 per month in 2013.
38 In the hotel and restaurant sectors, for instance, wages after the reforms fell to less than half of manufacturing wages. During the 1970s they were at 80 per cent of manufacturing pay.
39 Hassel 2014; Carlin and Soskice 2009; Dustmann et al. 2014.
40 Beramendi et al. 2015: 8. See also Busemeyer et al. 2018 and Hemerijck 2018.
41 Garritzmann et al. 2018: 585.
42 Amable and Palombarini 2009; Baccaro and Howell, 2017; Hacker and Pierson 2004; Korpi 2006.
43 Korpi 1983: 168; 2006; Esping-Andersen 1990; Huber and Stephens 2001.
44 Korpi 2006: 173.
45 For a recent review of the literature on unions and inequality, see Ahlquist 2017.
46 Korpi 2006; Esping-Andersen 1990.
47 Streeck 2016: 245.
48 For an overview of these developments, see Baccaro and Howell 2011; Peters 2008; Visser 2013.
49 Jaumotte and Buitron 2015; Töngür and Elveren 2014.
50 Visser 2013: 23.
51 Baccaro and Howell 2011: 540.

52 Baccaro and Howell 2017; Baccaro and Benassi 2017; Reisenbichler and Morgan 2012.
53 Brandl and Traxler 2011. The concept of 'competitive corporatism' is from Rhodes 1998.
54 Albo 1994.
55 Peters 2008.
56 Baccaro and Benassi 2014: 160; 2017; Baccaro and Pontusson 2016.
57 Baccaro and Howell 2017: 160.
58 Scharpf 1999: 3.
59 Doellgast and Greer 2007; Lippert et al. 2014; Holst 2014; Vidal 2013.
60 Dimova 2019.
61 Baccaro and Howell 2017: 198; Baccaro and Pontusson 2016; Howell 2020; Vidal 2013.
62 Adkins et al. 2019; Doling and Ronald 2010; Montgomerie and Büdenbender 2015; Norris and Fahey 2011; Schwartz 2012; Watson 2009.
63 Schwartz 2012 quoted in Mertens 2017: 477.
64 Kalina and Weinkopf 2018: 4.

Chapter 5 Corporate Governance

1 Bivens and Mishel 2013: 61.
2 Business Roundtable 1997.
3 Lazonick and O'Sullivan 2000.
4 Lazonick and O'Sullivan 2000: 14.
5 Wibbelink and Heng 2000: 5.
6 Berle and Means 1932: 312.
7 Boix 2019: 57.
8 Boix 2019: 58.
9 Lichtenstein 2014: 9; see also Boix 2019; Fligstein 1990; Mizruchi 2013; Schwartz 2016.
10 Chandler 1984: 475. See also Chandler 1977.
11 Lazonick and O'Sullivan 2000: 15.
12 Lichtenstein 2014: 10.
13 Vidal 2012: 546.
14 FitzRoy and Kraft 2005; Streeck 1987; Müller-Jentsch and Weitbrecht 2003.
15 Lazonick and O'Sullivan 2000: 15.
16 Dohse et al. 1984: 119; see also Naruse 1991.
17 Lazonick and O'Sullivan 2000: 15; see Lazonick 1998.
18 Lazonick and O'Sullivan 2000: 18.
19 'Equity' refers to the ownership of a firm: shareholders' equity is the net amount of a firm's total assets and total liabilities. RoE equals RoA multiplied by firm leverage (= value of assets/equity).
20 Fligstein 1990: 15.
21 Boix 2019: 113; see also Bayard et al. 2013; Bernard and Fort 2015; Kamal 2018.
22 Schwartz 2016: 214.
23 Unless stated otherwise, this box is based on Froud et al. 2012 and Fernandez and Hendrikse 2015.
24 Manne 1962; Fama and Jensen 1983; Jensen 1986.
25 Friedman 1962: 133.
26 Manne 1962: 113.
27 Fama and Jensen 1983; Jensen 1986.

28 This box is based on Mankiw 2018: 544–646.
29 Lazonick and O'Sullivan 2000: 16.
30 Mankiw 2018: 546–7.
31 Mankiw 2018: 546–7.
32 Davis and Kim 2015: 209; see also Davis 2009; Harmes 2001.
33 Harmes 2001: 10.
34 Jensen and Murphy 1990: 138.
35 Lazonick 2015: 8.
36 Knafo and Dutta 2020: 3.
37 Gourevitch and Shinn 2005.
38 Bebchuk et al. 2002; Bebchuk and Fried 2003; 2004.
39 Bebchuk and Fried 2004: 7.
40 Baker 2016: 538.
41 Hacker and Pierson 2011: 190; see also Angeles et al. 2016; Angeles and Kemmerling 2020.
42 Zysman 1983; see also Albert 1993; Dore 2000.
43 Deeg et al. 2016.
44 Pontusson 2005: 23; Rajan and Zingales 2003.
45 Pontusson 2005: 23–5; Culpepper 2005.
46 Schmidt and Tyrell 1997.
47 Hall and Soskice 2001; Hancké et al. 2007; Jackson and Deeg 2006.
48 Hall and Gingerich 2009: 465.
49 Hall and Gingerich 2009: 465.
50 Angeles et al. 2016; Jaumotte and Buitron 2015; Töngür and Elveren 2014.
51 Page 2009: 10.
52 Aguilera and Jackson 2003; Roe 2003.
53 Aguilera and Jackson 2003: 455.
54 Aguilera and Jackson 2003: 459.
55 Foroohar 2016: 96.
56 Porter 1990; Jackson and Deeg 2006.
57 Jackson and Deeg 2006: 20.
58 Schwartz 2016: 237.
59 Haskel and Westlake 2017: 4–5.
60 Schwartz 2016.
61 Krippner 2012; Orhangazi 2008. See Davis and Kim 2015 for a review of this literature.
62 Krippner 2012.
63 Fernandez and Hendrikse 2015.
64 Orhangazi 2008: 868.
65 Lazonick 2015: 4.
66 Mason 2015: 11.
67 Schwartz 2019: 3.
68 Schwartz 2019: 3.
69 Andrews et al. 2016.
70 Janssen 2017; Schwartz 2016.
71 Andrews et al. 2016.
72 Braun 2020: 14–15. Exchange traded funds are passive funds whose stock portfolio tracks the most important indices of the publicly listed firms (for example, the S&P 500, which is an index of the 500 largest pubicly listed US firms).
73 Fichtner et al. 2017: 317.

74 Boyer 2000.

75 Boyer 2000: 116.

76 Veblen 1994.

77 Frank et al. 2014. See Behringer and van Treeck 2019 and Michell 2015 for a discussion.

78 Davis 2009; Harmes 2001.

79 Epstein 2002: 2.

80 Bieling 2006; Mügge 2010.

81 Bieling 2006: 425.

82 See Watson 2001 for a critique of this agenda.

83 Engelen 2003: 1368.

84 Hassel et al. 2019: 487.

85 On the impact of the financialization of European non-financial firms on investment and wages see, respectively, Tori and Onaran 2018 and Guschanski and Onaran 2018.

86 On the role of vertical disintegration in the polarization of the German labour market, see Doellgast and Greer 2007; Lippert et al. 2014; Holst 2014; Vidal 2013.

87 Vitols 2005.

88 Howarth 2013.

Chapter 6 Financial Policy

1   Calomiris 2008; Richardson 2006.

2   Stern and Feldman 2009.

3   Rogoff and Reinhart 2009: xxxii.

4   Schularick 2012.

5   Schularick 2012: 882.

6   Admati and Hellwig 2013.

7   Gilbert 1986; Walter 2006. See also Calomiris 1997; Russell 2007.

8   Dorene Isenberg quoted in Russell 2007: 4.

9   The tax system, for example, favoured public bonds (particularly for housing and infrastructure) over industrial bonds. Double taxation of equities (corporation tax plus individual income tax) stunted the development of equities markets.

10 Vitols 2001: 187.

11 Vitols 2001.

12 Rogoff and Reinhart 2009; Wyplosz 1999.

13 Fuller 2016: 2.

14 Fuller 2016: 8.

15 Fuller 2016: 9.

16 Ertürk 2016a.

17 Mehrling et al. 2013; see also Nesvetailova 2019; Thiemann 2018.

18 Bezemer et al. 2017; Fuller 2016; Jordà et al. 2016.

19 Hardie and Maxfield 2013.

20 Fuchita et al. 2009: 1.

21 IMF 2006: 133.

22 Thompson 2012: 402; see also Schelkle 2012; Schwartz 2009.

23 Fabozzi and Kothari 2008.

24 https://www.federalreserve.gov/boarddocs/speeches/2005/20050408/default.htm.

25 Conforming (i.e. 'prime') loans required borrowers to make a 10 per cent down payment (i.e. be below a 90 per cent loan-to-value ratio), have a credit rating that put

them into the top 75 per cent of the population, and expend no more than 28 per cent of their gross income on direct housing expenses (principal, interest, property taxes and insurance). In addition, the loan amount was capped in most markets at 125 per cent of the national median home price.

26 For a very clear overview of the role of increasingly complex securitization in the subprime crisis, see Beitel 2009 and Schwartz 2008.
27 Beitel 2009.
28 Crotty 2009: 565.
29 Schwartz 2008: 197; Schwartz and Seabrooke 2008.
30 Schwartz 2008: 197.
31 Tooze 2018: 75.
32 Hardie and Howarth 2013: 25–6.
33 Gabor and Ban 2016; Gabor 2016.
34 Royo 2013.
35 Lane 2012; Milesi-Ferretti and Tille 2011.
36 Monnet et al. 2014: 2. See also Baker 2010; Johnson and Kwak 2011; Pagliari 2015.
37 FCIC 2011: xviii.
38 Bell and Hindmoor 2014: 3. See Pagliari 2015 for a review of instrumentalist and structural perspectives on financial industry power.
39 Helleiner 1994; Gill and Law 1989.
40 Monnet et al. 2014; Gabor and Ban 2016.
41 Pagliari and Young 2014.
42 Ansell 2014.
43 Pagliari et al. 2018.
44 See also Harmes 2001; Davis 2009.
45 Chwieroth and Walter 2019: 4.
46 Crouch 2009.
47 Adkins et al. 2019; Doling and Ronald 2010; Montgomerie and Büdenbender 2015; Norris and Fahey 2011; Schwartz 2012; Watson 2009.
48 Barnes 2016: 534–5; see also Fuller 2016; Hope 2016.
49 Fuller 2015.
50 https://www.ecb.europa.eu/pub/pdf/other/housingfinanceeuroarea0309en.pdf.
51 Fuller 2015; Fuller et al. 2020; Johnston and Regan 2017.
52 Johnston and Regan 2017.
53 Tranøy et al. 2020: 393.
54 Tranøy et al. 2020; see also Fuller et al. 2020.
55 Johnston and Regan 2017.
56 Braun and Deeg 2019.

Chapter 7 Macroeconomic Imbalances Before and After the Crisis

1 Cooper 1975.
2 Gilpin 1987; Helleiner 1994.
3 Bernanke 2004.
4 Dunaway 2009; Obstfeld and Rogoff 2009; Wolf 2008.
5 Lapavitsas et al. 2010; Shambaugh 2012.
6 Bernanke 2005; see also Dumas 2008; Wolf 2008.
7 Dooley et al. 2003. It is called the Bretton Woods II hypothesis because the configuration resembles the original Bretton Woods system during the 1950s and 1960s,

when Western countries strengthened their export competitiveness by pegging their exchange rate against the dollar.

8   Aizenman and Lee 2008; Ocampo 2007.
9   Chinn 2005; Roubini 2006; Obstfeld and Rogoff 2009.
10 Behringer and van Treeck 2019; see also Wolf 2015.
11 Boyer 2000; Stockhammer 2008.
12 Iversen and Soskice 2013: 37.
13 Lin and Tomaskovic-Devey 2013: 186.
14 Hacker 2004.
15 Hancké 2013; Hancké and Johnston 2009; Johnston et al. 2014.
16 Baccaro and Benassi 2017; Dustmann et al. 2014.
17 Its cyclically adjusted government primary balance – which measures discretionary changes in the government's fiscal policy by removing its net debt interest payments and correcting for the position of the economy in the business cycle – improved from −1.05 per cent of GDP in 2000 to 1.4 per cent in 2007. Therefore, despite the fact that the domestic economy was already weak during this period because of relatively high real interest rates, the German government's fiscal policy restrained it even further.
18 Martin 2016: 230.
19 Di Carlo 2020: 25.
20 Behringer and van Treeck 2019; Redeker 2019. There is indeed considerable empirical evidence that German manufacturing firms responded to the repression of labour costs by increasing their profit margins rather than cutting their prices. See Vermeiren 2017 for a discussion.
21 Thelen 2014.
22 Baccaro and Pontusson 2016; 2019.
23 Hancké 2009: 7.
24 Molina and Rhodes 2007; Karamessini 2008; Royo 2007.
25 Boyer 2002: 44.
26 Hall 2018: 12.
27 Hancké 2013; Iversen et al. 2016; Johnston et al. 2014.
28 Höpner and Lutter 2014: 7.
29 Hancké 2013: 77.
30 Lallement 2011: 237. This also explains why manufacturing sectors from the MMEs were hurt much more by the exponential rise in the nominal exchange rate of the euro from 2002 to 2007/9, as well as by the rise of China and other emerging markets in the world economy, than manufacturing firms from the CMEs. See De Ville and Vermeiren 2016 and Vermeiren 2017 for an elaboration of this argument.
31 Nölke 2015: 153.
32 G20 2008.
33 G20 2009.
34 G20 2009.
35 Frieden 2015; Frieden and Walter 2017.
36 Eichengreen 2011: 44; Helleiner and Kirshner 2009; Vermeiren 2014.
37 Gourinchas and Jeanne 2012: 24.
38 Fields and Vernengo 2013: 746. See also Vermeiren 2019.
39 Koo 2014.
40 See Dynan 2012 and Mian and Sufi 2016 for the United States and Bunn and Rostom 2014 for the United Kingdom.
41 Felkerson 2011, who estimates that its total bailout commitment was in excess of

US$29 trillion, gives a detailed overview of the Federal Reserve's actions in response to the crisis.

42 G20 2010.

43 G20 2010.

44 El-Erian 2016.

45 Reisenbichler 2020: 470.

46 Green and Lavery 2015; Hale 2018.

47 Bernanke 2010.

48 Bernanke quoted in Klein 2012. A 401(k) plan is a defined-contribution retirement account offered by many US employers to their employees, consisting typically of an assortment of stock and bond mutual funds.

49 Three reviews of the economics literature on QE came to sobering conclusions about its macroeconomic effects. Haldane et al. (2016) found that the effects of QE on the broader macroeconomy are state-dependent: the effectiveness of QE policies varies across both countries and time, with QE interventions being more effective when financial markets are disturbed. Borio and Zabai (2016) observed that the effectiveness of QE tends to diminish over time and that its side effects – e.g. on the profitability and resilience of the financial system – tend to grow. Rogoff (2017: 48) also concluded that 'unconventional monetary policy tools are poor substitutes for conventional interest rate policy and might well have more side-effects'.

50 Mason 2015: 3.

51 https://assets.publishing.service.gov.uk/government/uploads/system/uploads/attachment_data/file/817978/share-repurchases-executive-pay-investment.pdf.

52 Ertürk 2016b: 9.

53 OECD 2015b: 31.

54 Green and Lavery 2015: 899. See also Adolph 2018; Jacobs and King 2016; Montecino and Epstein 2015.

55 Cynamon and Fazzari 2016; Goda et al. 2017.

56 Lane 2008; Schmitz and Von Hagen 2011.

57 This section is mostly based on Vermeiren 2014; 2017.

58 An additional reason why the ECB's reluctance to provide a monetary backstop to peripheral sovereign bond markets destabilized these markets is related to the role of sovereign bonds as collateral in wholesale funding markets. Rising yields on the sovereign debt of distressed member states undermined the willingness of core Eurozone banks to use these securities as collateral in repos, raising the yields on these sovereign bonds even further. In the absence of a central bank willing to act as a lender of last resort to governments by backstopping sovereign bond and collateral markets, the provision of external liquidity evaporated for peripheral governments and banks that were faced with the declining attractiveness of these sovereign debt markets. As such, changing perceptions of funding risk in wholesale markets impacted the liquidity of collateral markets and triggered collateral discrimination in integrated funding markets (Gabor and Ban 2016; see also Allen and Moessner 2012).

59 De Grauwe 2013; Papadimitriou and Wray 2012; Corsetti 2010.

60 Henning 2016; Sacchi 2015; Woodruff 2015.

61 González-Páramo 2011.

62 European Commission 2011: 21.

63 European Council 2011: 6.

64 For an overview of major changes in national collective bargaining systems, see Schulten and Müller 2014.

65 See Vermeiren 2017 for a detailed analysis.
66 Scharpf 2016: 23.
67 Perez and Matsaganis 2019: 266. See also De Ville and Vermeiren 2016; Vermeiren 2017.
68 Jacobs and Mazzucato 2016.
69 Summers 2016: 2.
70 For a discussion of mainstream views on secular stagnation, see Teulings and Baldwin 2014; for a discussion of heterodox views, see Akyüz 2018.
71 Summers 2014: 69.
72 Summers 2016: 3.
73 Larry Summers quoted in Vinik 2013.
74 Kliman 2012; Magdoff and Foster 2014; Vidal 2013.
75 Palley 2012; Hein 2015.
76 Stockhammer 2015: 951; see also Hein 2015; Onaran 2016.

Chapter 8 The Future of Egalitarian Capitalism

1   Alvaredo et al. 2018: 10.
2   Berman 2017; Woods 2017.
3   Kalecki 1943.
4   Thelen 2014.
5   Iversen and Soskice 2019: 147.
6   Iversen and Soskice 2019: 149.
7   Howell 2015: 403.
8   Baccaro and Pontusson 2016; Behringer and van Treeck 2019; Manger and Sattler 2019.
9   Stockhammer and Kohler 2019: 3.
10 Summers 2016: 7; 2018.
11 Bunn et al. 2018; Lenza and Slacalek 2018.
12 Borio and Zabai 2016; Haldane et al. 2016; Rogoff 2017.
13 Blyth and Lonergan 2014; see also Muellbauer 2014.
14 Matthijs and Blyth 2018.
15 Bernanke 2013.
16 Draghi 2014.
17 Bernanke 2017: 4.
18 Mandelkern 2016.
19 Blanchard 2019.
20 Reinhart and Rogoff 2010.
21 Hager 2016; Arbogast 2020.
22 Akyüz 2018: 11.
23 Akyüz 2018: 11.
24 Turner 2015.
25 Haffert 2019: 3; see also Haffert and Mertens 2019.
26 Mandelkern 2016: 226.
27 Pontusson 2018: 3. See also Adolph 2018; Jacobs and King 2016.
28 Ahlquist and Ansell 2017; Ansell 2014; Schwartz and Seabrooke 2008; Schwartz 2009.
29 Ansell 2017: 7.
30 Sylvester Eijffinger quoted in den Haan et al. 2017.
31 Jones 2015: 83.

32 Mudde and Kaltwasser 2017: 7.
33 Müller 2018: 2.
34 Pappas 2019.
35 Hatton 2016; Becker and Fetzer 2017; Mayda et al. 2016; Kaufmann 2019.
36 Kaufmann 2018: 224.
37 Berman 2019: 2. See also Broz et al. 2019; Hopkin and Blyth 2019; Judis 2016; Rodrik 2017.
38 Funke et al. 2016: 276.
39 Inglehart and Norris 2019.
40 Gidron and Hall 2020: 1048.
41 Kurer and Palier 2019: 5.
42 Keskinen et al. 2016.
43 Röth et al. 2018.
44 Rennwald and Pontusson 2020.
45 Berman 2019; Hopkin and Blyth 2019; Hopkin 2020; Lynch 2019.
46 Lynch 2019: 671.
47 Hopkin and Blyth 2019: 207; Hopkin 2020.
48 Mouffe 2018.
49 Streeck 2019.
50 Streeck 2019. See also Mitchell and Fazi 2018.
51 Abou-Chadi and Wagner 2019; Abou-Chadi and Immergut 2019; Iversen and Soskice 2019.
52 Bremer 2018.
53 Bremer and McDaniel 2019.
54 Berman 2019: 666.
55 IPCC 2019.
56 Stern 2006.
57 https://unfccc.int/process-and-meetings/the-paris-agreement/.
58 Newell and Paterson 2010: 1.
59 Koch et al. 2016: 705.
60 https://eur-lex.europa.eu/legal-content/EN/TXT/PDF/?uri=CELEX:52018DC0773&from=EN.
61 Zachmann et al. 2018.
62 Koch 2018: 43. See also D'Alisa et al. 2015; Kallis 2009; Latouche 2009.
63 Gough and Meadowcroft 2012.
64 Pollin 2018: 25.
65 Lachapelle et al. 2017: 312. See also Jessop 2002; Lindblom 1977; O'Connor 1973.
66 https://eur-lex.europa.eu/legal-content/EN/TXT/PDF/?uri=CELEX:52018DC0773&from=EN.
67 Koch 2018: 39–49. See Newell and Paterson 2010: ch. 6 for an extensive critique of the EU ETS.
68 UN-DESA 2009.
69 https://ec.europa.eu/commission/sites/beta-political/files/political-guidelines-next-commission_en.pdf.
70 https://www.congress.gov/116/bills/hres109/BILLS-116hres109ih.pdf.
71 https://www.businessinsider.nl/alexandria-ocasio-cortez-says-green-new-deal-cost-10-trillion-2019-6.
72 Pollin 2018.
73 Claeys 2019.

74 Dafermos et al. 2018; Tooze 2019; van Lerven and Ryan-Collins 2017.
75 Blyth 2020.
76 Heimberger 2020a.
77 IMF 2020.
78 Blyth and Lonergan 2020.
79 Hiltzik 2020.
80 Bolton and Carney 2020.
81 Parker et al. 2020.
82 Chazan 2020.
83 IMF 2020.
84 Heimberger 2020b.
85 Dennis 2020.
86 ECB 2020.
87 Saez and Zucman 2019.
88 Editorial Board of the *Financial Times* 2020.
89 Blyth and Lonergan 2020; De Grauwe 2020; Tooze 2020; Turner 2020.
90 De Grauwe 2020.
91 Turner 2020.
92 Mitchell and Fazi 2018.
93 Adam Tooze quoted in Ackerman 2018.

References

Abbas, S. A., Blattner, L., De Broeck, M., El-Ganainy, M. A. and Hu, M. (2014). *Sovereign Debt Composition in Advanced Economies: A Historical Perspective*. Washington, DC: International Monetary Fund.

Abdelal, R. (2007). *Capital Rules: The Construction of Global Finance*. Cambridge, MA: Harvard University Press.

Abou-Chadi, T. and Immergut, E. (2019). Recalibrating Social Protection: Electoral Competition and the New Partisan Politics of the Welfare State. *European Journal of Political Research*, 58 (2), 697–719.

Abou-Chadi, T. and Wagner, M. (2019). The Electoral Appeal of Party Strategies in Post-Industrial Societies: When Can the Mainstream Left Succeed? *Journal of Politics*, 81(4), 1405–19.

Acemoglu, D. and Autor, D. (2011). Skills, Tasks and Technologies: Implications for Employment and Earnings. In Ashenfelter, A. and Card, D. (eds.), *Handbook of Labor Economics. Vol. 4B*. Amsterdam: Elsevier.

Ackerman, S. (2018). All That Was Solid: Interview with Adam Tooze. *Jacobin*, 29 November.

Adkins, L., Cooper, M. and Konings, M. (2019). Class in the 21st Century: Asset Inflation and the New Logic of Inequality. *Environment and Planning A: Economy and Space*, 9 September.

Admati, A. and Hellwig, M. (2013). *The Bankers' New Clothes: What's Wrong with Banking and What to Do about It*. Princeton: Princeton University Press.

Adolph, C. (2018). The Missing Politics of Central Banks. *PS: Political Science and Politics*, 51(1), 737–42.

Aglietta, M. (2001 [1979]). *A Theory of Capitalist Regulation: The US Experience*. London: Verso.

Aguilera, R. and Jackson, G. (2003). The Cross-National Divergence in Corporate Governance: Dimensions and Determinants. *Academy of Management Review*, 28(3), 447–65.

Ahlquist, J. S. (2017). Labor Unions, Political Representation, and Economic Inequality. *Annual Review of Political Science*, 20, 409–32.

Ahlquist, J. S. and Ansell, B. W. (2017). Taking Credit: Redistribution and Borrowing in an Age of Economic Polarization. *World Politics*, 4, 640–75.

Aizenman, J. and Lee, J. (2008). International Reserves: Precautionary versus Mercantilist Views, Theory and Evidence. *Open Economies Review*, 18(2), 191–214.

Akyüz, Y. (2018). Inequality, Financialisation and Stagnation. *The Economic and Labour Relations Review*, 29(4), 428–45.

Albert, M. (1993). *Capitalism vs. Capitalism*. New York: Four Walls Eight Windows.

Albo, G. (1994). Competitive Austerity. In Miliband, R. and Panitch, L. (eds.), *Between Globalism and Nationalism: The Socialist Register 1994*. London: Merlin.

Alesina, A. and Rosenthal, H. (1989). Partisan Cycles in Congressional Elections and the Macroeconomy. *American Political Science Review*, 83(2), 373–98.

Alesina, A. and Roubini, N. (1992). Political Cycles in OECD Economies. *Review of Economic Studies*, 59(4), 663–88.

Alesina, A., Perotti, R., Tavares, J., Obstfeld, M. and Eichengreen, B. (1998). The Political Economy of Fiscal Adjustments. *Brookings Papers on Economic Activity*, 1, 197–266.

Allen, W. and Moessner, R. (2012). *The Liquidity Consequences of the Euro Area Sovereign Debt Crisis*. BIS Working Paper 390.

Alvaredo, F., Chancel, L., Piketty, T., Saez, E. and Zucman, G. (2018). *World Inequality Report 2018: Executive Summary* Berlin: World Inequality Lab.

Amable, B. and Palombarini, S. (2009). A Neorealist Approach to Institutional Change and the Diversity of Capitalism. *Socio-Economic Review*, 7(1), 123–43.

Andrews, D. (1994). Capital Mobility and Monetary Adjustment in Western Europe, 1973–1991. *Policy Sciences*, 27, 425–45.

Andrews, D., Criscuolo, C. and Gal, P. N. (2016). *The Best versus the Rest: The Global Productivity Slowdown, Divergence across Firms and the Role of Public Policy*. OECD Productivity Working Papers 5.

Angeles, R. C. and Kemmerling, A. (2020). How Redistributive Institutions Affect Pay Inequality and Heterogeneity among Top Managers. *Socio-Economic Review*, 18(1), 3–30.

Angeles, R., Hopkin, J. and Linsi, L. (2016). The Global Diffusion of Inequality: US Multinationals as Exporters of the 'Winner-Take-All-Economy'. Mimeo.

Ansell, B. (2014). The Political Economy of Ownership: Housing Markets and the Welfare State. *American Political Science Review*, 108(2), 383–40.

Ansell, B. (2017). Wealth Inequality Beyond Piketty. Mimeo.

Ansell, B. and Gingrich, J. (2013). A Tale of Two Trilemmas: Varieties of Higher Education and the Service Economy. In Wren, A. (ed.), *The Political Economy of the Service Transition*. Oxford: Oxford University Press.

Arbogast, T. (2020). *Who Are These Bond Vigilantes Anyway? The Political Economy of Sovereign Debt Ownership in the Eurozone*. MPfIG Discussion Paper 20/2.

Argitis, G. (2008). Inflation Targeting and Keynes's Political Economy. *Journal of Post Keynesian Economics*, 31(2), 249–70.

Armingeon, K. and Beyeler, M. (eds.) (2004). *The OECD and the European Welfare States*. Cheltenham: Edward Elgar.

Armstrong, P., Glyn, A. and Harrison, J. (1991). *Capitalism Since 1945*. Oxford: Blackwell.

Autor, D. (2010). *The Polarization of Job Opportunities in the U.S. Labor Market: Implications for Employment and Earnings*. Washington, DC: Center for American Progress and the Hamilton Project.

Autor, D., Dorn, D. and Hanson, G. (2016). The China Shock: Learning from Labor Market Adjustment to Large Changes in Trade. *Annual Review of Economics*, 8, 205–40.

Baccaro, L. (2020). Do We Need Trade Unions? Presentation at the Philosophie Kontrovers organized by the University of Cologne, 14 January.

Baccaro, L. and Benassi, C. (2014). Softening Industrial Relations Institutions, Hardening Growth Model: The Transformation of the German Political Economy. *Stato é Mercato*, 3, 369–96.

Baccaro, L. and Benassi, C. (2017). Throwing Out the Ballast: Growth Models and the Liberalization of German Industrial Relations. *Socio-Economic Review*, 15(1), 85–115.

Baccaro, L. and Howell, C. (2011). A Common Neoliberal Trajectory: The Transformation of Industrial Relations in Advanced Capitalism. *Politics and Society*, 39(4), 521–63.

Baccaro, L. and Howell, C. (2017). *Trajectories of Neoliberal Transformation: European Industrial Relations Since the 1970s.* Cambridge: Cambridge University Press.

Baccaro, L. and Pontusson J. (2016). Rethinking Comparative Political Economy: The Growth Model Perspective. *Politics and Society*, 44(2), 175–207.

Baccaro, L. and Pontusson J. (2018). *Comparative Political Economy and Varieties of Macroeconomics.* MPIfG Discussion Paper 18/10.

Baccaro, L. and Pontusson, J. (2019). *Social Blocs and Growth Models: An Analytical Framework with Germany and Sweden as Illustrative Cases.* Unequal Democracies Working Paper 7.

Baker, A. (2005). Three-Dimensional Governance of Macroeconomic Policy in the Advanced Capitalist World. In Baker, A., Hudson, D. and Woodward, R. (eds.), *Governing Financial Globalization: International Political Economy and Multilevel Governance.* Abingdon: Routledge.

Baker, A. (2006). *The Group of Seven: Finance Ministries, Central Banks and Global Financial Governance.* Abingdon: Routledge.

Baker, A. (2010). Restraining Regulatory Capture? Anglo-America, Crisis Politics and Trajectories of Change in Global Financial Governance. *International Affairs*, 86(3), 647–63.

Baker, D. (2016). The Upward Redistribution of Income: Are Rents the Story? *Review of Radical Political Economics*, 48(4), 529–43.

Baldwin, P. (1992). *The Politics of Social Solidarity: Class Bases of the European Welfare State, 1875–1975.* Cambridge: Cambridge University Press.

Baldwin, R. (2016). *The Great Convergence: Information Technology and the New Globalization.* Cambridge, MA: Harvard University Press.

Barnes, L. (2016). Private Debt and the Anglo-Liberal Growth Model. *Government and Opposition*, 51(4), 529–52.

Barro, R. J. (1974). Are Government Bonds Net Wealth? *Journal of Political Economy*, 82(6), 1095–1117.

Barro, R. J. (1995). Inflation and Economic Growth. *Quarterly Bulletin of the Bank of England*, Q2, 166–76.

Barro, R. J. (1996). Inflation and Growth. *Federal Reserve Bank of St. Louis Review*, May/June, 153–69.

Barro, R. (1999). *Inequality, Growth and Investment.* NBER Working Paper 7038.

Barro, R. and Gordon, D. (1983). Rules, Discretion and Reputation in a Model of Monetary Policy. *Journal of Monetary Economics*, 12, 101–21.

Barta, Z. and Johnston, A. (2018). Rating Politics? Partisan Discrimination in Credit Ratings in Developed Economies. *Comparative Political Studies*, 51(5), 587–620.

Baumol, W. J. and Bowen, W. G. (1966). *Performing Arts: The Economic Dilemma.* Cambridge, MA: MIT Press.

Bayard, K., Byrne, D. and Smith, D. (2013). The Scope of U.S. 'Factoryless Manufacturing'. In Houseman, S. N. and Mandel, M. (eds.), *Measuring Globalization: Better Trade Statistics for Better Policy.* Kalamazoo: W. E. Upjohn Institute.

Bebchuk, L. A. and Fried, J. (2003). Executive Compensation as an Agency Problem. *Journal of Economic Perspectives*, 17, 71–92.

Bebchuk, L. A. and Fried, J. (2004). *Pay Without Performance: The Unfulfilled Promise of Executive Compensation.* Cambridge, MA: Harvard University Press.

Bebchuk, L. A., Fried, J. and Walker, D. (2002). *Managerial Power and Rent Extraction in the Design of Executive Compensation.* NBER Working Paper 9068.

Becker, S. O. and Fetzer, T. (2017). *Does Migration Cause Extreme Voting?* CAGE Online Working Paper 306.

Behringer, J. and van Treeck, T. (2019). Income Distribution and Growth Models: A Sectoral Balances Approach. *Politics & Society*, 47(3), 303–32.

Beitel, K. (2009). The Subprime Debacle. *Monthly Review*, 60(1), 27–44.

Bell, S. and Hindmoor, A. (2014). Taming the City? Ideas, Structural Power and the Evolution of British Banking Policy Amidst the Great Financial Meltdown. *New Political Economy*, 20(3), 454–74.

Bengtsson, E. and Ryner, M. (2015). The (International) Political Economy of Falling Wage Shares: Situating Working-Class Agency. *New Political Economy*, 20(3), 406–30.

Beramendi, P., Häusermann, S., Kitschelt, H. and Kriesi, H. (2015). Introduction: The Politics of Advanced Capitalism. In Beramendi, P., Häusermann, S., Kitschelt, H. and Kriesi, H. (eds.), *The Politics of Advanced Capitalism*. Cambridge: Cambridge University Press.

Berle, A. and Means, G. (1932). *The Modern Corporation and Private Property*. New Brunswick: Transaction.

Berman, E. (2017). *Does Factor-Biased Technological Change Stifle International Convergence? Evidence from Manufacturing*. NBER Working Paper 7964.

Berman, S. (2006). *The Primacy of Politics: Social Democracy and the Making of Europe's Twentieth Century*. Cambridge: Cambridge University Press.

Berman, S. (2019). Populism Is a Symptom Rather than a Cause: Democratic Disconnect, the Decline of the Centre-Left, and the Rise of Populism in Western Europe. *Polity*, 51(4), 654–67.

Bernanke, B. (2004). The Great Moderation. Remarks at the Meetings of the Eastern Economic Association, Washington, DC, 20 February.

Bernanke, B. (2005). The Global Saving Glut and the U.S. Current Account Deficit. The Sandridge Lecture, Virginia Association of Economics, Richmond.

Bernanke, B. (2010). Aiding the Economy: What the Fed Did and Why. *The Washington Post*, 4 November.

Bernanke, B. (2013). Semiannual Monetary Policy Report to the Congress. Testimony before the Committee on Banking, Housing, and Urban Affairs, US Senate, Washington, DC, 26 February.

Bernanke, B. (2017). Monetary Policy in a New Era. Paper prepared for the conference on Rethinking Macroeconomic Policy, Peterson Institute, Washington, DC, 12–13 October.

Bernanke, B. (2018). The Real Effects of the Financial Crisis. *Brookings Papers on Economic Activity*, 2018(2), 251–342.

Bernard, A. B. and Fort, T. C. (2015). Factoryless Goods Producing Firms. *American Economic Review*, 105 (5), 518–23.

Bernhard, W. (1998). A Political Explanation of Variations in Central Bank Independence. *American Political Science Review*, 92, 311–27.

Bernhard, W., Broz, J. and Clark, W. R. (2002). The Political Economy of Monetary Institutions. *International Organization*, 56, 693–723.

Bezemer, D., Samarina, A. and Zhang, L. (2017). *Shift in Bank Credit Allocation: New Data and New Findings*. DNB Working Paper 559.

Bieling, H. J. (2006). EMU, Financial Integration and Global Economic Governance. *Review of International Political Economy*, 13 (3), 420–48.

Birch, J. (2015). The Many Lives of François Mitterrand. *Jacobin*, 19 August.

Bivens, J. and Mishel, L. (2013). The Pay of Corporate Executives and Financial Professionals as Evidence of Rents in Top 1 Percent Incomes. *Journal of Economic Perspectives*, 27(3), 57–78.

Bivens, J., Gould, E., Mishel, L. and Shierholz, H. (2014). *Raising America's Pay: Why It's Our Central Economic Policy Challenge*. Economic Policy Institute Briefing Paper 378.

Blanchard, O. (2019). Public Debt and Low Interest Rates. *American Economic Review*, 109(4), 1197–229.

Blyth, M. (2002). *Great Transformations: Economic Ideas and Institutional Change in the Twentieth Century*. Cambridge: Cambridge University Press.

Blyth, M. (2009). An Approach to Comparative Analysis or a Subfield Within a Subfield? Political Economy. In Lichbach, M. and Zuckerman, A. (eds.), *Comparative Politics: Rationality, Culture, and Structure*. Cambridge: Cambridge University Press.

Blyth, M. (2013). *Austerity: The History of a Dangerous Idea*. Oxford: Oxford University Press.

Blyth, M. (2020). The US Economy Is Uniquely Vulnerable to the Coronavirus. *Foreign Affairs*, 30 March.

Blyth, M. and Lonergan, E. (2014). Print Less but Transfer More: Why Central Banks Should Give Money Directly to the People. *Foreign Affairs*, September/October.

Blyth, M. and Lonergan, E. (2020). This Time, Can We Finally Turn a Financial Crisis Into an Opportunity? *Foreign Policy*, 20 March.

Blyth, M. and Matthijs, M. (2017). Black Swans, Lame Ducks, and the Mystery of IPE's Missing Macroeconomy. *Review of International Political Economy*, 24(2), 203–31.

Boix, C. (2019). *Democratic Capitalism at the Crossroads: Technological Change and the Future of Politics*. Princeton: Princeton University Press.

Bolton, A. and Carney, J. (2020). White House, Senate Reach Deal on $2 Trillion Stimulus Package. *The Hill*, 25 March.

Borio, C. and Zabai, A. (2016). *Unconventional Monetary Policies: A Re-appraisal*. BIS Working Papers 570.

Boyer, R. (2000). Is a Finance-Led Growth Regime a Viable Alternative to Fordism? A Preliminary Analysis. *Economy and Society*, 29(1), 111–45.

Boyer, R. (2002). The Unanticipated Fallout of European Monetary Union: The Political and Institutional Deficits of the Euro. In Crouch, C. (ed.), *After the Euro: Shaping Institutions for Governance in the Wake of European Monetary Union*. Oxford: Oxford University Press.

Boyer, R. (2005). How and Why Capitalisms Differ. *Economy and Society*, 34 (4), 509–57.

Boyer, R. and Saillard, Y. (eds.) (2002). *Regulation Theory: State of the Art*. Abingdon: Routledge.

Brandl, B. and Traxler, F. (2011). Labour Relations, Economic Governance and the Crisis: Turning the Tide Again? *Labor History*, 52(1), 1–22.

Braun, B. (2020). American Asset Manager Capitalism. Mimeo.

Braun, B. and Deeg, R. (2019). Strong Firms, Weak Banks: The Financial Consequences of Germany's Export-Led Growth Model. *German Politics*, 26 December.

Braun, B. and Downey, S. (2020). *Against Amnesia: Re-Imagining Central Banking*. CEP Discussion Note 2020/1.

Bremer, B. (2018). The Missing Left? Economic Crisis and the Programmatic Response of Social Democratic Parties in Europe. *Party Politics*, 24 (1), 23–38.

Bremer, B. and McDaniel, S. (2019). The Ideational Foundations of Social Democratic Austerity in the Context of the Great Recession. *Socio-Economic Review*, March.

Brenner, R. (2006). *The Economics of Global Turbulence*. London: Verso.

Broz, L., Frieden, J. and Weymouth, S. (2019). Populism in Place: The Economic Geography of the Globalization Backlash. Mimeo.

Bruff, I. and Ebenau, M. (2014). Critical Political Economy and the Critique of Comparative Capitalisms Scholarship on Capitalist Diversity. *Capital and Class*, 38(1), 3–15.

Buchanan, J. M., Wagner, R. E., Meckling, W. H. and Olson, M. (1978). The Political Biases of Keynesian Economics. In Buchanan, J. M. and Wagner, R. E. (eds.), *Fiscal Responsibility in Constitutional Democracy*. New York: Springer.

Bunn, P. and Rostom, M. (2014). Household Debt and Spending. *Bank Of England Quarterly Bulletin*, Q3, 304–15.

Bunn, P., Pugh, A. and Yeates, C. (2018). *The Distributional Impact of Monetary Policy Easing in the UK Between 2008 and 2014*. Bank of England Staff Working Paper 720.

Burdekin, R. C. K. and Burkett, P. (1996). *Distributional Conflict and Inflation: Theoretical and Historical Perspectives*. London: Macmillan.

Burdekin, R. C. K. and Laney, L. O. (1988). Fiscal Policymaking and the Central Bank Institutional Constraint. *Kyklos*, 41(4), 647–62.

Busemeyer, M. R. (2009). Asset Specificity, Institutional Complementarities and the Variety of Skill Regimes in Coordinated Market Economies. *Socio-Economic Review*, 7(3), 375–406.

Busemeyer, M. R., de la Porte, C., Garritzmann, J. L. and Pavolini, E. (2018). The Future of the Social Investment State: Politics, Policies, and Outcomes. *Journal of European Public Policy*, 25(6), 801–9.

Busemeyer, M. R. and Iversen, T. (2012). Collective Skill Systems, Wage Bargaining, and Labor Market Stratification. In Busemeyer, M. R. and Trampusch, C. (eds.), *The Political Economy of Collective Skill Formation*. Oxford: Oxford University Press.

Business Roundtable. (1997). *Statement on Corporate Governance*. Washington, DC: Business Roundtable of CEOs.

Calgano, A. (2012). Can Austerity Work? *Review of Keynesian Economics*, 0(1), 24–36.

Calomiris, C. W. (1997). *US Banking Deregulation in Historical Perspective*. Cambridge: Cambridge University Press.

Calomiris, C. W. (2008). *Bank Failures in Theory and History: The Great Depression and Other 'Contagious' Events*. NBER Working Paper 13597.

Cameron, D. R. (1978). The Expansion of the Public Economy. *American Political Science Review*, 72, 1243–61.

Capie, F., Mills, T. and Wood, G. (1994). Central Bank Independence and Inflation Performance: An Exploratory Data Analysis. In Siklos, P. (ed.), *Varieties of Monetary Reforms: Lessons and Experiences on the Road to Monetary Union*. Dordrecht: Kluwer Academic.

Carlin, W. and Soskice, D. (2009). German Economic Performance: Disentangling the Role of Supply-Side Reforms, Macroeconomic Policy and Coordinated Economy Institutions. *Socio-Economic Review*, 7(1), 67–99.

Cerny, P. G. (1997). Paradoxes of the Competition State: The Dynamics of Political Globalization. *Government and Opposition*, 32 (2), 251–74.

Chandler, A. (1977). *The Visible Hand: The Managerial Revolution in American Business*. Cambridge, MA: Harvard University Press.

Chandler, A. (1984). The Emergence of Managerial Capitalism. *The Business History Review*, 58(4), 473–503.

Chazan, H. (2020). Germany Tears Up Fiscal Rule Book to Counter Coronavirus Pandemic. *Financial Times*, 21 March.

Chinn, M. (2005). *Getting Serious about the Twin Deficits*. CFR Special Report 10.

Christophers, B. (2018). Intergenerational Inequality? Labour, Capital, and Housing Through the Ages. *Antipode: A Radical Journal of Geography*, 50(1), 101–21.

Chwieroth, J. (2010). *Capital Ideas: The IMF and the Rise of Financial Liberalization*. Princeton: Princeton University Press.

Chwieroth, J. and Walter, A. (2019). *The Wealth Effect: How the Great Expectations of the Middle Class Have Changed the Politics of Banking Crises*. Cambridge: Cambridge University Press.

Cingano, F. (2014). *Trends in Income Inequality and its Impact on Economic Growth*. OECD Social, Employment and Migration Working Papers 163.

Claeys, (2019). The European Green Deal Needs a Reformed Fiscal Framework. Bruegel blog, 10 December.

Clarke, S. (1988). *Keynesianism, Monetarism and the Crisis of the State*. Cheltenham: Edward Elgar.

Clarke, S. (1994). *Marx's Theory of Crisis*. Basingstoke: Macmillan.

Clift, B. (2009). National or European Social Models? Contesting European Welfare Futures. In Gamble, A. and Lane, D. (eds.), *The European Union and World Politics: Consensus and Division*. Basingstoke: Palgrave Macmillan.

Clift, B. (2014). *Comparative Political Economy: States, Markets and Global Capitalism*. Basingstoke: Palgrave Macmillan.

Clift, B. (2018). *The IMF and the Politics of Austerity in the Wake of the Global Financial Crisis*. Oxford: Oxford University Press.

Coates, D. (2006). Paradigms of Explanation. In Coates, D. (ed.), *Varieties of Capitalism, Varieties of Approaches*. Basingstoke: Palgrave Macmillan.

Cooper, R. (1975). Prolegomena to the Choice of an International Monetary System. *International Organization*, 29(1), 63–97.

Corsetti, G. (2010). The 'Original Sin' in the Eurozone. *VOX*, 9 May.

Cox, R. W. (1987). *Production, Power, and World Order: Social Forces in the Making of History*. New York: Columbia University Press.

Crotty, J. (2008). If Financial Market Competition Is Intense, Why Are Financial Firm Profits So High? Reflections on the Current 'Golden Age' of Finance. *Competition & Change*, 12(2), 167–83.

Crotty, J. (2009). Structural Causes of the Global Financial Crisis: A Critical Assessment of the 'New Financial Architecture'. *Cambridge Journal of Economics*, 33(4), 563–80.

Crouch, C. (2009). Privatised Keynesianism: An Unacknowledged Policy Regime. *British Journal of Politics and International Relations*, 11(3), 382–99.

Culpepper, P. (2005). Institutional Change in Contemporary Capitalism: Coordinated Financial Systems Since 1990. *World Politics*, 57(2), 173–99.

Cusack, T. R., Iversen, T. and Soskice, D. (2007). Economic Interests and the Origins of Electoral Systems. *American Political Science Review*, 101(3), 373–91.

Cynamon, B. Z. and Fazzari, S. M. (2016). Inequality, the Great Recession and Slow Recovery. *Cambridge Journal of Economics*, 40(2), 373–99.

Dafermos, Y., Nikolaidi, M. and Galanis, G. (2018). Can Green Quantitative Easing (QE) Reduce Global Warming? *FEPS Policy Brief*, July.

D'Alisa, G., Demaria, F. and Kallis, G. (eds.) (2015). *Degrowth: A Vocabulary for a New Era*. Abingdon: Routledge.

Davis, A. and Mishel, L. (2014). *CEO Pay Continues to Rise as Typical Workers Are Paid Less*. Economic Policy Institute Policy Brief 380.

Davis, G. F. (2009). *Managed by the Markets: How Finance Reshaped America*. Oxford: Oxford University Press.

Davis, G. F. and Kim, S. (2015). Financialization of the Economy. *Annual Review of Sociology*, 41, 203–21.

Deeg, R., Hardie, I. and Maxfield, S. (2016). What is Patient Capital, and Where Does It Exist? *Socio-Economic Review*, 14(4), 615–25.

De Grauwe, P. (2013). The European Central Bank as Lender of Last Resort in the Government Bond Markets. *CESifo Economic Studies*, 59(3), 520–35.

De Grauwe, P. (2020). The ECB Must Finance COVID-19 Deficits. *Project Syndicate*, 18 March.

Dellepiane-Avellaneda, S. (2014). The Political Power of Economic Ideas: The Case of

Expansionary Fiscal Contractions. *British Journal of Politics and International Relations*, 17(3), 391–418.

Den Haan, W., Ellison, M., Ilzetzki, E., McMahon, M. and Reis, R. (2017). The Future of Central Bank Independence: Results of the CFM–CEPR Survey. *VoxEU.org*, 10 January.

Dennis, S. T. (2020). GOP Rekindles Deficit Concerns, Adding Snag to Talks on Aid. *Bloomberg*, 11 May.

De Ville, F. and Vermeiren, M. (2016). *Rising Powers and Economic Crisis in the Euro Area*. Basingstoke: Palgrave Macmillan.

Devine, J. (2000). The Cost of Living and Hidden Inflation. *Challenge*, 44(2), 73–84.

Di Carlo, D. (2020). Understanding Wage Restraint in the German Public Sector: Does the Pattern Bargaining Hypothesis Really Hold Water? *Industrial Relations Journal*, 6 May.

Dimova, D. (2019). *The Structural Determinants of the Labour Share in Europe*. IMF Working Paper 19/67.

Doellgast, V. and Greer, I. (2007). Vertical Disintegration and the Disorganization of German Industrial Relations. *British Journal of Industrial Relations*, 45(1), 55–76.

Dohse, K., Jürgens, U. and Nialsch, T. (1984). From 'Fordism' to 'Toyotism'? The Social Organization of the Labor Process in the Japanese Automobile Industry. *Politics and Society*, 14(2), 115–46.

Doling, J. and Ronald, R. (2010). Home Ownership and Asset-Based Welfare. *Journal of Housing and the Built Environment*, 25, 165–73.

Donado, A. and Wälde, K. (2011). *How Trade Unions Increase Welfare*. CESifo Working Paper 3618.

Dooley, M. P., Folkerts-Landau, D. and Graber, P. (2003). *An Essay on the Revived Bretton Woods System*. NBER Working Paper 9971.

Dore, R. (2000). *Stock Market Capitalism: Welfare Capitalism*. Oxford: Oxford University Press.

Draghi, M. (2014). Recovery and Reform in the Euro Area. Opening Remarks by the President of the ECB to the Brookings Institution, Washington, DC, 9 October.

Drahokoupil, J. (2007). Political Business Cycle. In Bevir, M. (ed.), *Encyclopedia of Governance. Vol. II*. London: Sage.

Dumas, C. (2008). *China and America: The Time of Reckoning*. London: Profile Books.

Dunaway, S. (2009). *Global Imbalances and the Financial Crisis*. New York: Council on Foreign Relations.

Dustmann, C., Fitzenberger, B., Schönberg, U. and Spitz-Oener, A. (2014). From Sick Man of Europe to Economic Superstar: Germany's Resurgent Economy. *Journal of Economic Perspectives*, 28 (1), 167–88.

Dutta, S. (2018). Sovereign Debt Management and the Globalization of Finance: Recasting the City of London's 'Big Bang'. *Competition & Change*, 22(1), 3–22.

Dynan, K. (2012). Is a Household Debt Overhang Holding Back Consumption? *Brookings Papers on Economic Activity*, 43(1), 299–362.

ECB. (2000). *Mergers and Acquisitions Involving the EU Banking Industry: Facts and Implications*. Frankfurt: European Central Bank.

ECB. (2020). ECB Announces €750 Billion Pandemic Emergency Purchase Programme (PEPP). Press Release, 18 March.

Editorial Board of the *Financial Times*. (2020). Virus Lays Bare the Frailty of the Social Contract. *Financial Times*, 3 April.

Eichengreen, E. (1996). *Globalizing Capital: A History of the International Monetary System*. Princeton: Princeton University Press.

Eichengreen, E. (2011). *Exorbitant Privilege: The Rise and Fall of the Dollar and the Future of the International Monetary System*. Oxford: Oxford University Press.

El-Erian, M. (2016). *The Only Game in Town: Central Banks, Instability, and Avoiding the Next Collapse*. New York: Random House.

Emmenegger P., Häusermann, S., Palier, B. and Seeleib-Kaiser, M. (eds.) (2011). *The Age of Dualization: Structure, Policies, Politics*. Oxford: Oxford University Press.

Engelen, E. (2003). The Logic of Funding European Pension Restructuring and the Dangers of Financialisation. *Environment and Planning A*, 35(8), 1357–72.

Epstein, E. (2002). Financialization, Rentier Interests, and Central Bank Policy. Mimeo.

Epstein, G. (1992). Political Economy and Comparative Central Banking. *Review of Radical Political Economics*, 24(1), 1–30.

Epstein G. (2005). Introduction. In Epstein, G. (ed.). *Financialization and the World Economy*. Cheltenham: Edward Elgar.

Epstein, G. and Jayadev, A. (2005). The Rise of Rentier Incomes in OECD Countries: Financialization, Central Bank Policy and Labor Solidarity. In Epstein, G. (ed.), *Financialization and the World Economy*. Cheltenham: Edward Elgar.

Erixon, L. (2008). The Swedish Third Way: An Assessment of the Performance and Validity of the Rehn–Meidner Model. *Cambridge Journal of Economics*, 32(3), 367–93.

Ertürk, I. (2016a). Financialization, Bank Business Models and the Limits of Post-Crisis Bank Regulation. *Journal of Banking Regulation*, 17(1/2), 60–72.

Ertürk, I. (2016b). *Post-Crisis Central Bank Unconventional Policies and Financialised Transmission Channels*. Foundation for European Progressive Studies Working Paper.

Esping-Andersen, G. (1990). *Three Worlds of Welfare Capitalism*. Princeton: Princeton University Press.

Estevez-Abe, M., Iversen, T. and Soskice, D. (2001). Social Protection and the Formation of Skills: A Reinterpretation of the Welfare State. In Hall, P. and Soskice, D. (eds.), *Varieties of Capitalism*. Oxford: Oxford University Press.

European Commission. (2011). *Quarterly Report on the Euro Area*, 10(3). Brussels: DG ECOFIN.

European Council. (2011). *Conclusions of European Council 24/25 March*. Brussels: European Council.

Fabozzi, F. J. and Kothari, V. (2008). *Introduction to Securitization*. Hoboken: John Wiley and Sons.

Fama, E. and Jensen, M. (1983). Separation of Ownership and Control. *Journal of Law and Economics*, 26, 301–25.

FCIC. (2011). *The Financial Crisis Inquiry Report: Final Report of the National Commission on the Causes of the Financial and Economic Crisis in the United States*. Washington, DC: Financial Crisis Inquiry Commission.

Felkerson, J. (2011). *$29,000,000,000,000: A Detailed Look at the Fed's Bailout by Funding Facility and Recipient*. Levy Institute Working Paper 698.

Fernandez, R. and Hendrikse, R. (2015). *Rich Corporations, Poor Societies: The Financialisation of Apple*. Amsterdam: Center for Research on Multinational Corporations (SOMO).

Fichtner, J., Heemskerk, E. and Garcia-Bernardo, J. (2017). Hidden Power of the Big Three? Passive Index Funds, Re-Concentration of Corporate Ownership, and New Financial Risk. *Business and Politics*, 19(2), 298–326.

Fields, D. and Vernengo, M. (2013). Hegemonic Currencies During the Crisis: The Dollar versus the Euro in a Cartalist Perspective. *Review of International Political Economy*, 20(4), 740–59.

FitzRoy, F. and Kraft, K. (2005). Co-Determination, Efficiency and Productivity. *British Journal of Industrial Relations*, 43, 233–47.

Fligstein, N. (1990). *The Transformation of Corporate Control.* Cambridge, MA: Harvard University Press.

Foa, R. S. and Mounk, Y. (2016). The Danger of Deconsolidation: The Democratic Disconnect. *Journal of Democracy,* 27(3), 5–17.

Foroohar, R. (2016). *Makers and Takers: How Wall Street Destroyed Main Street.* New York: Crown Business.

Frank, R., Levine, A. S. and Dijk, O. (2014). Expenditure Cascades. *Review of Behavioral Economics,* 1(1–2), 55–73.

Frieden, J. (2006). *Global Capitalism: Its Fall and Rise in the Twentieth Century.* New York: W. W. Norton.

Frieden, J. (2015). The Political Economy of Adjustment and Rebalancing. *Journal of International Money and Finance,* 52, 4–14.

Frieden, J. and Walter, S. (2017). Understanding the Political Economy of the Eurozone Crisis. *Annual Review of Political Science,* 20, 371–90.

Friedman, M. (1953). *The Methodology of Positive Economics.* Chicago: University of Chicago Press.

Friedman, M. (1962). *Capitalism and Freedom.* Chicago: University of Chicago Press.

Friedman, M. (1968). The Role of Monetary Policy. *The American Economic Review,* 58(1), 1–17.

Froud, J., Johal, S., Leaver, A. and Williams, K. (2012). *Apple Business Model: Financialization across the Pacific.* CRESC Working Paper 111.

Fuchita, J., Herring, R. and Litan, R. (2009). The Future of Securitization: An Introduction. In Fuchita, J., Herring, R. and Litan, R. (eds.), *Prudent Lending Restored: Securitization After the Mortgage Meltdown.* Washington, DC: Brookings Institution Press.

Fuller, G. (2015). Who's Borrowing? Credit Encouragement vs. Credit Mitigation in National Financial Systems. *Politics & Society,* 43(2), 241–68.

Fuller, G. (2016). *The Great Debt Transformation: Households, Financialization, and Policy Responses.* Basingstoke: Palgrave Macmillan.

Fuller, G., Johnston, A. and Regan, A. (2020). Housing Prices and Wealth Inequality in Western Europe. *West European Politics,* 43(2), 297–320.

Funke, M., Schularick, M. and Trebesch, C. (2016). Going to Extremes: Politics After Financial Crises, 1870–2014. *European Economic Review,* 88, 227–60.

G20 (2008). *Declaration: Summit on Financial Markets and the World Economy.* 15 November.

G20 (2009). *Leaders' Statement: The Pittsburgh Summit.* 24–5 September.

G20 (2010). *The G20 Toronto Summit Declaration.* 27 June.

Gabor, D. (2016). The (Impossible) Repo Trinity: The Political Economy of Repo Markets. *Review of International Political Economy,* 23(6), 967–100.

Gabor, D. and Ban, C. (2016). Banking on Bonds: The New Links Between States and Markets. *Journal of Common Market Studies,* 54(3), 617–35.

Galbraith, J. K. (1955). *The Great Crash, 1929.* Boston: Houghton Mifflin.

Galbraith, J. K. (2012). *Inequality and Instability: A Study of the World Economy Just Before the Great Crisis.* Oxford: Oxford University Press.

Garret, G. (1998). *Partisan Politics in the Global Economy.* Cambridge: Cambridge University Press.

Garritzmann, J. L., Busemeyer, M. R. and Neimanns, E. (2018). Public Demand for Social Investment: New Supporting Coalitions for Welfare State Reform in Western Europe? *Journal of European Public Policy,* 25(6), 844–61.

Genschel, P. and Schwarz, P. (2011). Tax Competition: A Literature Review. *Socio-Economic Review,* 9(2), 339–70.

Genschel, P. and Seelkopf, L. (2015). The Competition State: The Modern State in a Global Economy. In Leibfried, S., Huber, E., Lange, M., Levy, J. D. and Stephens, J. D. (eds.), *The Oxford Handbook of Transformations of the State*. Oxford: Oxford University Press.

Gereffi, G. (2018). *Global Value Chains and Development: Redefining the Contours of 21st Century Capitalism*. Cambridge: Cambridge University Press.

Gidron, N. and Hall, P. A. (2020). Populism as a Problem of Social Integration. *Comparative Political Studies*, 53(7), 1027–59.

Gilbert, A. R. (1986). *Requiem for Regulation Q: What It Did and Why It Passed Away*. Federal Reserve Bank of St. Louis, February.

Gill, S. (1998). European Governance and New Constitutionalism: Economic and Monetary Union and Alternatives to Disciplinary Neoliberalism in Europe. *New Political Economy*, 3(1), 5–26.

Gill, S. and Cutler, C. (eds.) (2014). *New Constitutionalism and World Order*. Cambridge: Cambridge University Press.

Gill, S. and Law, D. (1989). Global Hegemony and the Structural Power of Capital. *International Studies Quarterly*, 33(4), 475–99.

Gilpin, R. (1987). *The Political Economy of International Relations*. Princeton: Princeton University Press.

Glyn, A. (1995). Social Democracy and Full Employment. *New Left Review*, 211, 33–55.

Glyn, A. (2001). *Social Democracy in Neoliberal Times: The Left and Economic Policy Since 1980*. Oxford: Oxford University Press.

Glyn, A. (2007). *Capitalism Unleashed: Finance, Globalisation and Welfare*. Oxford: Oxford University Press.

Goda, T. and Lysandrou, P. (2014). The Contribution of Wealth Concentration to the Subprime Crisis: A Quantitative Estimation. *Cambridge Journal of Economics*, 38(2), 301–32.

Goda, T., Onaran, O. and Stockhammer, E. (2017). Income Inequality and Wealth Concentration in the Recent Crisis. *Development and Change*, 48(1), 3–37.

Godley, W. (2000). The Hole in the Treaty. In Gowan, P. and Anderson (eds.), *Europe in Question*. London: Verso.

Goldin, C. and Katz, L. (2008). *The Race Between Technology and Education*. Cambridge, MA: Harvard University Press.

Goodhart, C. (1988). *The Evolution of Central Banks*. Cambridge, MA: MIT Press.

González-Páramo, J. M. (2011). The Conduct of Monetary Policy: Lessons from the Crisis and Challenges for the Coming Years. Speech at the SEACEN-CEMLA Conference, Kuala Lumpur, 13 October.

Gough, I. and Meadowcroft, J. (2012). Decarbonizing the Welfare State. In Dryzek, S., Norgaard, R. and Schlosberg, D. (eds.), *The Oxford Handbook of Climate Change and Society*. Oxford: Oxford University Press.

Gourevitch, P. A. and Shinn, J. (2005). *Political Power and Corporate Control: The New Global Politics of Corporate Governance*. Princeton: Princeton University Press.

Gourinchas, P. and Jeanne, O. (2012). Global Safe Assets. Paper presented at the 11th BIS Annual Conference, 22 June.

Gowa, J. (1983). *Closing the Gold Window: Domestic Politics and the End of Bretton Woods*. Ithaca: Cornell University Press.

Grabel, I. (2003). Ideology, Power and the Rise of Independent Monetary Institutions in Emerging Markets. In Kirshner, J. (ed.), *Monetary Orders*. Ithaca: Cornell University Press.

Grabel, I. (2010). Instantiating Neoliberal Reform via Economic Theory and Small Group Agreements. In Fontana, G., McCombie, J. and Sawyer, M. (eds.), *Macroeconomics, Finance and Money: Essays in Honour of Philip Arestis*. Basingstoke: Palgrave.

Green, J. and Lavery, S. (2015). The Regressive Recovery: Distribution, Inequality and State Power in Britain's Post-Crisis Political Economy. *New Political Economy*, 20(6), 894–923.

Greenspan, A. (2001). Opening Remarks. In *Economic Policy for the Information Economy*, Federal Reserve Bank of Kansas City Symposium, 30 August to 1 September, 1–10.

Greenspan, A. and Kennedy, J. (2008). Sources and Uses of Equity Extracted from Homes. *Oxford Review of Economic Policy*, 24(1), 120–44.

Guschanski, A. and Onaran, O. (2018). *The Labour Share and Financialisation: Evidence from Publicly Listed Firms*. Greenwich Papers in Political Economy 19371.

Hacker, J. S. (2004). Privatizing Risk without Privatizing the Welfare State: The Hidden Politics of Social Policy Retrenchment in the United States. *American Political Science Review*, 98(2), 243–60.

Hacker, J. S. and Pierson, P. (2002). Business Power and Social Policy: Employers and the Formation of the American Welfare State. *Politics and Society*, 30(2), 277–325.

Hacker, J. S. and Pierson, P. (2004). Varieties of Capitalist Interest and Capitalist Power: A Response to Swenson. *Studies in American Political Development*, 18(2), 186–95.

Hacker, J. S. and Pierson, P. (2011). *Winner-Take-All Politics: How Washington Made the Rich Richer – and Turned Its Back on the Middle Class*. New York: Simon and Schuster.

Haffert, L. (2019). Tax Policy as Industrial Policy in Comparative Capitalisms. *Journal of Economic Policy Reform*, 13 September.

Haffert, L. and Mertens, D. (2019). Between Distribution and Allocation: Growth Models, Sectoral Coalitions and the Politics of Taxation Revisited. *Socio-Economic Review*, 30 July.

Hager, S. B. (2016). *Public Debt, Inequality, and Power: The Making of a Modern Debt State*. Oakland: University of California Press.

Hager, S. B. (2018). Varieties of Top Incomes? *Socio-Economic Review*, 23 August.

Haldane, A. G., Roberts-Sklar, M., Wieladek, T. and Young, C. (2016). *QE: The Story So Far*. Bank of England Staff Working Paper 624.

Hale, T. (2018). The Bank of England Has a Strange Idea of What QE Achieved. *Financial Times Alphaville*, 3 August.

Hall, P. A. (1997). The Role of Interests, Institutions, and Ideas in the Comparative Political Economy of the Industrialized Nations. In Zuckerman, A. (ed.), *Comparative Politics: Rationality, Culture and Structure*. Cambridge: Cambridge University Press.

Hall, P. A. (2018). Varieties of Capitalism in Light of the Euro Crisis. *Journal of European Public Policy*, 25(1), 7–30.

Hall, P. A. and Gingerich, D. W. (2009). Varieties of Capitalism and Institutional Complementarities in the Political Economy: An Empirical Analysis. *British Journal of Political Science*, 39(3), 449–82.

Hall, P. A. and Soskice, D. (eds.) (2001). *Varieties of Capitalism: The Institutional Foundations of Comparative Advantage*. Oxford: Oxford University Press.

Hancké, B. (2009). Varieties of European Capitalism and Their Transformation. Mimeo.

Hancké, B. (2013). *Unions, Central Banks, and EMU: Labour Market Institutions and Monetary Integration in Europe*. Oxford: Oxford University Press.

Hancké, B. and Johnston, A. (2009). Wage Inflation and Labour Unions in EMU. *Journal of European Public Policy*, 16(4), 601–11.

Hancké, B., Rhodes, M. and Thatcher, M. (eds.) (2007). *Beyond Varieties of Capitalism: Conflict, Contradictions, and Complementarities in the European Economy*. Oxford: Oxford University Press.

Hardie, I. and Howarth, D. (eds.) (2013). *Market-Based Banking and the Global Financial Crisis*. Oxford: Oxford University Press.

Hardie, I. and Maxfield, S. (2013). Market-Based Banking as the Worst of All Worlds: Illustrations from the United States and United Kingdom. In Hardie, I. and Howarth, D. (eds.), *Market-Based Banking and the Global Financial Crisis*. Oxford: Oxford University Press.

Harmes, A. (2001). Mass Investment Culture. *New Left Review*, 9, 103–24.

Harvey, D. (2006). *A Brief History of Neoliberalism*. Oxford: Oxford University Press.

Haskel, J. and Westlake, S. (2017). *Capitalism Without Capital: The Rise of the Intangible Economy*. Princeton: Princeton University Press.

Hassel, A. (2014). The Paradox of Liberalization: Understanding Dualism and the Recovery of the German Political Economy. *British Journal of Industrial Relations*, 52(1), 57–81.

Hassel, A., Naczyk, M. and Wiß, T. (2019). The Political Economy of Pension Financialisation: Public Policy Responses to the Crisis. *Journal of European Public Policy*, 26(4), 483–500.

Hatton, T. J. (2016). Immigration, Public Opinion and the Recession in Europe. *Economic Policy*, 31(86), 205–46.

Hay, C. (2009). Good Inflation, Bad Inflation: The Housing Boom, Economic Growth and the Disaggregation of Inflationary Preferences in the UK and Ireland. *British Journal of Politics and International Relations*, 11, 461–78.

Hay, C., Smith, N. J. and Watson, M. (2006). Beyond Prospective Accountancy: Reassessing the Case for British Membership of the Single European Currency Comparatively. *British Journal of Politics and International Relations*, 8(1), 101–21.

Heilbroner, R. L. (1995 [1953]). *The Worldly Philosophers: The Lives, Times and Ideas of The Great Economic Thinkers*. New York: Touchstone.

Heimberger, P. (2020a). European Burden Sharing of Corona Crisis Costs: Why Germany Should Lead the Way. Vienna Institute for International Economic Studies, 20 April.

Heimberger, P. (2020b). The Dynamic Effects of Fiscal Consolidation Episodes on Income Inequality: Evidence for 17 OECD Countries over 1978–2013. *Empirica*, 47, 53–81.

Hein, E. (2015). *Secular Stagnation or Stagnation Policy? Steindl after Summers*. Levy Institute Working Paper 846.

Hein, E., Paternesi Meloni, W. and Tridico, P. (2020). Welfare Models and Demand-Led Growth Regimes Before and After the Financial and Economic Crisis. *Review of International Political Economy*, 30 March.

Helleiner, E. (1994). *States and the Re-Emergence of Global Finance*. Ithaca: Cornell University Press.

Helleiner, E. (1995). Explaining the Globalization of Financial Markets: Bringing States Back In. *Review of International Political Economy*, 2(1), 315–41.

Helleiner, E. (2008). The Evolution of the International Monetary and Financial System. In Ravenhill, J. (ed.), *Global Political Economy*, Oxford: Oxford University Press.

Helleiner, E. and Kirshner, J. (eds.) (2009). *The Future of the Dollar*. Ithaca: Cornell University Press.

Hemerijck, A. (2018). Social Investment as a Policy Paradigm. *Journal of European Public Policy*, 25(6), 810–27.

Henning, R. (2016). The ECB as a Strategic Actor: Central Banking in a Politically Fragmented Monetary Union. In Caporaso, A. and Rhodes, M. (eds.), *Europe's Crises: Economic and Political Challenges of the Monetary Union*. New York: Oxford University Press.

Hiltzik, M. (2011). *The New Deal: A Modern History*. New York: Free Press.

Hiltzik, M. (2020). The Coronavirus Crisis Shows What Happens When a Country Puts Its Workers Last. *Los Angeles Times*, 20 March.

Holst, H. (2014). 'Commodifying Institutions': Vertical Disintegration and Institutional Change in German Labour Relations. *Work, Employment and Society*, 28(1), 3–20.

Hope, D. (2016). The Political Economy of Growth Models and Macroeconomic Imbalances in Advanced Market Economies. PhD thesis, LSE.

Hope, D. and Soskice, D. (2016). Growth Models, Varieties of Capitalism, and Macroeconomics. *Politics & Society*, 44(2), 209–26.

Hopkin, J. (2020). *Anti-System Politics: The Crisis of Market Liberalism in Rich Democracies*. Oxford: Oxford University Press.

Hopkin, J. and Blyth, M. (2019). The Global Economics of European Populism: Growth Regimes and Party System Change in Europe (The Government and Opposition/ Leonard Schapiro Lecture 2017). *Government and Opposition*, 54(2), 193–225.

Höpner, M. and Lutter, M. (2014). *One Currency and Many Models of Wage Formation: Why the Eurozone Is Too Heterogeneous for the Euro*. MPIfG Discussion Paper 14/14.

Howarth, D. (2013). State Intervention and Market-Based Banking in France. In Hardie, I. and Howarth, D. (eds.), *Market-Based Banking and the International Financial Crisis*. Oxford: Oxford University Press.

Howell, C. (2015). Review Symposium: On Kathleen Thelen, *Varieties of Liberalization and the New Politics of Social Solidarity*, New York, Cambridge University Press, 2014. *Socio-Economic Review*, 15(3), 399–403.

Howell, C. (2020). Rethinking the Role of the State in Employment Relations for a Neoliberal Era. *ILR Review*, 24 February.

Howell, D. (2003). Introduction. In Howell, D. (ed.), *Fighting Unemployment: The Limits of the Free Market Consensus*. Oxford: Oxford University Press.

Huber, E. and Stephens, J. D. (2001). *Development and Crisis of the Welfare State: Parties and Policies in Global Markets*. Chicago: University of Chicago Press.

Hung, H. and Thompson, D. (2016). Money Supply, Class Power, and Inflation: Monetarism Reassessed. *American Sociological Review*, 81(3), 447–66.

Ingham, G. (2008). *Capitalism*. Cambridge: Polity.

Inglehart, R. and Norris, P. (2019). *Cultural Backlash: Trump, Brexit and Authoritarian Populism*. Cambridge: Cambridge University Press.

IMF (2006). *Global Financial Stability Report*. Washington, DC: International Monetary Fund.

IMF (2020). *Fiscal Monitor, April 2020*. Washington, DC: International Monetary Fund.

IPCC (2019). *Global Warming of 1.5 °C*. IPCC: Geneva.

Iversen, T. and Soskice, D. (2006). Electoral Systems and the Politics of Coalitions: Why Some Democracies Redistribute More than Others. *American Political Science Review*, 100, 165–81.

Iversen, T. and Soskice, D. (2009). Distribution and Redistribution: The Shadow of the Nineteenth Century. *World Politics*, 61(3), 438–86.

Iversen, T. and Soskice, D. (2013). A Structural-Institutional Explanation of the Eurozone Crisis. Paper presented at the Political Economy Workshop at the London School of Economics, 3 June.

Iversen, T. and Soskice, D. (2015). Politics *for* Markets. *Journal of European Social Policy*, 25(1), 76–93.

Iversen, T. and Soskice, D. (2019). *Prosperity and Democracy*. Cambridge: Cambridge University Press.

Iversen, T., Soskice, D. and Hope, D. (2016). The Eurozone and Political Economic Institutions. *Annual Review of Political Science*, 16, 163–85.

Iversen, T. and Wren, A. (1998). Equality, Employment, and Budgetary Restraint: The Trilemma of the Service Economy. *World Politics*, 50(4), 507–46.

Jackson, G. and Deeg, R. (2006). *How Many Varieties of Capitalism? Comparing the Comparative Institutional Analyses of Capitalist Diversity.* MPIfG Discussion Paper 06/2.

Jacobs, L. R. and King D. (2016). *Fed Power: How Finance Wins.* New York: Oxford University Press.

Jacobs, M. and Mazzucato, M. (eds.) (2016). *Rethinking Capitalism: Economics and Policy for Sustainable and Inclusive Growth.* Hoboken: John Wiley and Sons.

James, H. (1996). *International Monetary Cooperation Since Bretton Woods.* Oxford: Oxford University Press.

Janssen, R. (2017). The Rise of the 'Super Firms' and Inequality. *Social Europe*, 9 February.

Jaumotte, F. and Buitron, C. O. (2015). Power from the People. *Finance and Development*, 52(1), 29–31.

Jensen, M. C. (1986). Agency Cost of Free Cash Flow, Corporate Finance, and Takeovers. *American Economic Review*, 76, 323–9.

Jensen, M. C. and Murphy, K. J. (1990). CEO Incentives: It's Not How Much You Pay, But How. *Harvard Business Review*, 68(3), 138–53.

Jessop, B. (1997). Survey Article: The Regulation Approach. *Journal of Political Philosophy*, 5(3), 287–326.

Jessop, B. (2002). *The Future of the Capitalist State.* Cambridge: Polity.

Johnson, S. and Kwak, J. (2011). *13 Bankers: The Wall Street Takeover and the Next Financial Meltdown.* London: Vintage.

Johnston, A. and Regan, A. (2016). European Monetary Integration and the Incompatibility of National Varieties of Capitalism. *Journal of Common Market Studies*, 52(2), 318–36.

Johnston, A. and Regan, A. (2017). Global Finance, Labor Politics, and the Political Economy of Housing Prices. *Politics and Society*, 45(3), 327–58.

Johnston, A., Hancké, B. and Pant, S. (2014). Comparative Institutional Advantage in the European Sovereign Debt Crisis. *Comparative Political Studies*, 47(13), 1771–800.

Jones, E. (2015). Europe's Tragic Political Economy. *Current History*, 114, 83–8.

Jordà, O., Schularick, M. and Taylor, M. A. (2016). The Great Mortgaging: Housing Finance, Crises and Business Cycles. *Economic Policy*, 31(85), 107–52.

Judis, J. B. (2016). *The Populist Explosion: How the Great Recession Transformed American and European Politics.* New York: Columbia Global Reports.

Kaldor, N. (1983). *The Economic Consequences of Mrs. Thatcher: Speeches in the House of Lords, 1979–1982.* London: Fabian Society.

Kalecki, M. (1943). Political Aspects of Full Employment. *Political Quarterly*, 14(4), 322–31.

Kalina, T. and Weinkopf, C. (2018). *Niedriglohnbeschäftigung 2016.* IAQ-Report 2018–06.

Kalinowski, T. and Hlasny, V. (2017). Can a Comparative Capitalism Approach Explain Fiscal Policy Activism? *Journal of Post Keynesian Economics*, 40(3), 376–412.

Kallis, G. (2009). Socialism Without Growth. *Capitalism Nature Socialism*, 30 (2), 189–206.

Kamal, F. (2018). *A Portrait of U.S. Factoryless Goods Producers.* NBER Working Paper 25193.

Karamessini, M. (2007). *The Southern European Social Model: Changes and Continuities in Recent Decades.* Geneva: International Institute for Labour Studies.

Karamessini, M. (2008). Still a Distinctive Southern European Employment Model? *Industrial Relations Journal*, 39(6), 510–31.

Karwowski, E. (2019). Towards (De-)Financialisation: The Role of the State. *Cambridge Journal of Economics*, 44(4), 1001–27.

Katzenstein, P. J. (1985). *Small States in World Markets*. Ithaca: Cornell University Press.

Kaufmann, E. (2018). Good Fences Make Good Politics: Immigration and the Future of the West. *Foreign Affairs*, September/October.

Kaufmann, E. (2019). *Whiteshift: Populism, Immigration and the Future of White Majorities*. New York: Penguin.

Kaya, A., Golub, S., Kuperberg, M. and Lin, F. (2019). The Federal Reserve's Dual Mandate and the Inflation–Unemployment Trade-Off. *Contemporary Economic Policy*, 37(4), 641–51.

Keskinen, S., Norocel, O. C. and Jørgensen, M. B. (2016). The Politics and Policies of Welfare Chauvinism Under the Economic Crisis. *Critical Social Policy*, 36(3), 321–9.

Keynes, J. M. (1970 [1936]). *The General Theory of Employment, Interest and Money*. London and Basingstoke: Macmillan.

Kirshner, J. (1999). The Political Economy of Low Inflation. *Journal of Economic Surveys*, 15(1), 41–70.

Kirshner, J. (2000). The Study of Money. *World Politics*, 52(3), 407–36.

Klein, M. C. (2002). Trickle-Down Central Banking. *The Economist*, 10 October.

Kliman, A. (2012). *The Failure of Capitalist Production: Underlying Causes of the Great Recession*. London: Pluto Press.

Knafo, S. and Dutta, S. (2020). The Myth of the Shareholder Revolution and the Financialization of the Firm. *Review of International Political Economy*, 27(3), 476–99.

Koch, M. (2018). Sustainable Welfare, De-Growth and Eco-Social Policies in Europe. In Vanhercke, B., Chailari, D. and Sabato, S. (eds.), *Social Policy in the European Union: State of Play 2018*. Brussels: ETUI.

Koch, M., Gullberg, A. T., Schoyen, M. A. and Hvinden, B. (2016). Sustainable Welfare in the EU: Promoting Synergies Between Climate and Social Policies. *Critical Social Policy*, 36(4), 704–15.

Konzelman, S. (2014). The Political Economics of Austerity. *Cambridge Journal of Economics*, 38(4), 710–42.

Koo, R. (2014). Balance Sheet Recession Is the Reason for 'Secular Stagnation'. *VoxEU.org*, 11 August.

Korpi, W. (1983). *The Democratic Class Struggle*. Abingdon: Routledge.

Korpi, W. (1991). Political and Economic Explanations for Unemployment: A Cross-National and Long-Term Analysis. *British Journal of Political Science*, 21(3), 315–48.

Korpi, W. (2002). The Great Trough in Unemployment: A Long-term View of Unemployment, Inflation, Strikes, and the Profit/Wage Ratio. *Politics and Society*, 30(3), 365–426.

Korpi, W. (2006). Power Resources and Employer-Centered Approaches in Explanations of Welfare States and Varieties of Capitalism: Protagonists, Consenters, and Antagonists. *World Politics*, 58(2), 167–206.

Kraemer, K. L., Linden, G. and Dedrick, J. (2011). *Who Captures Value in the Apple iPad and iPhone?* PCIC Working Paper.

Krippner, G. (2012). *Capitalizing on Crisis: The Political Origins of the Rise of Finance*. Cambridge, MA: Harvard University Press.

Kristal, T. (2010). Good Times, Bad Times: Post-War Labour's Share of National Income in Capitalist Democracies. *American Sociological Review*, 75(5), 729–63.

Kumhof, M. and Rancière, R. (2010). *Inequality, Leverage and Crises*. IMF Working Paper WP/10/268.

Kurer, T. and Palier, B. (2019). Shrinking and Shouting: The Political Revolt of the Declining Middle in Times of Employment Polarization. *Research and Politics*, 28 March.

Lachapelle, E., MacNeil, R. and Paterson, M. (2017). The Political Economy of Decarbonisation: From Green Energy 'Race' to Green 'Division of Labour'. *New Political Economy*, 25(3), 311–27.

Lallement, M. (2011). Europe and the Economic Crisis: Forms of Labour Market Adjustment and Varieties of Capitalism. *Work, Employment and Society*, 25(4), 627–41.

Lane, P. (2008). *EMU and Financial Market Integration*. IIIS Discussion Paper 248.

Lane, P. (2012). The European Sovereign Debt Crisis. *Journal of Economic Perspectives*, 26(3), 49–68.

Lapavitsas, C., Kaltenbrunner, A., Lindo, D., Michell, J., Painceira, J. P., Pires, E., Powell, J., Stenfors, A. and Teles, N. (2010). *Eurozone Crisis: Beggar Thyself and Thy Neighbour*. RMF Occasional Report, March.

Latouche, S. (2009). *Farewell to Growth*. Cambridge: Polity.

Lavery, S. (2019). *British Capitalism After the Crisis*. Cham: Palgrave Macmillan.

Lazonick, W. (1998). Organizational Learning and International Competition. In Michie, J. and Smith, J. (eds.), *Globalization, Growth, and Governance: Creating an Innovative Economy*. Oxford: Oxford University Press.

Lazonick, W. (2015). *Stock Buybacks: From Retain-and-Reinvest to Downsize-and-Distribute*. Center for Effective Public Management at Brookings, April.

Lazonick, W. and O'Sullivan, M. (2000). Maximizing Shareholder Value: A New Ideology for Corporate Governance. *Economy and Society*, 29(1), 13–35.

Lenza, M. and Slacalek, J. (2018). *How Does Monetary Policy Affect Income and Wealth Inequality? Evidence from Quantitative Easing in the Euro Area*. ECB Working Paper 2190.

Lichtenstein, N. (2014). Two Cheers for Vertical Integration: Corporate Governance in a World of Global Supply Chains. Mimeo.

Lijphart, A. (1999). *Patterns of Democracy: Government Forms and Performance in Thirty-Six Countries*. New Haven: Yale University Press.

Lin, K. and Tomaskovic-Devey, D. (2013). Financialization and US Income Inequality, 1970–2008. *American Journal of Sociology*, 118(5), 1284–329.

Lindblom, C. (1977). *Politics Against Markets*. New York: Basic Books.

Lipietz, A. (1987). *Mirages and Miracles: The Crises of Global Fordism*. London: Verso.

Lippert, I., Huzzard, T., Jürgens, U. and Lazonick, W. (2014). *Corporate Governance, Employee Voice, and Work Organization: Sustaining High-Road Jobs in the Automotive Supply Industry*. Oxford: Oxford University Press.

Lynch, J. (2019). Populism, Partisan Convergence, and Mobilization in Western Europe. *Polity*, 51(4), 668–77.

McBride, S. and Williams, R. (2001). Globalization, the Restructuring of Labour Markets and Policy Convergence: The OECD 'Jobs Strategy'. *Global Social Policy*, 1(3), 281–309.

McNamara, K. (2002). Rational Fictions: Central Bank Independence and the Social Logic of Delegation. *West European Politics*, 25(1), 47–76.

Magdoff, F. and Foster, J. B. (2014). Financialization and Stagnation: The Nature of the Contradiction. *Monthly Review*, 66(1), 1–24.

Mandelkern, R. (2016). Explaining the Striking Similarity in Macroeconomic Policy Responses to the Great Recession: The Institutional Power of Macroeconomic Governance. *Comparative Political Studies*, 49(2), 219–52.

Manduca, R. (2019). Selling Keynesianism. *Boston Review*, 9 December.

Manger, M. S. and Sattler, T. (2019). The Origins of Persistent Current Account Imbalances in the Post-Bretton Woods Era. *Comparative Political Studies*, 10 July.

Mankiw, N. G. (2013). Defending the One Percent. *Journal of Economic Perspectives*, 23(3), 21–34.

Mankiw, N. G. (2018). *Principles of Economics*. Boston: Cengage Learning.

Manne, H. G. (1962). Mergers and the Market for Corporate Control. *Journal of Political Economy*, 73(2), 110–20.

Mares, I. (2003). *The Politics of Social Risk: Business and Welfare State Development*. Cambridge: Cambridge University Press.

Marglin, S. A. and Schor, J. B. (eds.) (1990). *The Golden Age of Capitalism: Reinterpreting the Postwar Experience*. Oxford: Oxford University Press.

Marsh, D. (1983). Interest Group Activity and Structural Power: Lindblom's Politics and Markets. *West European Politics*, 6(2), 3–13.

Martin, C. J. (2000). *Stuck in Neutral: Business and the Politics of Human Capital Investment Policy*. Princeton: Princeton University Press.

Martin, C. J. (2016). Economic Prosperity Is in High Demand. *Politics and Society*, 44(1), 227–35.

Martin, C. J. and Swank, D. (2010). *The Political Construction of Business Interests: Coordination, Growth, and Equality*. Cambridge: Cambridge University Press.

Marx, K. (1967). *Capital. Vol. 3*. New York: International.

Mason, J. W. (2015). *Disgorge the Cash: The Disconnect between Corporate Borrowing and Investment*. Roosevelt Institute Working Paper.

Mason, J. W. and Jayadev, A. (2013). Strange Defeat: How the New Consensus in Macroeconomics Let Austerity Lose All the Intellectual Battles and Still Win the War. *Economic and Political Weekly*, 48(32), 102–11.

Matthijs, M. and Blyth, M. (2018). When Is It Rational to Learn the Wrong Lessons? Technocratic Authority, Social Learning, and Euro Fragility. *Perspectives on Politics*, 16(1), 110–26.

Mayda, A. M., Peri, G. and Steingress, W. (2016). *Immigration to the U.S.: A Problem for the Republicans or the Democrats?* NBER Working Paper 21941.

Mehrling, P., Pozsar, Z., Sweeney, J. and Neilson, D. (2013). *Bagehot Was a Shadow Banker: Shadow Banking, Central Banking, and the Future of Global Finance*. INET Working Paper, 6 December.

Mentz, G. (2017). *Comparative Political Economy: Contours of a Subfield*. Oxford: Oxford University Press.

Mertens, D. (2017). Borrowing for Social Security? Credit, Asset-Based Welfare and the Decline of the German Savings Regime. *Journal of European Social Policy*, 27(5), 474–90.

Mian, A. and Sufi, A. (2016). *Who Bears the Cost of Recessions? The Role of House Prices and Household Debt*. NBER Working Paper 22256.

Mian, A., Straub, L. and Sufi, A. (2020). *The Saving Glut of the Rich and the Rise in Household Debt*. NBER Working Paper 26941.

Michell, J. (2015). Income Distribution and the Financial and Economic Crisis. In Hein, E., Detzer, D. and Dodig, N. (eds.), *The Demise of Finance-Dominated Capitalism: Explaining the Financial and Economic Crises*. Cheltenham: Edward Elgar.

Milesi-Ferretti, G. M. and Tille, C. (2011). The Great Retrenchment: International Capital Flows During the Global Financial Crisis. *Economic Policy*, 22(66), 285–342.

Mitchell, B. and Fazi, T. (2018). *Reclaiming the State*. London: Pluto Press.

Mizruchi, M. (2013). *The Fracturing of the American Corporate Elite*. Cambridge, MA: Harvard University Press.

Molina, O. and Rhodes, M. (2007). The Political Economy of Adjustment in Mixed Market Economies: A Study of Spain and Italy. In Hancké, B., Rhodes, M. and Thatcher, T. (eds.), *Beyond Varieties of Capitalism: Conflict, Contradictions and Complementarities in the European Economy*. Oxford: Oxford University Press.

Monnet, E., Pagliari, S. and Vallée, S. (2014). *Europe Between Financial Repression and Regulatory Capture.* Bruegel Working Paper 2014/08.

Montecino, J. A. and Epstein, G. (2015). *Did Quantitative Easing Increase Income Inequality?* PERI Working Paper 407.

Montgomerie, J. and Büdenbender, M. (2015). Round the Houses: Homeownership and Failures of Asset-Based Welfare in the United Kingdom. *New Political Economy*, 20(3), 386–405.

Mosley, L. (2000). Room to Move: International Financial Markets and National Welfare States. *International Organization*, 54(4), 737–73.

Mosley, L. (2005). Globalisation and the State: Still Room to Move? *New Political Economy*, 10(3), 355–62.

Mouffe, C. (2018). *For a Left Populism.* London: Verso.

Mudde, C. and Kaltwasser, C. R. (2017). *Populism: A Very Short Introduction.* Oxford: Oxford University Press.

Muellbauer, J. (2014). Combating Eurozone Deflation: QE for the People. *VOX*, 23 December.

Müller, J.-W. (2018). The Rise and Rise of Populism? In BBVA (ed.), *The Age of Perplexity: Rethinking the World We Knew.* Madrid: Penguin Random House Grupo Editorial.

Mügge, D. (2010). *Widen the Market, Narrow the Competition: Banker Interests and the Making of a European Capital Market.* Colchester: ECPR Press.

Müller-Jentsch, W. and Weitbrecht, H. (2003). *The Changing Contours of German Industrial Relations.* Munich: Rainer Hampp.

Naruse, T. (1991). Taylorism and Fordism in Japan. *International Journal of Political Economy*, 21(3), 2–48.

Neilson, J., Pritchard, B. and Yeung, H. W. (eds.) (2016). *Global Value Chains and Global Production Networks: Changes in the International Political Economy.* Abingdon: Routledge.

Nesvetailova, A. (ed.) (2019). *Shadow Banking: Scope, Origins and Theories.* Abingdon: Routledge.

Newell, P. and Paterson, M. (2010). *Climate Capitalism: Global Warming and the Transformation of the Global Economy.* Cambridge: Cambridge University Press.

Nolan, B. and Weissstanner, D. (2020). Has the Middle Secured Its Share of Growth or Been Squeezed? *West European Politics*, 18 February.

Nölke, A. (2015). Economic Causes of the Eurozone Crisis: The Analytical Contribution of Comparative Capitalism. *Socio-Economic Review*, 44(1), 141–61.

Norris, M. and Fahey, T. (2011). From Asset Based Welfare to Welfare Housing? The Changing Function of Social Housing in Ireland. *Housing Studies*, 26(3), 459–69.

Obstfeld, M. and Rogoff, K. (2009). *Global Imbalances and the Financial Crisis: Products of Common Causes.* CEPR Discussion Paper 7606.

Ocampo, J. (2007). *The Instability and Inequities of the Global Reserve System.* DESA Working Paper 59.

O'Connor, J. (1973). *The Fiscal Crisis of the State.* New York: St. Martin's Press.

OECD. (1994). *The OECD Jobs Study: Facts, Analysis, Strategies.* Paris: OECD.

OECD. (2015a). *The Future of Productivity.* Paris: OECD.

OECD. (2015b). *OECD Business and Finance Outlook 2015.* Paris: OECD.

OECD. (2018). *Tax Policy Studies: The Role and Design of Net Wealth Taxes in the OECD.* Paris: OECD Publishing.

Okun, A. (2015 [1975]). *Equality and Efficiency: The Big Trade-Off.* Washington, DC: Brookings Institution Press.

Onaran, O. (2012). A Wage-Led Recovery Would Help Reverse Inequalities, Increase Demand, and Help the EU to Get Out of its Crisis. EUROPP blog, 12 April.

Onaran, O. (2015). *State and the Economy: A Strategy for Wage-Led Development.* Greenwich Papers in Political Economy.

Onaran, O. (2016). Secular Stagnation and Progressive Economic Policy Alternatives. *European Journal of Economics and Economic Policies: Intervention,* 13(2), 229–40.

Onaran, O., Stockhammer, E. and Grafl, L. (2011). Financialisation, Income Distribution and Aggregate Demand in the USA. *Cambridge Journal of Economics,* 35(4), 637–61.

Orhangazi, O. (2008). Financialisation and Capital Accumulation in the Non-Financial Corporate Sector: A Theoretical and Empirical Investigation on the US Economy, 1973–2003. *Cambridge Journal of Economics,* 32(6), 863–86.

Ostry, J. D., Berg, A. and Tsangarides, C. T. (2014). *Redistribution, Inequality, and Growth.* IMF Staff Discussion Note SDN14/02.

Overbeek, H. W. and Jessop, B. (eds.) (2018). *Transnational Capital and Class Fractions: The Amsterdam School Perspective Reconsidered.* Abingdon: Routledge.

Page, R. (2009). *Co-Determination in Germany: A Beginner's Guide.* Hans Böckler Stiftung Arbeitspapier 33.

Pagliari, S. (2015). Financial Industry Power and Regulatory Policies: What Lessons from the Global Financial Crisis? *Rivista Italiana di Politiche Pubbliche,* 2, 209–32.

Pagliari, S. and Young, K. L. (2014). Leveraged Interests: Financial Industry Power and the Role of Private Sector Coalitions. *Review of International Political Economy,* 21(3), 575–610.

Pagliari, S., Phillips, L. and Young, K. (2018). The Financialization of Policy Preferences: Financial Asset Ownership, Regulation and Crisis Management. *Socio-Economic Review,* 24 July.

Palley, T. I. (2012). *From Financial Crisis to Stagnation: The Destruction of Shared Prosperity and the Role of Economics.* Cambridge: Cambridge University Press.

Panitch, L. and Gindin, S. (2012). *The Making of Global Capitalism: The Political Economy of American Empire.* London: Verso.

Papadimitriou, D. and Wray, R. (2012). *Euroland's Original Sin.* Levy Institute Policy Note 2012–08.

Pappas, T. S. (2019). *Populism and Liberal Democracy: A Comparative and Theoretical Analysis.* Oxford: Oxford University Press.

Parker, G., Giles, C. and Payne, S. (2020). Sunak Turns on Financial Firepower to Help Workers. *Financial Times,* 20 March.

Paudyn, B. (2013). Credit Rating Agencies and the Sovereign Debt Crisis: Performing the Politics of Creditworthiness Through Risk and Uncertainty. *Review of International Political Economy,* 20(4), 788–818.

Peck, J. and Theodore, N. (2007). Variegated Capitalism. *Progress in Human Geography,* 31 (6), 731–72.

Perez, S. and Matsaganis, M. (2019). Export or Perish: Can Internal Devaluation Create Enough Good Jobs in Southern Europe?. *South European Society and Politics,* 24(2), 259–85.

Peters, J. (2008). Labour Market Deregulation and the Decline of Labour Power in North America and Western Europe. *Policy and Society,* 27, 83–98.

Petry, J. (2016). Intellectual Monocultures, Black Swans, and the Failure of Economics: Lessons from the Global Financial Crisis and Austerity. *Social Science Works,* 16 November.

Pierson, P. (ed.) (2001). *The New Politics of the Welfare State.* Cambridge: Cambridge University Press.

Piketty, T. (2014). *Capital in the 21st Century.* Cambridge, MA: Harvard University Press.

Polanyi, K. (1944). *The Great Transformation*. New York: Farrar and Rinehart.

Pollin, R. (2018). De-Growth vs a Green New Deal. *New Left Review*, 112.

Pontusson, J. (2005). *Inequality and Prosperity: Social Europe vs Liberal America*. Ithaca: Cornell University Press.

Pontusson, J. (2018). The Fed, Finance, and Inequality in Comparative Perspective. *PS: Political Science and Politics*, 51(4), 1–5.

Porter, M. (1990). *The Competitive Advantage of Nations*. Cambridge, MA: Harvard Business Review.

Portes, J. (2016). *Capitalism: 50 Ideas You Really Need to Know*. London: Quercus.

Posen, A. (1995). Declarations Are Not Enough: Financial Sector Sources of Central Bank Independence. *NBER Macroeconomics Annual*, 10, 253–74.

Prescott, E. (2016). *RBC Methodology and the Development of Aggregate Economic Theory*. NBER Working Paper 22422.

Przeworski, A. (1986). *Capitalism and Social Democracy*. Cambridge: Cambridge University Press.

Rajan, R. (2010). *Fault Lines: How Hidden Fractures Still Threaten the World Economy*. Princeton: Princeton University Press.

Rajan, R. and Zingales, L. (2003). *Banks and Markets: The Changing Character of European Finance*. NBER Working Paper 9595.

Rauchway, E. (2007). *The Great Depression and the New Deal: A Very Short Introduction*. Oxford: Oxford University Press.

Redeker, N. (2019). *The Politics of Stashing Wealth: The Demise of Labour Power and the Global Rise of Corporate Savings*. CIS Working Paper 101.

Reinhart, C. and Rogoff, K. (2010). *Growth in a Time of Debt*. NBER Working Paper 15639.

Reisenbichler, A. (2020). The Politics of Quantitative Easing and Housing Stimulus by the Federal Reserve and European Central Bank, 2008–2018. *West European Politics*, 43(2), 464–84.

Reisenbichler, A., and Morgan, K. J. (2012). From 'Sick Man' to 'Miracle': Explaining the Robustness of the German Labor Market During and After the Financial Crisis 2008–09. *Politics and Society*, 40(4), 549–79.

Rennwald, L. and Pontusson, J. (2020). *Paper Stones* Revisited: Class Voting, Unionization and the Electoral Decline of the Mainstream Left. *Perspectives on Politics*, March.

Rhodes, M. (1998). Globalization, Labor Markets and Welfare States: A Future of 'Competitive Corporatism'? In Rhodes, M. and Meny, Y. (eds.), *The Future of European Welfare: A New Social Contract?* London and Basingstoke: Palgrave Macmillan.

Richardson, G. (2006). *Bank Distress During the Great Depression: The Illiquidity–Insolvency Debate Revisited*. NBER Working Paper 12717.

Rodrik, D. (1998). Why Do More Open Economies Have Bigger Governments? *Journal of Political Economy*, 106(5), 997–1032.

Rodrik, D. (2017). *Populism and the Economics of Globalization*. CEPR Discussion Paper 12119.

Roe, M. (2003). *Political Determinants of Corporate Governance: Political Context, Corporate Impact*. Oxford: Oxford University Press.

Rogoff, K. (2017). Dealing with Monetary Paralysis at the Zero Bound. *Journal of Economic Perspectives*, 31(3), 47–66.

Rogoff, K. and Reinhart, C. (2009). *This Time Is Different: Eight Centuries of Financial Folly*. Princeton: Princeton University Press.

Rohlf, W. D. (2010). *Introduction to Economic Reasoning*. Boston: Addison-Wesley.

Rommerskirchen, C. (2020). Foreign Bond Investors and Market Discipline. *Competition & Change*, 24(1), 3–25.

Röth, L., Afonso, A. and Spies, D. (2018). The Impact of Populist Radical Right Parties on Socio-Economic Policies. *European Political Science Review*, 10(3), 325–50.

Roubini, S. (2006). The Unsustainability of the US Twin Deficits. *Cato Journal*, 26(2), 343–56.

Rowthorn, B. (1980). *Capitalism, Conflict and Inflation*. London: Lawrence and Wishart.

Royo, S. (2007). Varieties of Capitalism in Spain: Business and the Politics of Coordination. *European Journal of Industrial Relations*, 13(1), 47–65.

Royo, S. (2013). A 'Ship in Trouble': The Spanish Banking System and the International Financial Crisis. In Hardie, I. and Howarth, D. (eds.), *Market-Based Banking and the International Financial Crisis*. Oxford: Oxford University Press.

Rueda, D. (2007). *Social Democracy Inside Out: Government Partisanship, Insiders, and Outsiders in Industrialized Democracies*. Oxford: Oxford University Press.

Rueda, D. and Pontusson, J. (2000). Wage Inequality and Varieties of Capitalism. *World Politics*, 52(3), 350–85.

Ruggie, J. (1982). International Regimes, Transactions, and Change: Embedded Liberalism in the Postwar Economic Order. *International Organization*, 36(2), 379–415.

Russell, E. (2007). *New Deal Banking Reforms and Keynesian Welfare State Capitalism*. London: Routledge.

Ryan-Collins, J. and van Lerven, F. (2018). *Bringing the Helicopter to Ground: A Historical Review of Fiscal-Monetary Coordination to Support Economic Growth in the 20th Century*. Post-Keynesian Economics Society Working Paper 1810.

Sacchi, S. (2015). Conditionality by Other Means: EU Involvement in Italy's Structural Reforms in the Sovereign Debt Crisis. *Comparative European Politics*, 13, 77–92.

Saez, Z. and Zucman, G. (2019). *The Triumph of Injustice: How the Rich Dodge Taxes and How to Make Them Pay*. New York: W. W. Norton.

Sargent, T. J. (1985). Reaganomics and Credibility. In Ando, A. Hikdekazu, E., Farmer, R. and Suzuki, Y. (eds.), *Monetary Policy in Our Times*. Cambridge, MA: MIT Press.

Sattler, T. (2013). Do Markets Punish Left Governments? *Journal of Politics*, 75(2), 343–56.

Scharpf, F. (1999). *The Viability of Advanced Welfare States in the International Economy: Vulnerabilities and Options*. MPfIG Working Paper 99/9.

Scharpf, F. (2016). *Forced Structural Convergence in the Eurozone: Or a Differentiated European Monetary Community*. MPIfG Discussion Paper 16/15.

Schelkle, W. (2012). A Crisis of What? Mortgage Credit Markets and the Social Policy of Promoting Homeownership in the United States and in Europe. *Politics and Society*, 40(1), 59–80.

Schmidt, R. and Tyrell, M. (1997). Financial Systems, Corporate Finance and Corporate Governance. *European Financial Management*, 3(3), 333–61.

Schmitz, B. and von Hagen, J. (2011). Current Account Imbalances and Financial Integration in the Euro Area. *Journal of International Money and Finance*, 30(8), 1676–95.

Schularick, M. (2012). Public Debt and Financial Crises in the Twentieth Century. *European Review of History*, 19(6), 881–97.

Schulten, T. (2004). *Foundations and Perspectives of Trade Union Wage Policy in Europe*. WSI Working Papers 129.

Schulten, T. and Müller, T. (2014). *Wages and Collective Bargaining During the European Economic Crisis: Developments in European Manufacturing Industry*. industriALL European Trade Union Report.

Schwartz, H. (2008). Origins and Consequences of the US Subprime Crisis. In Schwartz, H. and Seabrooke, L. (eds.), *The Politics of Housing Booms and Busts*. Basingstoke: Palgrave Macmillan.

Schwartz, H. M. (2009). *Subprime Nation: American Power, Global Capital and the Housing Bubble.* Ithaca: Cornell University Press.

Schwartz, H. (2012). Housing, the Welfare State, and the Global Financial Crisis: What Is the Connection? *Politics and Society*, 40(1), 35–58.

Schwartz, H. (2016). Wealth and Secular Stagnation: The Role of Industrial Organization and Intellectual Property Rights. *RSF: The Russell Sage Foundation Journal of the Social Sciences*, 2(6), 226–49.

Schwartz, H. (2019). American Hegemony: Intellectual Property Rights, Dollar Centrality, and Infrastructural Power. *Review of International Political Economy*, 26(3), 490–519.

Schwartz, H. and Seabrooke, L. (eds.) (2008). *The Politics of Housing Booms and Busts.* Basingstoke: Palgrave Macmillan.

Schwartz, H. M., & Tranøy, B. S. (2019). Thinking about Thinking about Comparative Political Economy: From Macro to Micro and Back. *Politics & Society*, 47(1), 23–54.

Shambaugh, J. (2012). The Euro's Three Crises. *Brookings Papers on Economic Activity*, Spring, 157–231.

Shapiro, A. and Wilson, D. (2019). *Taking the Fed at its Word: A New Approach to Estimating Central Bank Objectives Using Text Analysis.* Federal Reserve Bank of San Francisco Working Paper 2019–2.

Sinclair, T. (2005). *The New Masters of Capital: American Bond Rating Agencies and the Politics of Creditworthiness.* Ithaca: Cornell University Press.

Slobodian, Q. (2018). *Globalists: The End of Empire and the Birth of Neoliberalism.* Cambridge, MA: Harvard University Press.

Soskice, D. (2007). Macroeconomics and Varieties of Capitalism. In Hancké, B., Rhodes, M. and Thatcher, M. (eds.), *Beyond Varieties of Capitalism: Conflicts, Contradictions, and Complementarities in the European Economy.* New York: Oxford University Press.

Steil, B. (2013). *The Battle of Bretton Woods.* Princeton: Princeton University Press.

Stephens, J. D. (1979). *The Transition from Capitalism to Socialism.* London: Macmillan.

Stern, G. H. and Feldman, R. J. (2009). *Too Big to Fail: The Hazards of Bank Bailouts.* Washington, DC: Brookings Institution Press.

Stern, N. (2006). *The Economics of Climate Change: The Stern Review.* Cambridge: Cambridge University Press.

Stiglitz, J. (2015). Inequality and Economic Growth. *Political Quarterly*, 86(S1), 134–55.

Stockhammer, E. (2008). Some Stylized Facts on the Finance-Dominated Accumulation Regime. *Competition & Change*, 12(2), 184–202.

Stockhammer, E. (2015). Rising Inequality as a Cause of the Present Crisis. *Cambridge Journal of Economics*, 39(3), 935–58.

Stockhammer, E. (2016). Neoliberal Growth Models, Monetary Union and the Euro Crisis. A Post-Keynesian Perspective. *New Political Economy*, 21(4), 365–79.

Stockhammer, E. (2018). *Demand Regimes, Financialisation and Hysteresis: New Keynesian and Post-Keynesian Macroeconomic Underpinnings of the Varieties of Capitalism.* Post-Keynesian Economics Society Working Paper PKWP1809.

Stockhammer, E. and Kohler, K. (2019). *Financialization and Demand Regimes in Advanced Economies.* Post-Keynesian Economics Society Working Paper PKWP1911.

Stockhammer, E. and Onaran, O. (2013). Wage-Led Growth: Theory, Evidence, Policy. *Review of Keynesian Economics*, 1(1), 61–78.

Stolz, S. M. and Wedow, M. (2010). *Extraordinary Measures in Extraordinary Times: Public Measures in Support of the Financial Sector in the EU and the United States.* ECB Working Paper 117.

Storm, S. and Naastepad, C. W. M. (2009). Labour Market Regulation and Productivity

Growth: Evidence for Twenty OECD Countries (1984–2004). *Industrial Relations*, 48(4), 629–54.

Streeck, W. (1987). The Uncertainties of Management in the Management of Uncertainty: Employers, Labour Relations and Industrial Adjustment in the 1980s. *Work, Employment and Society*, 1(3), 281–308.

Streeck, W. (2010). *E Pluribus Unum? Varieties and Commonalities of Capitalism.* MPIfG Discussion Paper 10/12.

Streeck, W. (2014). *Buying Time: The Delayed Crisis of Democratic Capitalism.* London: Verso.

Streeck, W. (2016). Varieties of Varieties: 'VoC' and the Growth Models. *Politics & Society*, 44(2), 243–7.

Streeck, W. (2019). Four Reasons the European Left Lost. *Jacobin*, 30 May.

Summers, L. (2014). U.S. Economic Prospects: Secular Stagnation, Hysteresis, and the Zero Lower Bound. *Business Economics*, 49(2), 65–73.

Summers, L. (2016). The Age of Secular Stagnation: What It Is and What to Do About It. *Foreign Affairs*, March/April.

Summers, L. (2018). Secular Stagnation and Macroeconomic Policy. *IMF Economic Review*, 66(2), 226–50.

Sweezy, P. (1942). *The Theory of Capitalist Development.* New York: Monthly Review Press.

Swenson, P. A. (2002). *Capitalists Against Markets: The Making of Labour Markets and Welfare States in the United States and Sweden.* Oxford: Oxford University Press.

Swenson, P. A. (2004). Varieties of Capitalist Interests: Power, Institutions, and the Regulatory Welfare State in the United States and Sweden. *Studies in American Political Development*, 18, 1–29.

Taylor, M. (ed.) (2008). *Global Economy Contested: Power and Conflict Across the International Division of Labour.* Abingdon: Routledge.

Teulings, C. and Baldwin, R. (eds.) (2014). *Secular Stagnation: Facts, Causes and Cures.* London: CEPR Press.

Thelen, K. (1994). Beyond Corporatism: Toward a New Framework for the Study of Labor in Advanced Capitalism. *Comparative Politics*, 27(1), 107–24.

Thelen, K. (2012). Varieties of Capitalism: Trajectories of Liberalization and the New Politics of Social Solidarity. *Annual Review of Political Science*, 15, 137–59.

Thelen, K. (2014). *Varieties of Liberalization and the New Politics of Social Solidarity.* Cambridge: Cambridge University Press.

Thiemann, M. (2018). *The Growth of Shadow Banking: A Comparative Institutional Analysis.* Cambridge: Cambridge University Press.

Thompson, H. (2012). The Limits of Blaming Neo-Liberalism: Fannie Mae and Freddie Mac, the American State and the Financial Crisis. *New Political Economy*, 17(4), 399–419.

Tickell, A. and Peck, J. A. (1995). Social Regulation After Fordism: Regulation Theory, Neo-Liberalism and the Global–Local Nexus. *Economy and Society*, 24(3), 357–86.

Töngür, U. and Elveren, A. Y. (2014). Deunionization and Pay Inequality in OECD Countries: A Panel Granger Causality Approach. *Economic Modelling*, 38, 417–25.

Tooze, A. (2018). *Crashed: How a Decade of Financial Crises Changed the World.* New York: Penguin.

Tooze, A. (2019). Why Central Banks Need to Step Up on Global Warming. *Foreign Policy*, 20 July.

Tooze, A. (2020). Should We Be Scared of the Coronavirus Debt Mountain? *The Guardian*, 27 April.

Tori, D. and Onaran, O. (2018). Financialization, Financial Development and Investment.

Evidence from European Non-Financial Corporations. *Socio-Economic Review*, 22 December.

Tranøy, B. S., Stamsø, M. A. and Hjertaker, I. (2020). Equality as a Driver of Inequality? Universalistic Welfare, Generalised Creditworthiness and Financialised Housing Markets. *West European Politics*, 43(2), 390–411.

Turner, A. (2015). The Case for Monetary Finance: An Essentially Political Issue. Paper presented at the 16th Jacques Polak Annual Research Conference, Washington, DC, 5–6 November.

Turner, A. (2020). Monetary Finance Is Here. *Project Syndicate*, 20 April.

UN-DESA. (2009). *A Global Green New Deal for Sustainable Development*. UN-DESA Policy Brief 12.

Van Apeldoorn, B. (2002). *Transnational Capitalism and the Struggle over European Integration*. London: Routledge.

Vandenbroucke, F. (2000). *Op Zoek naar een Redelijke Utopie: De Actieve Welvaarsstaat in Perspectief*. Leuven: Garant.

van der Zwan, N. (2014). Making Sense of Financialization. *Socio-Economic Review*, 12(1), 99–129.

Van Lerven, F. and Ryan-Collins, J. (2017). *Central Banks, Climate Change and the Transition to a Low-Carbon Economy*. New Economics Foundation Policy Briefing.

Veblen, T. (1994 [1899]). *The Theory of the Leisure Class*. North Chelmsford: Courier Corporation.

Vergeer, R. and Kleinknecht, A. (2014). Do Labour Market Reforms Reduce Labour Productivity Growth? A Panel Data Analysis of 20 OECD Countries (1960–2004). *International Labour Review*, 153(3), 365–93.

Vermeiren, M. (2014). *Power and Imbalances in the Global Monetary System: A Comparative Capitalism Perspective*. Basingstoke: Palgrave Macmillan.

Vermeiren, M. (2017). One-Size-Fits-Some! Sectoral Interests, Capitalist Diversity and the ECB's Monetary Policy in the Euro Area. *Review of International Political Economy*, 24(6), 929–57.

Vermeiren, M. (2019). Meeting the World's Demand for Safe Assets? Macroeconomic Policy and the International Status of the Euro after the Crisis. *European Journal of International Relations*, 25(1), 30–60.

Vidal, M. (2012). On the Persistence of Labour Market Insecurity and Slow Growth in the US: Reckoning with the Waltonist Growth Regime. *New Political Economy*, 17(5), 543–64.

Vidal, M. (2013). Postfordism as a Dysfunctional Accumulation Regime: A Comparative Analysis of the USA, the UK and Germany. *Work, Employment and Society*, 27(3), 451–71.

Vinik, D. (2013). Larry Summers Gave an Amazing Speech on the Biggest Economic Problem of Our Time. *Business Insider*, 17 November.

Visser, J. (2013). *Wage Bargaining Institutions: From Crisis to Crisis*. European Economy Economic Paper 488.

Vitols, S. (2001). *The Origins of Bank-Based and Market-Based Financial Systems: Germany, Japan, and the United States*. WZB Discussion Paper FS I 01–302.

Vitols, S. (2005). Changes in Germany's Bank-Based Financial System: Implications for Corporate Governance. *Corporate Governance: An International Review*, 13(3), 386–96.

Vlandas, T. (2018). Grey Power and the Economy: Ageing and Inflation across Advanced Economies. *Comparative Political Studies*, 51 (4), 514–52.

Wade, R. (2009). Beware What You Wish For: Lessons for International Political Economy from the Transformation of Economics. *Review of International Political Economy*, 16(1), 106–21.

Wallerstein, M. (1999). Wage-Setting Institutions and Pay Inequality in Advanced Industrial Societies. *American Journal of Political Science*, 43(3), 649–80.

Walter, J. R. (2006). The '3-6-3' Rule: An Urban Myth?. *Federal Reserve Bank of Richmond Economic Quarterly Volume*, 92(1), 51–78.

Watson, M. (2001). Embedding the 'New Economy' in Europe: A Study in the Institutional Specificities of Knowledge-Based Growth. *Economy and Society*, 30(4), 504–23.

Watson, M. (2009). Planning for a Future of Asset-Based Welfare? New Labour, Financialized Economic Agency and the Housing Market. *Planning Practice and Research*, 24(1), 41–56.

Whapshott, N. (2012). *Keynes Hayek: The Clash That Defined Modern Economics*. New York: W. W. Norton.

Wibbelink, R. P. and Heng, M. S. H. (2000). Evolution of Organizational Structure and Strategy of the Automobile Industry. Research Memorandum, VU Amsterdam.

Wolf, M. (2008). *Fixing Global Finance*. Baltimore: Johns Hopkins University Press.

Wolf, M. (2015). *The Shifts and the Shocks*. New York: Penguin.

Woodruff, D. (2015). Governing by Panic: The Politics of the Eurozone Crisis. *Politics and Society*, 44(1), 81–116.

Woods, J. G. (2017). The Effect of Technological Change on the Task Structure of Jobs and the Capital–Labor Trade-Off in US Production. *Journal of the Knowledge Economy*, 8, 739–57.

Wren, A., Fodor, M. and Theodoropoulou, S. (2013). The Trilemma Revisited: Institutions, Inequality, and Employment Creation in an Era of ICT-Intensive Service Expansion. In Wren, A. (ed.), *The Political Economy of the Service Transition*. Oxford: Oxford University Press.

Wright, E. O. and Dwyer, R. (2003). The Patterns of Job Expansions in the USA: A Comparison of the 1960s and 1990s. *Socio-Economic Review*, 1, 289–325.

Wyplosz, C. (1999). Financial Restraint and Liberalization in Post-War Europe. CEPR Discussion Paper 2253.

Zachmann, G., Fredriksson, G. and Claeys, G. (2018). *The Distributional Effects of Climate Policies*. Brussels: Bruegel.

Zysman, J. (1983). *Governments, Markets, and Growth*. Ithaca: Cornell University Press.

Index

and growth models 189–202
and QE 192, 195–7
and secular stagnation 175–6, 211
Macroeconomic Imbalance Procedure (MIP)
    200
macroeconomic imbalances 174–205
  after financial crisis 175
  before the crisis 175, 176–89, *176*, 202
  current account 176–80
  and global savings glut view 176
  and growth models before the crisis
    182–9
  sectoral financial 180, *181*, 182
  and secular stagnation 202–5
macroeconomic policy 6, 62–89
  CMEs 82, 86–7, 184–6
  and growth models 86–9
  and increased public spending 214
  Keynesian era 49, 64–71, 208
  LMEs 88–9, 182–4
  MMEs 87, 187
  neoliberal and Keynesian compared *85*
  neoliberalism 8, 21, 69–86, 97, 213
  reasons for transition from Keynesianism
    to neoliberalism 63
  secular stagnation and reform of 212–16
manager compensation 119, 129–30, 136
  performance-related 129
  stock options 129–30
  see also CEO compensation
managerial capitalism 122
managerism 130
Mankiw, Greg
  Principles of Economics 5, 28
Manne, Henry G. 127
manufacturing
  decline in 218
  factoryless 124–5
  fall in labour share in total economy
    115–16, *115*
  hourly compensation costs 99, *99*
  widening productivity gap between global
    frontier firms and other firms *141*
marginal propensity to consume (MPC) 32
market-based banking 9–10, 146, 147–8
  balance sheet 157–8, *157*
  and expansion of household credit 147,
    148
  and Eurozone crisis 164–6
  and expansion of household credit 147,
    148
  financial liberalization and rise of 154–8

funding of by repo finance 157
key features of 147, 157–8
originate-and-distribute model *see*
    originate-and-distribute model
and regulatory capture 167
securitization of loans 158–63
and structured investment vehicles (SIVs)
    157
and subprime mortgage crisis 160–4
and transatlantic financial instability
    158–69
market-based corporate finance 132–4, 134,
    134
market-based financial systems 135, 148
market equilibrium 3–4
market price mechanism 25–7, *26*, *27*, 39
markets
  capital 127–8, 139
  disciplinary effect of financial 215
  and efficient market hypothesis 4
  free *see* free markets
  labour *see* labour markets
  neoliberalism and open 5, 74–7
Markey, Edward 225
Marx, Karl 34, 81
  Capital 30
Marxism 34, 204
  an economic stagnation 204
  and capitalism 19
Mason, J.W. 140
Matthijs, Matthias 86
maturity transformation 149
MBSs (mortgage backed securities) 160,
    161, 162, 165, 193, 195
Means, Gardiner 121
Mehrling, Perry 157
MEWs (mortgage equity withdrawals) 163,
    164
Mian, Atif 33
middle 40 per cent
  income share 16–17, *17*
  wealth share 24
middle-class households 169
minority shareholder protection (MSP) 133,
    134
Mitterand, François 76
MMEs (mixed market economies) 6, 10, 11,
    56–7, 186–9
  consumption-led growth 186, 189
  current account balance 178, *179*
  effect of European monetary integration
    on growth model 187